Praise for *The Industrial Revolutionaries:*

"Refreshingly old-fashioned. . . . In this lively study, there is little room for the dry academic prose that so often makes economic histories a painful reading experience. Instead we have a wealth of vivid portraits of figures from the eighteenth and nineteenth centuries. . . . Weightman is excellent at demolishing some of the myths of the industrial revolution."
                                                          —*Literary Review*

"Ambitious [and] clear-sighted . . . Instead of simply replacing one set of triumphalist myths with an alternative one, he practises real history."
                                                          —*Sunday Herald* (UK)

"Think the planet is experiencing the most rapid period of technological progress in its history? Then think again. The average citizen in 1820 could neither travel nor communicate faster than the speed of a horse. Just thirty years later, after a tsunami of machines had swept over the world, he or she could ride a speeding train and send telegraph messages instantaneously over hundreds of miles. In *The Industrial Revolutionaries*, Gavin Weightman tells these stories and much, much more. Swirling with seers, savants, and sorcerers of the mechanical age, every page of this epic saga will dazzle even the most jaded reader."
                                          —William J. Bernstein, author of
                              A Splendid Exchange: How Trade Shaped the World

"Gavin Weightman makes heroic inventors, engineers, and entrepreneurs come alive in his thoroughly engaging recounting of the story of industrialization. His book is full of memorable characters."
                                          —Henry Petroski, Aleksandar S. Vesic
                          Professor of Civil Engineering and Professor of History,
                              Duke University, and author of *Engineers of Dreams*

"Eye-opening."   —Steve Goddard, Historywire.com

"Amid tales of escapees from the guillotine, indentured laborers, and no small number of scoundrels, Weightman introduces some fascinating people."   —*BBC History Magazine*

"For Weightman, modernity was created not only by ingenious inventers but by talented entrepreneurs. . . . The interconnectedness of this world of invention and technology is extraordinary. . . . There are many wonderful details that I feel I am a better person for knowing."   —*The Sunday Telegraph* (UK)

"The author of some fine business histories, Weightman elevates his game in this work. Skeptical of theoretical explanations of the Industrial Revolution, he highlights entrepreneurs behind inventions symbolic of the world's transformation from agrarianism to manufacturing. Beginning with innovators of iron smelting and winding up with the founders of the chemical industry, Weightman profiles the often obsessed personalities whose technical advances made watching capitalists take notice and invest. His narrative of the iron story sets the tone: it depicts the man who introduced coke into the smelting process, which rendered previous methods obsolete, and whose effusion of business schemes earned him the sobriquet John "Iron Mad" Wilkinson. Indeed, eccentricity seems a common trait in Weightman's cast of characters. . . . Integrating lively biography with technological clarity, Weightman converts the Industrial Revolution into an enjoyably readable period of history."
                    —Gilbert Taylor, *Booklist*

THE
INDUSTRIAL
REVOLUTIONARIES

—◆—

THE MAKING OF THE MODERN
WORLD 1776–1914

GAVIN WEIGHTMAN

Grove Press
New York

First published in Great Britain in 2007
by Atlantic Books, an imprint of Grove Atlantic Ltd.

Printed in the United States of America

ISBN-13: 978-0-8021-4484-3

Grove Press
an imprint of Grove/Atlantic, Inc.
841 Broadway
New York, NY 10003

Distributed by Publishers Group West
www.groveatlantic.com

10 11 12 13 14   10 9 8 7 6 5 4 3 2 1

CONTENTS

————•◆•————

	List of Illustrations	vi
	Acknowledgements	ix
	Introduction	1
1	Spies	10
2	Mad About Iron	22
3	The Toolbag Travellers	37
4	The Cornishman's Puffer	48
5	They Kept Their Heads	67
6	Some Yankees in the Works	90
7	The Railway Men	117
8	Cowcatchers and Timber Tracks	136
9	Les Rosbifs Go To Work	152
10	A Prophet Without Honour	173
11	A Blast of Hot Air	190
12	Morse Decoded	197
13	The Palace of Wonders	213
14	'A Very Handsome Tail'	232
15	The Petroleum Pioneers	252
16	The Steel Revolution	270
17	Of Scots and Samurai	285
18	Horsepower	299
19	The Wizard of Menlo Park	324
20	The Terror of the Torpedo	342
21	The Synthetic World	361
	Postscript	383
	Notes	394
	Bibliography	402
	Index	407

LIST OF ILLUSTRATIONS

————— ◆ —————

Integrated Illustrations

p.10. Spinning Jenny, 1811. Arbraham Rees, *The Cyclopaedia of Arts, Sciences and Literature*, plates, vol. iv, Longman, Hurst, Rees, Orme & Brown, 1820.

p.22. Cannon boring machine, 1812. Arbraham Rees, *The Cyclopaedia of Arts, Sciences and Literature*, plates, vol. ii, Longman, Hurst, Rees, Orme & Brown, 1820.

p. 37. Canal scene, 1809. Arbraham Rees, *The Cyclopaedia of Arts, Sciences and Literature*, plates, vol. ii, Longman, Hurst, Rees, Orme & Brown, 1820.

p.48. Richard Trevithick's portable steam engine, *Catch-me-who-can*, 1814. Courtesy of the Trevithick Society.

p.67. Guillotine, 1790s. Courtesy FCIT.

p.90. Fulton's nautilus, 1798. Public domain.

p.117. Portable theodolite, 1817. Arbraham Rees, *The Cyclopaedia of Arts, Sciences and Literature*, plates, vol. iv, Longman, Hurst, Rees, Orme & Brown, 1820.

p.136. Steam train with cowcatcher, *c.*1850. Courtesy FCIT.

p. 152. Navvy. *Punch*, vol. 28, 1855.

p.173. German customs, *c.*1830. Public domain.

p.190. Welsh iron works, *c.*1840. Public domain.

p.197. Morse code machine, 1877. Courtesy of the Library of Congress, LC-USZ62-110409.

p.213. Crystal palace, 1851. Mary Evans Picture Library, 10071391.

p.232. John Manjiro, *c.*1852. The Museum of Art, Kochi, Japan.

p.252. James Young's paraffin lamp, *c.*1864. Courtesy of Strathclyde University Archives.

p.270. Henry Bessemer's moveable converter, *c.*1860. Henry Bessemer, *An Autobiography*, Offices of Engineering, 1905.

p. 285. Steam vehicle in Tokyo, Japan, 1870. Courtesy of the Library of Congress, LC-USZC4-10643.

p. 299. Early motor car. *Observer*, 9 December 1827.

p. 324. Thomas Edison's electric lamp, 1880. Courtesy of the U.S. National Archives and Records.

p. 342. Outrigged Torpedo Pinnace attacking an Iron-clad. *Harper's Weekly*, 14 July 1877. Courtesy of the U.S. Navy Art Collection, Washington, D.C.

p. 361. Justus von Liebig's laboratory at Giessen, *c.* 1840. Public domain.

First Picture Section

1. Cromford Mill in Derbyshire, 1771. Mary Evans Picture Library, 10090218.

2. John Wilkinson, *c.*1780s. Science Museum, 10419510.

3. Du Pont powder mills, 1804. Hagley Museum and Library.

4. Marc Isambard Brunel, *c.*1802. Science Museum, 10300792.

5. Warship, early 1800s. Mary Evans Picture Library, 10043435.

6. Fulton's pioneer steamboat, the *North River* or *Clermont*, 1807. Science Museum, 10318047.

7. Richard Trevithick, 1816. Science Museum, 10198838.

8. Paris to Rouen railway line, 1800s. Science Museum, 10419999.

9. Opening of Crystal Palace, 1851. Mary Evans Picture Library, 10022873.

10. Challenge board for Bramah padlock, 1801. Science Museum, 10305355.

11. The McCormick reaper, *c.*1850. Mary Evans Picture Library, 10002154.

Second Picture Section

12. Railway conveyances on the Liverpool to Manchester railway, 1834. NRM, 10302114.

13. South Sea whaling, 1835. Courtesy of The New Bedford Whaling Museum.

14. American steamer in Japan, 1861. Courtesy of the Library of Congress, LC-USZC4-1274.

15. The Battle of Chemulpo Bay, 8 February 1904. Arthur M. Sackler Gallery, Smithsonian Institution, Washington, D.C., Gift of Gregory and Patricia Kruglak, S2001.37a-c.

16. Bicycling, *c.*1887. Courtesy of the Library of Congress, LC-USZC4-3043.

17. The first bicycle fitted with inflatable tyres, 1888. Mary Evans Picture Library, 10129078.

18. Motoring in England, 1903. Mary Evans Picture Library, 10040114.

19. Advertisement for 'Extractum Carnis Liebig', 1800s. Copyright Bibliotheque des Arts Decoratifs, Paris, France/Archives Charmet/The Bridgeman Art Library.

Third Picture Section

20. American expedition at Yokuhama, Japan, 1854. Courtesy of the Library of Congress, LC-USZ62-8127.

21. The 'Choshu Five', 1863. Courtesy of University College London.

22. Justus Liebig, 1843. Science Museum, 10267609.

23. Henry Bessemer, c.1870. Rischgitz/Getty Images.

24. Thomas Edison, 10301363.

25. Robert Whitehead, 1875. Public domain.

26. Daimler motocycle, 1885. Science Museum, 10322617.

27. John Dunlop, c.1890. Science Museum, 10301166.

28. Horse-drawn bus in London, early 1900s. Mary Evans Picture Library, 10193105.

29. Vice-Admiral Petrovich Rozhestvensky, 1904. RIA Novosti/TopFoto, 0828045.

30. Postcard celebrating the signing of the Treaty of Portsmouth, 1905. Courtesy of the Library of Congress, LC-DIG-ppmsca-08199.

31. Army recruits, 1914. Imperial War Museum, Q 53581.

ACKNOWLEDGEMENTS

For those of us who work alone, without the companionship and broad knowledge of academic colleagues, the internet has proved to be invaluable. There is now on the web a wealth of original documentation available for instant download as well as easy access to useful reference books through e-libraries. These resources lift some of the loneliness of the author's desk, but much more significant is the contact made with a global network of experts and enthusiasts, not all of them mainstream academics. In researching *The Industrial Revolutionaries* I had the good luck early on to find in the London Library a book called *The Transfer of Early Industrial Technologies to America*. In short, succinct chapters there were accounts of the way in which European industrial know-how had been taken across the Atlantic during the late eighteenth and early nineteenth century. The book had been published nearly twenty years earlier, in 1987, and I wondered if I would be able to find the author, Darwin H. Stapleton. It turned out to be as simple as tapping his name into a search engine to discover that he was the Executive Director of the Rockefeller Archive Centre in Sleepy Hollow, New York.

An email to Darwin Stapleton elicited an immediate response and the beginnings of a dialogue which has been absolutely vital to the authorship of this book. I was introduced to the historical discipline known as 'technology transfer' and provided with a hugely rewarding reading list. For well over a year, from the first contact, Darwin Stapleton and I never spoke on the phone. Everything was by email. And, of course, we have never met. Without the internet I doubt that I would have got beyond the book I found in the London Library. As it is, I am hugely indebted to its author.

Without the London Library I would not have found that important book in the first place and I would once again like to thank all the staff for their help. Most of the eighteenth- and nineteenth-century works I consulted I found in the British Library which still astonishes me with the depth of its holdings, such as the potter Josiah Wedgwood's 1783 pamphlet urging his skilled workforce not to be attempted abroad by French manufacturers. I have also had the privilege of access to the library of the Reform Club where Simon Blundell, the librarian, was helpful as always.

On the subject of early railways, and the life of William James the railway promoter, I am indebted to Miles Macnair who corrected my chapter and put me right on a number of significant points. His biography of James is to be published in late 2007 by the Railway & Canal Historical Society. In search of information on John Holker, the greatest industrial spy of the eighteenth century, I had the help of Michael Hindley who scoured the libraries of Lancashire for the scant details there are of this Jacobite rebel, who was branded a traitor in England and a hero in France. Brian Stewart in Canada made some helpful suggestions on the Postscript.

At Atlantic Books I would like to thank Toby Mundy and Angus MacKinnon for suggesting the subject of this book to me and for the kind attention paid to it by Angus, Sarah Norman and Louisa Joyner. At Peters, Fraser and Dunlop I would like to thank Charles Walker and Lydia Lewis for looking after my interests, as always.

Gavin Weightman
Highbury
May 2007

INTRODUCTION

In a photograph taken at University College London, in 1863, the five young men look like a modern pop group with their dark suits and oddly cropped hair – a Japanese imitation of the Beatles perhaps. They were, in fact, young revolutionaries, brave-hearted stowaways to London, who were to become powerful and famous in their own country a few years later. In Japan they became known as the Choshu Five, after the clan to which they all belonged, and were celebrated for the part they played in modernizing their country and transforming it into an industrial power.

The Choshu Five had left Japan illegally and risked their lives to discover the secrets of the success of Western nations. Their rulers, the Shogunate, had effectively sealed Japan off from foreign influences for more than two centuries, tolerating only a few trading posts such as that at Nagasaki in the south. Though in its art and culture Japan was highly sophisticated, the country had remained almost medieval in its economy and industry. In effect, its rulers had abdicated from the modern world and had been able to ignore it until ships were sighted off its coast belching black smoke and moving without sails. When engaged in battle, these dragon-like invaders possessed a firepower that no Japanese battery could match, and when their crews were finally allowed to land, they displayed strange engines which could pull entire carriages of people along a sort of track, and also a device which produced astonishing, almost instant portraits. So the five young samurai had set out to discover how the sort of society which produced such technological marvels might be established in Japan.

It was in the late 1860s that reformers such as the Choshu Five overthrew the old order, reinstated the fifteen-year-old Emperor and ushered in the Meiji (Enlightened Rule) era which began with a crash course in industrialism. This was so spectacularly successful that Japan was able to inflict a humiliating defeat on Russia in 1904, destroying a large part of the Tsar's navy. As the lines of battle were drawn up in Europe in the summer of 1914, Japan took the side of the British, whose English and Scots engineers and merchants had taught them in a few years the technological and administrative skills that had been forged over the previous century during the most remarkable period of practical inventiveness in world history.

The first 'Industrial Revolution' had taken shape in Britain a mere hundred years before the Japanese were confronted with its consequences. Nobody had planned this revolution: the rise of the machine age and the mill in a new kind of town – one in which the smoking factory chimney dwarfed the church steeple – had come about in an explosion of innovation, the origins of which remain a matter of historical dispute. What it meant in Britain, however, was the rapid rise of towns such as Liverpool and Manchester, whose populations soared from the 1760s onwards. There was simultaneously a nationwide population explosion as birth rates rose and death rates gradually fell. Britain became reliant on coal for its heating and to fuel its steam engines. In the countryside, if there was coal underground, mining was much more profitable than farming. Digging coal and iron ore and other metals for industry employed a rising proportion of the nation's workforce. The nation became less rural and more urban as the number of jobs rose in factories and workshops, taking families away from the land. Steam-powered mechanization produced unprecedented wealth as well as new kinds of hardship. But there was no stopping the advance of industrialism once it had begun.

It took some half a century for the new industrial forces to change the fabric of British society significantly, and for that reason there are those who still argue that the use of the term 'revolution' is misleading, if not downright wrong. It seems a Frenchman first coined the sobriquet 'industrial revolution' in the 1820s as a kind of counterpart to the earlier, political and non-industrial French Revolution. The term gained currency in the nineteenth century but it was not until 1884 that it became widely used, inspired by the publication, after his death at the age of thirty, of Arnold Toynbee's *Lectures on the Industrial Revolution*.

For Toynbee, the success of Britain in pioneering industrial change and ushering in a new era in world history was not the result of mere mechanical inventiveness. The essential ingredient was a political culture which was receptive to change and – to borrow the eighteenth-century term – 'improvement'. Old working practices had to be abandoned, old rights had to be torn up, new forms of financing had to be devised, and the whole social and economic fabric of a country had to be loosened up if innovation were to take effect. It was one thing to learn how to build a steam railway – and you could buy the thing lock, stock and barrel with driver and guard by the 1830s – but it was quite another to know where the money was to come from to pay for it, or to decide whose land was going to be annexed for the line and what the fares would be. These were issues the Japanese had to deal with in the 1870s and which other nations, notably France, Germany and Russia, grappled with when they sought to emulate Britain's industrial successes. For the newly emergent United States, which gained independence at precisely that historical turning point when a new industrial society was taking shape, the impulse to innovate and make use of new technologies was much less inhibited than it was in tradition-bound Europe.

The Industrial Revolutionaries, therefore, is not just about inventors, nor is it a catalogue of the kind of machines that drove the novelist Charles Dickens to distraction at the time of the Great Exhibition in London's Hyde Park in 1851. Lay readers of this book, whose minds numb at the mention of pistons and air pressure, will sympathize with Dickens, who escaped London for most of the Exhibition summer, renting out his house in Tavistock Square and hiding away at Broadstairs on the Kent coast. From there he wrote:

3

I find I am 'used up' by the Exhibition. I don't say 'there is nothing in it' – there's too much. I have only been twice; so many things bewildered me. I have a natural horror of sights, and the fusion of so many sights in one has not decreased it. I am not sure that I have seen anything but the fountain and perhaps the Amazon. It is a dreadful thing to be obliged to be false, but when anyone says, 'Have you seen?' I say, 'Yes,' because if I don't, I know he'll explain it, and I can't bear that.[1]

A certain amount of technical explanation is necessary in this book, but it is not intended as a guide to the functioning of any kind of 'engine' and it is written in the firm belief that you do not have to know how to build a motor car to be able to say something interesting about the uses to which it has been put and its impact on society at large. In fact, it is argued here that the over-emphasis on the mechanical inventiveness of the British in forging the first Industrial Revolution is extremely misleading. Promoters of railways such as the land surveyor William James were, for example, just as important to their establishment as the men – the Stephensons, say, or the Hackworths – who built them. Plagiarism was, in any case, rife in the early years of industrialism and it is almost invariably impossible to say with any certainty who first invented what. It is much easier, in fact, to knock a few tenacious myths on the head, such as the still-repeated nonsense that the dour and sickly Scot James Watt 'invented' the steam engine after watching the lid rise on a boiling kettle.

Many of the characters whose lives and achievements are recalled in this study of the spread of industrialism after the mid-eighteenth century are not well known at all today, though some enjoyed celebrity in their own lifetime. John Holker, the Catholic rebel from Lancashire, who escaped both London's Newgate prison and almost certain execution, was much better known in France, where he made a career of stealing the secrets of English textile machinery and enticing workmen to his factory in Rouen. Industrial espionage was common in the eighteenth century and was partly responsible for planting the seeds of British industrialism in Europe and North America.

Some industrialists, however, were so confident of the superiority of their workmanship that they had no qualms about setting up factories abroad, as did John 'Iron Mad' Wilkinson, replicating his cannon- and pipe-making manufactory in the Loire.

The United States, in particular, benefited from the time of its eventual independence in 1783 from an influx of skilled artisans, mostly from Britain but some also from France and Germany, who founded the earliest industries there. American industrialization was the more remarkable in its first fifty years because the country had virtually no coal-mining industry and relied for fuel on the abundance of timber in its forests. Its canals and early railways were all laid out with the help and advice of British engineers and its first locomotives were shipped across the Atlantic. Like pilgrims visiting an industrial Mecca, ambitious young Americans then embarked for Britain to school themselves in the arts of surveying and engineering: men such as Horatio Allen, who was the first man in the United States to drive a steam locomotive on native soil. However, it was not always a one-way traffic. The adventurous American Robert Fulton, who visited Europe first as a painter, was bitten by the inventive bug and, having failed to convince either Napoleon or the British Admiralty of the effectiveness of his torpedoes and submarines, returned home to inaugurate the world's first passenger steamboat service in 1807. His first steamers, with British engines, ran on the Hudson but the riverboat was soon the symbol of America's first industrial boom, carrying bales of cotton on the Mississippi and the other rivers of the southern 'slave' states.

Another very prolific American inventor was Jacob Perkins, an engraver and steam enthusiast who packed up his tools, gathered a few workmen around him and in 1818 sailed for London in the hope of winning the competition to print forge-proof banknotes for the Bank of England. He failed in that ambition but stayed on in London for the rest of his life: his firm printed the very first Penny Black postage stamps, which were issued in 1840, and on one occasion Perkins himself demonstrated what was in effect a steam-powered machine-gun to the astonished Duke of Wellington.

The nation which seemed destined to under-achieve in the first century or so of the spread of industrialism was Britain's most formidable rival, France. It would be wrong to blame the backwardness of French technology entirely on the Revolution and the guillotine, but that gruesome machine was certainly used to behead many leading scientists and intellectuals. It also drove into exile one of the most brilliant engineers and inventors of his generation, Marc Isambard Brunel, who fled to America before settling in Britain with his English wife Sophia Kingdom. It was their son, Isambard Kingdom Brunel, who became an engineering superstar of the Victorian era, but it is his father who features in this book as he was more the true innovator. The Du Pont family also fled the guillotine and founded in the United States a gunpowder factory with know-how brought from France, much of it in fact developed by the great chemist Antoine Lavoisier, who was beheaded in the Terror. Today, Dupont (this is the Americanized spelling of the name) is one of the world's giant chemical companies.

What post-Revolutionary France was good at was theoretical science and its famous chemists such as Gay-Lussac taught many aspiring Germans and some Americans the rudiments of chemical experimentation and analysis. British engineers, however, remained much superior in the practical application of technology and were so far in advance of the French that, in the 1840s, they built that country's first significant railway line between Paris and Rouen, one which was extended to Le Havre. In fact, the British built railways all around the world in the mid-nineteenth century, with contractors such as Thomas Brassey and William Mackenzie often taking with them a veritable army of 'navvies' who excavated the cuttings and raised the embankments for thousands of miles of line.

Indeed, it is quite remarkable in retrospect the degree to which British expertise was called upon around the world by any individual or any nation which coveted the wealth and power that industrial production generated. Almost everyone of any significance spent some time in Britain, if only to soak up the atmosphere of the first industrial nation or in an effort to sell some innovation. The German chemist Justus Liebig was lionized in England, and his star pupil August-Wilhelm von Hofmann was the first teacher of modern chemistry in London. Though gas and petrol engines were first devised in France and Germany, brilliant engineers such as Gottlieb Daimler spent time in England to observe how factories were run.

Yet the most extraordinary example of the wholesale adoption of British expertise is undoubtedly that of the rapid industrialization of Japan. Once the old Shogunate was overthrown, with some British assistance, engineers were invited into the country to teach everything from road- and bridge-building to the laying down of railway lines and the building of lighthouses. Whereas the Russians, who had for more than a century relied on the importation of foreign expertise, failed to learn much from it, the Japanese were intent on creating their own manufacturing industry from the start. There are Scottish heroes in Japan who are barely known in their own homeland, men such as John Blake Glover, the merchant who helped the Choshu Five escape to Britain, or Richard Brunton, who built Japan's first lighthouses. The Japanese also recognized the importance of education, bringing in the many academics and teachers who founded their universities. The inevitable result, when the rival imperial ambitions of Russia and Japan brought them into conflict, was the near-total annihilation of the Russian fleet at the battle of Tsushima in 1905. As early as 1863, when they were bombarded by British gunboats, the Japanese had learned the lesson that industrialism equals military might and that, if they refused to modernize, they ran the risk of becoming a mere colony of a great power.

Choosing the cast for a book such as this has inevitably involved some arbitrary selection: tens of thousands of significant individuals were involved in the creation and spread of industrial societies in eighteenth-century Britain up to the outbreak of the First World War. The narrative stops in 1914, for to take it any further into the twentieth century would be too cumbersome and, anyway, all the essentials are by then in place: petrol as well as steam engines, electronic communications including wireless, electric light and electric motors, iron ships and heavier-than-air flying machines. As the first industrial nation, Britain had by then already lost ground to the United States and Germany, and a familiar pattern had emerged as the built-in obsolescence of all technologies was revealed.

At one time there was an assumption that the forces of industrialism were such that all nations were bound in the end to succumb, and that the whole world would live in great cities, its workforce nailed to production lines, while farming and food production would everywhere become highly mechanized, requiring only a handful of workers in a depopulated countryside. In the 1960s, economists imagined that by studying the rise of industrial society in Britain and Europe they could predict where it would move next. There was a belief that many countries, in particular the newly independent African nations, were on the verge of 'industrial take-off'. All nations moving towards an industrial form of society would go through 'stages of growth' which were themselves predictable. The reality has turned out to be very different: technological innovation and the creation of a new kind of global economy have confounded the crystal-gazing of the economists.

The study of industrial change is full of paradoxes. There was a time when the wealthiest countries were the leading manufacturers, but now the most prosperous nations do not present an industrial image at all: most of their factories have been closed down and the work farmed out to much poorer countries where the wages are lower. There are countries which never developed any industries and have no factories to speak of yet are immensely wealthy because they own oil reserves. And then there is the enduring paradox of a machine such as the primitive cotton gin – a labour-saving device which vastly increased the demand for labour and helped perpetuate slavery in the American South.

There is no easy answer to the question of why industrialism has become established in some countries and not in others, or why, for example, in Europe it is more associated with the northern regions than with the southern. In the past, it was a popular notion that the countries which seemed to lag behind did so because of some failing of national character, a criticism often made of Italy and Spain. Certainly, even today, there are serious and knowledgeable commentators who regard certain cultures as resistant to industrialism and modernism, or lacking in some 'essential' component such as free speech or widespread education: they ask, for example, whether an orthodox Muslim nation could embrace industrialism. It is not the purpose of this book to try to answer such questions, although some explanations are touched upon in accounts of the industrial development of Europe. *The Industrial Revolutionaries* tells a different story – that of the extraordinary spread of industrialism from the middle of the eighteenth century up until the beginning of the twentieth.

CHAPTER ONE

SPIES

There were spies everywhere in eighteenth-century Britain. Though they disguised themselves in a variety of ways, they all had one ambition – to unearth the secrets of Britain's industrial success. They came from many different European countries, from Russia, Denmark, Sweden and Prussia, but the most eager of the spies were from Britain's greatest rival, France. Many were very erudite men who posed as disinterested tourists, compiling reports which they presented as purely academic treaties. Others posed as workmen in the hope of getting close to some fiendishly clever piece of machinery. And wherever the spies failed to gain entry, they were often reduced to lurking around local inns, hoping to engage knowledgeable workmen in conversation and induce them to cross the Channel for some splendid reward.

It was already evident to the French and other Europeans that Britain was gaining an industrial lead in the first half of the eighteenth century. There was, for example, the newly acquired technique of smelting iron with purified coal or 'coke' instead of charcoal, a fuel which was becoming prohibitively expensive. There were processes for the preparation of raw wool which were trade secrets and much sought after, as were some of the arcane skills of watchmakers. In the absence of any really reliable textbooks or journals which might disseminate information on how things were done, the most effective way to steal an innovation was simply to bribe a skilled workman to leave his employer. Indeed, in 1719 the British government had passed a law forbidding craftsmen to emigrate to France or any other rival country and put a penalty on attempted enticement. At that time the chief concern was the loss of iron founders and watchmakers. But after the mid-century it was the astonishing developments in textiles which were the chief target of foreign spies and the subject of protectionist legislation outlawing the export of tools and machinery as well as skilled men. It was in this trade that the English turncoat, John Holker, the master of all French spies, began an extraordinary career which spanned half a century of rapid innovation.

The invention of machines for preparing and spinning raw cotton into a strong, even yarn was exclusive to a few pioneers in England, some of whom grew rich in just a few years. They built the first spinning mills which were worked night and day by children and women on thirteen-hour shifts. Much of the cotton thread was turned by hand-loom weavers into cheap and colourful cotton cloth which was sold around the world. Millions of miles of thread was exported to countries that had not learned the secrets of how to make machinery that would produce yarn of such quality so cheaply. The first of the revolutionary cotton-spinning mills was built in 1771 in the Derbyshire countryside on the River Derwent, the flow of which provided its power: it was not until a few years later that steam engines were devised which could drive spinning or other machinery.

Cromford Mill, as it was named, was the work of two men: Richard Arkwright, a former barber-surgeon and wig-maker, and Jedediah Strutt, a Nottingham manufacturer of stockings and inventor of an ingenious 'frame' for the machine-knitting of ribbed stockings. The novelty of Cromford Mill and the great secret the stone building kept hidden was the 'water frame', a complex piece of mostly wooden machinery, a confusing mass of cogs and pulleys and subtle devices which could turn ninety-one spindles at a go – the equivalent of nearly a hundred cottagers sitting on their porches with a single-bobbin spinning wheel. Cotton thread produced on spinning wheels or spinning jennies was not generally strong enough to be used as the warp as well as the weft of cloth, which meant that it had to be interwoven with linen or wool yarn. However, the spindles of the Arkwright water frame turned out a high-quality yarn which could be used for both warp and weft so that cloth could be woven which was 100 per cent cotton.

In the last quarter of the eighteenth century, and for long after, the spinning of thread and the making of cloth was the single most important industry in Britain and much of Europe. By tradition, home-grown sheep's wool was the basic raw material, along with linen, which is made from the pounded stalks of blue-flowered flax. The very finest cloth was made of silk which came from China or was produced in some regions of Italy and France where the planting of mulberry trees, on which silk worms feed, was successful. Cotton, grown in Egypt or India, could not be raised in the temperate climate of northern Europe and was, until the 1770s, relatively unimportant. A speciality of one part of Lancashire, cotton yarn was generally woven with wool or linen thread to produce a variety of cloths.

For hundreds of years, colourful, lightweight and washable pure cotton cloth had been produced in India and was sold on a world market into which Europeans entered in the sixteenth and seventeenth centuries. The British East India Company, founded in 1600, for many years picked up Indian cotton cloth at the Malabar coastal town of Calicut and traded it in Indonesia for spices. Towards the end of the seventeenth century, the Company, seeking new ways of making money, brought back to England some cargoes of colourful Indian cotton cloth. It was a sensation, not only in England but throughout Europe. When it was washed, the dyes did not run, though how this was achieved nobody outside India knew. As the East Indiamen returned from the Thames to the Malabar coast, they carried instructions as to which kinds of pattern might be popular in England.

But the East India Company was soon in trouble, accused of unpatriotic profiteering. In the woollen-weaving and silk-producing districts of England, cotton became a dirty word. In France and other European countries too, the threat that these wonderful Indian goods presented to the established textile industries brought a swift reaction. Women seen wearing cotton gowns were attacked in the Spitalfields district of London in what became known as the 'calico riots' – calico being the term for all cotton goods derived from the entrepot of Calicut. The selling and wearing of pure cotton goods was outlawed to protect indigenous industries. In Britain the ban lasted from 1721 until 1776, though many ingenious ways were found to get around it. Similar bans were imposed in Europe.

The popularity of cotton was established, however, and while British dyers puzzled over the secrets of the fast colours of Indian cottons, others set out to discover how the yarn could be produced in greater quantities and more cheaply. There were a number of false starts in the 1740s with machines that could spin cotton but for one reason or another were not successful. It was in the 1760s, although it is impossible to say exactly when, that the first 'spinning jennies' appeared. The invention is generally attributed to a Lancashire textile worker called James Hargreaves, who fashioned the first prototype with a penknife. It was a small machine which could revolve up to nine bobbins at a time with the turn of a single wheel which was worked by hand. There was a certain knack to it as a tension had to be kept in the threads, but it could be operated by a child and could fit into the rooms of a cottage. Revolutionary though it was, reproductions based on the original patent application show a piece of machinery that looks primitive, if not decidedly medieval.

Hargreaves was allegedly driven out of Lancashire and developed his jennies in Nottingham. The new machines were quickly copied and soon there were hundreds and then thousands at work. Not long after, Richard Arkwright arrived in Nottingham with his plans for a spinning machine that could be driven by 'gin' (an abbreviation of 'engine') horses or a waterwheel. Arkwright had no background in textiles and appears to have consulted a clock-maker about the mechanisms he needed, and he found a ready and skilled partner in Jedediah Strutt. Once their Cromford Mill began to whirr, it drew from other parts of the country, and from all over Europe, fascinated visitors, many of whom were quite obviously industrial spies.

If you glance at a diagram of the first of Arkwright's water frames, it is immediately apparent that copying it would be no easy task. There were those who bribed workmen to allow them a glimpse of spinning machines and other British technological novelties and attempted to fathom how they worked. But with all this early equipment there was no substitute for finding someone who had spent time in the Mill and might be enticed abroad with the prospect of higher wages and a more comfortable life. Any workman who accepted such offers was taking a considerable risk, for under English law any possessions they left at home could be confiscated and they faced jail if they wanted to return.

The threats did not, however, do much to inhibit the efforts of John Holker, who was successful in enticing large numbers of English artisans to work in France. Holker was born in 1719 in Stretford near Manchester, the son of a blacksmith who died when John was in his infancy. When he was in his early twenties, Holker worked in the Manchester textile trade as an apprentice calenderer, a skilled job in which cloth was pressed between rollers to make it smooth. He went into partnership with a man called Peter Moss, who had money, and by 1745 they owned a thriving business. It was in that year that the forces supporting the claims of the 'Young Pretender' to the English throne, Bonnie Prince Charlie, reached Lancashire. Both Holker and Moss were Catholic and joined a rapidly assembled Manchester Regiment under Colonel Townley to fight for the Pretender in the uprising known for ever after as the '45. It was a mad venture which was quickly and brutally crushed, the decisive victory going to the Duke of Cumberland at Culloden. Moss and Holker were taken prisoner at Carlisle in Cumberland and, along with other officers and men involved in the rebellion, were sent to London's Newgate prison to await trial.

Newgate was a grim fortress in the mid-eighteenth century but run on commercial lines. Prisoners could pay for privileges and Peter Moss managed to bribe their jailer to sell them rope and tools to bore a hole in the prison wall. Holker was a big man and after Moss had eased through he became stuck and his friend had to go back to widen the gap. According to Holker, who would regale his French friends with the story many years later, they lowered themselves on knotted sheets to a roof which enabled them to leap across on to a merchant's house adjoining the prison. Holker missed a jump and landed in a barrel of water, but was still able to make his escape. One version of the story has Holker hidden for six weeks by a London woman with a greengrocer's stall before he got away to Holland and on to Paris, which he reached in 1746.

In France, Holker joined a regiment of Scottish infantry fighting in Flanders and, by his own account, once again risked his neck by accompanying Bonnie Prince Charlie on a secret mission to England in 1750. The following year, he found himself a home in Rouen, Normandy, where there was an established homespun textile industry in which he took a professional interest. He went into partnership with two French associates, making velvet, but still in 1753 appears to have had a desire to return to England. Peter Moss's daughter had married into the prominent Gartside family and through them Holker asked if he might be pardoned for his treacherous Jacobite activities. Either he was refused this amnesty, or he received no reply, for in 1754 he accepted an offer to set up a textile works in Rouen. This was before the invention of the spinning jenny or the water frame, but in England at the time there were machines for preparing raw wool or cotton for spinning, and Holker persuaded the French Inspector of Cloths at Rouen that it would be worth importing some Lancastrian expertise. He was introduced to the head of the French Bureau of Commerce, Daniel Charles Trudaine, creator of the postal system and the bridges and roads department, who was convinced of Holker's abilities and knowledge.

Trudaine quickly found the money (about £350) to pay for Holker to return to England in disguise so that he could snoop around Manchester and other Lancashire towns. Holker's mother was still alive and helped him find samples of cloth and key workers with knowledge of particular processes. He worked frantically for three months, dispatching workers to be greeted by his wife at a temporary reception centre and then sent on to Rouen. In a short time a textile business with royal patronage was established in Saint-Sever on the outskirts of the town. Under Holker's direction, there was a team of English workmen including carpenters, joiners, calenderers and others. In October 1754, out of a total of eighty-six artisans at Saint-Sever, there were twenty English skilled workers and over the next few years they became influential in developing machinery for preparing and spinning cotton, not only there but in other parts of France as well.

Under Trudaine's patronage Holker flourished, earning a large salary and almost certainly prospering more than he might have done as a manufacturer back in Lancashire. That his main duty was as a spy is made clear in a letter in Trudaine's files: 'If one proposes to bring to France foreign skills, and principally those of England, where industry has made more progress than anywhere else, one can first use Sieur Holker to set up and maintain a secret correspondence with England to get thence surely and quickly all the models of machines and the samples and tools one needs.' Holker himself appears to have experienced little difficulty in bypassing the English customs officers, favouring the overcrowded port of London for transporting skilled artisans and machines to France. He chose ships sailing from the Thames to Rotterdam to allay any suspicion that cargoes were heading to Rouen. All the latest pieces of equipment – the spinning jennies from the 1760s onwards and the water frames and mules, which were hybrids of the jenny and water frame, from the 1770s – were shipped across to France illegally.

Some spies were caught. Charles Albert, a native of Strasburg, came to England in 1791 as the agent for a Toulouse firm which had cotton mills. While trying to recruit skilled workers, including a man called Geoffrey Scholes, he was arrested. He was tried in 1792 at Lancaster Assizes, where he was convicted, fined £500 and sentenced to one year in jail. Albert was unable to pay the fine and spent five years in Lancaster prison before returning to France where, undaunted, he set up his own spinning mill with the help of expatriate English artisans. He never looked back, establishing himself in Paris as a manufacturer of textile machines for which he was awarded a gold medal at the Paris Industrial Exhibition of 1806. Albert then moved into the manufacture of steam engines, for which he and his partner won more medals. Nevertheless, he ended his career simply buying in foreign inventions from England and America before his eventual retirement to Strasburg.

Holker was never caught, and in time he persuaded the French authorities that if he were given a high-ranking official position and were well paid, his conspicuous success would encourage more British artisans to follow. In April 1755 he was made one of just seven Inspectors General of Manufactures and attempted to encourage the best in British industrial practice in his adopted country, not only in textile manufacture but other areas as well. Towards the end of his life Holker became a distinguished figure, elevated to the French aristocracy and honoured by the Academy of Sciences. He was visited by the American publisher, scholar and inventor, Benjamin Franklin, and was friendly with Thomas Jefferson, who took over from Franklin as ambassador to France in 1784. Holker was anxious to forge a closer relationship with the United States, but he died in 1786, just three years after America's victory in its War of Independence from Britain.

In the year before Holker died, a piece appeared in *The Daily Universal Register*, the forerunner of the London *Times*, which stated unequivocally that at one stage Holker (his name was spelt 'Haulker') had wanted to return to England and had asked for a pardon. Haulker was then already established in France but, so the piece claimed, offered to abandon his manufactory in Rouen if the Duke of Newcastle would allow him to establish a business again in England. According to the newspaper report, the Duke responded: 'It's all a mere trick to get a pardon, which he never shall obtain; and he may carry on what trade he pleases.' So Haulker 'reluctantly concluded with the Court of France and began to fabricate cotton cloth'.

The Duke of Newcastle then realized his mistake and offered Holker not only a pardon but a bribe of £400 if he would abandon his French factory. 'His answer,' says the *Universal Register*, 'was noble, and does him credit, though us an injury. "All I wanted [said he] was a pardon – this offer is now too late, as several gentlemen have embarked their property with me, depending on my honour to fulfil my agreement." From this cause was the cotton manufacture introduced into Normandy, and from that period, the French have done all in their power to encourage it. Spies have been repeatedly detected at Manchester and other places with models of the machinery.' In the opinion of the *Universal Register*, Holker had 'entailed more ruin and mischief on this kingdom than perhaps even the loss of America'.[1]

Holker was a spy, pure and simple. But there were many other visitors from France who did not travel cloak and dagger but were, on the face of it, honoured guests. Travellers such as Faujas de Saint-Fond and Monsieur Le Turc, and indeed carriageloads of distinguished Frenchmen, wrote up their observations on the wonders of English industrialism in all apparent innocence. On their tours they were bound to take in Cromford Mill and might observe it at night with the spindles whirring under candlelight or the fiery hell of Coalbrookdale's iron foundries in the steep-sided gorge of the River Severn. Here, indeed, was the world's very first iron bridge, opened to traffic in 1781. Then there were the works at Soho just outside Birmingham where Matthew Boulton made what were known in the eighteenth century as 'toys' – buttons and buckles and all manner of metal trinkets. From the 1770s Boulton's factory also manufactured the most celebrated stationary steam engines of the day designed by the Scot, James Watt. And any serious tourist was bound to visit Etruria, where Josiah Wedgwood had his world-famous pottery which made splendid crockery and tea sets always with an eye to the latest fashions.

There was a dilemma for the leading industrialists of the day when confronted with a visitor from abroad. Men like Boulton and Wedgwood sold their wares all over Europe and they did not want to upset potential customers. It was always possible, too, that a visitor might want to order some of their wares or one of their machines and they were not necessarily averse to selling. And on occasion a foreigner might let slip some really useful piece of technical information, as happened from time to time. Matthew Boulton, for example, used his French contacts to discover the secret of or moulu (literally, 'ground gold') for gilding and employed at his Soho works some celebrated engravers, including the Frenchman Jean-Pierre Droz and Conrad Heinrich Kuchler from Flanders. On the other hand, they could never be quite sure if their guest had an eye to steal their trade secrets, and a decision had to be taken about how much to show them, or whether to let them in at all. Quite a few distinguished visitors were disappointed by their arm's-length treatment.

Josiah Wedgwood was one who felt seriously threatened by attempts to lure his skilled workmen away to France. In 1783 he published a little pamphlet he titled *An Address to the Workmen in the Pottery on the subject of Entering into Service of Foreign Manufacturers*, signing it 'Josiah Wedgwood FRS, Potter to her Majesty'. Prefacing his pamphlet with the proverb 'A rolling stone gathers no moss', Wedgwood put forward a telling argument to the effect that any of his workmen who were enticed abroad by the offer of higher wages were bound to end up poorer than when they left his employ. Why could French property masters, for instance, afford to pay them at a rate six times higher than the local wage rates? 'Now they certainly cannot be gainers, so long as we are able to send among them a better and cheaper commodity than they can make themselves: and surely we shall not find it difficult to do this whilst they give double the wages that we do.'[2]

Inevitably, therefore, the foreign potter would seek to use the Englishmen to train up French apprentices and, once they had learned the trade, the English instructors would no longer be necessary and would certainly not command very high wages. In fact, in the long run they would probably be offered *less* than the locals. 'And such low wages would afford but miserable subsistence to Englishmen brought up from their infancy to better and more substantial fare than frogs, hedgehogs and the wild herbs of the field.'

It was not necessarily inventiveness that was stolen when a skilled worker went abroad but his knowledge of industrial technique. And that, in the eighteenth century, was what the British were thought to be especially good at: turning novel ideas into successful commercial ventures. Daniel Defoe, in his *A Plan of the English Commerce*, had written in 1728: 'It is a kind of Proverb attending the Character of English Men, that they are *better to improve than to invent,* better to advance upon the Designs and Plans which other People have laid down than to form Schemes and Designs of their Own; and which is still more, the Thing seems to be really true in Fact and the Observation very just ...'[3] As another proverb had it, 'For a thing to be perfect it must be invented in France and worked out in England.'

Within Britain, the theft of techniques and the enticing away of workmen from one firm to another was widespread. And it is quite probable that the celebrated inventors of textile machinery, James Hargreaves and Richard Arkwright, were really plagiarists. Conclusive evidence of who invented what does not exist. Either way, claiming an invention did not guarantee success. Hargreaves was, in the end, a failure, while Arkwright became a very rich man. It is extremely unlikely that Arkwright had the know-how or technical ability to invent any complex machinery. He was more in the way of a fixer, who said what he wanted and got others to solve the problem. In the case of the water frame, the inventive genius was quite likely a watchmaker called John Kay whom Arkwright had met in his days as a travelling peruke- or wig-maker. Kay challenged the validity of Arkwright's patent for the water frame and won the legal battle, but only long after Arkwright had already become wealthy and been honoured with a knighthood.

The laws against the export of men and machines, which were extended throughout the eighteenth century and into the nineteenth, were the subject of a parliamentary review in 1824. Though the Select Committee, which took evidence from a wide range of manufacturers, found that espionage and the enticement of workmen abroad was still rife, the new enthusiasm for 'free trade' put an end to attempts to stem the flow of native know-how out of the country. The committee wondered if it was still true that finding workmen with special skills was so important in an age where the nature of inventions had become much more complex, the patent laws more rigorously applied and more information was available in technical publications. Skilled workers were now free to go abroad without fear of having their luggage searched for specialist tools. But the ban on the export of key machinery – the steam engine was a puzzling exception – remained until the 1840s.

In any case, as the French were to discover, transferring industrialism in bits and pieces across the Channel was never just a simple matter of enticing workmen away from home. In the age of the steam engine, an abundant and relatively cheap supply of coal was needed. Either industry had to be established on the coalfields or there had to be reasonably priced transport, which meant by boat before the coming of the railways. Britain had the huge advantage of rich coalfields lying along tidal rivers linked to each other by coastline. Most of France's coalfields were in the north while much of its textile industry was on the Rhone in the region of Lyons. That was just one fundamental difference between the two countries. There were many others to do with government's attitude to industry – which, for instance, was much more controlling in France than in Britain – as well as the attitude to manufacturing of the moneyed classes. As Arnold Toynbee was to argue in his

1888 *Lectures on the Industrial Revolution,* the key to 'take off' was a loosening of old guild restrictions and other cultural inhibitors of industrial growth.

The key figure, then, was perhaps not so much the skilled artisan as the talented entrepreneur or businessman. Men such as Matthew Boulton and Josiah Wedgwood combined both skills. In a later period they might well have considered moving their factories abroad to tap cheaper land and labour or to expand their business. As it was, they were content to sell to foreign buyers. However, there was a contemporary of theirs who seemed to suffer no fear at all of foreign competition, especially from the French. So assured was he of his superiority that he had no compunction in planting his industry on French soil, and it was not without reason that he became known as 'Iron Mad' Wilkinson.

CHAPTER TWO

MAD ABOUT IRON

Among the distinguished guests enjoying a banquet beneath the glittering chandeliers of the Hotel de Ville in Paris on 12 July 1786 were two Englishmen who were well known in France. The banquet was being held to celebrate the completion of an entirely new system of water supply for Paris for which the brothers William and John Wilkinson had supplied miles of iron piping. They had also arranged the installation of steam engines to pump water from the Seine into storage reservoirs. Like the iron pipes, the steam engines were made in England by the Wilkinsons' good friends and business partners, Messrs Boulton and Watt of Birmingham.

That the French should purchase iron pipes from England is not surprising, for their own iron industry had not advanced much during the eighteenth century and their foundries could not compete in terms of quality or price with the works of the senior of the two brothers, John, who was widely known as 'Iron Mad' Wilkinson. What was strange, and not a little inconvenient for both supplier and customer, was that more than one shipment of these iron water pipes was dispatched when England and France were at war with each other, as they were for a large part of the eighteenth century. Not only that, but John Wilkinson had made his name as a leading ironmaster with his production of superior iron cannon for the British Navy, and the barrel of a cannon did not look very different from a Paris water pipe.

The suspicion that Wilkinson was supplying the enemy with cannons disguised as water pipes has long lingered, but the issue has never been satisfactorily resolved. What is indisputable, however, is that Wilkinson had no compunction at all about trading with the enemy or entertaining visitors at his famous ironworks at Broseley in Shropshire. There is an account by two French aristocrats, the brothers La Rochefoucauld, of a visit they paid to the Broseley works while on a tour of the industrial areas of England in 1785. 'Mr Wilkinson is one of the greatest ironmasters in the world,' they wrote, '...He has acquired immense wealth, mostly by his genius ... We didn't find Mr Wilkinson: he was in bed with a heavy cold he had caught in London. He read the letter we had brought him and sent us to his nearest ironworks where his agent showed us everything they were doing.' There was no shutting of doors or silencing of workmen at Broseley – the French visitors were shown everything they wanted to see by workmen whose knowledge impressed them. They noted, too, how much good quality beef the workmen had to eat, quite different from the diet of French *ouvriers* – but also how tough the ironwork shifts were. François La Rochefoucauld, then still a teenager, wrote: 'Seeing them at work, I reflected as I very often have before: how lucky I am to be born into a position in which I don't have to work in order to live: and how unhappy I'd be if I had to work as hard as I could for three hours, then sleep for as long ... What a miserable fate! What a price our luxury costs!'[1] He would no doubt have been even more upset had he realized that a shift at Broseley was not three hours but twelve, a misunderstanding that arose in the translation into French.

The admiration that the French had for John Wilkinson went back a good ten years. It arose from the discovery that his ironworks had made the cannon for the British Navy which had been so successful against the French in the series of conflicts known as the Seven Years War which had ended in peace treaties agreed by half a dozen European protagonists in 1763. On land, the big field guns were forged from brass and so were lighter and more manoeuvrable than a heavy iron weapon. At sea, the favoured metal was iron. The French cast their cannon with the barrel fashioned in moulds and then smoothed out, but these had proved to be treacherous, often blowing up at the point of firing and killing the crew: hidden hollows and impurities in the metal made for dangerous weak spots. English cannon had performed much better and with fewer accidents, and given that John Wilkinson was their chief supplier to the Royal Navy, it was not long before French traveller-spies were knocking on his door.

In 1764, Gabriel Jars, a young engineer from a Lyonnais family of metal smelters, was sent to Britain to investigate the way in which iron was produced, not with charcoal as a fuel, as was universal in France and the rest of the world, but with a modified form of coal. Jars, whose itinerary was organized by John Holker, described how the ironworks he visited at Carron in Scotland, and in other parts of the country, had a method of turning raw coal into something called 'courke' by getting it to burn slowly. It was a similar process to charcoal-burning in which the slow combustion of a stack of wood over several days rid the fuel of its impurities, particularly sulphur. The use of 'courke' or, as the English had it, 'coke', made available for iron production a huge abundance of fuel which the coppice woods of the charcoal burners would never have been able to match.

The breakthrough in coke-smelting had been made as early as 1709 in the gorge of the River Severn in Shropshire at a place called Coalbrookdale. It was the achievement of a family of Bristol Quakers who had been in the business of casting brass and copper goods which were valuable currency in the British trade in African slaves. (Then, Quaker families were involved in the slave trade, though they were later abolitionists.) When Abraham Darby, getting on in years, bought up a more or less defunct ironworks in Coalbrookdale and experimented with the use of coke for iron-smelting he was able to produce workable pig iron by this method.

Why this breakthrough should have occurred in England rather than some other part of Europe remains something of a mystery. But coal was mined and burned in huge quantities in Britain long before it became a significant fuel in other European countries. A whole range of British manufacturers had switched to coal from wood fuel in the sixteenth century: blacksmiths, glass-makers, dyers, brick-makers and so on. The coalmines of the north-east of England along the River Tyne were by 1700 sending thousands of tons of coal to London on a fleet of collier ships, which made up the single largest fleet of the English merchant navy. Captain James Cook first learned seamanship on the colliers that were built in Whitby for the east coast coal trade, and his exploration ship in 1778 was a collier vessel, the *Earl of Pembroke*, refitted and armed at Chatham dockyard and renamed the *Endeavour*.

There was one major limitation to the widespread use of coal in manufacturing: it could not be used to smelt iron ore. The reason for this was chemical: ore heated with raw coal became contaminated with sulphur, which made it friable and useless. Iron ore could only be smelted with charcoal, wood that had had the impurities smoked out of it. This pig or bar iron could then be worked in coal furnaces. The quality of bar iron varied according to the iron ore used and the skills of the smelter, and England imported a great deal of high-quality bar iron from Sweden and Russia up until the second half of the eighteenth century. Both countries had an abundance of timber to turn into charcoal as well as good-quality ores. The Sheffield cutlery industry was reliant on imported bar iron which it turned into fine steel using a process invented by Benjamin Huntsman in which the iron was heated to very high temperatures in clay crucibles (see Chapter 16).

The smelting of iron ore is best understood as a kind of 'cooking' process in which the basic ingredients could vary greatly in quality. Iron implements were being made in Egypt and ancient countries of the Middle East at least four thousand years ago, so the technique of melting down ore found in bogs or, more commonly, in rocks has a long prehistory. A major advance, which came from Europe to England, was the use of a blast of air to raise the temperature of the furnace, the bellows worked by men, horses or a water-driven mill wheel. In the seventeenth century, the iron industry in England was confined to regions which had adequate supplies of timber for charcoal, rivers which would drive mill wheels, and a supply of ore which was close by as the transport of heavy materials was prohibitively expensive.

Smelting iron with coking coal was therefore revolutionary, which is the reason the French were so keen to learn the secrets of the process. It would free the iron industry from dependence on woodland and, as the first coal-fuelled steam engines began to provide power for the bellows, from reliance on river sites. All that took time, however. Old Abraham Darby, who had begun the revolution, was long dead by the time coke-smelted iron became common and the old charcoal furnaces began to close down.

John 'Iron Mad' Wilkinson was born around 1728 (nobody is quite sure of his date of birth) and from an early age was familiar with iron-smelting. His father, Isaac, worked at various coke-fired furnaces and had a number of patents to his name, the most successful of which was for a hollow 'box-iron', used in the textile business for smoothing cloth, especially linen. Isaac took his family to Bersham in North Wales, where he worked for twenty years trying to make a go of various projects, taking out another patent on an iron-blowing engine for furnaces.

His son, John, was no rude mechanic. He had been educated at Dr Caleb Rotheram's Dissenting Academy at Kendal before he set up as a wholesale ironmonger. He married in 1755 a woman with a small personal fortune which provided him with the funds to establish a coke-fired furnace in the Black Country of the Midlands. He made pig iron which others turned into pots and pans and cannon for the navy. Acquiring a reputation as an ironmaster, he went into partnership with a syndicate of merchants and landed gentry who wanted to set up a new furnace close to the pioneering works of the Darbys at Coalbrookdale. This was established at Wiley on the other side of the River Severn from the Darby works.

Wilkinson settled in Broseley and soon had complete charge of the works, which made great profits casting naval cannon and shot for the British government, and indeed for anyone else prepared to pay, including privateers. At the same time, John went into partnership with Isaac, his father. But their commercial ventures together failed and they fell out. Old Isaac died a bankrupt while John went on to make a success of the business. In 1774 he took out a patent which was to become his greatest claim to fame: an elaborate mechanism for boring out the barrels of iron cannon from a solid mould. Versions of this boring system had been in existence for a number of years, but Wilkinson's machine was an improvement on them, with the cannon itself being rotated while the cutter was held steady.

Just at the time when Wilkinson's fame at home and abroad was becoming established, he was visited by an infantry brigadier, Marchant de la Houlière, from Perpignan in southern France, who made a tour of English iron foundries in 1775. This was an official visit, backed by Louis XVI with a grant from the Languedoc estates where de la Houlière had already experimented smelting iron with coke. There had been a number of French attempts to emulate the English success with coke-smelting but none had been really successful. De la Houlière, travelling with a chaplain, a Mr MacDermott, who acted as interpreter, wondered if there was something special about the varieties of iron ore and coal mined in England which gave it an advantage. Or was it just a knack of the ironmasters there that he could acquire?

The Frenchman concluded that there really was not much difference in the ores or coal and that it was the process of making the coke and the 'cooking' or the ore in the furnace that was crucial. He was quite wrong about this – the qualities of iron ore and coal were very important – but he was sure he could establish a French industry comparable with that in Britain if he could buy in specialist knowledge from Iron Mad Wilkinson. 'Being a zealous military man and having the interests of the King's service at heart, he [de la Houlière referred to himself in the third person] was suddenly seized with the idea of bringing to France an experienced man capable of fulfilling this object, and he ventured to drop certain vague hints to an eminent ironmaster [none other than Wilkinson] who owns four foundries and has brought the casting of cannon to the highest pitch of perfection, to the effect that an Englishman who would come to France and cast them in a similar manner, would make a large fortune.'

De la Houlière had been given a letter of introduction to Wilkinson by Messrs Boulton and Watt. After visiting Wilkinson, who made Boulton and Watt's cylinders, he wrote to thank them and to say how he had been received with 'every mark of politeness'. Wilkinson had entertained de la Houlière and his translator in his home in Broseley and had given them a tour of Coalbrookdale.

Wilkinson considered the Frenchman's offer to set up in business across the Channel but shook his head at the idea of any funding arrangement with the French government, which he thought would be unreliable. However, if it were a *private* arrangement with de la Houlière, then he would be interested and could see a 'tidy profit in it'. His terms were tough: a guaranteed market for twelve years for the products of a French ironworks, exemption from all tax on coal, the freedom to export cannon and cannon balls when and where he liked, as well as 'bombs manufacture in excess of service requirements'. To all this the Frenchman agreed, accepting an equal partnership in the prospective enterprise, and making just the one proviso that, in the event of war between the two countries, the weaponry of the new foundries could be sold only to 'neutral powers'.

John Wilkinson said there was no question of going to France himself, but his younger brother William, who was in charge of the foundries at Bersham in North Wales, might well be keen to take up the offer. De la Houlière reported: 'Next day I was at Bersham foundry near Wrexham, which is managed by this younger brother of his, a man of thirty to thirty-five years of age [William was thirty-two]. I gave him an account of my conversation with his brother. He appeared to me to agree with all the views expressed and had a great desire to see France.'[2] And so de la Houlière reported back that he could, provided the terms were agreed, ship over English expertise in the manufacture of cannons, cannonballs and bombs. He argued that cannon made in France with English expertise would be no more costly than those made in France, that they would be better quality, that there would be income from exports and that, when other English manufacturers saw how profitable it was to set up across the Channel, many more would follow, bringing their expertise with them.

William Wilkinson crossed the Channel in 1775 as the guest of Marchant de la Houlière and the French government. An ironworks for the manufacture of cannon was set up on the Isle Indret in the Loire, close to Nantes. Following the practice of the Bersham works, iron was not smelted here: instead, the raw material used was broken pieces of iron which were re-melted and then cast into sand moulds, a Wilkinson innovation. The machine used for boring cannon, however, was not the one patented by John Wilkinson but one similar and modified from a French model that was formerly used for boring brass barrels.

William was initially paid a salary of 12,000 livres per year to manage the Indret foundry, rising to an astonishing 50,000 livres (more than £130,000 in today's money) in 1779. Two years later he was offered even more money (about £160,000) to establish a new works at Le Cruesot near Montcenis in Burgundy, the site of one of the important coalfields in France. The Montcenis foundry became the first successful coke-smelting plant in Europe and continued operating after William returned to England a rich man. But both Indret in the Loire and the Burgundy venture suffered in the turmoil of the French Revolution and the export of expertise by the Wilkinsons did not, in the end, present the British iron industry with any real competition.

When, in 1777, a scheme for providing Paris with a more adequate supply of water was approved by the French government, those who promoted the scheme immediately set off for England to acquire the necessary equipment. The water scheme was a commercial venture put up by two brothers, Jacques-Constantin and Augustin-Charles Périer, and it required pumping engines to draw water from the Seine and miles of iron pipes to distribute it to customers. William Wilkinson was the first contact before the Périer brothers visited John Wilkinson at Broseley and went on to Matthew Boulton and James Watt's Soho works. All three – Wilkinson, Boulton and Watt – invested in the Paris scheme, offering their iron pipes and steam engines at very modest prices as they believed they would make handsome profits from their shares.

The whole enterprise was nevertheless fraught with danger. In 1776 war, which would continue until 1783, had broken out with the American colonies whose cause was supported by the French. Apart from the problem of supplying an ally of the enemy with iron pipes which were easily mistaken for cannon, the sea routes around Britain became hazardous. The navy was impressing ships and men and the Militia Bill would have a domestic army standing by to repel invasion. Nevertheless, through their government contacts and with great perseverance, Wilkinson, Boulton and Watt managed to get 'passports' for their export of steam engines and pipes and engaged Captain John Williams of the ship *Mary* at Chester to carry some of the cargo, which they hoped would get as far as Rouen on the tidal limit of the River Seine.

Captain Williams, however, set his own terms. John Wilkinson wrote to

Watt on 4 July 1779: 'He says it is not possible for him to go up to Rouen under £5 per ton freight – nay, indeed, that his vessel cannot on any account go there without being discharged one half at Havre. He has been at both places and knows the river, ports and custom well, and from what he says it would be madness going further than Havre; says charges in that river for going up, would he do so, would cost him £70 sterling, besides the delay which might be two months. His wages now stand in about £50 a month and on the most extravagant terms – men are not to be had at present …'[3]

The British had in fact put an embargo on all ships sailing to foreign ports in the summer of 1779, so it was not clear the *Mary* would get away. She loaded up at Dawpool, Chester's port, making sure she was well armed against attack with twelve guns, but before she could sail the Press Gang seized her entire crew. Captain Williams assembled a replacement crew, but that was seized too, as was a third before the ship got away. Eventually, part of the cargo arrived not in Le Havre but in the Normandy port of Honfleur and Captain Williams returned via Plymouth to take a second consignment. But again there were problems with permissions and the Paris water pipes lay for months on a dock at Chepstow, along with engine parts.

By 1781 the pipes had still not left England and John Wilkinson was concerned that the Périer brothers had not paid up for the first consignment, owing him about £9,000 or more than £500,000 in today's money. All Wilkinson had was his shares in the Compagnie des Eaux de Paris, which was not paying any dividends. It was, he surmised, an enterprise with 'too many Dukes and courtiers'. Meanwhile the iron pipes piled up on the quay at Chepstow were rusting and arousing suspicions. The Hon. John Byng made a note of them in his diary for 16–17 June 1781: 'On the quay were … incredible numbers of iron water pipes (like cannon) each nine feet long and weighing about 800 weight which are going to France (by permission). Nearly twenty-one miles of them are sent.'[4]

In March 1782, a Coalbrookdale shopkeeper sent a report to the Treasury complaining that Wilkinson had used the wayleave to export innocent water pipes as a cover for sending the French 'Cannon Balls, Cylinders of Most unusual Thickness and that Ball to the amount of twenty-four thousand tons in Six Weeks supposed for France as all were put on Board those Vessels employed by Wilkinson for exporting the Iron Pipes'. The Treasury passed this intelligence on to the Lords Commissioners of Customs but their investigation proved nothing and Wilkinson, Boulton and Watt were not pursued.

It is unlikely Wilkinson made any money out of the Paris project. Although he and his brother attended the celebration marking the completion of the works, the Revolution of 1789 swept away the water company and with it any chance of a profit from the shares. But the long drawn-out saga illustrates the fact that practically nothing could inhibit the trading impulse of a fierce capitalist such as John Wilkinson, and that he had no compunction at all about fraternizing with the enemy.

The French, seeking foreign expertise, always had in mind that they would learn from it and become proficient themselves at whatever the form of manufacturing involved. Other nations appear to have simply coveted foreign know-how and set out to implant it in their own otherwise stagnant economy. Russia especially made many attempts to buy up English industrialists and met with some success; Catherine the Great, who came to power in 1762 possessed of a reforming zeal, was very much in favour of importing expertise from abroad. A manifesto of 1763, translated into a quaint English, stated:

> If any of those Foreigners that have settled themselves in Russia shall erect Fabricks or Works, and manufacture there such Merchandizes, as have not been made yet in Russia: We do allow and give leave to sell and export the said Merchandizes out of our Empire for ten Years, without paying any inland Tolls, Port duties or Customs on the Borders ... If any Foreign Capitalist will erect Fabricks, Manufactures or Works in Russia, We allow him to purchase for the said Fabricks, Manufactures and Works a requisite Numbre of Bond-People and Peasants ... To those Foreigners which have settled themselves in Our Empire by Colonies or Places, we do allow and give leave to appoint such Markets and Fairs, as they themselves shall think most proper, without paying any Toll or Custom into our Treasury.[5]

In the 1770s the Carron ironworks, established in Scotland with workmen poached from Coalbrookdale, had become celebrated for its production of a powerful little cannon that was known by sailors as 'The Smasher' for its devastating effect in broadside encounters. It was also known as the Carronade and was coveted by the Russians, who were able to entice some workers away from the Carron works to establish a similar foundry in St Petersburg. Carron was founded by John Roebuck and Samuel Garbett but had been effectively taken over by the charming but unreliable Charles Gascoigne, who had married Garbett's daughter. When he got into financial difficulties, Gascoigne emigrated to St Petersburg, where he joined some of his workmen and prospered, enjoying the patronage of Catherine. He became a member of the Russian government and was known as State Councillor Karl Karlovich Gaskoin. He died in St Petersburg in 1806.

Another apprentice from the Carron works, Charles Baird, joined Gascoigne in Russia in 1786 and, after three years, established an iron foundry and gunworks with a partner in St Petersburg. Born in 1766, and one of ten children of the superintendent of the Firth and Clyde canal, Baird was both an engineer and manufacturer. He specialized in making steam engines and built the first steamship in Russia, the *Elizaveta,* which plied between Kronstadt and St Petersburg. He also provided the material for some of the first Russian iron bridges. His reputation for operating a streamlined factory gave rise to a saying in Russian '*Kak u Berda na zavode*', meaning to run smoothly 'like a Baird works'. Matthew Boulton himself had a lively trade with Russia and was asked to set up the machinery for a mint. Earlier James Watt had been sorely tempted to go. In 1771 a friend, John Robison, who had obtained an academic post in Russia, recommended Watt as 'Master Founder of Iron Ordnance to Her Imperial Majesty'. Watt dithered, then wrote in the nicest possible terms to say he would not go. His friend Erasmus Darwin wrote to him after a further attempt to entice him away in 1775: 'Lord how frightened I was when I heard a Russian bear had laid hold of you with his great paw, and was dragging you to Russia – Pray don't go, if you can help it. Russia is like the Den of Cacus, you see the Footsteps of many Beasts going thither but of few returning.'[6]

There had been a time when Matthew Boulton was tempted by overtures from Sweden. In 1753, the king had offered special privileges to foreigners who would emigrate to work in that country's important iron and steel industries. (At the time, Sweden produced about a quarter of the world's iron in forest foundries.) Boulton's business was not always buoyant and he appears to have given some indication that he might be willing to go. Indeed, in 1765 a firm offer was made to him. He would receive £500 for travelling expenses, an advance of £1,500 on equipment including waterwheels and a cut of 20 to 25 per cent on everything exported. He would be free to set up in business wherever he liked in Sweden and enjoy exemption from duty on English coal. He would have a wealthy partner and special arrangements would be made for the receipt of payments from overseas. Boulton turned the offer down, as he did later advances from Prussian manufacturers who wanted him to go into partnership with them. However, in 1800, to the consternation of other Birmingham manufacturers, Boulton was given government permission to sell to the Russians his own specialized equipment for stamping coins for the imperial mint. It was the same equipment that he would use to modernize the British mint at the Tower of London just before his death in 1809.

As for the Wilkinsons, after the French venture William returned to England and fell out with his older brother. William stirred up trouble between John and Boulton and Watt, providing evidence that his brother had been secretly selling their patent steam engines without permission. John Wilkinson rode out all these storms as his business ventures prospered and he continued to live up to his 'Iron Mad' sobriquet. He was a major promoter of that great wonder of the eighteenth-century world, the first cast-iron bridge which spans the River Severn downstream from Coalbrookdale. It was completed in 1779 with iron from the Darby works and opened to traffic in 1781.

John Wilkinson also launched on the River Severn on 6 July 1787 one of the first, if not the very first, boat made entirely of iron (there is an account of an iron pleasure boat built ten years earlier and floated on the River Foss). Wilkinson called his boat the *Trial* and gave it a fine salute from some of his own 32-pounder cannon as a large crowd of spectators gathered to watch the launch of this unlikely vessel, which was 70 feet long and 6' 8" wide and weighed eight tons. Wilkinson proudly penned this brief account of the event to a James Stockdale:

Broseley 14 July 1787

Dear Sir, – Yesterday week my Iron Boat was launched. It answers all my expectations, and has convinced the unbelievers, who were 999 in 1,000. It will be a nine days' wonder, and be like Columbus's Egg.

I remain, dear Sir, yours very truly

Signed John Wilkinson[7]

If the reference to Columbus's Egg seems obscure, Wilkinson was just making the point that what had seemed impossible one day would be regarded as nothing special the next. What he had fashioned with iron was a good deal more impressive than the trick Columbus played to show how to stand an egg on one end – he cracked one end on the table so that it was flattened. As Columbus is said to have exclaimed to those who had tried to set an egg upright and failed : 'Anybody can do it, after he has been shown how!'

Wilkinson's supreme confidence freed him of the anxieties that most other manufacturers had about the theft of trade secrets, and his brother's enterprises in France would undoubtedly have had a brighter future had it not been for the upheavals of revolution. The works at Le Cruesot in Burgundy (nothing to do with Le Creuset cast-iron kitchenware) did revive after the defeat of Napoleon, however, when France and other European countries began to industrialize rapidly.

Wilkinson never ceased trying out new projects, whether it was growing grapes in a greenhouse and harvesting 1,800 bunches from one vine, or reclaiming barren land or acquiring country houses. He did not, though, have an entirely peaceful old age. His first wife died young, leaving him with one daughter who was brought up by adoptive parents. He was married again, in the same year his first wife died, to Mary Lee, who provided him with enough money to set up on his own as an ironmaster but remained childless. Having fallen out with his younger brother, Wilkinson had no heir to his business. A nephew, Joseph Priestley, the son of the celebrated parson and chemist of the same name, was given a chance to take over, but Wilkinson did not keep him on.

It was said by a former clerk of his that Wilkinson spent a great deal of time in France, especially Paris, where he picked up 'French notions regarding morals'. In other words, he had affairs, often with the maids he employed in his various houses. His childless wife appears to have tolerated this, although there is no correspondence relating to their private lives. At the age of seventy-seven, Wilkinson set up home with a servant girl, Mary Anne Lewis, who gave birth to three children, two girls and a boy, the last born when John was eighty years old.

One of his 'iron mad' schemes was the manufacture of cast-iron coffins – a sensible enough idea in days when grave robbers were still supplying surgeons with the corpses they needed for teaching and study. Wilkinson kept his own coffins in each of his grand houses and sometimes liked to hide in them when he had guests and then pop up to frighten them, a practical joke so alarming that ladies of the party were apt to faint. He left instructions that he should be buried in one of his coffins in the grounds of whichever house was closest when he died. However, after his death on 14 July 1808, his executors had first to keep his body in a lead and wood coffin, which they loaded on to a hearse and set out for his remote coastal property at Castlehead in Cumberland where one of his iron coffins awaited. The driver took a short cut across the sandy beach near Holme Island in Morecambe Bay. It was a regular route but the hearse was caught in an unusually strong incoming tide and sank into the sand. The driver had to abandon the heavy coffin until the tide had gone out again. It took weeks to get Wilkinson buried at Castlehead and the lead coffin proved too big to fit into the iron coffin he had left in readiness. Then the site chosen for the burial proved too shallow for the grave-diggers, who struck rock.

Wilkinson wrote his own epitaph, which he liked to read out to friends:

Delivered from persecution of malice and envy, here rests John Wilkinson, Iron Master, in certain hopes of a better estate and Heavenly Mansion, as promulgated by Jesus Christ in whose Gospel he was a firm believer. His life was spent in action for the benefit of man, and he trusts in some degree to the glory of God, as his different works remain in various parts of the Kingdom are testimonies of increasing labour, until death released him the —— day of 18—— at the advanced age of ——.[8]

The epitaph was to have gone on to an iron obelisk marking his burial place, but his executors edited it down to something rather more modest. Wilkinson had died at Bradley, where his famous ironworks were established, and a rumour arose that seven years after his death he would reappear there, riding his grey horse. On 14 July 1815 several thousand people gathered to witness the second coming of 'Iron Mad' Wilkinson, but he failed to appear. Not long after his death, his iron empire fell apart as his will was disputed, new methods of forging iron were introduced and the iron industry suffered a short slump with the end of the Napoleonic wars after Waterloo. Through his own efforts and those of his brother William, John Wilkinson had planted in France the seeds of an industry which in the nineteenth century would become well established.

Wilkinson's influence did not extend much beyond France, however, and certainly had no bearing on the other side of the Atlantic, where the first seeds of American industrialization were taking root at the end of the eighteenth century. At the time, the United States had no coal to speak of, and no coke-fired iron industry. But there were other skills being taken across to America from Britain which were to be of immense value for the emerging nation once independence was won.

CHAPTER THREE

THE TOOLBAG TRAVELLERS

In the years just before the outbreak of the War of Independence, between 1773 and 1776, some 6,000 emigrants left Britain for America and the West Indies, a fifth of them settling in Philadelphia, which was to become a centre of the textile industry. They were not all, of course, skilled craftsmen. Just over half, according to the records kept in England, were 'indentured' servants – that is to say, they were under a contract of some kind with an employer in America and their passage across the Atlantic was paid. There were families, including women and children and a few elderly emigrants, but the typical passenger was a man in his early twenties, paying his own way and hoping for a better living than he had back home. There were a few who put themselves down as 'labourer' but the majority had some kind of trade or business: enameller, peruke-maker, muff-maker, mathematical instrument-maker and so on. More than 250 different skills were recorded. The great majority were headed for the eastern seaboard of America, only 5 per cent staying in the West Indies, and half of those in Jamaica. In the American colonies, Maryland, a staging post for migrants moving elsewhere, was the most favoured destination, followed by Pennsylvania, Virginia and Nova Scotia.

With these immigrants came some textile workers who were familiar with the latest innovations in spinning wool and cotton. The spinning jenny was not that difficult to reproduce as it was a clever but relatively simple piece of equipment and it was already being put together in colonial America in 1775. Joseph Hague, who had had his own weaving company in Derbyshire, sailed from Liverpool in 1774 to Philadelphia, Pennsylvania. He wanted to set up in business but found there was a severe shortage of yarn – the stimulus to the invention of the original jenny. His petition to the Pennsylvania Assembly in March 1775 to recoup the costs of bringing the invention to America stated:'... finding the high Price paid for Spinning a very great Discouragement to his Undertaking, he gave instructions for making a Machine similar to those lately invented, and used in England for that Purpose, whereby the Expence of Labour is exceedingly reduced; that not being furnished with either a Plan or Model of such Machine, he has been at the Expence of much Time and of some Money in causing one to be constructed.'[1]

Such enterprise as that displayed by Joseph Hague might have led to the establishment of an indigenous textile industry, but the outbreak of the Revolutionary War, which lasted from 1775 to 1783, hardly provided the conditions for the development of this or any other industries. And when the fighting ceased, the victorious United States of America, which then comprised the thirteen states of the eastern seaboard, was no longer a British colony but a foreign country to which all the prohibitions on the emigration of skilled men and machines applied. From that time on, until the lifting of the emigration ban, artisans leaving Britain for America had to indulge in the same subterfuge as those heading to France or other European countries.

By the 1780s the most advanced spinning machinery – whether Arkwright's frame and versions of it or Crompton's mule – was coveted in America. But there was a real difficulty getting working models past customs or constructing them from scratch in America. Inevitably there were some disasters, perhaps the most tragically comical that which befell Benjamin H. Phillips in 1783. Phillips planned his evasion of customs with care, packing several machines, including a version of Crompton's mule, in casks which he impudently labelled 'Queens Ware', the hugely popular pottery made by Josiah Wedgwood. He sent his son ahead to Philadelphia and boarded the same ship out of Liverpool as his secret cargo. However, when the ship put in at Cork in Ireland, a regular stop en route, Phillips fell ill. His cargo continued to Philadelphia while he returned to Liverpool, where he died shortly afterwards.

His son received the machines in Philadelphia but had no idea how to assemble them, so he sold them on to Joseph Hague and his partners. They too had trouble assembling the equipment and managed only to get a small jenny and a carding machine to work. Hague had them put in store and eventually sold them in 1787. The buyer shipped them back to England, much to the horror of the Pennsylvania Society, which was intent on enticing textile workers to Philadelphia and was soon demanding that the United States should have its own protectionist legislation to stop inventions being spirited out of the country and back to Britain.

Shipping whole machines was less practical anyway than taking abroad working models and sketches. These were frequently used, yet there was really no substitute in this era for the men who knew how things worked and had actually put them together in England. And in the last decade of the eighteenth century, more and more machines were being built – Arkwright's empire had spread right across northern England and into Scotland – so there was now a growing army of artisans with both the tools and the expertise to put them together.

In 1789 the newly created United States Congress passed laws which it hoped would encourage the development of manufactures, and the state of Pennsylvania offered a reward to anyone who could construct a working water frame for cotton-spinning on the lines of those then churning out miles of yarn in Britain. The inducement came to the notice of a young man who had worked since the age of fourteen in Cromford Mill, the pioneering example of modern industry set up by Jedediah Strutt and Richard Arkwright. Samuel Slater was born close to Cromford Mill at Belper, Derbyshire, in 1768, his family being described as 'yeomen', which suggests they were modestly wealthy farmers. By the age of twenty-one, Slater was a manager at Cromford and well thought of by his employers. Though he clearly had a promising future in British textiles, the Pennsylvania prize was enticing: not long after he heard about the American award, Slater was boarding a boat at Liverpool and heading across the Atlantic.

It is said that Slater did not risk taking with him any tools or drawings in case he was stopped. There is a story that he adopted a disguise to evade inquisitive customs officers, but a memoir written by someone who knew him says simply that he dressed 'like a farmer' anyway and would have had no need to pretend he was not an artisan. As it was, Slater arrived safely in America in 1789 with the complex machinery of the water frame and the mule committed to memory. He was set up in business at Pawtucket in Rhode Island financed by a merchant family, the Browns. Though he soon had a spinning mill working, his relationship with his backers was never easy. Apparently the Browns did not afford Slater the respect he felt he deserved, treating him as an uncouth mechanic rather than a skilled engineer or business partner.

Samuel Slater eventually set up on his own and developed a sophisticated spinning and weaving industry in America, later aided by his sons. He is still described as the 'Father of the American Industrial Revolution' as he was the first to successfully transplant one of the great innovations of early industrialism to the United States and to sustain its development well into the nineteenth century. In doing so, he found he had to adjust and adapt to American social conditions. There was no ready supply of women and children to work in his factories as there was in Britain, so he had to make arrangements for whole families to settle close by with work also provided for the husband. This became known as the Rhode Island system, although in fact it was not so very different from the arrangements Arkwright and Strutt made when looking for child labour for Cromford and the other early mills. Cromford had a public house, annual events and feasts and homes with attics in which weavers, who were invariably men, could work.

American history accords Samuel Slater a special place because what he achieved was both remarkable and conspicuous and it involved something obviously new and 'industrial'. Yet at the same time he was being enticed across the Atlantic, there were fellow travellers from England whose special expertise was highly prized and sought after by the Americans. They were men such as William Weston and Benjamin Henry Latrobe, young engineers who had learned their trade working with the pioneer builders of bridges and canals which had brought about a transport revolution in Britain before the development of railways. During the colonial era, Britain had done nothing to improve the roads or waterways of the North American colonies, which were regarded merely as producers of raw materials to be shipped across the Atlantic. Those anxious to modernize the eastern seaboard after the winning of independence realized that nothing much could be done until new transport routes were cut out and there was no longer a reliance on the seaborne carriage of heavy materials.

A great advantage Britain had over its continental rivals was, of course, that its main centre of population, London, was linked to the coalfields of the north-east, the grain-growing areas of Kent and Essex, the stone quarries of Portland on the south coast and the mines of Cornwall by a coastal trade in shipping which penetrated inland on tidal rivers. So coal could be loaded in collier ships at Newcastle on the River Tyne, which would be carried out to the North Sea on the ebb tide. When they reached the mouth of the Thames, they awaited the flood tide which ran at a good six knots up to London, sixty miles inland but still on the tidal river. All around England, these tidal rivers connected one town with another.

What limited this British transport system in the early 1700s was the state of the rivers upstream of their tidal limits. Here there were shallows and mills and all kinds of inconveniences which made the journey by boat, especially inland and against the current, very difficult. The first schemes to improve transport of heavy materials, in particular coal and clay and stone, were to dredge and widen rivers, and sometimes to divert their course within a valley so that sections were 'canalized'. The work was usually undertaken by a trust comprised of local dignitaries and manufacturers eager to free themselves of their reliance on cumbersome lines of pack animals. Roads up to the late eighteenth century were rutted and rough, with potholes so deep that in winter people were drowned in them.

With river improvements came the first moves to join them up with canals so that there might be a continuous waterway between one place and another. If, for example, you could connect the headwaters of the River Thames with the River Severn running into the Bristol Channel, there would be a waterway from east to west. Locally in the Midlands you could link one manufacturing region with another, or coal mines with river ports. The Mersey and Irwell navigation joined Liverpool and Manchester in 1740 and in 1755 what was called the Sankey navigation involved the creation of locks on the Sankey Brook which enabled barges to go from the coal mines of St Helens to Liverpool.

The technique of cutting canals, maintaining water levels and providing locks to carry barges up and down inclines was not entirely new in Europe. In the seventeenth century the famous Canal du Midi had been completed, joining Bordeaux with Sète on the Mediterranean and providing a short cut for cargoes that previously had to sail around the Atlantic coast of Portugal to reach southern France. It was this canal, in fact, which was one of the inspirations for the young Francis Egerton, Duke of Bridgewater, to resurrect his father's plans to build a canal which would carry coal from his family mines at Worsley to the growing town of Manchester. At this time, and well into the nineteenth century, most coal was burned in domestic fireplaces rather than as fuel for steam engines or manufactures. It would have been quite impossible for the towns of early industrial Britain to use wood for domestic heating and gas was not available for most people until the mid-nineteenth century.

Together with a cousin and his land agent, Francis Egerton worked up a scheme for a canal to carry coal into Salford near Manchester from his mines at Worsley to the north-west. Any such schemes – this was true for new roads and, later, railways as well as canals – required approval by Parliament, which was, by and large, in favour of any improvements to the country's transport. The Act giving the go-ahead for what became known as the Bridgewater Canal was passed in 1759 and the first sections were completed in 1763. By that time, the first of the 'canal manias' was underway in which manufacturers and landed gentry promoted and took shares in schemes to criss-cross the industrial areas of the country with new waterways.

As there had been no tradition of canal-building before the 1750s, the engineers who took on the task had to learn new engineering skills – surveying the ground, determining the best course for the water and planning where locks and tunnels might be needed. In the eighteenth century the experts in the use of large-scale machinery were mostly millwrights – it was they who knew about cogs and gears and harnessing water power. One such, James Brindley, was born at Leek in Derbyshire in 1716. At the time the first section of the Bridgewater canal was under construction, Brindley had a much more ambitious scheme for creating what he called a Grand Junction Canal which would link river navigations all over the north-west and the Midlands. He was hired by the Bridgewater Canal promoters and would drive himself to an early death, creating what were regarded as new wonders of the industrial age. For Brindley's canals did not just follow the course of rivers or join existing river navigations over short distances: they cut across country. They were even built *over* rivers, carried on marvellous brick aqueducts, with clay being used to seal them. The most celebrated of the first aqueducts that Brindley constructed was at Barton near Manchester and, as one excited observer put it, ran 'as high as the tree tops'. He was the great canal-builder of his day and both inspired and trained a small number of acolytes who were able to carry on his work.

Adam Smith had written in his *An Inquiry into the Nature and Causes of the Wealth of Nations*, published in 1776:

> Good roads, canals, and navigable rivers, by diminishing the expence of carriage, put the remote parts of the country more nearly upon a level with those in the neighbourhood of the town. They are upon that account the greatest of all improvements. They encourage the cultivation of the remote, which must always be the most extensive circle of the country. They are advantageous to the town, by breaking down the monopoly of the country in its neighbourhood. They are advantageous even to that part of the country. Though they introduce some rival commodities into the old market, they open many new markets to its produce.[2]

All this was well understood in America, and though Adam Smith believed the wealth of nations would be better served if the colonists remained tobacco-growing farmers, the revolutionaries fighting for independence were intent on emulating British industrial advances. After 1783, canal projects were proposed everywhere in New York, Massachusetts and Pennsylvania as seaboard cities sought connections with inland waterways, often competing with each other for a new transport route which might make or break their future prosperity. The enthusiasm was there and a modicum of funds, but there were no engineers in America who knew about canal-building and the hunt began for talent in Britain.

The legislation intended to stem the outflow of industrial expertise from Britain does not appear to have been applied to professionals such as the canal engineers, who took with them across the Atlantic the specialist gear used for surveying. An American canal was not seen as presenting the same kind of threat to British industry as a stolen machine, though in the long run improvements to transport were of greater importance to the emerging economy of the United States. In Adam Smith's terms, without a decent transport system, markets for goods would remain local, and this would limit production and reduce the incentive to innovate through division of labour.

Benjamin Franklin had written from London in 1772:

> I think it would be saving money to engage at a handsome Salary an Engineer from here who has been accustomed to such Business. The many canals on foot here under different great Masters, are daily raising a number of Pupils in the Art, some of whom may want Employment hereafter, and a single Mistake thro' Inexperience in such important Works, may cost much more than the Expense of Salary to an ingenious young man already well acquainted with both Principles and Practice.[3]

By the 1790s, Franklin's advice was to prove invaluable. A small but influential group of Pennsylvanian merchants and artisans formed a Society for the Improvement of Roads and Inland Navigation, which had its first meeting at the beginning of 1791. The president of the society was Robert Morris, who had been born in England in 1738 and had emigrated with his family at the age of thirteen. Morris was a close friend of George Washington and had been an important financial broker during the War of Independence. The Society drew up plans for a series of canals which they hoped would not only improve transport of goods in the region but also ensure that trade would not go elsewhere in America. As soon as work was begun, however, they ran into trouble and very soon heeded the advice of Franklin.

Urgent requests were made through a correspondent in London, Patrick Colquhoun, a West Indian merchant who had spent his youth in Virginia, for a British bridge and canal engineer. After several failed attempts to find his man, Colquhoun came up with William Weston, who was then twenty-nine years old and had some experience of bridge-building and possibly some tutelage from the ageing James Brindley. A month before he was due to sail, Weston met and married Charlotte Whitehouse, who agreed to emigrate with him provided that he gave her a 'solemn promise' that, if her family needed her, she could return home. Weston was presented with a huge contract to work on the various Philadelphia plans and, after some hesitation, accepted. The newly married Westons sailed from Falmouth on 23 November 1792 bound for New York and William's American salary of about £45,000 in today's money was paid from the moment the ship left harbour; that date was confirmed by the captain of the packet *Carteret*. He was contracted for only seven months of the year as it was anticipated he would be in demand elsewhere in America, as indeed he soon was.

Apart from the experience he had had working on the Oxford canal with those who were then the world experts in the construction of navigations, Weston took with him to America a levelling instrument of a kind that had not been used before on that side of the Atlantic. He arrived in Philadelphia in January 1793 and started work immediately. His salary was soon doubled and he was treated like a visiting celebrity – anyone in need of an engineer clamoured for both his experience and expertise. It is not known exactly when Weston returned to England but it is thought to have been after 1801. In the years he was in America he worked as an engineer or acted as consultant on six canal projects and one turnpike road. He was also called in to propose a means of increasing the fresh water supply for New York City, then still a relatively small town of 50,000 (in 1800 London's population was around 900,000). The supply from New York's wells was inadequate and Weston drew up an elaborate scheme to bring water from the Bronx River into town via several reservoirs. He was paid $799.67 and thanked for his advice, which was promptly ignored. New York eventually obtained a distant supply of water forty years later from the Croton River.

When Weston left, his place was taken by another Englishman with a rather French-sounding name, Benjamin Henry Latrobe, who had emigrated in 1796. Henry Latrobe, as he generally liked to be called, had worked with the leading engineers John Smeaton and William Jessop. He too brought his English surveying instruments with him as well as his technical books. He too was asked to help not only with the cutting of canals and building of locks but the creation of a new water supply system for Philadelphia. When the steam-powered system began operation in 1801, the Philadelphia Waterworks was considered the most advanced engineering plant in America. Despite all this, the whole enterprise proved to be a financial disaster. To make the steam engine economic, a scheme was devised to harness it to a series of mills for rolling out copper and iron sheets and for slitting these to make bars and nails. Latrobe designed the ironworks well enough, but the performance of the steam engine was disappointing: it was one of only a very few that had been built in the United States by 1800 and the expertise which made British Boulton & Watt engines so efficient was simply not there.

Latrobe had also studied architecture and he was involved in the design and building of both the original White House, home of American presidents from 1800, and the Capitol. It is said that he was the first professional architect in America. Not all the projects he worked on were successful or lucrative, however, and towards the end of his life he was declared bankrupt. In an effort to recoup his losses, he went to New Orleans to begin work on a new project, but died there of yellow fever in 1820 before he could complete it.

The real legacy of Weston and Latrobe was not so much what they achieved in terms of pushing through canal, road and water-supply projects but their influence on a generation of indigenous American engineers. When it came to the great project of the Erie Canal which, by 1825, was to link New York via the Hudson River with the rapidly developing interior of the United States, Weston, then back in England, was consulted. In 1811 he had written to the Erie Canal Commissioners: 'Should your noble but stupendous plan of uniting Lake Erie with the Hudson, be carried into effect, you have to fear no rivalry. The commerce of the immense extent of the country, bordering on the upper lakes, is yours forever, and to such an incalculable amount as would baffle all conjecture to conceive. Its execution would confer immortal honour on the projectors and supporters, and would in its eventual consequences, render New York the greatest commercial emporium in the world...'⁴ Plans were duly made to lure Weston back to America in 1813, but they were abandoned. By then the men who had worked with him and Latrobe were able to survey and build the Erie Canal without the aid of foreign expertise. In fact, by the 1820s it was widely believed that the American engineer was better because he was more aware of the need to modify British building techniques, which had become too costly for a young nation.

The toolbag travellers had done their job and thus were no longer needed after the 1830s. In his introduction to *Das Kapital*, first published in 1867, Karl Marx wrote of an inevitable progression, once industrialism took hold, with Britain's experience as the blueprint: 'It is a question of these laws themselves, of these tendencies working with iron necessity towards inevitable result. The country that is more developed industrially only shows, to the less developed, the image of its own future.'⁵ While there is a broad truth in this, it should have been clear by then that not all industrialization followed the same pattern. Rather like a plant that takes on a different shape and hue in a variety of soils, so the trail-blazing inventions were adopted in a variety of ways by different countries. Steam engines, for example, were less important in the early days of industrialization in the United States than in Britain because of the lack of coal and the abundance of strong, fast-flowing streams to power machinery. And Americans were soon to evolve their own way of adopting and adapting the first great British invention of the nineteenth century and that great icon of Victorian industrialism, the steam railway.

CHAPTER FOUR

THE CORNISHMAN'S PUFFER

It was not the first time anyone had seen a steam engine: such machines powered by a furnace and a boiler had been in existence for a hundred years. But nobody before had seen one – other than a little model – which moved along under its own power. The first excursion of a full-scale steam locomotive was a momentous event, yet it caused no immediate sensation. The engine was fired up and began its maiden journey in the Cornish mining town of Camborne on Christmas Eve 1801. The son of the man who invented it collected eyewitness accounts many years later. One of the locals, William Fletcher, recalled: 'When we saw Trevithick was going to turn on steam, we jumped on as many as could, maybe seven or eight of us. 'Twas a stiffish hill going up to Camborne Beacon, but she went off like a bird. When she had gone about a quarter of a mile, there was a rough piece of road, covered with loose stones. She didn't go up quite so fast, and it was a flood of rain, and we were very much squeezed together. I jumped off. She was going faster than I could walk, and went up the hill about half a mile further when they turned her, and came back again to the shop.'

The pioneer Cornish 'puffer', so called because it blew clouds of steam from its funnel with a rhythmic whoosh, was the work of one of those tragicomic figures of invention, Richard Trevithick. Though he came to a sad end, Trevithick had many claims to fame, not the least of which was his longstanding and bitter falling out with James Watt, the famous Scottish engineering genius whom half the world still believes invented the steam engine. To his dying day, Watt vilified Trevithick, who, near the end of his own life, wrote in despair to his close friend and scientific mentor Davies Gilbert:

> I have been branded with folly and madness for attempting what the world calls impossibilities, and even from the great engineer, the late Mr James Watt, who said to an eminent scientific character still living, that I deserved hanging for bringing into use the high-pressure engine. This so far has been my reward from the public; but should this be all, I shall be satisfied by the great secret pleasure and laudable pride that I feel in my own breast from having been the instrument of bringing forward and maturing new principles and new arrangements of boundless value to my country. However much I may be straitened in pecuniary circumstances, the great honour of being a useful subject can never be taken from me, which to me far exceeds riches.[1]

To understand the origin of the dispute between James Watt and Richard Trevithick it is necessary to know something of the history of the steam engine, one which goes much further back into history than is often realized. In particular, the garbled fable about Watt and his boiling kettle sets you off on the wrong track. It suggests that the young Scott experiences a eureka moment when he realizes that the vapour given off by boiling water raises the lid of a kettle and therefore might be harnessed to power a machine. He then sets to work to invent such an engine. In fact, the pressure exerted by steam that lifts a kettle lid when the water bubbles at 100 degrees Centigrade was anathema to the cautious Watt: it was called 'strong steam' and regarded, with considerable justification, as dangerous.

When Watt was born in Greenock on the Clyde in 1736 steam engines of a kind had been in commercial operation in England – and one or two abroad – for more than twenty years. And the potential power of expanding steam had been understood since antiquity. The priests in Greek temples made a wicked use of it to hoodwink worshippers into believing they could open the heavy gates to a tomb by supernatural powers. The visitors would be told that if they lit a devotional fire, the gods would open the doors to the tomb. And lo and behold, when the fire had burned for a while, the doors opened, apparently of their own accord or by an invisible hand, to the wonderment of the devotees. But there was nothing magical about it: the fire boiled a container of water which then spilled into another container, the weight of which pulled the tomb doors open.

In the seventeenth century, the French scientist and inventor Denis Papin, who worked all over Europe, often in London, devised a form of steam-pressure engine using a cylinder and a piston. But there was a big problem with harnessing steam to drive machinery: boilers and cylinders and all the essential parts of such an engine would have to be not only airtight and watertight but also immensely strong, for the steam would be generated under pressure. If you boil water in a sealed cylinder, it will explode: there was always a danger attendant on working with steam engines.

One of the first practical attempts to harness the power of steam was made by Thomas Savery, a well-educated scientist and inventor who was granted a patent in 1698 for his machine for 'raising water by fire'. Savery drew on the earlier experiments of Papin and others, such as the Marquess of Worcester, to design a pumping engine which incorporated two different ways of utilizing steam to generate power. Steam would be pumped into a cylinder and then cooled so that a vacuum was formed and atmospheric pressure drew water up. In another cylinder, the pressure of steam itself forced water out. For this pumping engine to work continuously, all kinds of stopcocks and valves had to be opened and closed every minute or so by a frantic engineman. Savery's pumping engine worked – he demonstrated models at Hampton Court and to the Royal Society and installed some to work fountains or raise water from the River Thames. However, they were not effective for the task he really wanted them to perform, which was draining water from tin, copper and coal mines. He called his treatise on the machine *The Miner's Friend*.

What Savery did have was a catch-all patent, which meant that anyone else devising a steam-powered pumping engine would have to negotiate terms with him or risk prosecution. And so it was when the Dartmouth ironmonger

Thomas Newcomen, after more than a decade of experimentation with his engineer colleague John Calley, devised a new kind of steam-driven pumping engine: he was obliged to go into partnership with Savery. This was hard on Newcomen but no more distressing than the bitter disputes that were to attend the development of the steam engine over the next century. The issue was not so much piracy by foreigners as infighting among the rival inventors and their champions.

Thomas Newcomen was descended from a distinguished English family which, over several generations, had fallen on hard times. He was a skilled craftsman making equipment for the mines of Devon and Cornwall which produced tin and copper. As with coal mines, the exhaustion of seams near the surface forced the miners to dig deeper wherever they could. They quickly found that mines of any depth were unworkable unless water was pumped out of them continuously. A variety of horse-driven, windmill or manual pumps were used but they were limited in the amount of water they could raise. Keeping and feeding 'gin' horses was also extremely expensive.

Savery had the right idea but the wrong machine for mines. His pumps could only draw water from a limited depth, while his partial use of high-pressure steam was potentially hazardous. Newcomen and Calley came up with the answer: they would rely on atmospheric air pressure to work their pumps, a system which would be safe, if rather slow. What they devised and brought to efficient working order was the first really reliable steam engine in the world. It did not matter that it was a leviathan of a structure with its great pivoted beam see-sawing back and forth alarmingly. There was no question of this engine going anywhere: it was stationary and set up in a brick shell of a building next to the mine it was draining.

The big, rocking overhead beam was the key to the whole thing. From one end hung a chain which was attached to the top of a kind of crude piston encased in a cylinder. A coal-fired boiler generated steam which was fed into the cylinder, filling it and driving out most of the air. The steam in the cylinder was then cooled. In the early models this was done by running cold water over the outside. Later it was discovered that an injection of cold water into the cylinder was much more effective. Suddenly cooled, the steam condensed, creating a partial vacuum in the cylinder so that the air pressure above the piston forced it down. As the piston moved, it dragged down the beam, the other end of which was attached to a rod which sucked up water from the mine. The end of the beam away from the piston was also weighted so that the beam would nod back as more steam was fed into the cylinder and the piston rose to repeat the process. The prototype Newcomen engines required the opening and closing of valves for releasing steam, injecting water and so on. In time, however, machinery was devised so that such operations worked automatically: this was the 'self-acting' engine.

Newcomen's first engine was installed in 1712 at a mine not in his native Devon but at one belonging to the Earls of Dudley in Staffordshire. The West Country had no coal of its own and it was expensive to import it. The Newcomen engine was greedy and was really only suited to coal-mining regions, or at least those which had access to a ready supply of cheap coal. Savery and Newcomen's patent was sold on to group of speculative investors who did not, apparently, pursue vigorously those who infringed it. Certainly, Newcomen engines were being installed in the north-east before the patent ran out in 1733 and the nodding of the giant beams became a familiar sight in mining areas. They were also useful for recycling river water needed to turn mill wheels as they could pump a body of water round and round, topping up the flow of a river when it became low. In Coalbrookdale they were used in this way to keep the bellows of the iron foundries going.

These so-called 'atmospheric engines' were modified over time by a number of engineers and one or two were also built in Europe. For their time they were revolutionary, offering a source of tireless and reliable power that neither water nor wind, nor any beast of burden had ever been able to provide. Before Newcomen's death in London in 1729 several engines – nobody is sure how many – had been erected in England either by him or others who had learned how to construct them. In the north-east, where they were in great demand in the mines, a man named John Potter appears to have acted as some kind of agent for the erection of Newcomen-type engines, as the following advertisement appeared in the *Newcastle Courant* on 27 January 1724: 'This is to give notice to all gentlemen and others, who have occasion for the fire engine, or engines for drawing water from collieries, &c to apply to Mr John Potter of Chester-le-Street, who is empowered by the proprietors of the said fire engine to treat about the same.'

It was around this time that the first Newcomen engines were constructed on the Continent. While on tour in England, Joseph Emanuel Fischer von Erlach, the son of a leading architect at the Court of Vienna, persuaded one Isaac Potter, who was perhaps a relative of John Potter's, to go to Königsberg (now Kaliningrad) in what was then Upper Hungary to erect 'fire engines' to drain the mines. The first of these was working around 1722. Again in the 1720s, Newcomen engines were constructed in France, one being used for pumping water from the Seine to the city of Paris in a scheme which was a precursor of the Wilkinson brothers'. The Paris engine, which excited much interest from French scientists, was erected by two Englishmen who had a stake in the old Savery patent, John May and John Meyers, though sadly Meyers died in Paris shortly after the engine began to work. Another engine appears to have been constructed at Toledo in Spain. However, during this time and until the 1750s, the engines were used almost exclusively either for pumping water out of mines or for supplying water to cities. In 1726 water was pumped from the Thames in London at York Buildings with a Newcomen engine working side by side with an earlier Savery model.

The first Newcomen-type engine to be erected in America arrived in 1753 from Cornwall. It had been ordered five years earlier by Colonel John Schuyler, who owned and ran a very profitable copper mine with two brothers at New Arlington, New Jersey. Once the mine's surface ores had been exhausted, it had become unworkable because of flooding. But it was well worth the expense of shipping over a steam pumping engine because Schuyler sold copper to the Bristol Copper and Brass Works, which paid a good price per ton. The order for the engine went to Jonathan Hornblower, another West Country engineer, who was a successor to Newcomen and a forerunner of Trevithick. It took five years after the purchase was accepted for the parts to be ready for shipment across the Atlantic. Hornblower sent his son Josiah to supervise the engine's erection, and legend has it that Josiah was so frightened and sick on the Atlantic crossing that he refused to suffer the return journey

and stayed in New Jersey. It took him two years to get the engine working –
the timber for the beam and other parts had to be fashioned and the stone
for the housing laboriously quarried – but Josiah was eventually offered the
job of supervising the running of the Schuyler copper mine. Over the years
this Hornblower engine had a chequered history: it caught fire in 1768, lay
in ruins for the duration of the revolutionary war, but was set to work again
in 1793 by the now ageing Josiah.

What is most notable about the New Jersey Hornblower engine, however,
is that it was for a very long time the only steam engine in America. There
was not much demand for coal on the eastern seaboard in colonial times as
there was an abundance of timber for domestic fires and there was little
industry requiring more than charcoal for heating. What coal there was in the
region was found on the surface and so no deep pits were dug, therefore there
was no need for pumping engines, except in the special case of the copper
mine. Later, when modified steam engines were harnessed to drive machinery,
they were only of value if they proved cheaper or more efficient than water
mills. But again, the eastern seaboard had an abundance of fast-flowing rivers
to drive its mill wheels. In fact, in 1794 Josiah Hornblower, who was still
working for the copper mine, built an ore-stamping mill for its then owners,
Messrs Roosevelt, Mark and Schuyler.

Improvements were made to the Newcomen engine and new possibilities
for the making of boilers and other parts opened up with the rapid
development of an iron industry in which coke-smelting was becoming
common by the 1760s. In most of the early models of what became known
as 'old smoking engines', the boilers were made from copper. Once the
production of iron increased and methods of working it improved, cast-iron
boilers, which were cheaper and stronger, were adopted. The brilliant engineer
and millwright John Smeaton built some very sophisticated Newcomen-type
engines and had the idea of using them to pump water on to a mill wheel,
thus providing an early form of rotary motion powered by steam.

A big problem with these Newcomen engines, however, was that they were
great guzzlers of coal. Cornish mine-owners, or 'adventurers' as they were
known, had to import their coal from South Wales and the cost of transport

made it expensive. It was therefore a boon to them when a Birmingham manufacturer offered them a new kind of steam engine which was much more economical in its use of coal. These new models were the Boulton & Watt engines, regarded as the finest machines of their day.

The brilliant mechanism of the new engines, which offered a saving on fuel of around 75 per cent on the Newcomen models, was a 'separate condenser' into which steam was fed. The main cylinder did not therefore have to be continually reheated as in the Newcomen engine. The separate condenser was the inspired invention of James Watt, the young Scottish instrument-maker who had become interested in the workings of steam-powered machines when he was asked to repair a model of a Newcomen engine used for demonstrations at Glasgow University. Born in 1736, Watt had served an apprenticeship as a mathematical instrument-maker in London before returning to Glasgow in 1756. He first began to tinker with the Newcomen model in 1763 and was critical of the workmanship involved and dubious about the engine's efficiency. It was two years later, in 1765, that the twenty-nine-year-old Watt had a flash of inspiration which produced the separate condenser.

In Glasgow, Watt was friendly with a number of the leading scientists of his day and when he showed them his new device, he was told to patent it as soon as possible. This he did in 1769. However, like so many inventors, he did not have the money to turn the model into a full-scale working steam engine. Watt's chief scientific mentor, Dr Joseph Black, Professor of Chemistry at Glasgow University, put him in touch with the industrialist John Roebuck, who had made a fortune out of the manufacture of vitriol or sulphuric acid and had been a co-founder of the celebrated Carron Ironworks. Roebuck took Watt on, providing him with both a workshop and the funds to develop his engine in return for a two-thirds share in the patent. But while Watt was labouring to get his new, improved steam engine to work, Roebuck got into financial trouble and it looked as if that might be the end of the story.

To take out his patent, Watt had had to go down to London in 1769 to argue his case and on the way he had called to see the Birmingham 'toy'-maker Matthew Boulton at his Soho works. For many of the ingenious processes he had devised to turn out buckles, buttons and a huge variety of metal pieces, Boulton relied on machines powered by a waterwheel. He had tried a Savery engine but it did not work efficiently. Watt and Boulton got on well at their first meeting and it was to Birmingham that Watt returned when Roebuck could no longer fund him. As it happened, one of Roebuck's creditors was Boulton, who agreed to take over the two-thirds share of Watt's patent. The Watt family then moved lock, stock and barrel to Birmingham along with the various parts of the revolutionary engine.

Before he would give Watt financial backing, however, Boulton insisted that the patent, with only eight years to run, should be extended to twenty-five years. This meant petitioning the House of Commons and beating off the opposition of rival engineers. By 1775 the two men had their patent, valid until 1800, and Watt was well on the way to perfecting his steam engine. As luck would have it, just when Watt needed a very accurately bored cylinder for his separate condenser, 'Iron Mad' Wilkinson had perfected his cannon-boring machine and was able to produce these crucial components for the new engines. The large boilers were made elsewhere in the Midlands, while Boulton's own workshops could turn out most of the smaller working parts.

A complete engine had to be shipped in pieces to wherever it was to be put to work and a competent engineer had to be on hand to assemble it. The cost of buying a Boulton & Watt engine outright was very high, so they were not sold as such but rather leased in return for a payment to the makers equivalent to a third of the savings in the cost of fuel these engines produced compared with the older Newcomen-type engines. Wherever coal was expensive, the Boulton & Watt engine offered substantial savings and its makers recognized early on their best market would be in the Cornish tin and copper mines. With no cheap local coal, the Cornish companies were all for fuel efficiency. However, the relationship with the Cornish miners was never easy, and Boulton and Watt had to contend with much resentment at the fees they charged as well as a rival's claim to have developed a better engine. This was built by Jonathan Hornblower of the celebrated Hornblower family, whose male members were hard to distinguish by their Christian names as they all began with the letter J, a foible of the Anabaptist set to which they belonged.

The Hornblower engine was a dual-cylinder machine which Jonathan asserted was both more efficient and economical than the Watt engine. For support, he looked to a fellow Cornishman, Davies Gilbert (or Giddy, his original surname), who was an amateur scientist and politician who advised many of the great engineers of the day on theoretical problems.

Battle was duly joined in Cornwall, and for the twenty-five years that Boulton and Watt's patent lasted there would be claims and counter-claims as well as legal challenges and persistent attempts to evade the payment of fuel premiums. During this time, the steam engine, which had been limited to pumping water, was eventually harnessed to machinery, thereby freeing industry from reliance on river water for power. But before this could happen, a way had to be found of transferring the vertical movement of a pumping engine into the rotary movement of a wheel. The first and simplest method was the crank, an idea Watt claimed was his own but had been stolen from him by one of his workmen and then patented by another. To get around this he – or possibly his excellent engineer and fellow Scot, William Murdoch – came up with a cog system known as the 'sun and planet'. Later, Watt devised the brilliant 'parallel motion' mechanism which he always regarded as his greatest achievement.

The new rotary engines had to run more smoothly than the old Newcomen models. Mills, especially those driving complex machinery such as Arkwright's water frame, required a steady and adjustable power source, and the addition of flywheels and 'governors' which controlled the supply of steam automatically brought this about. All this was achieved with the basic mechanism of the 'atmospheric' engine, working under low pressure but now incomparably more efficient than the Newcomen model and harnessed to factory machinery of various kinds, for grinding corn or rock ore, working the bellows of iron foundries or turning the cotton-spinning spindles.

There is no doubt that Watt solved a great many problems and turned the lumbering old Newcomen engine into a much more streamlined machine which quickly won a worldwide reputation. But he was a cautious and conservative man and at every stage had to be cajoled into inventiveness by his partner Boulton. Left to his own devices, it is unlikely he would have produced much at all for at first he opposed the idea of the 'rotary engine' and, when William Murdoch built a small working model of a steam-driven carriage, Watt saw no future in it. Nevertheless the idea was patented, but only in case someone else was daft enough to come up with something similar.

That person turned out to be none other than Richard Trevithick, who was born in 1771, the son of a greatly respected 'captain' in the Cornish mines. From boyhood Trevithick was familiar with all kinds of steam engines and knew from his father about the battles with the Boulton and Watt patents. Watt, of course, would not tolerate Murdoch's little steam car because it was driven by 'strong steam'. In Watt's view, this was not only foolhardy; it was also a challenge as these high-pressure engines did not use his patented separate condenser. And even though Watt's patent had nearly expired by the time Trevithick began to work on high-pressure steam engines, he still poured scorn on the whole idea of propelling a carriage with an explosive kettle.

In Newcomen's day, the high-pressure engine was not really practical because cylinders and boilers could not be made strong enough. But by the end of the eighteenth century, much tougher cast-iron casings could be made to withstand the steam pressures and new kinds of boilers had been devised. At the same time, the theoretical possibilities of 'strong steam' were being discussed, and Davies Gilbert had encouraged both Jonathan Hornblower and later Trevithick to experiment with it.

In fact, the inaugural run of Trevithick's 'puffer' was supposed to have taken him over Camborne Beacon to meet Davies Gilbert and others, but he was unable to finish the journey and so returned to the inn at Camborne, with his cousin Andrew Vivian at the helm. But this pioneering moving steam engine, of which no contemporary illustrations survive, was very soon to meet an unhappy end. They had parked it up in a shed but forgotten to put the boiler fire out and so, even as they were toasting their success, the puffer caught fire and all its wooden parts were consumed by the flames. Undaunted, Trevithick went on to build a number of steam road vehicles, one of which he ran in London. Upon hearing of these engines, one Samuel Homfray, the owner of a Welsh ironworks, wrote to the Cornishman in 1803, asking if he thought he could run one of his engines on iron rails.

Homfray had in mind solving a specific problem he and other iron founders had in transporting bulk goods from their works down to the port of Cardiff. For a long while they had used a canal in which they had all invested. Then one of the iron founders, Richard Crawshay, had argued that his barges should have precedence on the canal because he owned the largest share in it. In response, the other owners had laid down an iron railway nine and a half miles long which ran parallel to the canal. This railway was horse-drawn and typical of those already operating in mining districts. However, keeping a stable of horses was expensive and Homfray hoped a Trevithick steam engine might replace them, especially as there was plenty of coal at his ironworks at Penydarren near Merthyr Tydfil.

Trevithick, a giant of a man with immense energy, was never one to turn down a challenge and he began to construct a high-pressure engine at Homfray's works. Soon enough, Richard Crawshay heard of the scheme to send a steam engine into competition with his canal and declared the whole idea ridiculous. To settle the matter, Homfray and Crawshay agreed to a wager of 500 guineas – about £25,000 in today's money. If Trevithick could build an engine which could haul five trams loaded with ten tons of coal the length of the railway and pull the empty trams up the gentle incline – something one horse could achieve – then Homfray would have won the bet. A Richard Hill was to hold the money and act as referee for the trials.

The engine built at Homfray's works performed well in its trial runs and the inevitable teething troubles were sorted out. Trevithick himself was in a high state of excitement as the day drew near for the run which would decide the wager. He begged his friend and champion Davies Gilbert to come out to witness it. He had also heard that a man from the Navy Board would be present (one of Trevithick's madder schemes was to power a boat laden with explosives into Boulogne harbour to blow up Napoleon's invasion fleet). As ever, nothing quite went to plan. Gilbert did not get there on time and Samuel Homfray missed the trial when his carriage overturned and he was confined to bed with injuries. Nevertheless, on 21 February 1804 Trevithick's Penydarren-built engine hauled ten tons of bar iron and seventy passengers along the entire railway at a speed of around five miles per hour. One of the passengers was Richard Crawshay, who accepted that he had lost his bet with Homfray and paid up.

By Trevithick's account, the Penydarren railway was a considerable success. Even so, Davies Gilbert told another story. Although the little engine had performed well, it was too heavy for the rails, which had cracked and been distorted in many places. The line could cope with the relatively light goods trucks, while the horse exerted no pressure on the rails at all. But the steam engine would need a much stronger set of rails if it were to run regularly and efficiently. In fact, the problem of the track was at the time fatal to the whole notion of a steam-driven railway. Trevithick did run his locomotive again as a tourist attraction in London, calling his little engine *Catch-me-who-can* at the suggestion of Davies Gilbert's sister and charging the public one shilling for a ride around a circular track. The newspapers of the time are strangely silent on this epoch-making event: it was advertised but nobody wrote a report of the engine's performance. Like most of Trevithick's ventures, it was a financial failure and not long after he abandoned steam locomotives to work on other projects. One of these was an abortive attempt to dig a tunnel under the Thames and another was to dredge the river with a steam-driven boat.

It was not long after Trevithick had lost interest in steam locomotion that engines very similar to his prototype were being built in the north-east of England at Wylam Colliery on Tyneside. The engineer responsible was one John Steel, who had been working in Merthyr Tydfil and was involved with Trevithick's Penydarren venture. And it was at Wylam that George Stephenson and his son Robert would build the first steam engines to run on commercial lines (see Chapter 7). In the meantime, Trevithick's life took an astonishing turn as he set out for the silver mines of Peru.

Silver had been mined high up in the Andes of Peru from early in the seventeenth century and was an important source of income for the Hapsburg Empire. The mining district, Cerro de Pasco, was a strange, isolated place at an altitude of 14,000 feet, and all provisions had to be brought to it on narrow tracks, just as the mined ore had to be carried down to the coast for shipment. Near the surface, over a wide area, there were huge deposits of low-grade silver ore which could be excavated without the sinking of deep shafts. Over time, the miners had gone down as far as they could go before, inevitably, the mines became water-logged. Then, in the early 1800s, it occurred to the adventurers in Peru that British mining expertise, and steam pumping engines in particular, could provide the answer.

A Swiss watchmaker, Francisco Uville, who had formed a partnership with two Peruvian businessmen in 1812, was sent to England to seek out the new technology. He went to Birmingham to consult Boulton and Watt, who told him that steam engines, and certainly any kind of 'atmospheric' engine, would not be much good at 14,000 feet. Uville could see, anyway, that the big Birmingham engines were far too bulky to haul into the Andes and he might have returned empty-handed if he had not noticed in a shop in London's Fitzroy Square a working model of a Trevithick engine. How the model came to be there is a mystery, but Uville bought it for twenty guineas and took it back with him to Peru. It worked perfectly well in the rarefied atmosphere of the Andes, and Uville was soon back aboard ship to Falmouth with the money to buy high-pressure steam engines if he could find the man who made them. As it happened, a fellow passenger knew Trevithick and so was able to make the introduction.

Uville had money and the promise of riches if Trevithick himself invested in the silver mines. It seemed to the luckless Cornish giant, known to all as 'Captain Dick', as if his ship had come in. He bought shares in the Peruvian enterprise and then set to work ordering boilers and machine parts; he eventually had ready for shipment four Cornish pumping engines, four winding engines, one portable steam engine, four spare boilers, two mills for grinding ore, and a box of blacksmith's tools. To make sure the engines were erected properly, he also sent along three Cornish engineers. They were given permission to leave by the government, which was still concerned about the exodus of artisans. The lawyer who had arranged for the purchase of shares also sailed with Uville and all the equipment on a ship that left England on 1 September 1812.

It was January before the ship, named *Wildman*, arrived at the port of Callao in Peru and another eighteen months before the steam engine parts had been carried up into the mountains for assembly. In Peru's capital, the *Lima Gazette* was wild with enthusiasm for the Cornish mining engineers: 'Immense and incessant labour ... and boundless expense, have conquered difficulties hitherto esteemed altogether insuperable; and we have, with unlimited admiration, witnessed the erection and astonishing operation of the first steam engine ... we are ambitious of transmitting to posterity the details of an undertaking of such prodigious magnitude, from which we anticipate a torrent of silver, that shall fill surrounding nations with astonishment.'

In reality, although the production of silver had risen, there were serious problems with the boilers because they had not been assembled well and had to burn wood, something for which they were not suited. At the same time, Cornish mining was heading into one of its regular recessions, a circumstance which probably persuaded Captain Dick to head for Peru himself – an enterprise which did not please either his long-suffering wife or his children. On 20 October 1816 he sailed with a South Seas whaler, the *Asp*, taking along with him some more equipment, an experienced boiler-maker, James Sanders from Camborne, and the London lawyer Richard Page to act as his agent. Far from his native Cornwall, Trevithick was greeted like a conquering hero and awarded an unofficial academic qualification by the *Lima Gazette*, which gushed: 'This professor, with the assistance of workmen who accompany him, can construct as many engines as shall be wanted in Peru, without the necessity of sending to Europe for any part of these vast machines ... let us hope that his arrival in this kingdom will form the epoch of its prosperity, through the enjoyment of its internal riches, which could not be realized without such assistance, or if the British government had not permitted the exportation from England; an object hitherto deemed unattainable by all who know how jealous that nation is of all her superior inventions in the arts of industry.'

Back in Camborne, his wife Jane had no news of him for three years. She wrote to him, her letters being forwarded by Davies Gilbert to a shipping agent in London who had dealings with the South Seas whalers. But he never received her admonitions for leaving the rent unpaid, even if he claimed he had a year's worth put by. The first that was heard of him was when the lawyer Richard Page returned and called on Davies Gilbert. He said Trevithick had turned down the offer of a good job. But in truth the London shareholders in the mine had treated him badly, accusing him of mismanagement. He had left them and with the permission of the Spanish viceroy taken a tour of other Peruvian mines before moving on to Chile.

Trevithick had many adventures, among them a spell in the forces of Simon Bolívar, *El Libertador,* before he returned to the silver mines where a coal seam was found which enabled the engines to work much better. Just as everything was running smoothly again, political unrest swept the country and many had to flee. Uville, who had brought Trevithick out there, fell ill and died and his two partners lost most of their fortune. Though some news reached Camborne, nobody in England knew of the Cornishman's whereabouts, and a rumour was rife that he had married again in South America and started another family.As it turned out, this was one of the very few things Trevithick had not attempted. He did a little pearl fishing, some trading too, and then teamed up with a Scot called James Gerard, who persuaded him the place to be was Costa Rica on the isthmus between Mexico and the mainland of South America: here there was gold which could be mined and traded.

Gerard and Trevithick decided that they needed to return to Britain to get the necessary equipment to develop the Costa Rican gold mines. But they were based on the Pacific seaboard and did not much relish the prospect of the sea voyage around Cape Horn. Though they had no map, the two set off over the hills and through dense jungle with the idea of reaching the Atlantic coast, from where they could take ship to the Caribbean and back to England. Their party included Gerard's servant, six local men to help hack through the forest and two young boys whose family wanted them to get to England so that they could better themselves. Both of these boys, José Maria and Mariano Montelegre, survived the hazardous journey and prospered. José eventually studied at the Royal College of Medicine in Edinburgh while Mariano became an engineer. In later life they both returned to Costa Rica, where José was elected president in 1860, and took with them the European taste for coffee and the coffee bean, which had originated in North Africa.

Inevitably, Gerard and Trevithick's party became lost and one of them drowned, but in the end they reached Colombia and the port of Cartagena.

Here Trevithick nearly lost his life. His son Francis, who compiled his father's biography years later, had the story third-hand, but it still rings true: 'Mr Trevithick had been upset at the mouth of the River Magdalena by a black man he had in some way offended, and who capsized the boat in revenge. An officer of the Venezuelan and the Peruvian services was fortunately nigh the banks of the river, shooting wild pigs. He heard Mr Trevithick's cries for help, and seeing a large alligator approaching him, shot him in the eye, and then, as he had no boat, lassoed Mr Trevithick, and by his lasso drew him ashore much exhausted and all but dead.'

It turned out that the Venezuelan officer was in fact British. He got Trevithick back to Cartagena, where they found a fellow engineer whom Trevithick, as if in a dream, addressed cordially as 'Bobby'. He turned out to be Robert Stephenson, the son of George Stephenson, whom Trevithick must have met as a toddler when he went to Tyneside some time around 1805. Twenty years later, it was the Stephensons who were to become associated in the public mind with steam locomotives, having run them on part of the Stockton to Darlington line in 1825. According to the scant record of this meeting, Robert, who had been in Colombia on some mining venture which had not come off, was at first a little wary of Trevithick, but when he heard what trouble he had been in, lent him £50 for the journey home.

After his return to England on 9 October 1827, Trevithick lived another six years, always inventing – he offered the navy a new kind of cannon that could be worked by two men rather than nine but they turned it down – and always losing money. While he had been in South America, his high-pressure engine had been developed by others and was proving more useful and popular than the older style of engine made by Boulton and Watt, whose sons continued the business into the nineteenth century. The Trevithick engine was novel in so many ways, its advantages summed up neatly by his biographers, H. W. Dickinson and A. Titley:

> We have to think of the steam engine as it then existed to realise what a tremendous change Trevithick introduced. Cylinder, condenser, air pump, ponderous beam slowly sea-sawing in a

massive engine house, occupying large space and costly – what could be said when Trevithick dispensed with the beam, air pump, acted directly on the crank-shaft, increased the speed, decreased the space needed, made it capable of being manufactured in small (i.e. low) powers and of going anywhere, doing anything cheaply? The innovation was revolutionary and it may be best brought home to present-day readers by comparing its advent with that of the internal combustion engine.[2]

Trevithick took Cornish technology and Cornish mining techniques to South America and in time the expertise learned in this otherwise remote region of Britain was sought after around the world. A diaspora of Cornish miners dug for minerals everywhere from Peru to Australia, invariably calling themselves 'Cousin Jack', a nickname of obscure origins which they had first acquired in the West Country of England. The high-pressure engine proved to be much more exportable than the Boulton & Watt engine, and by the 1830s, when steam first became really important in the United States, it was high-pressure engines which were favoured, some of them evolved, as we will see, by one of a handful of home-grown American engineering geniuses of the Trevithick era.

Among the Cornishman's many projects after his return from South America was the development of a steam engine with one John Hall of Dartford in Kent. It was here that Trevithick fell ill in 1833 and, after a week of fever which confined him to his bed at the Bull Inn, he died on 22 April. Four days later, he was buried in an unmarked grave in Dartford after a funeral paid for by his workmates. Trevithick himself was broke but the good management of his wife, who lived to the age of ninety-six, kept the children from penury and two of his sons went on to become notable engineers themselves. One of them, Francis Trevithick, born in 1812, became the chief engineer of the London and North-Western Railway Company and rescued his father from historical oblivion with a biography published in two volumes in 1872. Later, two of Trevithick's grandsons were pioneer railway-builders in Japan.

Trevithick's many trials, though, were as nothing compared with those of Frenchmen caught up in the treacherous and bloodthirsty years of the Revolution. Britain could with some justification be accused of taking too little notice of its native geniuses such as Trevithick and allowing them to die in poverty. But the French revolutionaries, while extolling the virtues of science over superstition and religion, either killed or drove into exile many of their most gifted men, and they did so at the very time that industrialism was becoming established in their country.

CHAPTER FIVE

THEY KEPT THEIR HEADS

In just seven weeks of the Great Terror of June and July 1794, as the French revolutionaries led by Robespierre indulged in an orgy of what might now be called 'social cleansing', some 1,400 men and women were guillotined in Paris alone. The head of the king, Louis XVI, had gone the previous year, while on 8 May 1794 all the tax collectors of the old regime, the fermiers-général, had been executed, among them one of the great European chemists of the day, Antoine Lavoisier, who had been in charge of the government production of gunpowder. As the Parisian publisher Nicholas Ruault wrote to his brother on 21 June 1794:

> In recent weeks we have seen the deaths of all the greatest and most famous still surviving in France, and the richest too … They all died at the foot of a tall and hideous plaster statue called Liberty which has been set up on the remains of the plinth where the effigy of Louis XV stood. Is it possible to believe that all those who are sacrificed at her feet are her enemies? What well-born, well-educated men could fail to support properly organized civil and political liberty? Who will ever believe that Lavoisier and the others were supporters of slavery or tyranny? No, but they were noble, rich and enlightened; they had to be put to death.[1]

It is tempting to suggest that the guillotine was France's only significant contribution to mechanical innovation during the turbulent years of the Revolution. However, it was not a French invention at all, though the form it took was a consequence of the cruel logic of the revolutionary mind in the 1790s. The instrument of efficient decapitation took its name not from the inventor but from a member of the French Assembly who was anxious to usher in a new era of egalitarianism. Dr Joseph-Ignace Guillotin had proposed that all French men and women condemned to death should at least be entitled to the same form of execution which had formerly been reserved for aristocrats. Horrible tortures, such as breaking on the wheel, had been inflicted on the poor, whereas the aristocrat had been dispatched with a few blows of a sword to the neck. In the new France, Guillotin envisioned plebeian heads rolling off the same block as those of quality.

Guillotin was all too aware that execution with an axe or a sword could be a horrible and messy business. He therefore consulted a friend, Dr Antoine Louis of the Academy of Surgery, for advice on improvements that might be made to the mode of decapitation. Dr Louis produced a considered report which reviewed the range of techniques that had been used by other countries and took a close look at the bone structure of the human neck. He concluded that a chopping machine was preferable to an axeman and mentioned that such a device was used in England. In this he was somewhat behind the times, as hanging was now the favoured mode of execution across the Channel. Use had, however, been made of the Halifax Gibbet as well as the Scottish Maiden, both of which resembled the guillotine.

Once the law in favour of decapitation for all was passed in 1792, ratified by the king himself, tenders were sought for the best device. A model produced by the chief gibbet-maker was rejected in favour of one put forward by a German, Tobias Schmidt, who was a self-styled inventor and piano-maker living in Paris. Schmidt's machine was tested on live sheep and then the corpses of some robust criminals whose necks were still intact. The best shape for the blade was a subject of much discussion until Louis XVI was consulted and he, being a man of a technical turn of mind, suggested the obvious solution: a triangular blade that would sever the neck neatly.

At least, that is the story the novelist Alexandre Dumas told later to make the point that the French king helped devise the instrument of his own execution. The first plebeian beneficiary of the guillotine was a violent robber, Nicholas-Jacques Pelletier, who was beheaded on 25 April 1792. From then on, the grim roll of drums and baying of the crowds was to accompany the fall of the guillotine blade on some very distinguished necks.

There is no knowing how many men and women who might have played some part in the modernization of France in the Napoleonic era and afterwards were victims of the successive waves of killing in the Revolution. The Terror was all-consuming. It was not only Royalists who were in danger: those who had worked for revolution in the early years after the fall of the Bastille in 1789 were often judged enemies later on. Notoriously, even Robespierre, who had been instrumental in whipping up the frenzy of killing in 1794, was himself guillotined on 28 July of the same year.

Among those who fled France in the revolutionary years was a twenty-four-year-old naval officer named Marc Isambard Brunel, who had been born into a respected Normandy family in 1769. When he was just seven years old, his mother died and his father sent him to a school for army officers. There he carried a sword and wore a cocked hat, even though he was barely eleven years old when he left. According to Brunel's biographers, who have perhaps exaggerated his youthful struggles, his father Jean Charles dismissed as useless his son's interest in music and drawing and making things. Marc was instead sent to a seminary in Rouen to train for the priesthood, a career which was traditional for the second son – it was the first-born who would inherit the farm – but one he flatly refused to contemplate.

Marc was fortunate that a sympathetic priest recognized his talents and set him on a different course. At the age of thirteen he was sent to lodge with a cousin in Rouen, Madame Carpentier, and her husband François, who had become the city's American consul. Here he had as a tutor Professor Dulague, an astronomer and hydrographer at Rouen's Royal College who taught him navigation and mathematics. It is said the young Brunel was able to verify the height of Rouen Cathedral with a home-made theodolite when he had only just started to learn trigonometry. A brilliant student, he was rewarded with a position as officer in the French navy and sailed from Rouen for the Caribbean in 1786. Practically nothing is known about the next six years of his life, but it appears that he learned some English, possibly in American ports, and he would have returned home in 1792 with a thorough knowledge of navigation and the workings of a ship.

Brunel went back to stay with the Carpentiers in Rouen. Three years after the outbreak of the Revolution, there were skirmishes in many provincial towns. Rouen formed a 'national guard' after news arrived of the imprisonment of Louis XVI and his family in Paris. Brunel and François Carpentier both joined the guard and in August 1792 Brunel noted in his diary that he had been involved in a fight in which a mob of republicans was just held off at the gates of his barracks. The following winter, as social order began to break down even further, Brunel and Carpentier took a trip to Paris, only to become embroiled in an argument which forced them to flee the city.

When they slipped back into Rouen, they discovered Mme Carpentier had taken in a young English girl who had been sent to France by an elder brother so that she could learn the language. Sophia Kingdom came from Plymouth, where her father had been a naval contractor until his death a few years earlier. She was chaperoned by a Frenchman and his English wife, but they had to hurry back to England after a friend of theirs was killed by a band of revolutionaries who had heard him playing a royalist tune. Sophia was not well enough to travel with them and so stayed in Rouen under the protection of Mme Carpentier. Sheltering together in the house as Rouen endured riots and killings, Marc and Sophia fell in love, but it seemed at the time to be a hopeless romance and Mme Carpentier, aware of Marc's ardour, warned him off, saying Sophia was not for him.

And so it seemed that fate would have it. When the Jacobins – extremists who took their name from their meeting place in the rue Jacob in Paris – gained power, Brunel's position became untenable and he feared the guillotine awaited him. He decided to make his escape and to head for America. But he needed a passport and somehow managed to persuade the authorities he was on a mission to buy grain and would be back within a year. In July 1793 he set out on horseback, only to find himself sprawled on the main road out of

Rouen after his horse had stumbled. According to his own account, he had the good fortune to be picked up by the then Navy minister, Gaspard Monge. Monge took him in a cabriolet to the port of Le Havre, from where he sailed on 7 July in the American ship *Liberty*. As Richard Beamish, an English engineer who knew Brunel, remarked, 'Thus did the iniquity of her government deprive France of the services of one of her most gifted sons.'

It could be argued that the brutal dismantling of old privileges and forms of corruption by the revolutionaries laid the ground for the future economic advance of France, and that the brief rule of Napoleon from 1799 until his final defeat at Waterloo in 1815 introduced much-needed modernization. But during the years of political unrest which began with the outbreak of Revolution in 1789 and continued with the military excesses of Napoleon, not only was any significant industrial advance in France hindered, it also rid itself of many of its best brains – beheading some, like Antoine Lavoisier, and sending others, like Brunel, into exile. Furthermore, all Englishmen were declared dangerous aliens in October 1793: no longer sought for their skills, they were hunted down and imprisoned. Even the teenage Sophia Kingdom was arrested, but fortunately for her the prisons were full and she remained under house arrest with impoverished nuns, ever fearful of the busy guillotine.

Oblivious to the plight of his loved one, Brunel had arrived in New York and soon after had found himself taken on by two Frenchmen he had met on the *Liberty* who were planning to survey a huge tract of land through which the Mohawk River ran inland from New York up by Lake Ontario. Like the French trappers, the *couriers du bois*, Brunel and his companions went with native American guides into the wilds. They met by chance an American from New York who was one of those intent on opening up the interior, and Brunel found some work surveying for potential canals and navigational improvements. He showed a flair, too, for architecture, submitting award-winning plans for the Capitol in Washington, a scheme turned down on account of its expense. (Instead, his plans in modified form became the Park Theatre in New York which was destroyed by fire in 1821.) He was, briefly, appointed the Chief City Engineer for New York, a position which gave him access to the most elevated sections of society and some influential diplomats. At the home of Alexander Hamilton, aide-de-camp to George Washington, he met another Frenchman who had fled to England and then across the Atlantic. This Monsieur Delabigarre talked animatedly about British naval victories but made the point that the efficiency of the ships was threatened by a shortage of pulley blocks, the demand for which had greatly increased in wartime. The ease and speed with which a sailing ship could be manoeuvred and its guns brought into action was dependent not only on the skills of the captain and crew but also on the smooth running of its equipment, and pulley blocks were vital in ensuring this.

It is not clear what brought Brunel to England: the scheme he devised for the mass production of pulley blocks which he hoped to sell to the navy, or the desire to find again the English girl he had met and fallen in love with in Rouen. He could certainly have stayed in America, where fellow exiles from France were becoming established, for Brunel had acquired American citizenship. It certainly would not have been safe for him to return to France. However, it was most likely his wish to be reunited with Sophia Kingdom that enticed him back across the Atlantic, for he had clearly managed to stay in touch with her and knew just where to find her. Sophia was then lodging in London and the two met and married on 1 November 1799 in Holborn, only nine months after Marc had docked at Falmouth and set foot in England for the first time.

Brunel had a few savings, but he needed money quickly. He filed his first patent in April 1799 for a contraption he called a polygraph, which had two pens attached to the one wielded by a writer or artist and so provided two copies of any original simultaneously. But it was his second patent for the machining of ships' pulley blocks which was by far the more significant. This was not filed until 1801, but from the time he arrived in England, Brunel was using his letters of introduction and personal contacts to find a way of realizing his scheme. All he had, though, was a series of drawings for pieces of machinery which were to perform various cutting and grooving operations and these would mean little or nothing to most senior navy men. Or so he assumed.

Through a French contact in London, he was told of a young engineer who had just opened up a workshop in Wells Street, which runs north of London's Oxford Street. This was Henry Maudslay, then twenty-nine and only recently established on his own after leaving the workshop of the celebrated locksmith Joseph Bramah. As a boy, Maudslay had been apprenticed in the dockyards of Woolwich Arsenal where he was a 'powder monkey', filling cartridges with gunpowder. From there he had progressed to the carpenter's shop and had taken a special interest in the blacksmith's iron workings. Bramah himself liked to advertise the quality of his locks by inviting scientists and others to break them open for a large reward and then advertising the results in *The Times* (see Chapter 13). Maudslay left his employ a skilled craftsman.

Working with Maudslay, Brunel found a way of turning some of his original drawings into the working models which would be needed to convince the powers that be they were practical and worth investing in. The first approach was made through Sophia's brother, who was Under-Secretary to the Navy Board in Portsmouth. On Brunel's behalf, he wrote to the firm of Messrs Fox and Taylor in Southampton, the chief suppliers of blocks to the navy. Confident that nobody could produce blocks more efficiently and of better quality than they did, Samuel Taylor, son of the firm's founder, wrote back to say they would not be interested in Mr Brunel's inventions.

Fortunately, Brunel had made some excellent contacts while he was in America and he began to call on them. These led him to George John, 2nd Earl Spencer and an ancestor of Lady Diana Spencer. The Member of Parliament for Nottingham, Spencer was a highly educated man who had studied at Cambridge and also had seafaring connections as a Master of Trinity House. He introduced Brunel to many luminaries of the day but most importantly to Brigadier-General Samuel Bentham, brother of the Utilitarian philosopher Jeremy Bentham. In 1795, Samuel Bentham had been appointed Inspector-General of the Royal Dockyards and he had embarked on a major programme of modernization. Much of his experience had been gained in Russia, where he had spent twelve years under the patronage of Catherine the Great. During that time, although he was officially an army officer, he had been more involved with the Russian navy, assisting Admiral Potemkin with his ship-building programme.

Bentham was no dull bureaucrat. While in Russia he had invented a wood-planing machine which, with a change of cutters, could fashion a variety of mouldings. Back in England he devised dovetailing, boring and veneer-cutting machines which could be used to make sash windows. By 1793 he had two patents registered and was recognized as being in the forefront of the development of new woodworking techniques. He wanted to bring these techniques into the Royal Dockyards, and to that end had begun to establish at Portsmouth a new building containing the first steam engine used by the navy. This would drive a sawmill and possibly other machinery, including some new devices for making ships' blocks.

Earl Spencer was a close friend of Bentham and his recommendation of Brunel was enough for the French emigré, formerly an officer in the enemy fleet, to gain an introduction to the great modernizer of the dockyards. It did not take long for Bentham to recognize that Brunel had come up with a scheme which was worth trying. The need for more pulley blocks was pressing. The Royal Navy had grown from 272 warships in 1702 to 498 in 1793 and was rapidly expanding, so that by 1805, the year of the battle of Trafalgar, it could boast 949 vessels. The quantity of pulley blocks required on each ship was related to its rigging and the number of guns it carried. Admiral Nelson's *Victory* needed 768 pulley blocks for the 26 miles of rope in the rigging and 628 for the guns. In 1800 the Royal Navy needed at least 100,000 blocks a year, for new ships and for replacements and spares.

The shell of a pulley block was carved from elm and the inner 'sheave' which revolved inside the shell on an iron pin was made from a hardwood called lignum vitae. Blocks came in different standard sizes and at the time Brunel arrived at Portsmouth were largely hand-crafted, though both main suppliers to the navy – the Taylors of Southampton and Dunsterville in Plymouth – did have some ingenious horse-powered machinery for sawing lengths of wood. What Brunel proposed in his patent, and what Maudslay was striving to turn into a practical series of machines, amounted to a pioneering form of mass production. The skilled craftsman could be replaced by a machine set to cut everything exactly to order. When Bentham visited Brunel and saw what he was working on, he was immediately excited and recommended that the Frenchman be given a contract to work on his invention at Portsmouth. (A claim by Bentham's widow that he was the real inventor of the machines is not supported by any historical evidence.) Brunel was to be paid first on a daily basis as and when he attended to the work at Portsmouth and later to be given a further stipend for the savings his machines would make on the cost of producing one year's supply of pulley blocks.

In 1802, Brunel and Sophia moved to a small house in Britain Street, Portsea, close to the Portsmouth dockyard. By 1803, the first of a total of forty-five of Maudslay's machines had been delivered and were in operation. More were delivered over the next two years, all of them finally hitched to a steam engine in the block mills. Most of the machines bore some resemblance to Brunel's original patent designs but had been greatly improved upon by Maudslay and Brunel working together. The labour saved was spectacular: four men could now make as many elm block shells as fifty under the old craft system of manufacture, and six men could make as many sheaves as sixty. Overall, the labour force was reduced from over one hundred to ten men, affording a huge reduction in cost, and the Portsmouth block mills were soon supplying the whole of the Royal Navy, turning out 130,000 pulleys per year.

Just as the last of Maudslay's machines were being installed, Admiral Nelson paid a brief visit to Portsmouth Dockyard and inspected the block mills. This was in September 1805, a month before the rout of the French and Spanish at Trafalgar and Nelson's death aboard the *Victory*. It is even possible that some of Brunel's blocks were used when Nelson's ship was refitted at Chatham, and they would certainly have been available for other ships of the line in 1805.

The pulley-block system of manufacture inspired by Brunel and developed by Bentham and Maudslay was really the first successful application of precision 'machine-tool' working which both improved the quality of a product while reducing labour and cost. Indeed, it was a form of mass production which saved the British navy a fortune. As always, however, the Admiralty was slow in paying up, but eventually Brunel got back the money he had invested from his own savings and the cut he had been promised. In

1810 he received precisely £17,093 18s 4d, or some £600,000 in today's money.

By that time Brunel had moved back to London from Portsmouth, taking a house on the Thames at Chelsea in 1807. He had established with a business partner a sawmill at Battersea which was doing well, slicing up timber for all purposes with large circular saws driven by steam engines. Many of the teething troubles of this new form of wood-cutting had been solved at Portsmouth. Now Brunel and his partner, a Mr Farthing, were reaping the rewards. But, rather like Richard Trevithick, Brunel was always involved in several enterprises at once and would invariably leave others to run the businesses he had established. Next to his Battersea sawmills, which had become an attraction for foreign tourists, he established another novel factory, this one producing army boots.

The inspiration for the boot factory had been the pathetic sight of the British regiments of foot as they returned from northern Spain. They had been driven out of the country by Napoleon's armies following a last stand at Corunna in Galicia where their general, Sir John Moore, had been killed and buried. Brunel had found himself by chance among the flag-waving crowds at Portsmouth as the bedraggled infantrymen hobbled ashore, their feet often wrapped in rags. They had endured a long and arduous retreat and many were crippled. Noting the state of their boots, Brunel obtained a few pairs and was horrified to discover when he cut them open that they were filled with clay, a lining intended to give the impression of toughness by suggesting the weight of leather; unsurprisingly, in wet weather the clay had dissolved into a kind of liquid mud. The demand for boots remained huge while Napoleon fought for control of Europe, and by 1811 Brunel's factory was producing several grades of fine leather boots. It seems his shoeing of the army endeared him to Sir Arthur Wellesley, the Duke of Wellington, whose Thirty-Third Regiment of Foot is said to have worn Brunel-made boots at Waterloo in 1815.

Brunel was now a very highly regarded figure in England, feted in London society, a man with more than modest wealth and a growing family that now included a son, Isambard, who had been born in 1806 and was already showing an interest in his father's schemes and drawings. In recognition of his work, Marc was elected a Fellow of the Royal Society in March 1814. The Russians, ever vigilant of the talent of other nations, acknowledged Brunel too, and Tsar Alexander I presented him with a gold ring on a visit to Portsmouth earlier in the same year. It was not long before Brunel was being asked to design Russian bridges and offers were being made to entice him away from England. In fact, Russia was soon to save Brunel's bacon.

Between 1812 and 1814 he had been fantastically creative, working on an elaborate timber mill at Chatham dockyard involving all kinds of new-fangled means of loading up huge logs for his circular saws; he had installed a steam engine in a Thames boat and been to Margate and back, hoping the Admiralty would buy his new tugs; and he was still churning out army boots by the thousand. However, he never managed to hang on to his riches for very long as he would spend the earnings from one project on research for another. And when things went wrong financially, they did so disastrously.

In 1814, a fire on the riverfront at Battersea spread to Brunel's sawmill, which was wrecked. The loss was all Brunel's for his partner had gone. Still, there were the boots to make, although after Wellington's victory at Waterloo there was a post-war slump: demand for all kinds of military equipment effectively ceased. But Brunel had other projects: the Russians wanted him to design a bridge, and so did the French; Paris wanted a new waterworks. He was truly an international star. But for one reason or another, these schemes came to nothing and provided no income. Brunel was forever borrowing money to keep afloat, relying on his bankers, Sykes and Company, to settle with creditors. Then, in 1821, the bank declared itself insolvent and closed down.

Brunel could not pay his debts and he and his wife Sophia were arrested and put in the debtor's prison – not the Marshalsea, which featured in the novels of Charles Dickens, but the King's Bench. Visitors noted that Brunel continued to work on his designs and calculations while Sophia darned his stockings. They were imprisoned on 18 May 1821 and were still there, without much hope of redemption, in late July. From prison Brunel continued to write to the Tsar Alexander and let it be known that he might buy himself out by agreeing to shift his operations to Russia. This prompted the government, with a nudge from the Duke of Wellington, to reassess Brunel's contribution to the national good and to offer him £5,000 for services rendered, enough to set him free. There is no doubt Brunel considered Wellington to be his saviour, for he wrote to him on 10 August in the most obsequious terms, thanking him for the 'adjustment to his affairs' made by the British government and his consequent liberation from confinement.

Before the collapse of his finances, meanwhile, Brunel had been contemplating a solution to the problem which Richard Trevithick had tried, and only just failed, to solve. This was the Thames tunnel, a project that had been abandoned in 1808 when funds ran out after a series of near disasters. While he was working at Chatham dockyard, Brunel had taken an interest in a wood-boring mollusc that could do serious damage to the hulls of ships, wooden piers and flood defences. The shipworm or *Teredo navalis* resembles an elongated mussel which, in its larval stage, cuts its way into timber with two sharp shells, feeding on wood as it goes. In the Atlantic these shipworms are normally about seven or eight inches long and half an inch in diameter, but in the Caribbean they can reach lengths of two feet. To protect ships against the attacks of these and other aquatic borers, their hulls were covered in copper sheeting.

The discovery of the way *teredo navalis* burrowed into timber by twisting the cutting shells at its head and then passing the chewed wood through its body to be excreted at the tail, inspired Brunel to take out yet another patent, this time for cutting tunnels through soft ground. This was registered in 1818 with two separate techniques in which the men digging moved a kind of shield forwards underground, backing up the tunnel as they went. It took a long time to generate interest in a new Thames tunnel, but Brunel was not about to abandon the project and the chance to test his ingenious mechanism, which he liked to call the Great Shield and was made by Henry Maudslay. He canvassed a large number of potential investors, including his old friend the Duke of Wellington, and eventually a company was formed which successfully floated £2 shares to raise the capital for the project. This new tunnel would be excavated much closer to London than the one Trevithick had worked on. Its function was no longer to facilitate troop movements from the south coast into Essex; what it promised was the easing of traffic between the docks being constructed east of London Bridge on the north side of the river, and the dock systems to the south. There was no possibility at that period of building a bridge with river traffic still so dense on the Thames. A tunnel from Rotherhithe in the south to Wapping on the north bank would undoubtedly divert a huge amount of road traffic.

Work began in 1825 with the sinking of the Rotherhithe shaft. The plan was to get down to a depth where the segmented metal 'shield' could begin to inch its way through the blue clay that lay below the Thames. When the first stage of the tunnel was completed, there would just be room for pedestrians who would pay a toll that would help raise revenue for the final stage in which a double tunnel would carry horse-drawn traffic. To avoid the expense of purchasing an extensive tract of land either side for entry to the tunnel, wagons would descend a tight spiral roadway.

Of all Marc Brunel's myriad engineering schemes and inventions, which ranged from a card-shuffling machine invented for a lady with arthritic hands to his pulley-block machines and many bridges, the tunnelling technique was perhaps the most original and far reaching in its influence on later developments. It was at the start of this project that Marc was first joined by his talented son, Isambard (it is confusing that they both called themselves Isambard), who had received a very cosmopolitan education, first in England and then in Paris. It has often been asserted that young Isambard was denied access to the Ecole Polytechnique in Paris because he was English, an apparently absurd twist of fate which, for his British biographers, exemplified the *hauteur* of French academia. In fact he failed the highly competitive exam.

For three years, the Brunels – father and son – worked on the tunnel together, confronting a huge array of difficulties, the most critical of which was the geology of the ground below the riverbed. This was not, as Marc Brunel had been led to believe, pure clay. His shield hit quicksands and water poured in on a number of occasions. Finally, on 12 January 1828, work on the tunnel was stopped. The money had run out, investors had lost heart and the tunnel was barely half completed. It was left untended for seven years. Work then began again with an improved shield and, after seven more years, the first section was opened to pedestrians in March 1843. It was never opened for road traffic but it later became a railway tunnel, which it remains to this day.

During his life, Marc Brunel was showered with honours while his brilliant son became the most celebrated engineer of his day. In 1829 Marc was awarded the French Legion d'Honneur; ten years later the Institution of Civil Engineers presented him with the Telford Medal for his tunnelling shield; in 1841 he received a knighthood. From the time of the Thames tunnel project, however, his health began to falter and in 1842 and 1845 he suffered strokes, dying on 12 December 1849 at his home by St James's Park. He was buried in Kensal Green cemetery.

What fate would have befallen Brunel and his inventive genius had he braved it out in Rouen in 1793 is impossible to say. Like Lavoisier, he might have been beheaded and his many inventions would have tumbled, along with his head, into a basket and oblivion. Had he survived the Revolution, he would no doubt have applied his genius to the demands of French industry, although he would have been working in a less favourable environment in the early 1800s than that he found in Portsmouth and London. Similarly, had he stayed in America – as he might well have done but for his desire to be reunited with Sophia Kingdom – he would have begun his inventive work in a less sophisticated industrial world than that offered by the young Henry Maudslay and his workshop off Oxford Street.

In 1800, America had barely begun to develop its own manufacturing industries. However, for another French emigré the very backwardness of the industry he found in the United States provided an opportunity to establish what turned out to be one of the greatest American companies of the nineteenth century and one which remains a world leader today: the chemical giant, Dupont.

The founder of du Pont (this was how the family name was always spelt) was the son of the distinguished Pierre Samuel du Pont de Nemours, the owner of an estate sixty miles south of Paris in the village of Chavannes in the district of Nemours. Styling himself du Pont de Nemours, Pierre was the Inspector General of Commerce in Louis XVI's cabinet. He was in favour of reform but not revolution and he and his younger son, Irénée, went to the defence of the king in the Tuileries on 10 August 1792. When rioters gathered in pursuit of the king, his Swiss Guards tried to protect him but were routed. With a company of sixty men, du Pont and Irénée went to the rescue, but they too were beaten and nearly all of them killed. A few stragglers, including du Pont and his son, escaped by pretending to be revolutionaries themselves. The elder du Pont, aware that he was a marked man, first hid in the dome of the Paris Observatory, then slipped out of Paris and back to Nemours disguised as an elderly physician. Irénée stayed in Paris running a successful printing and publishing business, which his father had founded, and also provided some family income.

The Jacobins caught up with the elder du Pont just after the guillotining of his friend, the brilliant chemist Antoine Lavoisier, and he was incarcerated in the Parisian prison known as La Force to await almost certain execution in 1794. The sudden reversal of Robespierre's fortunes and his own execution saved du Pont, who returned to the political scene. Together with Irénée, he published a journal, *L'Historien*, propounding his own moderate views on political reform.

Later in 1794, du Pont and his son once again found themselves on the wrong side of the revolutionary power struggle. A left-wing faction staged a *coup d'état*, hunted down monarchists and went in search of what they considered reactionary journals, one of which was du Pont's *L'Historien*. Pierre du Pont was ill in bed when General Jannes stormed into his home with a warrant for his arrest. Despite his protests, Pierre was marched off to La Force once more. He was soon joined by Irénée and the two of them spent the night in a cell with a murderer and three thieves. They were not, this time, in fear of their lives, as they knew the punishment that had been meted out to those in a similar position was deportation to French Guiana in the West Indies. While they were in jail, however, the police broke into their printing works in the rue de l'Oratoire, looking for incriminating evidence, and, when they found none, smashed the place up, causing damage Pierre estimated at 40,000 francs. The du Ponts were released after two days, almost certainly because Pierre had agreed to stay out of politics. *L'Historien* was closed down. Du Pont had been comfortably off and well connected at the outbreak of the Revolution. Now he was banned from public office and broke. He had been jailed twice, threatened first with the guillotine and then deportation. It was in these circumstances that he made the decision to head for America.

This was not an entirely novel idea at the time. The du Ponts were also well connected across the Atlantic. Pierre's elder son, Victor, had lived there for a number of years and was married; when Pierre and Irénée had been imprisoned in La Force, he had been enjoying life as the French consul in Charleston, South Carolina, and he numbered both Thomas Jefferson and Benjamin Franklin among his personal friends. Nevertheless, there really was nothing much the du Ponts could do in America and they would certainly have to abandon their publishing business in Paris. One day, Pierre announced a plan to gather money from investors to fund a scheme in which he would buy land in the United States and establish a new community. His family were aghast. It was a similar scheme to one in which Brunel had been involved when he first went to America. Victor, who had now returned to France, warned that the French were not always popular in America and that only some states allowed foreigners to purchase land. But Pierre was not to be deterred.

Two years elapsed between Pierre du Pont's resolution to leave France and the final exodus. Friends warned him that if he just upped and took a ship to the United States, he could lose his entitlement to land in France and that he had better find some official reason for going, just as Brunel had done. Du Pont managed to get himself registered as part of a team of explorers studying American natural history and culture. He was not, therefore, strictly speaking a refugee from revolutionary France, although the treatment meted out to him had been sufficient to see him off.

The du Ponts left France en masse on 2 October 1799, boarding the ship *American Eagle* on the Ile de Ré. There were seven adults and six small children. As well as Pierre, there was Victor with his wife and two children, Irénée with his wife and three children, the wife of another family member and her baby and a brother-in-law, Charles Dalmas. The escape across the therefore appealed for skilled workmen to come over from France, and made it known in French-speaking Canada that there was work to be had on the Brandywine. By April 1804 the mills were working and Irénée was selling gunpowder of a quality everyone agreed was well above the customary American grade and at least as good as that made in England. Government orders rolled in. One of the first uses by the Americans was in their battles with the so-called Barbary Pirates of the Mediterranean who harassed their fleet and took prisoners for ransom money. Du Pont made 22,000 pounds for the assault on the pirates. Orders came in from other countries, too, with Spain asking for huge quantities of powder.

But the early days of the business were still fraught. The powder was good and in great demand but Irénée was always strapped for cash, verging on bankruptcy every time he bought the raw materials for the manufacture of more powder. His brother Victor was in financial trouble, while his father Pierre had gone back to France in 1802, disillusioned with America and reassured that in his own country he would no longer be hounded by the authorities. From Paris, Pierre did what he could to help fund Irénée's business, though he too was often in financial straits. One of his tasks was to arrange for a skilled 'powderman', Charles François Parent, to sign a contract, witnessed in Paris by the American consul, to work for du Pont in Delaware for nine years at a salary of $500 per annum.

Parent arrived at New York with his two sons and a governess in April 1803. He was met by Victor du Pont, who was straight away alarmed at the Frenchman's 'gentlemanly' manners: anyone so affected was unlikely to succumb to the rustic charms of Wilmington, Delaware. Victor's impression was confirmed when Parent announced that he was not prepared to live in the backwoods of Brandywine and would consider only Philadelphia, then the first city of the United States, or up and coming New York. The powderman was even less happy to discover that Irénée had offered him a lower salary than his American counterparts in the belief that a Frenchman had lower expectations than over-priced native labour. As it happened, there was nothing much for Parent to do as the works were not fully functioning on his arrival. But when the time came there was a showdown, with Irénée

Atlantic was almost as treacherous as the weeks of the Terror. The *American Eagle* leaked badly and had both a captain whose navigational skills seem to have deserted him and a crew that mutinied and robbed the passengers. The du Ponts had to stand guard over their belongings with swords drawn, and there was so little food on board that the ship had twice to take in provisions from English vessels. They were at sea for ninety-one days before they put in at Newport, Rhode Island, on New Year's Day 1800. (Some say it was 3 January, but this was not nearly such a romantic date.) Pierre's second wife had gone on ahead with her son-in-law and his little daughter and were to meet the rest of the family at Newport. But the *American Eagle* was so delayed they had given up and assumed their relatives had drowned. A family legend even had it that they staggered ashore in search of food and shelter and found a house with a brightly lit room in which there was a table laid with a feast and bottles of wine. As they could get no answer, they went in, helped themselves and left a gold coin in thanks.

Like so many apocryphal stories, this none the less had a grain of truth to it. The grand schemes that Pierre du Pont had for developing land in America were a dream which was never likely to come true. However, it was not long before there was food on the du Pont family table. As a young man, Irénée had wanted to become a naturalist, but his father, who could be domineering, insisted he take up what he regarded as a more useful profession. He had managed to get him a place with his friend Antoine Lavoisier, who, among his other responsibilities, was then a Commissioner of the Gunpowder and Saltpetre Administration. This had become a state-run operation as the commercial production of gunpowder had been banned in France because its quality had been so poor. To work in Lavoisier's circle was a great honour as he was one of the most famous chemists in Europe – the man who coined the word 'oxygen' and many other chemical terms which remain in use today. Working at the gunpowder mills at Essonne outside Paris, Irénée had learned something of the manufacture of explosives and the techniques Lavoisier and others had developed to improve its quality. He had still been at Essonne when, in 1791, the hounding of Lavoisier had begun after his move to the Treasury, at which point Irénée had left the mills and joined his father in Paris.

The knowledge Irénée had gleaned at Essonne proved to be the salvation of the du Pont family. There was huge demand for gunpowder in America at that time and for years to come. Wildlife was abundant and hunting a universal pursuit. There were the battles with the 'Indians' as the colonists moved west and a great deal of ground to clear, a task which required explosives. What coal-mining and quarrying there was needed black powder to break up rock. And yet, unlike in Britain or France, the production of gunpowder in America was not especially advanced. Irénée himself had from childhood loved the outdoors and he now became a keen hunter, enjoying days spent shooting in the wild countryside along with fellow emigrés. There was a small French community established at Wilmington, Delaware, most of whom had fled not from France but from the island of San Domingo (later Haiti) to escape an uprising of plantation slaves. Among the French emigrés were a few men such as Colonel Louis de Toussard, who was French-born but had become an American artillery officer. It was on a hunting expedition with Toussard that Irénée commented that the quality of locally produced gunpowder was not very good.

With Toussard's encouragement, Irénée decided to set up a French-style gunpowder works in America and to make it the family business. He needed investors and equipment, and he and his elder brother Victor reasoned that they would need to go back to France to prepare for their American enterprise. Irénée was able to return to the gunpowder works at Essonne, where he was greeted enthusiastically and given instruction on the very latest developments in gunpowder technology. A critical issue was the supply and purity of the three constituents: saltpetre (potassium nitrate), sulphur and carbon. At that time there were huge natural deposits of saltpetre in Bengal (now Bangladesh) and it had become the world's major supplier. But the British had annexed this source and so France had to make do with older methods of collection and refinement: the nitrate was formed in earth saturated with urine, both human and animal, and so-called 'saltpetre men' had the task of gathering it. Lavoisier had had many schemes for increasing and improving the supply of saltpetre, and there was a similar quest for abundant sources of high-quality sulphur and charcoal.

It seems odd that Irénée should have been given such a warm reception in France shortly after the family had left. In his mind there was little doubt why this was, as he wrote to his father some time later when his gunpowder works was established: 'It is the commerce of the English only that American manufacturers can hurt. In four years I have made 600,000 pounds of powder that would have come from England if I had not made it; therefore it is only the English I have injured. This truth was well understood in France when I was given every facility for procuring my machinery.' As another family member, Bessie Gardner du Pont, wrote in her little history of the company: 'Napoleon's efforts to destroy the commerce of England seem to have been most fortunate for the equipment of the American powder mills.'[2] Napoleon's so-called Continental System banned all trade between Europe and Britain, leaving America a free hand to fill the gap.

Thomas Jefferson, who in 1800 was vice-president of the United States, knew Pierre du Pont well from his time as a diplomat in Paris a few years earlier. He was enthusiastic about the powder works scheme and suggested a site close to Washington. On his return from France, however, Irénée chose to return to Wilmington, Delaware, close to the home of Colonel Toussard. Here the Brandywine River provided the power for many mills and f machinery for grinding and compacting powder essential for the gunpow works. Irénée had established his company in France, calling it E. I. du F de Nemours et Cie, his first name being the unusual Eleuthère. He acqu a farm on the Brandywine by going into partnership with an emigré Santo Domingo who had become an American citizen and was therefo to sign the deeds. There were both French and American investors company.

As it took shape, the gunpowder works was named, at Pierre's su the Eleutherian Mills. Construction on the site followed the Frenc fairly closely, with the various processes of preparing the constituen kept at a safe distance from each other. Accidental explosions we in gunpowder works. At first Irénée complained bitterly about of workmen available in America; many of them were unski whom he could not understand and who could not under

Above: From 1771 Cromford Mill in Derbyshire housed the revolutionary 'water frame' for spinning cotton. French spies enticed skilled workers from Cromford and other mills to use their skills to set up rival mills across the Channel.

Right: The stern countenance of John Wilkinson (1728–1808), the foremost ironmaster of his day. Known as 'Iron Mad' John, he made cannon for the British Navy, sold water pipes to France and set up an ironworks in the Loire Valley.

Below: A sketch of the gunpowder mills founded by Irénée du Pont on the Brandywine River at Wilmington, Delaware in 1804. Hounded during the years of Revolution, the du Ponts left France in 1799 to found in America what became a chemical giant.

Above: The inventive genius Marc Isambard Brunel (1769–1849), who fled France during the Revolution. After a stay in America he came to England to marry Sophia Kingdom: their son, Isambard Kingdom Brunel, was born in 1806.

Above: Marc Brunel's design for machines to mass produce the thousands of pulley blocks needed for the rigging and guns of warships was his greatest achievement.

Below: The American Robert Fulton's pioneer steamboat, the *North River* or *Clermont* in 1807. The engine was made by Boulton and Watt and the boiler sent from London.

Left: Richard Trevithick (1771–1833), the great unsung hero of British engineering who built the first working steam locomotives, was vilified by James Watt for using 'strong steam' and died an ignominious death. His grandsons built the first railways in Japan.

Below: France's first major railway line from Paris to Rouen was built by British engineers who brought over an army of several thousand navvies, *les rosbifs*, whose diet impressed the locals. A roast ox was served when the line opened in 1847.

Above: When the Great Exhibition opened in Hyde Park in 1851, there was a good deal of sarcasm in the British Press about the poor contribution of the United States, which did not fill the space allotted to it. All that changed when Yankee ingenuity became evident.

Below: One of the great triumphs of the United States at the Great Exhibition: the McCormick reaper. An Essex farmer held a trial for rival reapers which had to cut green corn on a wet day. The McCormick reaper won the day and a Great Medal.

Above: Displayed in the window of James Bramah at 124 Piccadilly from 1801, this padlock challenged all-comers to win a prize of 200 guineas if they could open it without damage. In 1851 an American, A. C. Hobbs, picked it in fifty-one hours and was handed the money.

demanding that Parent start work and the reluctant powderman slinking off to Philadelphia. Irénée had him arrested and locked up in jail, where he remained for several months. In the end, Irénée gave in and provided Parent with the money to set up on his own in New Orleans in partnership with Charles Dalmas, Irénée's brother-in-law. Parent was doing well until he was drowned in an unfortunate accident in 1811.

In time, Irénée gathered around him a skilled and largely loyal workforce at Wilmington and the gunpowder works gained such a reputation in America that the name Du Pont (now written DuPont) became synonymous with gunpowder. This success created its own problems as rival manufacturers sought to steal the expertise of Du Pont workers. In 1808 a new company established in Richmond, Virginia, advertised in the Wilmington newspaper for master powdermen and received some replies from Du Pont workers, although Irénée was able to take legal action to stop an agent who arrived to negotiate terms with his men. There were other similar incidents. But the war with England in 1812 gave a great boost to trade, even if afterwards, with surpluses of powder left over, there was a slump. At times Irénée had to see off fierce competition, yet for nearly the whole of the nineteenth century the company he founded remained a major manufacturer of gunpowder for both the military and sportsmen.

It was, of course, a dangerous business, with the threat of fire and explosions being ever present. On 16 July 1817, a charcoal-burner at Wilmington made the mistake of assuming some cinders were no longer alight and left them in wooden barrels. Some embers rekindled the charcoal, which then set fire to the timber and the drying house burst into flames. The Du Pont works had a firebell which summoned workers from all over the district. Irénée was away on one of his many business trips, negotiating for new orders, but Pierre du Pont heard the bell and, even though he was seventy-seven and in poor health, dressed as fast as he could and went to help the fire-fighters who had formed a chain bringing buckets of water from the Brandywine river to douse the flames.

Pierre was back in America because events in France had once again caused him to flee. For a short while following his return, he had enjoyed political office. After Napoleon had abdicated in 1814 and been confined to the island of Elba, Pierre had been appointed Secretary to the provisional government of Talleyrand: in fact, he had even certified the abdication of Napoleon on 11 April. He had then become a counsellor of state and been made a Chevalier of the Legion d'Honneur. Domestically, life had been not so happy as his wife had fallen from a carriage and become seriously ill. Then Napoleon had made his astonishing reappearance at Cannes and marched north. Members of the provisional government had scattered. Pierre had managed to obtain a false American passport and sailed back across the Atlantic. He was never to see his wife again, for she died soon after he had fled.

The effort Pierre made to help fight the fire in July 1817 proved to be too much for him. He was buried in what was to become the du Pont dynasty's own family plot not far from the powder mills. His epitaph read: 'Sacred to the Memory of Pierre Samuel du Pont de Nemours, Knight of the Order of Vasa, of the Legion of Honor and of the order du Lis; Counsellor of State, member of the first Constituent Assembly, President of the Council of Ancients and member of the Institute of France. Born in Paris, December A.D. 1739. Died at the Eleutherian Mills August 17 A.D. 1817.' Though their paterfamilias had tried to return to France, this was the end of any such ambition on the family's part. The du Ponts were now thoroughly American.

On 19 March 1818, however, the company very nearly disappeared altogether. The peace of a sunny spring day which had brought people on to the streets of Wilmington was shattered by what many took to be an earthquake – or possibly one of the new steamships blowing up on the river. The effect of the blast was felt more than forty miles away. A glazing mill at the du Pont works, where powder was 'polished' to give the grain resistance to moisture and slow its burning, had exploded. It was never discovered whether or not this was an accident. The mill burned furiously and a flaming timber was hurled hundreds of yards, setting fire to another building. One huge explosion followed another, and when the fire ignited a powder store cut into a stone hillside, rocks were blown in all directions.

Once again, Irénée was away, this time in Philadelphia. He galloped back to the mills to find that thirty-six of his workmen and members of their families had died: flying rocks had smashed through some of the timber houses. A large part of the works was destroyed and Irénée was in danger of losing the business altogether. His father had borrowed money in France and it was now Irénée's responsibility to pay those debts as well as to meet the bills presented to him by suppliers. It was a very close thing, but the company survived and indeed was soon back in business, employing 140 workmen who produced 800,000 pounds of fine quality powder a year.

The first generation of du Pont emigrés did not live long. In 1827 Irénée's elder brother, Victor, whose gambling habits had caused the family difficulties, dropped dead in the street in Philadelphia at the age of fifty-nine. It appears he suffered a heart attack. A ticket he had bought in the New York Consolidated Lottery was found in his pocket, and when the family checked it they found that Victor had posthumously won $850. Irénée himself died in similar circumstances, also collapsing in a Philadelphia street in 1834 and dying in his hotel room at the age of sixty-three. After his death the firm was kept going by Jacques Antoine Bidermann, who had married Irénée's daughter Evelina in 1816. Bidermann returned to France, cleared all the family debts there and wound up the French company. He reorganized the du Pont business in America and set it up as a partnership composed of Irénée's seven children – three sons and four daughters. Bidermann himself stood aside.

The du Pont story is a classic example of what is termed the 'transfer of technology' from one country to another. French skill in producing gunpowder was taken to America, where a new industry was established. As long as the United States remained relatively backward industrially, the traffic in technological innovation was likely to be in just one direction – westwards – across the Atlantic. However, by the early 1800s there were the stirrings of indigenous inventiveness. Americans were devising machines unique to their own industry and there were still others who had the audacity to offer the French and the British fiendishly clever devices they had dreamed up on their own home soil.

CHAPTER SIX

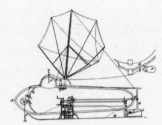

SOME YANKEES IN THE WORKS

On 15 October 1805, a crowd gathered on a beach on the south coast of England to witness the demonstration of a devastating new weapon. It was the invention of a young man whose name was said to be Robert Francis, although only a few men in the Admiralty knew his real identity. All eyes were on a ship, a 200-ton Dutch barque, anchored about three-quarters of a mile offshore. At some time previously, this old hulk had been taken as a prize of war and it was now eminently expendable. There was no crew on board: the ship was simply a target for the weapon being prepared on shore. A small group of men made ready a kind of crude twin-hulled canoe. They were watched by a crowd of intrigued locals as well as by some finely uniformed dignitaries. The beach chosen for the demonstration was immediately below Walmer Castle, the cliff-top residence of William Pitt, the British Prime Minister, and he was also there to witness the weapon that the inventor promised would put paid to Napoleon Bonaparte's plan to invade Britain. Just across the sea were the French ports of Boulogne and Calais, where Napoleon's armada was being assembled.

When the strange twin canoe was ready, it was pushed out towards the Dutch barque by a man lying low in the water and paddling. Progress was slow and a naval big-wig was heard to remark that he would have been happy enough 'to have dined' on the target ship for all the damage this inventor's so-called 'torpedo' would cause. Even so, as the weapon came close to the ship, the man propelling it aimed it in the direction of the anchor chain and then let it go, swimming back to the beach as fast as he could. Meanwhile a clockwork-activated fuse ticked away.

What happened next was reported the following day in *The Times*. There was just one short paragraph, which concluded:

> In a few minutes the clock-work of the machinery having performed its operation, a small cloud of smoke was seen to arise from the vessel, which in a moment after was blown to atoms, without any noise, or any appearance of fire. In about twenty-seven or twenty-eight seconds not a vestige of the brig was to be seen, as the fragments were then level with the water's edge. General Don, with a number of Military and Naval Officers, went with Sir Sidney Smith to Mr Pitt's, at Walmer Castle, to witness the experiment, and expressed the utmost astonishment at the destructive powers of the invention.[1]

This impressive demonstration of the destructive power of the torpedo was staged just a week before Admiral Horatio Nelson's defeat of the French and Spanish fleets at Trafalgar. The inventor had in fact written to Nelson personally some five weeks earlier, in the following terms:

> My Lord
>
> Had Mr Davison been in Town he was to do me the honor [sic] of introducing me to your Lordship; I am an inventor of what has been called submarine navigation carcasses and the kind [of] craft known by the name of Catamarans with which inventions I conceive your Lordship might do much execution in many cases of blockade – it is on the application of those engines I wish to see your Lordship and as I am convinced you will find the explanation of them interesting. I should be extremely happy to have a few minutes conversation before you leave Town, if you will be so good as to mention an hour when I may wait on you either

here or in town, you will much oblige your Lordships.

Most obedient and very humble
Servant
Robt Francis

September 4 1805
Sackville Street Piccadilly
No. 13[2]

Mr Davison, who was not in town, was Nelson's agent and we do not know if the admiral ever got to see this letter. It is unlikely, as he was on his way to Trafalgar shortly afterwards. Nelson knew, anyway, of the new weapons on offer and, unlike many senior navy men, was not entirely dismissive of them. But he felt confident that he could win any sea battle with traditional methods: that is to say, blasting the enemy broadside at close range.

It was typical of the foreigner who signed himself Francis that he should approach directly such an eminent figure as Nelson, for he had spent at least fifteen years touting his ideas around Britain and France, as well as his native America, making all sorts of claims for his inventive genius. His real name was Robert Fulton and he was one of a number of Americans born before the War of Independence who demonstrated a Yankee originality which not only drove forward the industrialization of the United States but influenced developments in Europe as well.

One other American also made a considerable impression in England. He was Jacob Perkins, born in Newburyport, Massachusetts, in 1766 and an astonishingly prolific inventor who sought his fortune in London, where he lived for the last thirty years of his life. Perkins was a great admirer of fellow American Oliver Evans, who built an automated flour mill and appears to have created independently a high-pressure steam engine around the same time as Trevithick. A fiercely independently minded man, Evans did not seek his fortune in Europe but contented himself with advancing American technology. So too did Eli Whitney, celebrated in American histories as the inventor of the 'cotton gin', a story even more obscured by claim, counter-claim and popular myth than that of the invention of the steam engine.

Of the four, Fulton was the most flamboyant and the least original – nearly all his discoveries were borrowed from others. Yet his perseverance paid off. Instead of realizing his ambition of rendering marine warfare impossible with a proliferation of torpedoes, he inaugurated one of the first passenger steamboat services in the world with trips on the Hudson River. The fact that Fulton managed as much is truly remarkable for he really had very little mechanical gift. He was a kind of 'inventomaniac' whose head was turned by the spirit of the times when he first set foot in an England gripped by canal mania and the steam revolution. Yet he had crossed the Atlantic as neither a mechanic nor an industrial spy, but to hone his talent as draughtsman and painter.

Fulton was born on 14 November 1765 on a farm at Little Britain Township (later named Fulton Township), twenty miles south of Lancaster, Pennsylvania. His father was a tailor and small-time trader whose experiment with farming proved a failure, so the family moved back to Lancaster when Robert was a toddler. According to a biography by Fulton's great-granddaughter, Alice Crary Sutcliffe, his father was a respected member of the community but not wealthy, leaving only a small legacy when he died two years after the family returned to Lancaster. There is no record of how the family survived the next few years, but Robert had some schooling and showed an early interest in the workshops of Lancaster, which had built a lot of the wagons that rolled westwards across America as well as much of the weaponry for the revolutionary forces.

When he was sixteen or seventeen, Fulton was working in Philadelphia for a jeweller, probably painting miniature pictures for cameos and the like. He appears to have gained quite a reputation as a miniaturist and one or two pieces which are said to be his survive. His name can be found in a trade directory of 1785: he is described as a miniaturist, apparently working on his own account. It was about this time that he somehow acquired enough money to settle his mother and her brother on a small farm and to provide further plots of land for his brothers and sisters. The recollections of those who knew Fulton all make it clear that his one overriding ambition was to become wealthy and all his schemes were directed to that end. It really did not matter to him how he achieved this, except that he was always in a hurry.

We do not know why Fulton decided in 1787 to travel to England for he left no account and there is precious little record of his early life. What we do know, however, is that he went as an artist and with an introduction to the American painter Benjamin West, who had established himself in London and was a founder member of the Royal Academy of Arts. West supposedly knew Fulton's parents and as a boy had painted their portraits. Whether or not this is true, West took care of Fulton, as he did of a number of other American hopefuls seeking their fortune in London, finding him digs with another artist. There is no doubt Fulton had great charm and powers of persuasion, if only modest talent as a painter, but the brush and the easel and his association with the celebrated Benjamin West did afford him an introduction to the British aristocracy. In particular, he was befriended by William Courtenay, the flamboyantly homosexual young Earl of Devon, who invited the struggling artist down to his estate at Powderham to paint his portrait. Fulton appears to have lived as the guest of the earl for eighteen months and when, a few years later, Courtenay was involved in a scandal and fled to America, he became one of the social outcast's few friends.

Fulton's first foray into the world of inventions was the design for a marble-cutting machine, a model of which won him a medal presented by the Royal Society for the Encouragement of Arts, Manufactures and Commerce. (The Society had been founded in a London coffee house in 1745 and was to be influential in the staging of the Great Exhibition of 1851.) To be awarded such a medal was a considerable honour, but there is no evidence that the marble sawmill ever worked and the model has disappeared. As with so many of his projects, Fulton did not stay long with this innovation, and he was soon writing to the proposer of a canal to link the Thames and the Bristol Channel to outline his own scheme for the works, despite the fact that he had absolutely no experience at all of canal engineering. Some time around 1794, Fulton gave up painting altogether and sought his fortune with canal projects.

One patent he took out was for a double inclined plane which acted rather like a funicular railway to carry goods up and down steep slopes as an alternative to a series of canal locks. He advocated the cutting of small-scale canals and wrote a treatise on them. He travelled to Manchester, the heartland of the newly prosperous cotton industry, where by chance he shared lodgings with a young man called Robert Owen, who had become a successful mill supervisor and would later establish his own revolutionary industrial development of New Lanark in Scotland. Owen took a share in Fulton's inclined plane project and a machine for digging canals, an investment that produced no return, like so many of Fulton's projects at this time. Back in London, Fulton met the eccentric clergyman Edmund Cartwright, who had invented the power loom. This was not then widely used but in modified form was to transform the weaving process in the woollen and cotton industries in the 1820s and 1830s. Wherever he went, Fulton made friends with influential people, though in reality all he had to offer was a great enthusiasm.

It seems that Fulton fancied himself a good republican in sympathy with the French revolutionaries, for in 1797, when there was a lull in the hostilities with England, he crossed the Channel and sought his fortune in Paris. Here he fell in straight away with fellow Americans Joel Barlow and his wife Ruth Baldwin. Barlow was a man of many interests, a speculator, poet and statesman, and was for a long time Fulton's closest friend, admirer and champion. Joel and Ruth were older than Robert, by seven and ten years respectively, and it is suggested by some that the fiery young inventor was taken on as a surrogate son. More recently, the close friendship has been interpreted as a ménage à trois. Certainly, Ruth and Robert spent a good deal of time together, apart from Joel, who always wrote very affectionately to Fulton, addressing him in his letters as 'Toot'.

These Paris years – a period which coincided with Napoleon's emergence as a great military leader – were undoubtedly the most influential on Fulton's future career. He shared a home with the Barlows for seven years and was well cared for so that he could concentrate on promoting his ideas. While his versions of the various inventions he patented or claimed for himself might have been original, the broad concept never was. The military devices he had made and tried to sell to Napoleon – the *Nautilus* submarine and the torpedo

– had histories going back to the seventeenth century. In Fulton's own time, his fellow countryman David Bushnell had tried with little success to attack the British navy in 1776 with a submarine. Fulton's *Nautilus* was a kind of cigar-shaped vessel, just large enough for two men who could submerge the craft with ballast tanks and survive for up to six hours, breathing a release of compressed air. It was powered by a hand-cranked propeller and was really no great advance on Bushnell's model. As for the development of the steamboat, for which Fulton ultimately became famous, there were literally dozens of precedents for the vessels he had built in Paris and tested on the Seine. Which is not to deny that Fulton did, in the end, achieve a breakthrough. He did so by becoming acquainted with British, French and American promoters of industrialism at a time when there was very fertile exchange of technologies between the three nations.

Henry Winram Dickinson, who was in charge of mechanical engineering exhibits at what is now the Science Museum, London, between 1924 and 1930 provided a detailed account of how Fulton came to be an innovator, writing in 1913:

> It is doubtful whether Fulton would have done anything in steam navigation … had it not been for the arrival in France of Chancellor Robert R. Livingston, Minister Plenipotentiary of the United States to France. The first thing he [Livingston] heard on his arrival in Paris in November 1801 was the news of the cession of Louisiana and the Floridas by Spain to France. Their new neighbour was viewed with great alarm by the States, and it is a matter of history that they succeeded in coming to terms on April 30, 1803, by the payment of eighty million francs, Napoleon thus astutely putting Louisiana in the hands of a power unfriendly to England and at the same time supplying himself with the funds he needed so badly for carrying on his schemes of conquest.
>
> Now, Livingston was deeply interested in the subject of steamboats; indeed, he had an idea or two of his own, and, as a result of his experiments, had gone so far as to procure an Act to be passed

in March 1798 vesting in himself the 'exclusive right and privilege of navigating all kinds of boats which might be propelled by the force of steam or fire on all the waters within the territory or jurisdiction of the State of New York for the term of twenty years from the passing of the Act; upon condition that he should within a twelvemonth build such a boat, the mean of whose progress should not be less than four miles per hour'.[3]

Livingston had laid the groundwork and had gone to the trouble of writing to Boulton & Watt in Birmingham to ask about the feasibility and cost of making a steam engine which might be used to power a boat. His brother visited Paris and learned something of Fulton, who seemed to be the very man that Livingston was looking for. At the time, Fulton had an agreement with the French that he would be rewarded on a fixed scale for the destruction by his submarine and torpedoes of any ships he managed to blow up in the English Channel. The promised fees were 400,000 francs for those of more than thirty guns, 200,000 francs for those of more than twenty up to thirty guns, 150,000 francs for those from twelve to twenty guns, and 60,000 francs for those of up to ten or twelve guns. Now Fulton could add the project Livingston proposed of building a peacetime steamboat to provide passenger services in America.

In pursuit of the proffered French bounty, Fulton had spent some frustrating days off the Channel port of Le Havre, trying to get close enough to blow up an English ship. Dickinson duly wrote of the escapade:

> The hardihood of Fulton in going in this cockle shell a voyage of about 70 miles upon what was really a warlike expedition upon the high seas seems almost incredible. His attempt to blow up the English brigs that were cruising along the coast was frustrated not by accident but by design because Fulton's movements generally were known to the British Admiralty. Captain S. H. Linzie, H. M.S. *L'Oiseau* off Havre, writing on Sept. 21, 1800: 'Thanks the Secretary to the Admiralty for his letter 1 [?] of the 14th giving an account of Mr.

Fulton's Plan respecting the possibility of destroying the ships on this station,' and says: 'I shall be very much on my guard.' So that it is explained why the brigs so quickly slipped from their anchorages.[4]

Not only were Fulton's submarine and torpedo adventures a practical failure: there was then an entrenched view amongst senior naval officers on both sides of the Channel that blowing ships up was not fair play and should not be contemplated. Fulton could, and indeed did, argue that his devices would put an end to naval warfare and make the seas safe for everyone. Alternatively, they might instead make the seas so treacherous that all trade would cease, a prospect he does not seem to have considered.

Much more successful was Fulton's first attempt to put Livingston's steamboat scheme into practice. Working as a partnership, they did not wait for a Boulton & Watt engine but had one supplied by none other than Monsieur Périer, one of the brothers who had engaged Wilkinson for the Paris waterworks scheme. A contemporary account in a Paris newspaper read:

> On the 21st Thermidor (9 August) a trial was made of a new invention of which the complete and brilliant success should have important consequences for the commerce and internal navigation of France. During the past two or three months there has been seen at the end of the quai Chaillot, a boat of curious appearance, equipped with two large wheels, mounted on an axle as in a chariot, while behind these wheels was a kind of large stove with a pipe, as if there were some kind of small fire engine intended to operate the wheels of the boat.[5]

The report goes on to say that an early version of this contraption was smashed up, presumably by river boatmen anxious about their future. However, the steamboat was repaired and worked well enough to give some distinguished Frenchmen an inaugural trip. At the same time, Fulton was planning with Livingston to establish a riverboat service not in France, but back on the Hudson River. In a letter dated just days after the successful Seine voyage,

Fulton was writing to Boulton & Watt to ask them if it would be permissible in law for engine parts to be shipped to an address in New York. There were all kinds of requirements listed for the arrangement of the engine. Boulton & Watt replied that they would need government permission to send an engine to America, prompting Fulton to pull all the diplomatic strings he could with his distinguished English friends.

Meanwhile, with Napoleon's invasion force still massing in the French Channel ports, the British Admiralty concluded that it would perhaps be best to get the troublesome American Fulton on their side. A diplomat imaginatively disguised as a 'Mr Smith' arranged to meet Fulton secretly in Amsterdam and, after much negotiation, the torpedo man was enticed back across the Channel. He adopted the name Robert Francis, perhaps in a vain bid to fool the French into believing there was someone else about who was intent on blowing up ships with underwater explosives.

In much the same way as a Hollywood studio might now buy up the rights to a book simply to prevent anybody else making a film of it, so the British authorities were prepared to pay Fulton handsomely to experiment with his weapons. They gave him the run of the naval dockyard at Portsmouth, a substantial salary and all kinds of emoluments, not because they thought he would help them see off a French invasion but to make sure he left their own ships alone. Fulton's torpedoes were duly sent against the French at Boulogne but with little effect. Then in October the news came that Nelson's last heroic act had been the defeat of the French and Spanish at Trafalgar and all interest in torpedoes evaporated. Fulton's final claim was sent for arbitration. He had already been paid £14,000 and had to accept the remaining balance of exactly £1,646 14s 2d. Fulton wrote to his old friend Barlow that this left him with just £200 when he had paid off all his debts. Nevertheless, he had made a modest fortune as he could count on £500 a year in interest on the money he had invested.

Fulton was nothing if not dogged. Spurned by the English but with money in the bank, he returned to New York, where he repeated his ship-destroying demonstrations. *The Times* continued to take an interest in him and reproduced from the American newspapers an address he had made in

September 1807, the gist of which was familiar – that a recent demonstration in which he had blown up yet another ship with seventy pounds of gunpowder delivered below the hull and triggered by a clockwork mechanism could bring peace to the high seas and prosperity to the United States. His invention, Fulton claimed, would 'in a few years put a stop to maritime wars, and give the liberty of the seas, which has been long and anxiously desired by every good man, and secure to America that liberty of commerce, tranquillity and independence which will enable her citizens to apply their mental and corporal faculties to useful and humane pursuits, to the improvement of our country and the happiness of the whole people'.[6]

Fulton may have been frustrated in his ambition to end war at sea, yet this did not prevent him from designing a steam-driven warship for the Americans when hostilities broke out again with Britain in 1812: it was aptly named the *Fulton* and launched after his death in 1815. As it was, between his return to America in 1806 and the war of 1812, he put most of his energies into the long-delayed project of getting a commercial steamboat service running on the Hudson.

Components of a Boulton & Watt engine had been shipped from England and stored in New York, and Fulton set about constructing the hull and experimenting with various arrangements for the engine. Meanwhile, Chancellor Livingston sought to enforce and extend the patent monopoly as there was always the possibility that rivals would soon set up in competition. The first trials were made in 1807, running up and down from New York to Livingston's estate at Clermont on the Hudson. The name of this first boat is a matter of dispute: most sources say it was the *Clermont*, but others that it was the *North River*. As with Trevithick's pioneer runs with steam carriages and railways, there are no eyewitness accounts of this first commercial riverboat service. However, a biographer of Fulton, Thomas W. Knox, writing in 1887, gleaned the following account from a man, then in his nineties, of a chance ride on the first Hudson boat in 1808. Perry was twenty years old and on his way back to Massachusetts with a woman friend from Albany on the Hudson:

On reaching Albany, I found that none of the sail boats, then in use, were to start for several days. So I engaged a room for myself at a public house, the lady going to the house of some friends. Early the next morning a man, evidently a person who loved his glass, rushed into the bar-room and cried out that the steamboat had come in during the night and would go down the river at nine o'clock. It took so much time to hunt down my charge, and she so long in getting ready, that the boat had started when we reached the wharf. I hailed her, however, and a small boat was sent to take us on board. There were more than fifty passengers, many of them youths and children. I soon noticed Mr Fulton who was watching and directing everything ... The first part of the voyage was quiet enough, but in the afternoon we ran aground, as many thought, through the treachery of some of the crew, for the owners of sloops and other sailing craft were much in dread of the successful inauguration of steam power. I got off at Esopus – now Kingston – as did my companion, and so missed being present at the bursting of the boiler, which occurred near West Point ...[7]

It was in this year, 1808, that Fulton married Harriet Livingston, niece of his steamboat partner, and became a family man: by the time of his death in 1815, the Fultons had four children. Meanwhile, the success of the steamboat very rapidly began to transform America as it became the most important form of transport before the arrival of the railways. In particular, the sale of Louisiana by Napoleon to the United States in 1803 meant the Mississippi could now function as a sort of grand artery running through the very centre of the continent, and the Mississippi paddle-steamer became the great symbol of American industrial progress and wealth. The cumbersome low-pressure Boulton & Watt type of steam engine could be fitted to a boat much more readily than to a locomotive to run on road or rail because its weight did not matter to the same degree. This was also true of the smaller and lighter high-pressure steam engines, like Trevithick's, which would break the brittle tracks laid for horse-drawn railways but could easily be borne by a boat on water.

It was for that reason that commercial steamship services got going a good twenty years before steam railways, which had to await the manufacture of wrought-iron rails.

Whereas there had been little call for stationary steam engines in eighteenth-century America, once the value of the steamship was recognized, demand grew for home-built engines. In one of the most remarkable coincidences in the history of invention, it appears that an American, Oliver Evans, devised a high-pressure steam engine at more or less the same time as Richard Trevithick. Though there have always been suspicions that one of these inventors stole the basic idea from the other, there really is no evidence to suggest this.

Evans, who rather misleadingly became known as the 'Watt of America', was born in Newport, Delaware, and as a teenager was apprenticed to a wheelwright. In 1782, when he was twenty-seven years old, he bought a flour mill with the idea of making it fully automatic. Taking his power from a water mill, Evans devised a series of pulleys and cogs which hoisted bags of grain, emptied them, ground the grain into flour and automatically poured it into sacks. His mill was a forerunner of the production line. However, remarkable as this innovation was, Evans himself was always more interested in the potential of steam power than in automation. He felt frustrated with what he regarded as the pigheadedness of his fellow countrymen who were slow to accept his advanced ideas about the potential of steam.

Evans first learned about steam engines from a description of a Newcomen atmospheric engine he read in an encyclopaedia. As he told the story later, he was instantly struck by the limitations of this kind of engine, which failed to harness the tremendous power of steam under pressure. Evans completely bypassed what might be called the Newcomen era – which in England lasted for seventy-odd years before Evans began to work with steam – and proceeded instead straight to the kind of high-pressure steam Trevithick was experimenting with. That Evans was able to find the technicians capable of building a boiler and parts for such an engine as early as 1801–2, when the American metallurgic industry was half a century behind that in England, is surprising. But there is no doubt he managed it, encasing the thin skin of his copper boiler in a sturdy, barrel-like outer layer of three-inch-thick beams of wood held together with iron hoops. A good deal of timber was used in the construction of early American steam engines as this material was the most readily to hand and also the cheapest.

The first engines Evans had built were crude but functional. One of the first was used for grinding plaster of Paris which was both a fertilizer and the main ingredient of stucco, the mock stone facing popular for grander buildings at the time. Evans built an odd-looking amphibian vehicle in 1804 and in time established an iron foundry, known as the Mars Works, in Philadelphia for the manufacture of a range of engines. Like Trevithick's high-pressure engines, those built by Evans were compact, ideal for fitting to boats and for transporting over long distances. His 'Colombian' engine became standard on many American steamboats. Fulton, meanwhile, remained wary of high-pressure steam because of the danger of explosions.

Two centres of steam engine manufacture became established in the United States after 1800, one in New York and the other in Philadelphia. Very soon the high-pressure engine, compact and economical, made the old Boulton & Watt engines redundant. And the triumph of the American steamboat gave the United States a march on Europe. Fulton's fame was worldwide: he was awarded a monopoly of steamboat construction in Russia, which had watched with envy the opening up of a vast region after the Louisiana purchase. Though Fulton did not manage ever to deliver a boat to Russia, his anniversaries are still celebrated there, the last great acknowledgement of his influence having been staged in 1965, the 200th anniversary of his birth.

The man who built the first Russian steamships was none other than the former Carron Works emigré, Charles Baird. These were in operation on the coastal waters up to Kronstadt in 1815, and were built at the St Petersburg factory (by this time the Scotsman was known as Karl Nikolaevitch Baird). When the Baird boats began operation, the American chargé d'affaires in St Petersburg, a Mr Levett-Harris, protested that Fulton's monopoly was being broken. It was pointed out that the American inventor had done nothing to claim his rights as he sent no ships or even plans for them to Russia. That was still the case when his theoretical monopoly ran out in 1816, at which point

Baird himself applied for and was awarded a monopoly of steamship operation on all of Russia's European waters.

By the time of Fulton's death in 1815, the first steamer had gone into service on the Mississippi. Built to Fulton's design in Pittsburgh and called the *New Orleans*, it undertook its maiden voyage in October 1811. It had a rear paddlewheel as well as sails on two masts and its trial run was slow, but it was not long before there were dozens and then hundreds of steamers on the Mississippi and the Ohio Rivers. And all the talk on these steamers was of one thing: cotton, a crop that in 1800 had been of little significance other than on the sea coast of Florida. The single-minded obsession with this plant was described vividly by the English naval officer Captain Basil Hall who, with his wife Margaret, travelled throughout America between early 1827 and the autumn of 1828. Of his experience on a steamboat churning through Alabama, Hall wrote:

> Numberless persons came on board at each landing-place, some to take a passage, some merely to gossip – but whatever might be the ostensible gossip, cotton was the sole topic. Every flaw of wind from shore wafted of the smell of that useful plant; at every dock or wharf we encountered it in huge piles or pyramids of bales, and our decks were soon choked up with it. All day, and almost all night long, the captain, pilot, crew and passengers were talking of nothing else; and sometimes our ears were so wearied with the sound of cotton!cotton!cotton! that we gladly hailed a fresh inundation of company in hopes of some change – but alas! Wiggin's Landing, Chocktaw Creek, or the towns of Gaines, or Cahawba, or Canton, produced us nothing but fresh importations of the raw material. 'What's cotton at?' was the first eager inquiry. 'Ten Cents.' 'Oh that will never do!' From the cotton in the market, they went to the crops in the fields … the bad times, the over-trading and so round to the prices and prospects again, till I wished all the cotton in the country at the bottom of the Alabama![8]

The southern cotton state of Alabama that drove Captain Hall to distraction was newly established. When he toured on the paddle-steamer, it had been part of the Union for only eight years and Mississippi, of which it had been a part, had been a state for a mere ten years. This vast region, comprising much of what had been Louisiana north of the Mississippi delta, was transformed in a few years by slave labour force. At the time of the Louisiana Purchase, the land was not that valuable – the Americans had bought it from France for $80 million. The old plantations of the southern states on the eastern seaboard were struggling after the War of Independence, their crops of tobacco, indigo and rice of diminishing value. Fine, sea-island cotton could be grown only near the coast. Inland the cotton crop was hardly worth tending for it was a variety in which the fibres of the plant which could be turned into thread were matted with sticky green seeds. The tiresome work of cleaning this 'upland' cotton was done mostly by black slaves who had been shipped in from Africa over the previous century to work on the plantations.

A typical colonial plantation, which had belonged to the loyalist Lieutenant Governor John Graham before the War of Independence, was Mulberry Grove on the Savannah River near the town of Savannah in Georgia. It had been planted with mulberry trees for the raising of silkworms at a time when it was thought the raw silk could be a useful export to Britain. Thousands of mulberry trees were planted on the east coast, all the way up to New Haven, and there are still many Mulberry Streets on the town maps. After the war, Mulberry Grove was confiscated and given to a senior officer from George Washington's forces, General Nathanael Greene, who, with his vibrant and enthusiastic wife Catherine, known as 'Caty', set about improving it. The mulberry trees and much of the land had been rendered derelict during the war years. Shortly after the Greenes moved in 1785, the general wrote to a friend: 'We have got upwards of sixty acres of corn planted, and expect to plant one hundred and thirty acres of rice. The garden is delightful. The fruit trees and flowering shrubs form a pleasing variety. We have green peas ... and as fine lettuce as you ever saw. The mocking birds surround us evening and morning ... We have in the same orchard apples, pears, peaches, apricots, nectarines, plums of different kinds, figs, pomegranates, and oranges. And we have strawberries which measure three inches around.'[9]

In this long catalogue of the produce of Mulberry Grove, there is no reference to cotton growing on General Greene's land, which was tended by more than a hundred black slaves. And yet it was on this plantation that the machine was invented which transformed the southern states of America into a vast cotton region. This is how it came about.

General Greene engaged to teach his children at Mulberry Grove a young Yale graduate called Phineas Miller, a pleasant, erudite man who quickly became part of the Greene family and a favourite of Caty's. Though the plantation looked promising, the general had fallen into debt during the war, chiefly because he had compensated those whose property had been pillaged by his half-mad, half-starved troops. He worked hard – too hard – and drove himself to an early grave, dying in 1786, according to one version from a *coup de soleil* or sunstroke. Young Miller became more than a tutor, helping the general's widow run the plantation and care for her five children, who were all under the age of eleven.

Seven years later, another Yale graduate, Eli Whitney, was looking for some kind of paid employment to support himself while he continued studying to become a lawyer. Whitney was from Westborough, Massachusetts, about forty miles inland from Boston. Born in 1765, he was brought up on a modestly prosperous farm. His father had a workshop in which Whitney was introduced to a variety of tools for making simple farm implements and from an early age he showed an aptitude for making and mending things. His mother died when he was a schoolboy and he disappointed his father when he decided he did not want to study for a place at college. However, Whitney was never idle. While still a teenager, he had a small nail-forging business on his father's farm, and when the demand for nails fell, he took to making hatpins.

When Whitney decided he did want to study after all, his father, like many farmers, was short of cash. So Whitney taught to earn the money to learn, working as a schoolmaster until he had raised the funds to go to Yale. By that time he was twenty-three, older than other students. It was a broad education in maths and philosophy and law, amongst other subjects. He was always hard up, though his father, who had remarried, sent him money when he was able. When he graduated, Whitney thought he had a place to teach in New York but that fell through. Instead, he had to accept an offer from the South that came from Phineas Miller, who was introduced to him by the Reverend Ezra Stiles, President of Yale University. All his letters at the time express apprehension about heading to the steamy climate of South Carolina, a foreign country to someone from the Puritan north of the United States.

Arrangements were made in late 1793 for Whitney to take the packet ship from New Haven down to New York, where he could meet up with Phineas Miller, who was there with Catherine Greene and the family. Whitney was horribly seasick, his ship ran aground and he and six other passengers abandoned it, waded ashore and took a wagon into New York. Here he shook hands with an old acquaintance whom he noticed too late was covered in the terrifying rash of smallpox. At Miller's suggestion, Whitney got himself inoculated or, as he wrote it, 'enochulated'. This was the procedure which had been adopted in England and colonial America in the early eighteenth century: the infection was introduced to the arm in the hope that it would produce a mild bout of the disease and confer immunity from then on. Vaccination – the use of cowpox instead of smallpox itself – was about to be introduced by the English doctor Edward Jenner, but would not reach the United States until 1801 or thereabouts.

The generous and sociable widow Catherine Greene took a liking to Whitney and suggested that Miller lend him the money to take the same packet down to Savannah. Whitney would then go on to South Carolina to act as tutor for the family of a General Dupont, who had asked Miller for his recommendations. As it turned out, Whitney stayed at Mulberry Grove and never took up his appointment with the Dupont family. The reason appears to have been that he and Phineas Miller were working in some secrecy on a plan to produce a new kind of machine for cleaning sticky, green-seed upland cotton.

At the time Whitney travelled to the South, the plantation economy was ailing: tobacco had exhausted the soil and was no longer a valuable crop. There was nothing much to be made out of rice or corn or indigo, and the planting of mulberry trees and raising of silkworms had not proved a great success as the production of silk thread was no simple matter. In fact, the old colonial slave economy was disappearing, a decline clearly signalled by the rapid fall in the price paid for slaves at the markets. However, everyone in the South was well aware that cotton was in great demand in Britain and that if they could only find a way of growing an economic crop, it would revive their fortunes. Experiments were made with different strains of plant but only the sticky-seeded upland variety grew readily away from the coast. There was a variety of machines used to separate the seed from the cotton fibres, some of them of great antiquity, such as the Indian *darka*. Most used a mechanism in which the cotton was fed through two rollers rather like a clothes mangle and the seeds were squeezed out. Some of these cotton 'gins' were worked by foot and nearly all of them were operated by slaves.

There is an enduring American fable that when Whitney arrived in the South all cotton was deseeded by hand and that, upon hearing planters talk of the problem of finding a more efficient way of preparing the fibre for export to England, he instantly devised a cotton 'gin' using a few tools he found on the plantation. As a result of his invention, the cotton crop became valuable and the price of slaves rose as planters extended the acreage of cotton planted. The story has been told and retold so many times that the reality of Whitney's contribution has been obscured. Furthermore, a good deal of the mythologizing has to do with the idea that a clever Yankee from up North was needed to solve the problem of the backward planters down South. What is not in doubt is that to make upland cotton a really economic crop, which British spinning mills would buy, a new kind of deseeding machine was needed. Ideally, it would be one that was less labour-intensive than those already in use. Clearly, Whitney was aware of this and, keen to make a great deal more money than he would as a tutor, he decided to try his hand at invention. He duly discussed this with Phineas Miller, who said he would put up the money to produce a deseeding machine if Whitney could find a way of designing it.

To make the prototype gins, Whitney went back north to New Haven, Connecticut, where the tools, materials and skills were all available. His expense books are the only detailed records surviving of his work, as the patent application and other documents were lost in fires. The books reveal a constant search for materials, such as wire of a certain calibre which would form hooks to catch the seeds. He laboured long and hard with little money to get his gin to work efficiently. He and Miller had hatched a kind of business plan in which they would make their money on the gins by charging planters a percentage of the extra fibre they could extract, which could be paid either in raw cotton or cash. They thought that gins would be too expensive for most of the Southern farmers to buy, so they would set them up to be worked by hand, gin-horse or water-mill wheel and have them superintended by their own men, who would then ensure the dues were paid. If anyone tried to steal their design, they had their patent, or so they thought.

While Whitney worked away in New Haven, Miller tried to set up the business in Georgia. In the hope of raising the funds to set the gin business going, he raised livestock and kept the Mulberry Grove farm going. Both partners were very short of cash and desperate to get their gin production established so that they could pay off debts and begin to enjoy some income. But events conspired to frustrate them. Miller unwisely invested in what turned out to be a fraudulent scheme known as the Yazoo Land Purchase in which large numbers of people lost money. Then, in March 1795, Whitney returned from a trip to New York to find his New Haven workshop razed to the ground by fire and all his special tools destroyed.

The partners could have withstood both calamities if their plan for the gins had worked. But it turned out to be a disaster. Planters were unwilling to pay a premium for the use of the Miller-Whitney gin despite the fact that this invention induced them to plant upland cotton on a scale never before imagined. Once the basic design was discovered, pirate gins were manufactured all over Georgia and the Carolinas. Modified designs appeared and the production of cotton grew at an astonishing pace without affording Miller and Whitney any profit at all. In 1795 the total cotton crop had been 8 million pounds: by 1800 it was 35 million and by 1807 80 million.

While happy enough to reap the profits, the planters nevertheless sought to damage the reputation of the men who had made this possible. Some of the cotton was sent north to Samuel Sadler's newly founded mills on Rhode

Island, but the real prize would be sales to Lancashire. A false rumour was put about by resentful planters that cotton deseeded by the Whitney gin was torn and no good for the English mills. Whitney contemplated travelling to England to put the record straight and to discuss how this new kind of upland cotton might be suitable for the Strutts and Arkwrights. But he simply did not have the fare to cross the Atlantic. In any case, as the production of cotton spread rapidly across the South, extending into the new territories of the Mississippi Delta after the Louisiana Purchase, American-grown cotton became the staple for English mills.

Paradoxically, the labour-saving device Whitney had invented vastly increased the demand for slave labour as the acreage under cotton spread over thousands of square miles. The back-breaking work of preparing the soils of the South was all done by slaves, as was the planting and the picking in the torrid heat of the day. So rapid was the spread of the cotton fields that by 1810 the American South was supplying half of England's annual consumption of 78 million pounds. It was reckoned that, for every hundred new acres planted in the Deep South, between ten and twenty slaves were needed to plant, hoe, weed, pick, sort and stack the cotton. This came at the same time as Britain outlawed the trade in slaves from Africa (1807) and, later, the institution of slavery in its own territories (1833). The price of slaves sold at markets in Virginia, a major supplier of labour to the South, rose sharply. Slaves who had been knocked down at auctions in the 1780s for $50 were now fetching $800 to $1,000 in the early 1800s.

Captain Basil Hall had sailed in many ships with black crewmen who were at least the equal in knowledge and ability as their white fellows. As he toured the South in the 1820s, he was therefore puzzled to hear planters expressing their belief that black men were incapable of intelligent work. Hall, of course, knew by now that black slaves were forbidden to learn to read or write and that, if they tried to escape north, as some did, they would be chased with dogs and guns. Indeed, he was very uneasy about being entertained by slave-owners who treated black Africans in this way. Yet it was this iniquitous system which was underpinning Britain's most prominent industry, the production of cotton cloth. In his *Travels in North America*, Hall wrote:

In condemning slavery, and scorning slave-holders, we are apt to forget the share which we ourselves contribute towards the permanence of the system. It is true, we are some three or four thousand of miles from the actual scene. But if we are to reproach the planter who lives in affluence in the midst of a slave population, it ought to be asked how he comes by the means to live at that rate. He gives his orders to the overseer, the overseer instructs the driver, who compels the negro to work, and up comes the cotton. But what then? He cannot make the smallest use of his crop, however luxuriant it be, unless, upon an invitation to divide the advantages with him we agree to become partners in the speculation – the result of slave labour. The transfer of the cotton from Georgia to Liverpool is certainly one step, but it is no more than a step, in the transaction. Its manufacture into the goods which we scruple not to make use of, and without which we should be very ill off, is but another link in the same chain, and the end of which is the slave.[10]

As Karl Marx put it succinctly in a letter written in 1848: 'Without slavery, no cotton; without cotton, no modern industry'. This was an over-simplification, for the cotton mill, and later the power loom, were not, by any means, the only modern industries. But cotton was, for a time, the staple of the most spectacular international manufacturing business the world had ever known. No doubt the British spinners would have found supplies of cotton somewhere in the world had the improved gin and slavery not served to make the Southern states the major supplier. Strangely, there is no record of any comment or opinion from Whitney on the 'peculiar institution' of Southern slavery to which his gin gave rise. However, the Reverend Ezra Stiles, who had introduced Whitney to Phineas Miller and so inadvertently had been partly responsible for the gin, was an ardent abolitionist.

Whitney and Miller tried to get their patent rights enforced but failed in their early attempts, partly because of the loose wording of the legislation, which was very new in the United States in the 1790s. They were not the only owners of a new invention who found that plagiarists robbed them of their profits. Whitney exchanged letters with both Oliver Evans and Robert Fulton on the patent issue and all three clearly felt hard done by, even though they went on to achieve success with later ventures. In Whitney and Miller's case, payments were eventually made in compensation for the gin's invention, although Whitney, out of desperation as much as anything else, branched out into the manufacture of muskets when in 1798 there was the threat of war between France and the United States.

It is a shame so little is known about Whitney's methods of production of both the cotton gin and, later, muskets, for he is credited by many authorities with introducing the concept of replaceable parts to American manufacture. This involved a kind of standardization of production in which cunningly constructed machinery operated by unskilled labour could achieve a precision which the hands of the skilled artisan rarely could, if ever, match. (The machines developed by the Bentham-Brunel-Maudslay partnership to make pulley blocks involved the same kind of standardized production on a large scale.) And such methods, of course, led the way to mass production.

It has been argued that because America was short of skilled artisans, despite the diaspora of workmen from Europe, there was a great incentive to develop 'labour-saving' devices. There is no doubt that Whitney's ambition was to produce huge quantities of muskets with standardized parts made with machine tools, and he did build a sizeable factory which turned out arms in their thousands. But there is precious little evidence that he was able to make a real breakthrough with the materials available to him at the time. He was invariably late in fulfilling his orders and his production techniques may not have been very different from the other suppliers of arms to the American government.

By way of explanation of what he was trying to achieve, Whitney had written around 1799: 'In short, the tools which I contemplate are similar to an engraving on copper plate from which may be taken a great number of impressions perceptibly alike.' Yet this process, as it happens, can be credited to another American, a contemporary of Whitney's born at Newburyport, Massachusetts, in July 1766. Jacob Perkins, whose name has so little resonance today, was surely the most brilliantly creative inventor of his generation, his genius being recognized on both sides of the Atlantic. He was from a family which had arrived in America from England in 1631. He had little education, as far as is known, and was apprenticed to a goldsmith at the age of thirteen. Two years later, he was left on his own to run the business when his master died unexpectedly. From the age of fifteen to twenty-one, he made a go of it, producing gold beads and other trinkets. He invented a way of silver-plating shoe buckles and learned about stamping patterns on metal. The State of Massachusetts mint ordered dies from him for striking copper coins, and he branched out into nail-making. He invented a machine for automatically cutting and heading nails and went into partnership with two English textile engineers, William Guppy and John W. Armstrong, who had crossed the Atlantic illegally some years before.

Nail-making, which Eli Whitney had tried in a small way before he went to college, was potentially big business. Large quantities were shipped across the Atlantic from the English Midlands, especially from Birmingham and Coventry, which both produced several thousand tons of nails a year, albeit by means of a grim cottage industry. Perkins, however, devised a tool which, with one pull of a lever, both cut and headed the nail. It proved a success in Massachusetts and then in England, where it was taken by another American, Joseph Chessborough Dyer.

A good deal younger than Perkins, Dyer was born the son of Captain Nathaniel Dyer in 1780 and grew up in prosperous circumstances. He had a hand in many schemes. As a young man, he criss-crossed the Atlantic promoting all kinds of projects, such as Robert Fulton's steamboat, which he tried to sell in England, although without success. He met Perkins in 1809 and under some kind of agreement – exactly what has never been discovered – took his nail-making machinery to Birmingham. Dyer patented the Perkins process in England and established the very successful Britannia Nail Works, which was the first company to 'cold cut' nails by machinery. He eventually settled in Manchester, where he became a founder member of the famous *Manchester Guardian* newspaper.

From nail-making, Perkins himself went into the business of printing illustrations and banknotes, working in a number of firms and forming a partnership with an engraver called Gideon Fairman. Forgery of bills and banknotes was rife and Perkins worked to produce a system of engraving printed notes that was difficult to copy exactly. He was disappointed when his method was not taken up in America and in 1818 took a big gamble. He packed up all his tools and, with his family and a team of skilled workmen, set sail for England. The Bank of England was offering a prize for the best method of printing banknotes which were difficult to forge and Perkins thought he had a good chance of winning. As it turned out, he and his team were judged runners up in the competition, almost certainly ruled out of first place by the veteran English inventor William Congreve, who was a rival printer and whose patriotism would not allow a rebel American to triumph. During the British-American war, which broke out in 1812, Congreve's military rockets had been launched in an attack on Fort McHenry and were immortalized in 'The Star Spangled Banner' as 'the rockets' red glare'.

Although they were beaten off by Congreve, the Perkins partnership used his steel plates for engraving printed notes for provincial banks and became well established in business. Before he left America, Perkins had become friendly with Oliver Evans and from that time had an obsession with high-pressure steam engines. He risked working with much higher pressures than even Trevithick would have used and at one time attracted the attention of the Stephensons when they were looking for improvements to their own steam engines. Yet the most extraordinary invention Perkins devised was a steam cannon, which in 1825 he demonstrated in London's recently laid out Regent's Park, close to where he had a factory.

According to *The Times,* patrols were sent out early to warn any horse-drawn traffic away from the area as early tests with the steam cannon had sent carriages careering dangerously when the terrified horses bolted. In his first show, before an invited audience which included the Duke of Wellington and the Duke of Sussex, the sixth son of George III, Perkins fired cannonballs a distance of thirty-five yards against an iron target on which they were flattened or shattered. He then demonstrated the exceptional power of his steam cannon which could fire a ball through eleven one-inch planks placed together. And then, in the *pièce de résistance,* cannonballs fed by gravity into the steam tube rattled off one after another – and this decades before the development of a workable machine-gun. In his autobiography, the American educationalist Samuel G. Goodrich recalled both his meeting with Perkins in London and the Regent's Park demonstrations. 'The whole performance was indeed quite formidable, and the Duke of Sussex – who was an enormous, red-faced man – seemed greatly excited. I stood close by, and when the bullets flew pretty thick and the discharge came to a climax, I heard him say to the Duke of Wellington, in an undertone – "Wonderful, wonderful d ... d wonderful" then again "Wonderful, wonderful, d ... d wonderful ..." And so he went on, without variation. It was, in fact, save the profanity, a very good commentary upon the performance.'[11]

Meanwhile, a piece of doggerel entitled *Steam* and published in the *New Monthly Magazine* included the verse:

> Five hundred balls, per minute, shot
> Our foes in fight must kick the beam
> Let Perkins only boil his pot
> And he'll destroy them all by steam.[12]

However, the only military power which showed much interest at the time was Greece, then embroiled in a war with Turkey. Perkins offered them a 36-pounder, which he said could be drawn by four or five horses with all its apparatus, including the steam boiler, and would fire at fifty times the rapidity of an ordinary cannon. But this was never delivered as there appears to have been some deal in which the British had exclusive rights to the cannon.

In this, as in so many other ventures, Jacob Perkins was way ahead of his time. But his skills as a printer had one final and lasting significance on the newly emerging world of nineteenth-century industrialism. One of the many companies he had left behind in America was one that made 'fire engines' – hand pumps – and it was left in the charge of a son-in-law with the wonderful name of Joshua Butters Bacon. Bacon later joined Perkins in London and together they ran an engraving and printing business which was known in 1832 as Perkins, Bacon and Petch with works in Fleet Street. It was this firm which was approached in 1839 by Henry Cole, who was assistant to Rowland

Hill, the man appointed by the government to introduce a new and revolutionary postal system to Britain. Cole asked Perkins and his partners whether they could make the master dies and print off hundreds of thousands of the new Penny Black stamp.

After some consideration, Perkins, Bacon and Petch replied that they could certainly carry out the work as required and they could start within a month, producing 41,600 'labels' a day, or double that for a 'day and a night' on each of its printing presses. The design of the stamp was the work of Frederick Heath, the son of an erstwhile partner of Perkins in his London venture. A contract to take on the work was signed at the beginning of 1840, and the production line was ready to go by April when Rowland Hill visited the Fleet Street works. Two presses were ready, and several others were being prepared. By 20 April, 200,000 stamps were delivered, and they were then turned out at the rate of 240,000 per day. The first issue of the Penny Black was on 6 May 1840, and when it was discontinued and replaced by stamps of different denominations and colours, Perkins, Bacon and Petch retained the contract.

Perkins died in London in 1849 and was buried in the same Kensal Green cemetery as Marc Brunel. His firm, called simply Perkins and Bacon after 1852, continued to print British postage stamps both for the British Post Office and the Empire until 1879. An enterprise founded in America had triumphed in the mother country, a portent of the future. Nothing much ever came of the many steam-engine enterprises of Perkins. He was an inventor who always had a great many irons in the fire, which is perhaps why he did not become more involved in the most momentous application of steam power – one that was taking shape at much the same time as he was firing his cannonballs in Regent's Park. The first steam railway lines were an entirely British achievement and the building of them would involve much more than simply mechanical genius.

CHAPTER SEVEN

THE RAILWAY MEN

In the summer of 1822, a hardy band of men could be seen in the countryside between Manchester and Liverpool, heaving across fields and through streams a series of chains which were exactly twenty-two yards long, the distance between the two sets of stumps on a cricket pitch. A muscle-bound minder, who regularly scanned the hedgerows and copses for trouble, stayed close to the man who carried a strange-looking instrument with a kind of viewfinder on a tripod. Some of the company were clearly men of some learning and substance and they had frequent and often animated discussions. They pointed and jotted in notebooks and then moved on warily. There was always the danger that the next field they entered would be defended by an army of keepers toting muskets or other weapons and threatening them with violence if they continued with their trespass. Whenever there was a confrontation, the minder, a prize-fighter hired for his strength and aggression, would take hold of the three-legged theodolite and hug it close, as if challenging anyone who wanted to destroy it to fight him first.

Such was the reality of their work for the surveyors of the earliest routes for prospective public railway lines in England. In charge of the team mapping out a projected line between Manchester and Liverpool in that summer of 1822 was William James, a remarkable man who, although one of the most forward-looking characters of his day, has been all but forgotten by the historians of

Britain's pioneer railways. James, the son of a Warwickshire solicitor, was born in 1771 at Henley-in-Arden in Warwickshire and, after a good education, trained for the law himself, establishing his own practice in 1797 in his home town. He was particularly drawn to the laws relating to the mining and enclosure of land, both of great interest to local landowners, and his talents brought him to the attention of the Earl of Warwick, who appointed him his land agent in 1801. From there, James broadened his practice and became associated with a great many schemes in different parts of the country. In London he was involved with draining the marshes of Lambeth south of the Thames. One of James's pursuits was searching out mineral wealth and he fancied himself as a prospector for coal in an era when geological knowledge was still very limited. By 1812 he owned six collieries in the Midlands and opened up a new coalfield at West Bromwhich on behalf of the Earl of Dartmouth.

James was an enthusiast for railways long before his promotion of the Liverpool–Manchester line. As a land agent and mine-owner, he was familiar with the many railway lines laid down in the mining regions of the country, all of which were horse-drawn. It has been estimated that there were 1,500 of these horse tramways in Britain in the early 1800s, most of them connecting a pit head to a canal or river navigation. As long as these lines did not cross any ground belonging to estates other than the coal-owners', and remained entirely private in their use, they could be laid down without the consent from Parliament which was necessary for the cutting of canals or the setting up of turnpike trusts for improved roads.

The very first public railway line which did need parliamentary sanction received it in 1801. It ran from the heavily industrial region of Wandsworth on the south side of the Thames in London to Croydon in Surrey. A canal had been proposed for some years but the capital could not be raised. The Surrey Iron Railway, as it was called, was cheaper than a canal. Entirely horse- or mule-drawn, it opened in 1803 with William James as one of its backers and investors. There was no question then of using steam locomotives on the line as even Trevithick's pioneer engine did not run at Penydarren in Wales until the following year. The trucks on the Surrey Iron Railway ran on L-shaped cast-iron plates.

It is likely that when he was in London in 1808, James was one of those who saw Trevithick's *Catch-me-who-can* engine running on its circular track and envisaged such steam locomotives forming a national network of railways. As he travelled the country, visiting estates and prospecting for minerals, James imagined railways everywhere and he began to promote the idea of them, sometimes drawing up plans for the routes they might take. The canal system remained horse-drawn, as did nearly all road traffic: there were just a few steam vehicles running before the 1820s. The horse-drawn railways had been a valuable innovation in mining areas, but if they could be steam-driven then the whole nature of transport would change. James began to envisage the end of the canal era.

In the north-east of England some of the coal-owners were becoming concerned about the cost of horse feed, which had risen alarmingly during the Napoleonic Wars. It is a modern prejudice, it has to be said, to imagine horses are a cheap form of power: in reality, the cost of 'running' them could rise or fall alarmingly with the price of hay and oats and the military demand for mounts. It was his concern about the rising cost of horse-power that prompted Christopher Blackett, owner of the Wylam Colliery on the Tyne in Northumberland, to ask in 1804 for a Trevithick-style engine to be built as an experiment. It seems Trevithick himself was to some extent involved in this project, visiting Tyneside on a number of occasions. (This was when he had met the toddler Robert Stephenson and, according to the giant Cornishman, 'dangled the lad on his knee'.) The Wylam locomotive was built at a Tyneside foundry under the supervision of a young man called John Steele (or sometimes Steel) who had worked with Trevithick at Penydarren. Although the engine worked, Blackett did not buy it as the problem of the rails had not been solved. Wylam rails were typical of those north-eastern tramways: oak logs with a replaceable strip of beachwood nailed on top. They were laid on stone or iron sleepers over which a layer of cinders formed the track for the horses who trod between the rails.

But there remained great incentives to find an alternative to the cutting of new canals for the transport of heavy goods. With existing canals there was great resentment at the charges made by the companies, who were anxious to pay their shareholders some dividends despite the huge costs of construction. A railway which was a rival to a canal, rather than a short link between pithead and canal port, was an increasingly attractive proposition and one considered by more and more merchants and mine-owners anxious to keep costs down. But it was not at all clear that a steam locomotive would be an improvement on the horse.

The first breakthrough came not in the north-east, as might have been expected, but further south, at the Middleton colliery in Yorkshire, close to the town of Leeds. Here the mine agent, John Blenkinsop, was asked by the pit-owner to see what he could do to produce a working steam engine running on rails. Blenkinsop must have examined the Trevithick engine because the inventor was paid £30 in lieu of his patent. But Blenkinsop came up with a rather different design, which worked even if it looked a little eccentric. It was still unclear what kind of grip a smooth engine wheel might have on a smooth rail. Evidently the weight of the engine would help, but then the heavier the engine was the more likely the rail would be to break. The Blenkinsop solution was an engine which had a cog wheel interlocked with sprockets on the side of the rail. The first two engines were named the *Prince Regent* and the *Salamanca* – this a reference to the battle which was a decisive victory for Wellington in Spain in 1812, the year the Middleton Colliery Railway first began to run.

The Middleton railway was not quite the future, but it worked and continued to run for many years, making it the first truly functioning steam railway in the world. It attracted a certain amount of international attention and fired the enthusiasm of a Nottingham man, Thomas Gray, who wrote a treatise on railways, published in 1820, in which he argued that the Blenkinsop cog-wheel locomotive could operate between London and Edinburgh. Grand Duke Nicholas, later Tsar Nicholas I, also visited the Middleton railway and was impressed, though it was to be a long time before Russia had any railways of significance.

Though the Trevithick-type locomotive built for Blackett at Wylam colliery had been used only as a stationary engine, development of locomotives did not stop at Wylam colliery. One of the workmen there, William Hedley, experimented with different kinds of rails, testing the grip of smooth wheels on smooth rails. Around 1811 Hedley built an engine he called the *Wylam Dilly*, which ran successfully. He and others partially solved the problem of rail breakage by distributing the load of the locomotive over eight rather than four wheels. Timothy Hackworth, the foreman blacksmith at Wylam who was to become a major engine-builder, was also experimenting at the same time as Hedley. And then, of course, there was George Stephenson.

Born in 1781, Stephenson was brought up in the Tyneside coalfields, the son of a steam engine fireman. At the age of eighteen he could neither read nor write but he had an intimate knowledge of the workings of the mines, in particular the steam pumping and winding engines. When he was twenty, George got the job of brakesman at the Dolly Pit in a place called Black Callerton, which is where he met his first wife, Fanny Henderson, the daughter of a poor farmer. Fanny was one of three sisters who worked as servants in the house in which George lodged. When one of the younger sisters rejected him, he lighted upon Fanny, twelve years his senior, who had been betrothed to the village schoolmaster before his untimely death. They moved on to a place called Willington with Fanny's life savings of gold coins as a dowry. Here their son Robert was born in October 1803, although he would always celebrate his birthday in November.

A self-taught man, Stephenson, like many colliery workers, took on a variety of freelance jobs, notably clock-cleaning and mending and shoe-making. In the early days this supplemented his income from his pit work. He kept on the move, taking a new post at West Moor colliery and setting up home in the town of Killingworth. Fanny was sickly and seemed to be in better health there. However, after the birth of a daughter who lived for only three weeks, she fell seriously ill and died in the spring of 1806. It was some years before George remarried, and Robert was cared for by a series of housekeepers and sent to local schools.

It was not until 1813 that George Stephenson first took on the task of building a steam locomotive. The year before, the engine-wright of Killingworth colliery had died and George was offered his job. At Middleton the practicability of the steam locomotive had been proved and Stephenson's employers, the mine-owners Sir Thomas Liddell, Stuart Wortley and the Earl of Strathmore – known locally as the Grand Allies – now decided they would have their own engine built. Sir Thomas asked George Stephenson to supervise the job at West Moor colliery workshops. The result was a little engine that was named the *Blücher* after a Prussian hero of the Napoleonic Wars. It first ran past George's own modest cottage at West Moor on 25 July 1814.

This was almost certainly the first locomotive to run under its own steam with flanged wheels on iron rails. It greatly impressed William Losh, a distinguished senior partner in the Newcastle ironfounders Losh, Wilson & Bell, who invited Stephenson to work with them for two days a week while he held his job at Killingworth. In 1816 Losh and Stephenson took out a patent for making steam engines as well as cast-iron rails and everything was manufactured at Losh's ironworks. While Stephenson and others began to improve the efficiency of the steam engine, the problem of the rails remained. Wood was far too soft and perishable a material and cast iron too brittle for the impact of heavy engines. Once again, the breakthrough came from an unexpected quarter, in this case an ironmaster in Morpeth, Northumberland, called John Birkinshaw who produced the first wrought-iron rails which were rolled out in handy lengths for laying track. Wrought iron is malleable and has much greater tensile strength than cast iron.

William James followed all these developments. His eldest son, also called William Henry James, began to work on a steam road vehicle and the two of them suggested a new kind of boiler which they later patented. For James, the Middleton railway was a first breakthrough, though the cog-wheel system would obviously be unsuitable for a high-speed service. However, there was the news that locomotives were being built up on Tyneside and James decided to visit the centre of locomotive development at Killingworth and was introduced to George Stephenson and William Losh. James looked at the variety of engines on offer and came to the conclusion that Stephenson's were the best. He signed an agreement with Losh and Stephenson in September 1821 to promote their system in England and Wales in the region below a line drawn between Liverpool and Hull in return for a quarter of the ensuing profits. In return, he offered Stephenson use of a tubular boiler developed and later patented by his son for use in steam road vehicles. As it turned out, this boiler arrangement was not used, but the 1821 agreement illustrates how enthusiastic James was about the Stephenson-Losh patent locomotive. One of his first attempts to promote it was on the Surrey Iron Railway, which was by then in financial trouble. But James had no success here or with other horse-drawn lines in southern and western England, even though his efforts brought George Stephenson's name to the attention of important people in the regions.

It was still not at all clear to those coal-owners, manufacturers and merchants who were keen to improve the transport links between their mines and factories and the ports that a railway was any better than a canal. After all, canals worked and the procedure of getting them built was well established. The greatest drawback was the cost. Expenses for carrying out surveys and getting a chosen route approved by Parliament were about the same for a canal or a railway. But cross-country canals requiring locks and aqueducts and tunnels as well as a reliable supply of water to top them up took years to complete and had not always proved to be profitable, despite the charges made. A railway – whether horse-drawn or steam-driven – might be a cheaper alternative.

There was one other possibility, which for a time seemed to be quite promising. Canals had been promoted to provide a cheaper and less hazardous means of transporting heavy goods than the roads. However, just as railways were emerging as a possible alternative to canals, dramatic improvements had been made in the road system in England by a man with absolutely no engineering background at all and who was sixty years old when he first took responsibility for any highways. In a short time his name, Macadam, became synonymous with road-building both in Britain and North America and he raised the hopes of those who imagined that steam road vehicles, by then much more efficient than Trevithick's Camborne puffer, would solve the transport problem.

Born in 1756, the youngest of ten children of a minor Scottish laird and the daughter of an earl, John Loudon Macadam was left with a legacy of

£1,000 at the age of fourteen when his father died. He had an uncle who was a distinguished and successful merchant in New York and he went to work with him. This was still colonial America and Macadam found a good living as a 'prize master', valuing the spoils of cargoes captured by the British in various skirmishes. But during the War of Independence Macadam picked the wrong side: he was a loyalist. He had married the daughter of a prominent Long Island lawyer, who was in charge of the New York Assembly when it declared itself independent of Britain. This put Macadam in an impossible position and he realized he could no longer stay in America. With his American wife, he returned to Britain in 1783 and bought himself an estate in Ayrshire in the Scottish Lowlands. Here he developed a business which extracted tar from coal, not for the surfacing of roads – that came long after his death – but for water-proofing ships. Macadam also took an interest in roads as he was one of the trustees of the turnpike trusts in the region.

Very little is known about Macadam's business dealings. However, at some point near the close of the eighteenth century his tar company hit trouble and he got into debt. He moved to Falmouth in Cornwall, which was then a major port for passengers sailing to and from America – it was where Marc Brunel had first set foot in England in 1799. Macadam possibly worked again as a prize agent for the navy, although this is uncertain. What we do know is that when he was in his fifties, he began to travel a great deal, up to Scotland and back again. By his own estimation he travelled 30,000 miles between 1798 and 1814, an astonishing 1,875 miles a year or 156 miles a month. Over time, Macadam questioned many surveyors and those responsible for the upkeep of roads and became a self-appointed expert on the subject. He arrived at a stunning conclusion: what was needed was not an improvement in the suspension of carriages but better road surfaces. This could be achieved by laying a top layer of stones no larger than a walnut, which, when compressed by carriage wheels, would form a smooth, well-drained surface.

Macadam's amateur expertise became known to various Members of Parliament and he was asked to give evidence to a House of Commons Select Committee on Highways. He put forward his cheap, simple remedy for the broken roads of England, but for a while he got nowhere. He was then offered the job of surveyor of the roads run by the Bristol turnpike trusts and took it on at the age of sixty. Very soon he set about reorganizing the administration of the roads, firing corrupt or incompetent superintendents and introducing piecework rates for the stone-breakers. In due course he brought in members of his own family to run roads all over Britain and soon had a clannish control of something like 3,000 miles of highway in England and Wales.

The engineer Thomas Telford, who built government-funded roads in Scotland and north Wales, advocated a much more robust kind of construction than Macadam and the two were rivals for a time. In his last years, Macadam travelled the country in a two-horse carriage with a pony tethered behind for local excursions. His companion was a Newfoundland dog that made sure his horses and pony did not stray too far. He died in Moffat, Ayrshire, in 1836 at the age of eighty. He had, at the very last, shown an interest in steam railways. By that time, however, it was abundantly clear that Macadam's roads, immensely valuable though they remained, were not to be the real excitement of the age.

Anyone with even the vaguest concept of the geography of Britain might wonder why it was that the first great breakthrough in railway-building beyond the pithead should have been between the town of Darlington in the north-east of England and the river port of Stockton-on-Tees. Was it, many people have wondered, because that is where the steam engine was invented? There are, after all, many familiar illustrations of the triumphant inaugural excursions on this line of an engine called *Locomotion*, hauling trucks full of hat-waving enthusiasts. In reality, the origin of the Stockton to Darlington railway is quite prosaic.

For mine-owners, transport costs were crucial. If they could not get their coal to market at a competitive price, they were out of business. A great deal of industry which had once relied on water or horse power to drive its machinery moved to the coalfields. But there were still regions in which vital transport links were poor. The single biggest market was London, the great consumer of what was known as sea coal shipped down the east coast and up the Thames in a fleet of hundreds of sailing colliers. The coasting route afforded a perfect link for the Tyneside pits. But those near Darlington had to shift their coal across country to the riverport of Stockton-on-Tees, a road journey which increased the cost to the point where it was no longer economic.

A proposed canal surveyed in the 1760s was regarded as too expensive. All that had been done by 1810 was the digging of a small cut to the river before Stockton. Yet another canal proposal was considered and the engineer John Rennie engaged to survey and mark out a route in 1812. This was shelved and the next scheme, six years later, was for a horse-drawn railway. Again Rennie was taken on, this time with the help of Robert Stevenson, a member of the celebrated Scottish lighthouse-building family and the grandfather of the author Robert Louis Stevenson. There then arose a deep disagreement between the businessmen of Darlington and Stockton about whether they backed a canal or a railway.

Among those vehemently in favour of a railway were the Quaker brothers Edward and Joseph Pease, bankers and woollen merchants in Darlington. The railway advocates brought in an engineer from Wales, George Overton, to conduct yet another survey. This was completed in 1819 but there was such opposition from two landowners on the route that the Bill put before Parliament for approval of the line was thrown out. Yet another survey and another approach to Parliament was needed before the first Stockton–Darlington Railway Act was passed on 19 April 1821.

Getting a railway started in these early days was a long-drawn-out and tedious business and it needs to be stressed once more that all the technological, political and social problems involved in the process were hammered out in England, so that when steam railways were taken abroad, everything was in virtually readymade kit form and could be laid and up and running in an astonishingly short space of time. The world of the railway promoter in these early days was also quite small, as there were only a handful of locomotive manufacturers and an interest in railways was still regarded as unrealistic by many businessmen. The enthusiasm of a man such as William James was therefore vital and his promotion of George Stephenson of huge significance.

After his first visit to Killingworth, James had written to a man involved in the Stockton–Darlington project who was a friend of Edward Pease: 'The locomotive engine of Mr Stephenson is superior beyond comparison to all other Engines I have seen. Next to the immortal Watt I consider Mr Stephenson's Merit in the invention of this engine.'[1] Just before the Stockton–Darlington Act was passed, Pease invited George Stephenson, along with a friend and colleague, Nicholas Wood, to visit him in Darlington. By this time Stephenson was very much a self-made man with considerable confidence in his abilities, and he greatly impressed Pease, thus winning the job of surveying this trail-blazing line. His son Robert, who was apprenticed to Nicholas Wood, was released to help with the survey and was allowed to put his signature on some of the documents. The partnership of Stephenson, father and son, was founded. There were other momentous developments associated with this line. Although Stephenson shared a patent with Losh for cast-iron rails, these were never really satisfactory and he was won over to William James's case for wrought-iron rails, adopting them for part of the new railway. The original Act for the line had not, however, specified the use of steam engines and so Parliament had to be approached again for their use to be approved. George Stephenson travelled to London for the first time in his life in 1823 to present the case, one which was accepted with little opposition.

However, Stephenson's recommendation of Birkinshaw's wrought-iron rails so angered William Losh that the two fell out and their partnership split up. Approaches were made to a number of ironmasters, including the manufacturers of Blenkinsop's cog-wheel engines, which were still running. But there were no offers. The only solution was for the Stephensons to establish their own works and this they were able to do with the backing of Edward Pease and others. The new company, set up at Forth Street Works, Newcastle-upon-Tyne, was called Robert Stephenson & Company, with George's son made a managing partner at the age of twenty.

The engines for the Stockton–Darlington line were now ordered from this new company, the first two named *Locomotion* and *Hope*, the third and fourth *Black Diamond* and *Diligence*. Quite a number of technical changes were made to these engines and George Stephenson was able to say with confidence that they would be more efficient than anything constructed before. *Locomotion* certainly looked more like a familiar steam engine than many previous models, with its pairs of wheels linked by connecting rods rather than with chain and sprockets. Weighing something over five tons, it was loaded on to a wagon drawn by a team of horses from the haulage firm of Pickersgill and, with much cracking of the whip and steaming of flanks, taken on a warm September day in 1825 to the newly laid track. Once it was on the rails, one of the men went off to fetch a candle lantern with which they would light the fire in the boiler. He was gone a while when Robert Metcalf, waiting with the others, noticed a piece of oakum or old rope that might do as a wick. The sun was still up and he had been lighting his pipe using a magnifying glass to focus the rays. Metcalf turned this on the oakum, which smouldered and flamed, and with this and a bit of kindling he lit the fire of the first functioning steam-driven public railway locomotive in the world.

The official opening of the railway on 27 September 1825 was a spectacular success, despite the occasional derailment, and the triumphant arrival of George Stephenson and his brother James on *Locomotion*, along with their 300 passengers, at Stockton quay was greeted with a six-gun salute, the cheers of a crowd of about 40,000 and a rendition of 'God Save the King'. But sceptics were still not convinced of the value of this new form of transport – at least, not in England. This first public steam railway still included two stationary engines which pulled coal trucks over a steep incline and also used horse-drawn carriages on one section. Doubts remained about what weight of heavy goods the new-fangled steam trains could pull.

Amid the triumphs of the Stockton–Darlington opening, there were also great anxieties. Three years earlier, in 1822, William James had got the job, on behalf of a powerful consortium of Liverpool and Manchester manufacturers and traders, of surveying a line between their two burgeoning cities. When the survey was complete, the promoters of the line waited impatiently for the results as they wanted to present their Bill before a closing date in Parliament. But the paperwork which was promised was slow in coming. James was in some trouble as a number of schemes had gone wrong and he was having to attend to his various interests. In frustration, the promoters, led by the Liverpool merchant Joseph Sandars, gave up on James and brought in George Stephenson to produce the survey necessary for an application to Parliament for the line's approval. This greatly upset James, who had been responsible for promoting Stephenson and could justly claim that the whole grand scheme was, to a large extent, his own inspiration.

For George Stephenson, however, the invitation from Liverpool was mouth-watering. In June 1824 he met his son Robert there and was invited to dinner by Joseph Sandars, along with Lister Ellis, another promoter of the line. Stephenson wrote of this occasion to his friend Michael Longridge:

> We dined with Mr Sandars on Saturday, and with Mr Ellis yesterday. He had three men-servants waiting in the entrance hall to show us to the drawing room. There was a party to meet us, and kindly we were received. The dinner was very sumptuous, and the wines costly. We had claret, hock, champagne, and madeira and all in good plenty; but no one took more than was proper ... What changes one sees! This day in the highest life, and the next in a cottage – one day turtle soup and champagne and the next bread and milk, or anything that one can catch.[2]

But while the rough-hewn Northumbrian he had championed was now literate, famous and sought after, William James himself was in deep trouble. He had already lost the surveying work on his favourite project, the Liverpool–Manchester line, and now he was replaced – again by Stephenson – on another, a Canterbury–Whitstable project. Furthermore, James's health was failing and, to make matters worse, in 1823 he was arrested for debt and held in the King's Bench prison in London. In fact, James was never to recover his position, even though he continued an active career as a land agent in Cornwall until his death in 1837. Understandably, James felt he had been poorly treated by George Stephenson and that all his work promoting railways and bringing together the very best engineers had gone unrecognized. It was a sad end for such a railway enthusiast but the fact that he ran out of steam was, to a large extent, his own doing.

The conditions under which George Stephenson and his team undertook another survey of the Liverpool–Manchester line were, if anything, more troublesome than those faced by James. Their lives were threatened, they were confronted by armed gamekeepers and had stones hurled at them. A propaganda war was waged in which it was said hunting preserves would be ruined, cows would not graze close to a railway, the countryside would be set alight by sparks from the train, horses would disappear from everyday life and therefore there would be no market for oats and hay, and farmers would be ruined.

To add to George's problems, Robert decided, very much against his father's wishes, to seek his fortune with a mining concern in Colombia. It was at Joseph Sandars' home that they were to see each other for the last time before Robert sailed in the summer of 1824. He was away for three years and therefore missed the triumphant opening of the Stockton–Darlington line and was out of the country when, in the same year – 1825 – Parliament threw out the Liverpool–Manchester Bill. George Stephenson was badly prepared for a gruelling cross-examination on his plans and estimates and it was generally agreed that his poor testimony was the reason the Bill was dropped.

In fact, notwithstanding the formation of a powerful committee to press for a railway line and the very public success of *Locomotion* on the Stockton–Darlington line, neither Parliament nor many leading engineers of the day were yet convinced that moving steam engines were viable. There were those who argued that stationary engines pulling carriages on cables could handle much greater quantities of coal than a moving engine with its smooth wheels sliding on the track. And there were still those who were not convinced that a Stephenson engine was more reliable and powerful than a team of horses. In evidence to the Committee on the Liverpool–Manchester Bill, the engine builder James Rastrick felt the need to point out under cross-examination:

> you can obtain a greater speed than you could conveniently do by horses; your engine is not tired at the end of the journey, it can keep up its speed during the whole of its journey, provided you supply it with the necessary fuel and water, so that you may go on all day, or work a whole day or a week, merely stopping it at such times as is necessary to take in the coal and water.[3]

That such an explanation of the advantages of a steam engine over horse power was thought necessary in 1825, more than a century after the first Newcomen engines began work, replacing a team of gin horses, and half a century after the steady installation of Boulton & Watt factory engines, emphasizes the novelty of the idea of a *mobile* engine. It would be another four years before Britain, and the rest of the world, was convinced that steam-driven railways were not only workable but could, with astonishing rapidity, transform the economy of a country. By then, Robert Stephenson had returned from Colombia, bringing back with him in 1827 the luckless Richard Trevithick, whom he had met by chance and bailed out with a loan of £50. (The latter was a small reward, really, for the man who had set the train wheels running more than twenty years earlier and had, indirectly, laid the foundations for the Stephenson fortune.) Yet at least the railway Robert had first surveyed with William James was now taking shape.

After his father's failure to get the Bill through in 1825, yet another survey was carried out by yet another surveyor. The man chosen for the job was one Charles Blacker Vignoles (about whom more later), and with whole teams of engineers, including the celebrated brothers George and John Rennie, staking out a new route, the line was finally accepted by Parliament. Estates where the owners were especially vociferous in their opposition were avoided and canal companies were appeased by conditions that bridges crossing their channels should be of a certain height. Though government did not fund the railways, those promoting them had to submit to a close scrutiny – to allay the fears of those who imagined locomotives in towns might jump the rails and go careering off down the high street, and to limit the damage they might cause to passengers and the countryside. One of the rules laid down was the strangely worded stipulation that locomotives should 'consume their own smoke'. In effect this meant that they were fuelled not with coal but with coke, which was virtually smokeless, and this remained the standard on mainline railways until the 1850s, when more efficient fireboxes were fitted on trains. This was not, it should be said, an environmental measure but an attempt to protect first-class passengers, and goods in open wagons, from red-hot sparks and soot.

After much discussion and disagreement among committee members of the Railway Company, George Stephenson was put in charge of construction of the Liverpool–Manchester line. This involved not only cuttings and bridges but the crossing of a peat bog called Chat Moss. William James had thought it possible to build a line across this treacherous, spongy mass and Stephenson kept to that plan. But the very idea was ridiculed in the parliamentary committee, with an expert witness, the engineer Francis Giles, stating, 'No engineer in his senses would go through Chat Moss if he wanted to make a railroad from Liverpool to Manchester ... No carriage would stand on Chat Moss short of the bottom.'[4] But Stephenson went ahead, confident that in the end he could stack enough brushwood and heather to form a floating platform for the four miles of the bog crossing. Helping him for some of the time was a young apprentice engineer, Joseph Locke, the son of one of George's old friends, William Locke. It was part of an apprenticeship for Locke, who also worked on the Edgehill tunnel which took the line into Liverpool and was in charge of the construction of colliery lines elsewhere. Joseph, in fact, had become a good friend of Robert Stephenson, then away in Colombia, and kept him informed about the progress on the line with regular letters.

Nine miles out of Liverpool there were steep inclines around Rainhill and it was decided here to use inclined planes, which resemble a funicular railway, rather than go to the expense of a cutting. It was a huge enterprise, though it proceeded much more quickly than the cutting of a canal. The rails – the quality of iron, length and shape determined by George Stephenson – were bought from several different ironworks, but the newly founded firm of Robert Stephenson & Company won the order for the rolling stock. It was still the case in 1829 that many engineers and founders of the Railway Company were unsure about the use of locomotives. Would trucks pulled by cable not be more efficient, at least for heavy goods? And, to the very end, there were those who continued to advocate the use of horses.

Finally, with the whole world watching, the Railway Company agreed to a suggestion by two of its engineers that the best way to decide on the type of motive power would be to hold a competition. This was advertised in April

1829 with a prize of £500 for the engine which could perform a variety of tasks laid down in the competition rules. The Company was inundated with suggestions, as Henry Booth, the prominent Liverpool backer of the railway and its treasurer and secretary at the time of the trials, remarked:

> from professors of philosophy down to the humblest mechanic, all were zealous in their proffers of assistance. England, America and Continental Europe were alike tributary ... The friction of the carriages was to be reduced so low that silk thread would draw them, and the power to be applied was to be so vast as to rend a cable asunder ... Every scheme which the restless ingenuity or prolific imagination of man could devise was liberally offered to the Company; the difficulty was to choose and decide.[5]

As it turned out, the rules of the competition, which was to be run over a stretch of line at Rainhill, were very demanding and the field of plausible contenders was strictly limited. Just before the trials, an inventory of all known steam locomotives in Britain or abroad had been made by the line's consulting engineers, who had then inspected those still in existence. They counted fifty that had been built in England since Trevithick's day, two that had been tried in Germany and failed, and one, just a model train, in the United States. Two British locomotives had already been sent to France and four to America. Of the twenty-six actually working then, four were on the rack-rail line at Middleton Colliery, three at Wylam Colliery, and eleven at Killingworth, Hetton and Springwell collieries in the north-east. All had been built by the Stephensons, who also constructed an engine called the *Lancashire Witch* that ran on a short goods line between the cotton town of Bolton and Leigh from August 1828, another of William James's initiatives. Finally, there was the *Agenoria*, built by John Rastrick, one of the three judges at Rainhill, for a colliery near Stourbridge where he had his engine works, Foster, Rastrick and Company.

In the end, there were only five competitors for the Rainhill prize, one of them an eccentric and daft engine powered by horses on a kind of treadmill and called the Cycloped. Large crowds turned out to watch as the four steam locomotives were put through their paces. For a while, the favourite was an engine made in London and christened *Novelty*. It was the design of a brilliant team consisting of John Braithwaite and John Ericsson, a Swedish engineer who came to England to promote his inventions and went on to the United States to build screw-propeller steamships. *Novelty* flew like the wind but then broke down at a crucial moment and was eliminated. A strong contender was the *Sans Pareil*, which had been entered by one of the very experienced locomotive engineers, Timothy Hackworth, the former blacksmith of Wylam who was appointed engineer of the Stockton–Darlington line once it was running. This worked well and was eventually bought by the Liverpool–Manchester Company and put to work on another line. A third entry was the *Perseverance*, but it performed so poorly that it was hardly in the running. Finally, and most famously, there was the Stephensons' *Rocket*, which won the day and subsequently received orders for engines from around the world. Hackworth, too, emerged as a serious rival and was soon taking orders, notably from Russia.

The Liverpool–Manchester line was a huge success, carrying in 1831 445,047 passengers, 43,070 tons of cotton and other merchandise and 11,285 tons of coal. Over the next four years the passenger total varied a good deal, but the tonnage of goods and coal went on rising steadily: the figures for 1835 were 473,847 passengers, 230,629 tons of merchandise and 116,246 tons of coal. On the turnpike roads between the two towns, the toll income fell sharply and the Bridgewater Canal Company had to drop its charges. The stagecoaches disappeared very quickly: only one remained in 1832, carrying mainly parcels rather than passengers. The substantial industry that revolved around the breeding and training of horses feared the worst, but, as it turned out, it was only the stagecoaches that really suffered. Very soon the railways increased the demand for horses since they carried a much greater volume of people and goods into the towns, where nearly all the road vehicles were horse-drawn.

The profitability of the Liverpool–Manchester line was a prelude to the first great railway boom in Britain. Parliament was deluged with Bills for new lines, one of them engineered by Robert Stephenson, covering the 112 miles between Birmingham and London. By 1837 there were something like eighty railway companies intent on adding to the network and in one year a thousand miles of track were laid down. The colliery railways, the Stockton–Darlington line and finally the Liverpool–Manchester project had created a trail-blazing band of railway engineers in Britain and they would soon be taking their knowledge and expertise and their workforce abroad. At the same time, some hard-won lessons had been absorbed by a generation of young engineers from the United States, intent by the 1820s on implanting British industrialism on American soil.

CHAPTER EIGHT

COWCATCHERS AND
TIMBER TRACKS

As early as 1852, an English observer of the emerging railway culture of Britain and other parts of the world noted how different this new technology was on the other side of the Atlantic. In the final chapter of *Our Iron Roads: their history, construction and social influences*, Frederick Smeeton Williams offered a few observations on the American railways on which he and other tourists, such as Charles Dickens, had travelled. Compared with the Liverpool–Manchester line with its wrought-iron rails on stone sleepers, its bridges and cuttings and tunnels, most American lines were almost comically makeshift. 'The appearance of American railways is very different from that of those in Britain. To select a level district of country, and to lay down wooden rails on roughly hewn sleepers, seems all that is necessary in some parts to make a line. Except where a branch-road joins the main, there is usually but one track of rails, so that the road is very narrow, and the view, as the traveller passes through interminable forests, is frequently by no means extensive.'

Dickens himself had made a tour of America, which he then wrote up as a travelogue that was published in 1842. Like all Englishmen, he was struck by the difference between the way American railroads (they never say rail*way*) had developed and those which, to date, had been built in England. Inevitably, the form a nation's railroads took reflected its social foibles as well as its general level of wealth and manufacturing sophistication. At this stage of America's industrial development, railway promoters, whether state-funded, as some were, or private, could not afford the stout structures of the British viaducts or canyon-like cuttings. Dickens first took a train from Boston to the newly founded New England textile works at Lowell.

> I made acquaintance with an American railroad, on this occasion, for the first time. As these works are pretty much alike all through the States, their general characteristics are easily described.
>
> There are no first- and second-class carriages as with us; but there is a gentleman's car and a ladies' car: the main distinction between which is that in the first, everybody smokes; and in the second, nobody does. As a black man never travels with a white one, there is also a negro car; which is a great, blundering, clumsy chest, such as Gulliver put to sea in, from the kingdom of Brobdingnag. There is a great deal of jolting, a great deal of noise, a great deal of wall, not much window, a locomotive engine, a shriek, and a bell.
>
> The cars are like shabby omnibuses, but larger: holding thirty, forty, fifty people. The seats, instead of stretching from end to end, are placed crosswise. Each seat holds two persons. There is a long row of them on each side of the caravan, a narrow passage up the middle, and a door at both ends. In the centre of the carriage there is usually a stove, fed with charcoal or anthracite coal; which is for the most part red-hot. It is insufferably close; and you see the hot air fluttering between yourself and any other object you may happen to look at, like the ghost of smoke ...
>
> The conductor or check-taker, or guard, or whatever he may be, wears no uniform. He walks up and down the car, and in and out of it, as his fancy dictates; leans against the door with his hands in his pockets and stares at you, if you chance to be a stranger; or

enters into conversation with the passengers about him ...
Everybody talks to you, or to anybody else who hits his fancy. If
you are an Englishman, he expects that that railroad is pretty much
like an English railroad. If you say 'No,' he says 'Yes?' (interrogatively),
and asks in what respect they differ. You enumerate the heads of
difference, one by one, and he says 'Yes?' (still interrogatively) to
each. Then he guesses that you don't travel faster in England; and
on your replying that you do, says 'Yes?' again (still interrogatively),
and it is quite evident, doesn't believe it. After a long pause he
remarks, partly to you, and partly to the knob on the top of his
stick, that 'Yankees are reckoned to be considerable of a go-ahead
people too;' upon which YOU say 'Yes,' and then HE says 'Yes' again
(affirmatively this time) ...

The train calls at stations in the woods, where the wild
impossibility of anybody having the smallest reason to get out, is
only to be equalled by the apparently desperate hopelessness of
there being anybody to get in. It rushes across the turnpike road,
where there is no gate, no policeman, no signal: nothing but a
rough wooden arch, on which is painted 'WHEN THE BELL
RINGS, LOOK OUT FOR THE LOCOMOTIVE.' On it whirls
headlong, dives through the woods again, emerges in the light,
clatters over frail arches, rumbles upon the heavy ground, shoots
beneath a wooden bridge which intercepts the light for a second
like a wink, suddenly awakens all the slumbering echoes in the
main street of a large town, and dashes on haphazard, pell-mell,
neck-or-nothing, down the middle of the road. There – with
mechanics working at their trades, and people leaning from their
doors and windows, and boys flying kites and playing marbles, and
men smoking, and women talking, and children crawling, and pigs
burrowing, and unaccustomed horses plunging and rearing, close
to the very rails – there – on, on, on – tears the mad dragon of an
engine with its train of cars; scattering in all directions a shower of
burning sparks from its wood fire; screeching, hissing, yelling,

panting; until at last the thirsty monster stops beneath a covered way to drink, the people cluster round, and you have time to breathe again.[1]

One distinctive feature of the American locomotives was the cowcatcher or, as it was rendered by amused English visitors, the 'cowketcher'. The railroads, as Dickens noted, were unprotected from any kind of trespass, while the steam trains ran through miles of wilderness inhabited by a rich diversity of beasts, both free-roaming farm animals and wild deer, bears and other potentially formidable obstacles. If a locomotive was travelling at twenty miles an hour – a good speed in America in the 1840s – it could easily be thrown off the line by an errant beast. The cowcatcher, an iron grating shaped rather like a snowplough, was attached to the front of the locomotive so that it pushed out in front close to the top of the rails. With luck, it would toss aside any stray animals that wandered on to the line or would carry the carcass along until the next stop. As one traveller remarked of the cowcatcher: 'It is by no means uncommon, on arriving at the station, to find a sheep or a hog dead or dying on it.'

In the very early days of canal projects, just after the American War of Independence, there was a clamouring on the eastern seaboard for British engineers with experience and expertise in building canals. However, by the 1820s there was already a considerable body of home-grown talent, and the manner in which up-to-date engineering skills were acquired had changed. Those states which were anxious to improve their roads and canals and intrigued by the possibility of building railways did not, for the most part, seek to buy in British talent. Instead they funded their own people to make exploratory trips to Europe, and Britain in particular, to learn how things were done and to bring back whatever equipment they could afford and thought would be useful. There were other engineers with private means who funded their own fact-finding tours.

There was no need for any of them now to travel in disguise or to hang around public houses, as the eighteenth-century French spies had done, in the hope of enticing a knowledgeable mechanic to emigrate with his expertise. Americans were confident that they would be greeted cordially in Britain and given all the help they might need. And so American engineers began to cross the Atlantic to learn how to build steam locomotives and how to lay down railway lines. The Pennsylvania Society for the Promotion of Internal Improvement appointed an architect engineer, thirty-eight-year-old William Strickland, to sail from Philadelphia to Liverpool in March 1825. The Society had been formed the year before with many members from the great American scientific body, the Franklin Institute, and they were very clear about what they wanted from Strickland. No whimsical scientific theories: just hard engineering facts. They did not want '… abstract principles, nor an indefinite and general account of their application to the great works of Europe … These we possess in books … What we earnestly wish to obtain, is the means of executing all those works in the best manner, and with the greatest economy and certainty … We desire to obtain working plans … so that those works may be executed in Pennsylvania, without the superintendence of a civil engineer of superior skill and science.'[2] Strickland, who had trained for a while in America with Latrobe, was encouraged to make a special study of railways, both horse-drawn and steam-driven.

With $3,000 dollars to spend and with an assistant, Samuel Kneass, who was an excellent draughtsman, Strickland spent six months meticulously recording the wonders of Britain's industrial world, comparing cast-iron and malleable iron rails, looking at the gauge of the lines, comparing canals and railways and so on. His findings were written up and illustrated and became one of the early textbooks for anyone seeking to build a railway up to the mid-nineteenth century. Typically too, Strickland went on to become the chief engineer of a number of railway projects.

The historian Darwin H. Stapleton has identified no fewer than fifteen American engineers who visited Britain between 1825 and 1838 to improve their understanding of their profession and the building of railroads in particular. A further eighteen engineers at one time or another worked with those who had been to Britain. All had at least some experience before they crossed the Atlantic, a few having trained at West Point military academy, which was criticized for being overly theoretical. Those who had British experience or were influenced by it, adapted the technology to the American landscape, training up more engineers as they did so. But they were not in a position initially to call upon an American iron industry to make their rails or their locomotives: these were all shipped across the Atlantic.

Most of the early railroads, like those in Britain, were horse-drawn or worked over hilly ground with inclined planes of one kind or another. But after the opening of the Stockton–Darlington line, an enthusiasm grew for steam engines. The first American to drive one on native soil was Horatio Allen, one of that band of industrial explorers who visited Britain in this pioneering period of American history. The son of a mathematics professor, Allen was born in 1802 in Schenectady, New York, and enjoyed one of the best educations available at the time, attending Columbia College (later Columbia University). At first attracted by the law, he realized his greatest interest was in canals and found work with the Delaware & Hudson Canal Company, where he rose rapidly to the post of engineer.

The canal company had been founded by brothers Maurice and William Wurts, two Philadelphia merchants who had acquired large tracts of land in Pennsylvania. In effect, they became the owners of huge reserves of hard anthracite coal which, for a while, was regarded as worthless. In England at this time only soft bituminous coal was burned in furnaces and steam engines, and anthracite was little used. Even when anthracite was found to be combustible, there was no way of getting the Pennsylvanian coal to New York, where it could be shipped by sea and river to other towns. The war with Britain in 1812 had cut off coal supplies from across the Atlantic and given rise to a new urgency to find a way of mining and using the indigenous coal of the United States (about which more later). Improved transport was vital and in 1825 the massive project of cutting the Delaware and Hudson canal was begun.

Modelled in part on the best English canals, the Delaware and Hudson had on completion fourteen aqueducts and 109 locks with inclined planes to haul coal over the steepest sections of the route. Horatio Allen learned a great deal of his engineering expertise building this canal. His boss, John B. Jervis, began to take a serious interest in railways from early in 1827. He had never seen one, not even a horse-drawn line, but he had read about them, and he was persuaded that a locomotive was cheaper to fuel and run than a horse. The canal company had planned to buy rails and locomotives from England when Allen announced he was going there anyway and was resigning from the company to free himself to travel. He wrote in a later account: 'Having come to the conclusion as to the locomotive ... and believing that the future of the civil engineer lay in the direction of the ... railroad era, I decided to go to the only place where a locomotive was in daily operation, and could be studied in all its practical details.'[3] The company promptly retained him and engaged him for the trip, for which they provided some funding. Allen sailed in late January 1828 with a pocketful of instructions from Jervis who pondered, among other things, the number of wheels a train should have and what its weight might be. Jervis thought a speed of three and a half to five miles an hour would be sufficient; he also reckoned $1,800 would be quite enough to buy one locomotive and that it would not be worth getting English ones if they cost more than that. Where he imagined he could find a locomotive in America in 1829 he did not say.

Not long after his arrival in Liverpool, Allen met George Stephenson, who was very friendly and showed him the Liverpool–Manchester railway as it was nearing completion. Some entries from Allen's diary indicate that at fifty years old George was still very robust. He took Allen by stagecoach up to Bolton, thirty-two miles from Liverpool, so they could look at the line built there. They then returned to the Liverpool–Manchester railway, walking seven miles of it until it got late and they realized they had missed the last coach from the town of St Helens back to Liverpool. As dusk fell, they set off to cover the ten miles on foot.

There were no objections to this American engineer sketching everything he saw, from the newly built Liverpool docks to the details of the track on Stephenson's railway. Allen became so absorbed in his study of locomotives that Jervis began to write to him with some testiness as he was anxious for a swift response. However, the company's agent was doing his work well. He spent some time on the Stockton–Darlington line, where he discussed the relative costs of horses and steam engines with Timothy Hackworth, the engineer in charge of the line. Eventually Allen wrote to Jervis to say he was convinced that steam locomotives were the future and, though they already worked well, they were bound to improve.

Before he returned to America, Allen put in an order for one engine from Robert Stephenson's company and three from Foster and Rastrick of Stourbridge in Worcestershire. Rastrick had been one of the judges at the Rainhill trials but his company engines were much heavier than Stephenson's and really, for that time, a poor choice. But they were relatively cheap – a very important consideration for Allen and Jervis. In May 1829 the first of these English engines, named the *Stourbridge Lion*, was delivered by ship to the wharf of the West Point Foundry Works at the foot of Beach Street, New York City. There was no line to put it on at first, but it was exhibited as a curiosity, propped up on blocks so that its wheels would turn, and thousands came to view it.

It was sometime in July that this locomotive was hauled to a rough and ready track that had been laid down as a canal-port connection by the Delaware and Hudson Company. Though Allen was convinced steam locomotives could work on the new railway line, it was intended to carry only horse-hauled trucks. Indeed, the general opinion of those who gathered on 8 August 1829 to watch the first run by a locomotive on American soil was that the journey would not last long as it was quite evident the engine was too heavy for the rails, which, in one section, ran over a timber viaduct.

Horatio Allen might have shouted 'All aboard!', but he desisted, for he knew there would be no takers. He later recalled:

> The circumstances which led to my being left alone on the engine were these: the road had been built in the summer, the structure was of hemlock-timber, and the rails, of large dimensions, notched on to caps placed far apart. The timber had cracked and warped from exposure to the sun. After about five hundred feet of straight line, the road crossed the Lackawaxen Creek on a trestle-work about thirty five feet high, and with a curve of three hundred and fifty or four hundred feet radius. The impression was very general

that the iron monster would either break down the road or that it would leave the track at the curve and plunge into the creek.[4]

Undaunted, Allen made the trip on his own:

> As I placed my hand on the throttle-valve handle, I was undecided whether I would move slowly or with a fair degree of speed: but believing that the road would prove safe, and preferring, if we did go down, to go down handsomely and without any evidence of timidity, I started with considerable velocity, passed the curve over the creek safely, and was soon out of hearing of the cheers of the large assemblage present. At the end of two or three miles, I reversed the valves and returned without accident to the starting place, having thus made the first railroad trip by locomotive in the Western Hemisphere.[5]

There were no accidents on the railway, as there were at the opening of the Manchester to Liverpool line the following year, when the MP William Huskisson was run over and died of his injuries. However, a celebratory cannon fired to mark the success of the inaugural run of the *Stourbridge Lion* injured a workman, who had to have a leg amputated.

In the various attempts made early on in America to emulate the British railway line, there was an element of regression or, as one commentator has put it 'a giant leap backwards'. It was not quite a case of reinventing the wheel, more a matter of repeating the folly of trying to run locomotives weighing several tons on wooden structures and with wood as fuel. The standard track was not much better than that laid down in the Tyneside pits when George Stephenson was a lad: wooden rails with, at best, a strip of iron along the top. Timber warped and rotted and, as Allen noticed, became twisted when exposed to the sun. For this reason, the *Stourbridge Lion* never went into service on the Delaware and Hudson and, like some of its predecessors in England, notably Trevithick's Penydarren engine, it was only used for stationary power.

At this stage in its development, the United States simply could not afford to build railways to the standards that were being established in Britain and elsewhere in Europe by British engineers. In a sense, Horatio Allen and other promoters of the locomotive were pushing America ahead too fast, trying to get it to run before it could walk. As industrialism spread, especially with the railways, a common problem was that the new technology arrived before any purpose could be found for it. In the United States there was, however, a clamour for improvements in transport for the movement of goods and raw materials along the eastern seaboard and across the spine of mountains that curtained off the developing lands to the west. There was also considerable competition between cities, which feared they would be left behind by their rivals if they did not create better communications with new roads or canals or, as they became feasible, railways. This all contributed to give the whole world of transportation a vibrancy in the first half of the nineteenth century which, in a sense, overrode the problem of resources.

Charles Dickens, in another of his descriptions of railroad travel in America, remarks on the monotony of the view when the trains ran through mile after mile of forest. Wood was, after all, the one resource the United States had, initially in superabundance. It has been estimated that in 1838 the fuel used for all purposes – from the heating of homes to the running of stationary and other steam engines to the baking of bread – was predominantly wood: 80 per cent timber, 14 per cent anthracite coal, 3 per cent charcoal and 2 per cent bituminous coal. It was a striking anomaly: a rapidly industrializing world largely made of wood and fuelled by it. Of the railroads, historian John H. White has written:

> During the first half of the nineteenth century everything about the American railroad was wooden. The track structure, stations, engine house, bridges, snow sheds, water tanks, coaling stations, freight and passenger cars, locomotives fuel – even the brake shoes and rail joints. Ironically, railroads were frequently called iron roads during the last century, when in fact they were actually wooden roads.[6]

A classic project of the period was the South Carolina Railroad, which ran from Charleston on the coast to Hamburg, a distance of 136 miles which made it, for a time, the longest railway in the world. It was promoted by the cotton merchants of Charleston and Hamburg as a means of siphoning off bales of cotton which were then bypassing them as they were shipped from Augusta, Georgia, by river down to Savannah. Horatio Allen was appointed chief engineer and he was proud to claim that this was the very first railroad which was intended from the outset to rely on the power of steam locomotives as opposed to horses. Famously, he expressed the following opinion: 'There is no reason to believe that the breed of horses will be materially improved, but the present breed of locomotives will furnish a power of which no one knows the limit.'[7]

It was a commercial venture in which investors took shares, and it was intended for both passengers and freight. In contrast with the English railway-builders, those in South Carolina had little or no trouble with landowners, who were nearly all keen to have a railway. They were prepared too to hire out their slaves as a workforce for the line. Horatio Allen supervised the work, placing his confidence in timber as the chief building material. To reduce the cost of creating a level line across undulating country, he decided on a structure which resembled an endless low bridge, the whole route elevated on a trestle arrangement. Allen argued that this would not only give a smooth ride, it would also allow livestock and slaves to pass under, rather than over, the railroad.

The South Carolina Railroad was opened in 1833 and Allen was soon ordering more locomotives, this time from American manufacturers. It was on this line that the first home-built American locomotive was to make a commercial run: called the *Best Friend of Charleston*, it was designed by E. L. Miller and built at the West Point Foundry in New York where the *Stourbridge Lion* had been displayed. For a time, it seemed as if the South Carolina Railroad would blaze a new and uniquely American trail. However, the wooden structure of the line was soon rotting and the *Best Friend* blew up within a year when its safety valve was held down by mistake. The locomotive ran along only one section of the line and it was soon replaced by the *West Point* from the same foundry, but the deterioration of the track proved extremely costly. Along much of the route, the space below the trellis work was filled in to form an embankment and iron rails had to be bought to replace the crumbling wooden track. In the end, the whole *raison d'être* of the line was undermined by further railway developments, but it was never a complete failure and it at least taught American engineers some important lessons. In England, one term for a railroad was a 'permanent way' and in time that is how they were built on the other side of the Atlantic.

Some of the American railway-builders tried to follow the English model more closely than Allen, though this did not necessarily mean using steam locomotives for the whole of a line's route. The first sections of the railroad that would eventually connect Baltimore in Maryland with the interior and the Ohio River were made of stouter materials than those used on the South Carolina line, but the use of stone cross-ties – or sleepers, as they are known in England – in imitation of the Liverpool–Manchester railway had its problems when the ground froze in hard winters. More successful was the use of stone for viaducts and bridges. The Baltimore and Ohio began running in 1830 with horse power at first and inclined planes for steep sections of line. One of the problems of introducing locomotives was the winding nature of the line as some of the curves were quite tight. So a miniature engine, the *Tom Thumb*, was designed by Peter Cooper of New York to cope with these sections. It was one of the first steam locomotives to be built in America and in 1830 Cooper gave it a run-out on the Baltimore and Ohio.

John Latrobe, a lawyer working for the Baltimore and Ohio company, has left this graphic account of *Tom Thumb*'s extraordinary maiden outing:

> The boiler of Mr. Cooper's engine was not as large as the kitchen boiler attached to many a range in modern mansions. It was of about the same diameter, but not much more than half as high. It stood upright in the car, and was filled, above the furnace, which occupied the lower section, with vertical tubes. The cylinder was but three and a half inches in diameter, and speed was gotten up by gearing. No natural draught could have been sufficient to keep up steam in so small a boiler; and Mr. Cooper used therefore a blowing-apparatus, driven by a drum attached to one of the car wheels, over which passed a cord that in its turn worked a pulley on the shaft of the blower ...

Mr. Cooper's success was such as to induce him to try a trip to Ellicott's Mills; and an open car, the first used upon the road, having been attached to his engine, and filled with the directors and some friends, the speaker [i.e., Latrobe himself] among the rest, the first journey by steam in America was commenced. The trip was most interesting. The curves were passed without difficulty at a speed of fifteen miles an hour; the grades were ascended with comparative ease; the day was fine, the company in the highest spirits, and some excited gentlemen of the party pulled out memorandum books, and when at the highest speed, which was eighteen miles an hour, wrote their names and some connected sentences, to prove that even at that great velocity it was possible to do so. The return trip from Ellicott's Mills – a distance of thirteen miles – was made in fifty-seven minutes.

But the triumph of this *Tom Thumb* engine was not altogether without a drawback. The great stage proprietors of the day were Stockton & Stokes; and on this occasion a gallant gray of great beauty and power was driven by them from town, attached to another car on the second track – for the Company had begun by making two tracks to the Mills – and met the engine at the Relay House ... From this point it was determined to have a race home; and, the start being even, away went horse and engine, the snort of the one and the puff of the other keeping time and tune.

At first the gray had the best of it, for his steam would be applied to the greatest advantage on the instant, while the engine had to wait until the rotation of the wheels set the blower to work. The horse was perhaps a quarter of a mile ahead when the safety valve of the engine lifted and the thin blue vapor issuing from it showed an excess of steam. The blower whistled, the steam blew off in vapory clouds, the pace increased, the passengers shouted, the engine gained on the horse, soon it lapped him – the silk was plied – the race was neck and neck, nose and nose – then the engine passed the horse, and a great hurrah hailed the victory.

But it was not repeated; for just at this time, when the gray's master was about giving up [sic], the band which drove the pulley, which drove the blower, slipped from the drum, the safety valve ceased to scream, and the engine for want of breath began to wheeze and pant. In vain Mr. Cooper, who was his own engineman and fireman, lacerated his hands in attempting to replace the band upon the wheel: in vain he tried to urge the fire with light wood; the horse gained on the machine, and passed it; and although the band was presently replaced, and steam again did its best, the horse was too far ahead to be overtaken, and came in the winner of the race.[8]

It was, of course, a minor setback for steam and there were still many Americans making the pilgrimage to view Britain's new railways. One who was to become very influential in American railroad-building in the South was Moncure Robinson. He was born in 1802 to a well-to-do merchant family of Richmond, Virginia. As a boy, he had a tutor who taught him French and he moved on to the College of William and Mary. But he left at the age of sixteen to take a job surveying for a prospective canal and was soon taken on as a surveyor on various projects. When he was twenty, he went to New York and, uninvited, introduced himself to some of the engineers then working on the Erie Canal. Returning to Virginia, Robinson got himself a job as engineer on the construction of the James River Canal Company. He worked there for two years, gaining valuable experience in building locks and bridges, but funding for the canal was tenuous and he decided that he needed to broaden his horizons.

In 1825 Robinson set out, at his father's expense, on his own idiosyncratic version of the Grand Tour of Europe, a popular expedition for well-off and cultured young men at the time. He had written to a friend earlier that he wanted to 'tread on classic ground' and for a while 'doff Roads & Canals, Aqueducts and Bridges ... to strut on the Boulevards and loll at the Théâtre Français'.[9] Whereas William Strickland and Horatio Allen had travelled on behalf of canal companies with an expense allowance and had focused almost exclusively on Britain, Robinson preferred to set himself down in Paris, where he could practise his French and absorb some 'classic' culture. He could make excursions to England and hoped to have a look at the Bridgewater Canal and perhaps knock on the door of Boulton and Watt's factory in Birmingham – now managed by their sons and the company's faithful servant, William Murdoch, as both Matthew Boulton and James Watt had died.

Robinson is especially interesting because he was an intelligent and well-informed young man who was able to compare and contrast the French and English approach to science and engineering at a period when Europe still lagged far behind Britain in practical matters. At the Sorbonne he attended the lectures of a number of brilliant French scientists such as the chemist Joseph Louis Gay-Lussac. Indeed, it was accepted there was no more advanced country in the world than France when it came to theories of structures and forces and the general principles of chemistry and engineering.

During his stay in Europe, which lasted two and a half years, Moncure Robinson spent seven months in England and it was the knowledge he had acquired here that would prove of real value when he returned to America and took on the supervision of many projects, including the surveying and engineering for a large number of railways. He walked the canals and was mightily impressed by London. In one letter home, he wrote: 'Much as I heard of the wealth of England I had no conception of it until I came to London ... To judge superficially one would suppose there was no poverty in the land, for even to live in England seems to require more money than to attain Comfort would anywhere else ... And yet with the immense expenditure of England its Capital seems to be accumulating in an unexampled manner. New buildings & Manufactures are springing up everywhere whilst every new scheme abroad is put into operation with English Capital. What a wonderful country.'[10]

Robinson himself had noticed the crucial difference between France and England as early as 1825, writing home after his first visit to England: 'In practical Mechanics the French must be at least one hundred years behind the English. It is indeed astonishing that in a country so contiguous to one where the mechanical arts are brought to the highest perfection their contrivances in everything should still be so rude...'While the French prided themselves, quite justifiably, on the brilliance of their scientists, they lacked the practical application of the British. They could not, for example, get to grips with the idea of a steam railway, and indeed they were to leave the laying out of the first major lines in France to their rivals across the Channel.

CHAPTER NINE

LES ROSBIFS GO TO WORK

In early September 1833, a distinguished French government officer, Adolphe Thiers, and his party were taken on a whistle-stop tour of the great public works of England. The visit was organized by the English soldier and surveyor Charles Blacker Vignoles, who had successfully steered the Liverpool–Manchester Railway Bill through Parliament and was now hoping to convince Thiers that the grand project of a railway line linking London and Paris, with a steamer across the Channel, would be both exciting and profitable. Vignoles had in fact spent a great deal of time before Thiers's visit talking to all the most influential individuals in Paris and at the court of Louis-Philippe: it was true that the French had been dithering over the project, but Vignoles was convinced he had finally won them over and that work on the line would soon begin. In a letter from Paris to London dated 25 August 1833, Vignoles had written:

> After a great dinner of ceremony at the Minister's yesterday, where
> I met most of the principal attachés and heads of departments and
> the leading engineers, I went about nine o'clock with M. Thiers
> to the King's evening party at St Cloud, which is about five or six
> miles from Paris, and had the honour of about half an hour's private
> audience with Louis-Philippe.

The King assured me that he felt the warmest interest in the matter, and would support the measure to the utmost … he desired M. Thiers to pay every attention to have the matter brought in the strongest possible manner before the Chamber of Deputies … He told me he was convinced that it would be exceedingly profitable to subscribers, but that it was not possible in his mind to measure the importance of the affair in its political relations. He mentioned as a matter of personal interest that he had a Chateau close to Dieppe, and all the royal family were fond of bathing; and that when four hours would take the Parisians to Dieppe, it would become as fashionable a watering place as Brighton … it is impossible for me to convey to you in writing the warmth and even eagerness of his manner for the promotion of the scheme.[1]

It was therefore with considerable confidence that Vignoles, having returned to England, went down to Dover to greet M. Thiers and his entourage to take them on a tour of the world's most advanced industrial nation. They travelled up to London, stopping en route to take in the Thames Tunnel and Chatham dockyard. On 9 September they left for the north by road, travelling overnight and reaching Birmingham around noon the following day. They visited Foster's Stourbridge works, which had made the *Stourbridge Lion* for Horatio Allen, admired – at least Vignoles did – Thomas Telford's handiwork on the Birmingham Canal and looked in on an ironworks. Travelling overnight once again, they were the following day able to take a look at the Menai Bridge and other structures before going on to Birkenhead, where they arrived after midnight. From there they crossed the Mersey to Liverpool, where Thiers was entertained by a number of railway promoters. He had a ride on a section of the now famous Liverpool–Manchester line and the St Helens–Widnes Railway. In the evening, the mayor of Liverpool gave a banquet in honour of the distinguished French official.

Next day – it was now 13 September – they took the train to Manchester, where they visited warehouses stacked with cotton, coal and other goods. There was one hiccup in this astonishing itinerary – the spinning mill of Birley and Kirk in Manchester refused to let them in. The old rivalry, it seemed, had not entirely disappeared from the textile trade. Later, though, they were able to see silk-spinning and weaving at Congleton outside Manchester and went on to the Potteries, where they visited the Wedgwood manufactory at Etruria. By 14 September, they had continued their tour through the Midlands and were back in London and therefore able to view the streets lit by gaslight, which Vignoles always rendered as '*gazlight*'. This was still something of a novelty in 1833, though a few London streets had been lit by gas since 1812 and it would not have been new to Thiers, even if the effect in the city's finer streets was considered by foreign visitors to be startling. There were more visits in London, including a call on the Spitalfields weavers, who, like Vignoles' own forebears, were descended from the Protestant Huguenot families that had fled France in the seventeenth century to escape religious intolerance. The French party lunched at a London tavern and were bid farewell before they travelled back overnight to Dover.

For all this, Thiers declared himself unimpressed by what he had seen in England and, once back in Paris, reported that railways were a waste of time and quite unsuited to French conditions. Years later, Vignoles offered a witty account of the whole sorry affair:

> Mr Vignoles, said the accomplished statesman, I am infinitely obliged to you, and I think you a very clever fellow; but, do you know, I did not believe a word of what you told me in Paris before I came over, and even now I cannot see the great advantages you were constantly dwelling on. You have good canals, but very small, and ours in France are much superior. As for your roads, they are very good, but I have not met a merchandise wagon on them in the whole course of our journeys! As to railways, I do not think them suited to France; and, as to your vaunted posting, we go quite as quickly in my own country ... Perhaps this last remark was not to be wondered at, as M. Thiers had insisted on bringing over to England his own heavy lumbering vehicle, quite à la Louis Quatorze, with immense lamps, like the old Paris reverberators, at

the four corners on the top of the carriage, which also carried heavy imperials, and eight or nine persons, outside and in, requiring six horses most of the way.[2]

And so it was that the inauguration of serious railway-building in France was delayed for a good ten years. The French traveller and campaigner for railways, Michel Chevalier, visited Liverpool in November 1833, taking the train from Manchester. He enjoyed being whisked along at thirty miles an hour 'without being the least incommoded and with the utmost feeling of security' and in a letter he wrote, 'Those who doubt the policy of introducing railroads to France, and think it prudent to wait for more light, cite, among other arguments, the experiments continually made in England to apply locomotive engines to common roads, the success of which, they think, would save the expense of rails.'[3] But most of the cost of a railway, Chevalier pointed out, lay in the creation of a line with slight gradients which required much excavating of tunnels and cuttings and the building of embankments, viaducts and bridges, and any road that could provide a track for a fast steam vehicle would surely require the same. (The cost of rails, by comparison, was minimal.) And while other nations had viewed the Liverpool–Manchester railway with admiration and sought to emulate the achievement, the French, Chevalier added, 'stand looking with folded arms' and would soon have 'fallen behind all Europe in manufactures and commerce'.[4]

Some short lines were built in France in spite of Thiers's diatribes against railways. Michel Chevalier was an enthusiast as was the financial journalist Emile Péreire, who, writing in the newspaper Le National, attracted the interest of financiers, notably James de Rothschild. There were pioneer railway-builders in France, notably Stephane Mony and Eugene Flachat. The first line to be financed and built was a short run from St Lazare in Paris towards St Germain-en-Laye, which was opened in 1837. It was an atmospheric railway powered by compressed air rather than a steam engine and it was a financial success. But the projects which followed it were to discourage French investors from getting involved in railway-building.

Emile Péreire, along with his brother Isaac, James de Rothschild and other financiers planned a line from Paris to Versailles starting on the right bank of the Seine. No sooner had the plans been put forward than a rival group of financiers set about building a line starting from the left bank and going to their own station at Versailles. Whereas in England there had been a sound basis for believing a line between, say, two great centres of the cotton trade would generate traffic, there was not much sense in one line from Paris to Versailles, never mind two. The result was that neither line made much of a profit, and the good name the Paris–St Germain-en-Laye line had won for railways was soon lost. For ten years the French gave up on railways altogether.

By the time the official French attitude had changed, Britain had already been through its first bout of railway mania: the line engineered by Robert Stephenson between London and Birmingham had opened in 1838 and permission had been granted for a good thousand miles of track in Acts of Parliament passed up to that date. This astonishing rate of development had created a new generation of talented and experienced surveyors, engineers and contractors, a number of whom had learned their trade in the long drawn-out saga of the Liverpool–Manchester line between the first surveys of the line in 1822 and its final completion in 1830. Charles Vignoles was one of these men, and the snub from Thiers after his attempts to get French backing for the Paris to London line was soon forgotten. There was, of course, no formal training for the railway engineer or surveyor at this time and those who went on to become prominent figures over the next few years as they built railways around the world tended to find their vocation by chance. Yet none of the leading characters in this saga had quite such an exotic education as Charles Blacker Vignoles himself.

After Vignoles' forebears had fled France in 1685 to escape religious persecution, they had settled in Ireland, where they enjoyed distinguished military careers. Charles was born in County Wexford in 1793, the son of an army officer, also named Charles Vignoles, and Camilla Hutton, the daughter of a distinguished teacher at the Royal Military Academy at Woolwich on the Thames. When Charles was just one, he and his mother accompanied his father when he was posted to Guadeloupe, where the French and English were constantly fighting for control. Captain Vignoles was badly injured in a skirmish and held captive. Both he and Camilla caught yellow fever and died, leaving the infant Charles to be cared for by his regiment. At the age of eighteen months, Charles was made an ensign on half-pay, a recognized way of providing for orphans until a boy's family could care for him. Then, two years after his parents had died, an uncle found him and delivered him to his maternal grandparents in England, who cared for him until he was a teenager. His grandfather, Dr Hutton, was very well connected and knew the famous Rennie brothers, eminent engineers.

Anxious to steer Charles away from the army, his grandfather encouraged him to study law. But this did not suit him and he chose instead to go to the cadet college at Sandhurst, thus possibly instigating a rift with his grandfather which was never mended. Vignoles met his future wife through social connections at Sandhurst and embarked on a military career with the patronage of the Duke of Kent. He saw action in Europe during the Napoleonic campaigns and provided comparative tables of French and English weights and measures for the Duke of Wellington. He was also able to turn his hand to surveying in the army, and after he had been sent out to fight with Simon Bolivar, the colourful leader of the South American struggle for independence from Spanish colonial control, he ended up in South Carolina, where he was appointed deputy to the state civil engineer. By this date – 1817 – he was married and seeking a living away from the army.

In 1821, Vignoles was appointed city surveyor at St Augustine, Florida, and produced a map of that disputed territory in 1823. But he was always short of money and at the news of his grandfather's death he returned to London and was reunited with his grandmother. He wrote articles on surveying and found work as assistant surveyor on the London Commercial Docks, which were then being built. His big breakthrough, however, came in 1825 when the Rennie brothers hired him to survey the Liverpool–Manchester line, a task he undertook successfully. He had backed the *Novelty* at the Rainhill trials after working in partnership with its engineers and was taken on to work on a section of the line being built. After falling out with George Stephenson, Vignoles was offered a position by Marc Brunel on the Thames Tunnel but fell out with Brunel too after a disagreement about how the project should proceed. None the less, by the time he was asked to persuade the French to embark on a London–Paris railway, he was an experienced surveyor with considerable railway experience.

While Vignoles himself went on to work on many different railways in Britain, other surveyors and contractors who had gained experience on the Liverpool–Manchester line were finally heading for France. The task of planning the first major railway line in that country fell to a surveyor a good deal younger than Vignoles but well known to him, for they had worked on many projects together. This was Joseph Locke, the son of William Locke, colliery manager and friend of George Stephenson. Born in 1805, Joseph Locke was both a contemporary of and, as we have seen, a friend of Robert Stephenson. He had attended grammar school and served a colliery apprentice before joining George Stephenson as a pupil engineer. By the age of thirty-five he had considerable experience of railway-building: he had worked on the so-called Grand Junction line between Birmingham and Warrington and in 1840 completed the London and South-Western line. The latter gave a great boost to the port of Southampton, from where steamships crossed the Channel to the French port of Le Havre.

In 1839 a French banker, Charles Lafitte, frustrated by his country's tardiness in railway-building, carried out a survey of traffic on the route from Paris to Rouen, which is at the tidal limit of the River Seine, and on to Le Havre. He calculated that there was ample movement of goods and people to make a line pay and approached his government with a proposition. If they would put up about a quarter of the capital, French investors might be induced to take a gamble on the line; the rest could come from British capitalists. With official sanction, he approached the board of directors of the newly completed London and South-Western Line for support. At a cordial meeting Locke was introduced to Lafitte and he made a preliminary survey of the terrain between Paris and Rouen. Compared with some of the lines he had worked on in the north of England, this route was a dream: chalk hills to tunnel through and shallow valleys to cross. Much of his work in Britain had been salvaging other people's failing projects. This French line, however, was to be his own, and he was duly appointed chief engineer when the French government decreed in August 1840 that it could go ahead.

Although Locke had imagined that he would find the workforce to build the railways in France, he soon discovered that there were really no contractors with anything like the experience of those he had worked with in Britain. A few tenders came in but Locke regarded the estimates as far too high. He therefore turned to the people he knew: one was Thomas Brassey and the other William Mackenzie. Together, Brassey and Mackenzie divided up the work of tunnelling and embanking and excavation on the eighty-two miles of the projected Paris–Rouen railway. An extension to Le Havre from Rouen, finally creating the London to Paris link by steamer, was to follow. The more direct routes from Paris to either Calais or Boulogne for a short Channel crossing were not feasible simply because there was not the financial backing from Britain which was necessary to get the scheme going in France.

By the time work started on the Paris to Rouen railway – four tunnels were the first structures to be tackled – there were other lines being authorized in France. In 1842, a new law enabled the government to become involved, deciding on the lines that should be built and offering loans to the railway companies. But it was the Paris to Rouen line – and, to an even greater extent, the completion of the considerably more demanding task of extending the line to Le Havre – which would demonstrate to the rest of the world that the British, whom the French liked to call, not without reason, *les rosbifs*, were the great masters of building steam locomotive railways.

When Locke appointed Thomas Brassey and William Mackenzie as contractors, he knew he was dealing with men who had proved that they could marshal hundreds or even thousands of men, from bricklayers and stonemasons to rugged labourers, make sure they were paid and looked after and that, whatever the project – whether a tunnel, a viaduct or ten miles of railway through a swamp – it would be finished on time. In the first railway boom in Britain, following the success of the Liverpool to Manchester line, the demand for contractors outstripped the supply. There was a great deal of shoddy workmanship, exploitation of labour and downright dishonesty, and many small outfits went bankrupt. Brassey and Mackenzie stood out from the crowd, however, and they had at times competed for the same work.

William Mackenzie was the senior of the partners and with much longer experience of engineering works than Brassey. He was born in 1794 at Nelson in Lancashire at the height of the canal-building boom. His father was a contractor on the Leeds and Liverpool Canal and Mackenzie began his working life apprenticed to a canal-lock carpenter. He then moved up to Scotland to work on dock-building and one of the bridges which were part of Thomas Telford's government-funded improvements of the Highland roads. In the 1820s Mackenzie took on more and more responsibility, often working alongside Telford and constructing cast-iron bridges or undertaking the cutting of new canals. He was not involved in railway-building until he won the contract to construct the Lime Street tunnel into Liverpool on that celebrated line. From there, he went on to work with Locke on the Grand Junction and other railways.

Thomas Brassey had also worked with Thomas Telford on the laying of new roads. Born to a modestly wealthy landowner in Cheshire in 1805, Brassey had a brief formal education before being articled at the age of sixteen to a land surveyor who was the agent for a number of landed gentry with property across a wide area of the north-west. One of Brassey's first assignments was to work with a surveyor mapping the route for a new road from Shrewsbury to Holyhead being built by Telford for the growing traffic across the sea to Ireland. By the time he was twenty-one, Brassey was offered a partnership in the land-surveying firm he had joined five years earlier and was given his own office in Birkenhead, a district of Cheshire across the Mersey from booming Liverpool but itself not then much developed.

Brassey guessed Birkenhead was bound to grow and persuaded his father to lend him the money to buy a brickyard and some lime kilns. Working as both an agent and a builder's merchant, he began to save money to provide the capital necessary to bid for big projects, if they came along. One of his interests was in a stone quarry at Stourton and it was here that he was introduced to George Stephenson, who was out prospecting for building materials for a viaduct to span the Sankey canal on the Liverpool to

Manchester railway. Stephenson was impressed with Brassey and advised him to have a go at tendering for railway work when it came up. Sure enough, an opportunity arose when tenders were called for the building of a viaduct at Dutton on the Grand Junction railway. He lost that one – to William Mackenzie, who put in a bid £5,000 lower – but Brassey was now on his way as a railway contractor.

In the lives of the industrial revolutionaries, wives are not often mentioned, except in passing as the begetters of broods of children or as the source of some important finance for the ambitious ironmaster, potter or engineer they brought as a dowry at their wedding. But throughout his life Brassey attributed a great deal of his success to Maria Harrison, the young woman he met and married when he became established at Birkenhead. Her father, Joseph Harrison, was a well-to-do shipping agent and one of the far-sighted enthusiasts for the Liverpool–Manchester railway, who travelled to London to speak for the project in Parliament. Thomas and Maria were married a year after the line opened, in 1831, and she urged him to go on looking for railway contracting work. His chance came in 1835 when he put in a bid to build a viaduct at Penkridge on a new line between Stafford and Wolverhampton. Joseph Locke had taken over from George Stephenson as chief engineer on the line, and when Brassey bid £26,000, Locke suggested £20,000 less. They finally agreed on £6,000.

To supervise the work, Brassey moved house from Birkenhead to Stafford, the beginning of a nomadic lifestyle to which his ambitious wife agreed, though every time they upped sticks they had to sell their furniture as it was too costly to move. To make sure he had workmen he could rely on, Brassey persuaded bricklayers and masons to move from Birkenhead to Stafford, where they were put up in lodgings. He also began to attract a following of loyal labourers who knew they would be paid on time and in full and that, if they were injured, he would seek medical help for them. The excavation of cuttings and tunnels was especially hazardous as gunpowder was used in great quantities.

Brassey's next move was south to Hampshire, where Joseph Locke had been asked to take over the supervision of the London–Southampton line which had run into trouble because of the incompetence of the first senior engineer. It was customary to award the contract for different sections of line to particular contractors and Locke asked Brassey to take on a missing piece between the towns of Basingstoke and Winchester. And from Hampshire, the next step was across the Channel to set up home in Rouen, where Mrs Brassey was quite at home as a fluent French speaker.

As Brassey and Mackenzie began to put together their teams of workers in France, it became clear to them that they would not be able to recruit all, or even a majority, locally. French blacksmiths and carpenters were considered perfectly competent, but miners from various parts of Britain were recruited for tunnelling and the immense muscle power needed to shift thousands of tons of earth proved to be, at least in the first years of railway-building in France, an attribute exclusive to the British navvy. These labourers were, in effect, a self-selecting group who in an earlier era would have moved from agricultural work on to the building of roads and then canals. It was their labour with barrows and spades, excavating the inland waterways of Britain, that gave them the name 'navigators', which was in turn shortened to navvies. Inevitably, they led a nomadic existence, going wherever there was work to be found. And now, as they built railways, they travelled even greater distances than they had when constructing roads or canals.

In Britain, the navvy in his moleskin jacket with trousers tied at the knee became a figure of popular myth and fear. The reformer Edwin Chadwick wrote in a paper read to the Statistical Society of Manchester in the 1840s: 'The labourer has been detached from the habits and influences of his home and his village, and set to work amongst promiscuous assemblages of men attracted from all parts, has received double the ordinary amount of wages, and has been surrounded by direct inducements to spend them in drink and debauchery.'[5] A House of Commons Select Committee examined the lifestyle of the railway labourer in 1846 and heard evidence from prison chaplains all over the country of cells filled up with these navvies, of the efforts to provide them with some religious instruction – even the Archbishop of Canterbury had preached to them on the Dover line – and of the establishment of schools for those who had wives and children. The greatest difficulties tended to be when lines were built across barren moors where there were no lodgings for the men and they had to live in turf huts. Here, too, the contractors could make untold profits selling beer and whiskey and food to the men at inflated prices – the iniquitous 'truck' system clawing back money from the high wages they paid.

When these wild men of the railways went to France, however, their image was transformed. Perhaps only the better sort crossed the Channel – Brassey and Mackenzie possibly brought over as many as 5,000 – but the French were mightily impressed when they watched them at work. Their tools were picks, shovels and wheelbarrows. To shift earth out of a cutting and to build embankments, they would attach the barrow at its lowest point to a rope, the other end of which was hitched to a horse at the top. When the barrowload of earth was ready to be raised, the horse would be set off and the navvy would race up a plankway hanging on to the barrow, which he would tip at the top. It was reckoned a navvy could shift twenty tons of earth in a day. Joseph Locke recorded in his memoirs that many a time he heard the exclamation, 'Mon Dieu, ces anglais: comme ils travaillent!' (My God, these English: how they work!)

In 1843 the French publication *Journal des Débats* ran a piece on the difference between French and English labourers on the Paris–Rouen line, which *The Times* abridged under the headline 'The Effect of Diet on the Labourer':

> The English workman gets through more work in a given time than a Frenchman. Is this because he is more intelligent, more supple of limb, quicker or more dextrous than the Frenchman? No; but he has more muscular power, and is provided with better tools. Place a Frenchman in the same circumstances with regard to food and tools, and he will very soon be equal to the Englishman. A hundred times we have seen instances of it. At the forges of Charenton, about twenty years ago, when the consequences of a strike forced Messrs Manly and Wilson to employ French workmen in some of their most difficult operations, it was found that these

men, heretofore inferior, did the same quantity of work as the English from the moment that, like them, they were fed with beef and mutton, washed down with copious drafts of beer and wine.

On the Rouen Railway the same proof was afforded. At the bridge of Tourville, the piles of stonework were divided between the French and English, separated one from the other, but provided with the same tools, and living in the same manner. A love of roast beef having spread among the masons of Normandy, there was such a trial of strength between the two, and the French gained it.[6]

For the first ten miles of the railway, Brassey and Mackenzie had imported the iron rails from England. But shipping them up the River Seine was expensive. The solution was to bring over William Buddicom, another veteran of the Liverpool–Manchester Railway and an acolyte of Joseph Locke. As an engineer, Buddicom had come to specialize in the building of locomotives and rolling stock. To supply the Paris–Rouen line with both these and with rails, he set up in business at Sotteville, a district of Rouen, in partnership with Brassey and Mackenzie and other financiers involved in the line. Buddicom married and made his home in France, only later returning to an estate in Flintshire. He built many of the first locomotives to run on French railways. Forty English engine-drivers were also brought in when the Paris–Rouen line was opened.

Again, according to the *Journal des Débats* the key to English success was – roast beef.

At Rouen, the splendid establishment founded, almost in a day, by English people, drawn thither by the necessities of the railway, and devoted to the construction of carriages and engines, was carried on by means both of French and English workmen. In all those kinds of work requiring more skill and nicety than the manual strength, the French very rapidly became equal to the English; in the smithies the English were far in advance. But the French, as soon as they began to imitate their mode of work, and more especially to feed upon beef as they did, were soon as powerful as they. This is one more proof of the necessity of extending, by all possible means, the use of meat among the labouring classes of France.[7]

The mingling of European cultures on the Paris–Rouen line was instructive for all concerned. On some works there were Germans, Belgians and workers from northern Italy, alongside the English, Scots, Irish and Welsh. Much instruction was given in a kind of sign language, accompanied by the word 'Damn!' The British navvies, who generally took on the more dangerous or strenuous work, were paid at a better rate than all the others, a cause of occasional resentment. Railway directors from England were, however, taken aback when they were instructed to pay damages for workmen injured on the line, as a great many were. There was an instance where an Irishman, retrieving a charge of gunpowder which had apparently failed to blow, was hit full-face by an unexpected blast. He lost his sight and both his arms. The English directors argued that he had been careless and therefore did not deserve any compensation. But in French law the hapless navvy was entitled to a payment and he was sent home with £200.

The contractors Brassey and Mackenzie did not face many claims from British workmen and Brassey certainly ensured he made donations to local hospitals wherever his men were working in France. At this stage in their careers, both men stayed very much on the job. Whereas Brassey set up home in Rouen, Mackenzie took to Parisian life, renting an apartment in a fashionable district in the summer of 1840. He could travel to England with ease, taking the steamer on the crossing between Calais and Dover and then a train northwards, but he spent at least six months of the year in France from 1842 to 1847 as he and Brassey took on more and more railway work. On the Paris–Rouen line, Mackenzie's diaries show that he travelled the whole route 130 times before it was completed, taking boats on the Seine up to Paris or travelling by road.

The extension of the Paris to Rouen line to the port of Le Havre would finally complete the through route to London via Southampton and the

South-Western railway, but it was going to be a tough engineering job. First, out of Rouen there had to be a bridge across the Seine, and then a sequence of cuttings and tunnels, embankments and viaducts so that for much of the line's fifty-eight miles there was little in the way of straightforward track-laying. Twelve miles out of Rouen, Mackenzie and Brassey built a fine brick viaduct which towered above the little town of Barentin. Looping in a great curve one hundred feet above a valley on twenty-seven arches, it was nearly a third of a mile long and cost £50,000 to build. It had a sweep and elegance which was much admired by the French.

As it was nearing completion, but before it carried any trains, there were several days of torrential rain. Then one morning a local boy who was taking ballast up to the track with a team of horses heard a crashing sound and looked up to see the fifth arch of the viaduct crumbling, the bricks and masonry falling to the ground. With one arch gone, the whole of the viaduct tumbled down like a pack of cards. It was fortunate that the edifice fell down almost vertically, for had it toppled sideways it would have killed and injured an untold number of the inhabitants of Barentin. As it was, it destroyed a mill on the river below and the one person at work there suffered only a cut finger. The rubble, however, blocked the flow of water in the river, putting a whole line of water-wheels out of action, while the lime from the brickwork and mortar poisoned the fish.

In France there was an outcry. If a viaduct was not safe without a locomotive on it, what would it be like when the trains were running? The government department responsible for ensuring the safety of structures put all bridges and viaducts through severe tests. Brassey and Mackenzie took the news of the collapse of the viaduct philosophically. Locke told them there would be no extra funds for rebuilding and the two contractors agreed immediately to foot the bill themselves. Notices appeared in the French papers to say that rebuilding would delay the completion of the line by only two months and it was running ahead of schedule anyway. (The contractors were due for a bonus of £10,000 for finishing within a given time.) It was generally agreed that the reason for the collapse of the viaduct was the poor quality of the materials, especially the mortar. The viaduct was redesigned and, when it was complete, subjected to many test runs with trains and carriages weighing together up to eighty tons. It withstood every test and is still there today, vaulting over the French countryside.

By the time the Rouen–Le Havre section was ceremonially opened in 1847, Brassey and Mackenzie were already engaged in building several other lines in France. In 1842 a law had been passed authorizing the French government to direct the future of railway-building and, though latecomers to the new technology, the French were already imposing a degree of rationality on a potentially anarchic bundle of projects. By contrast, in the mid-1840s, Britain was gripped by a new bout of railway mania. In just one year – 1845 – Parliament authorized the construction of 2,170 miles of railways to add to the existing 2,234 miles. The cost, according to *The Times*, would be some £500 million. The following year another 477 Bills were passed for lines that would cost a further £200 million.

Already the way in which railways were developed was diverging in Europe. For contractors like Brassey and Mackenzie, who avoided hare-brained schemes, the French determination to control the development of new lines was a great improvement on the free-for-all prevailing in Britain. It was, in a way, a turning point in industrial history. The early development of railways had been hard won by clear-headed businessmen who wanted to exploit a new, faster and cheaper form of transport which would be of great value to them. It was for this reason that the first really successful line ran between two great commercial cities, Liverpool and Manchester. However, once the idea caught on, rather less consideration was given to where it was actually worth building a railway. And if the true costs of running a railway were not that clear at the outset, in time there came the inevitable accretion of staff, along with an entirely novel range of jobs such as those of guard and ticket collector, driver and fireman, clerk and station master.

Just as Charles Dickens and other English travellers were amused by the style of the early American railroads, so were the visitors to France who travelled on the lines built mostly by the British. In his book *Our Iron Roads*, published in 1852, Frederick Williams had this to say:

Continental railways have peculiarities unknown in this country, which appear very strange, and are sometimes rather annoying, to Mr Bull when he crosses the Channel. In England, the traveller goes to the station when he pleases, lounges in the waiting-room, consumes Banbury-cakes, and drinks scalding coffee *ad libitum*, wanders about the platform, and superintends his own luggage, and, in fact, so long as he does not violate the 'bye-laws' of the Company, he may do what he likes without let or hindrance.

In France the system is very different: instead of the traveller managing himself, he is managed. On procuring his ticket, he delivers up his luggage, pays a sous or two, and obtains a receipt, and is then marched into a waiting-room, according to the class of his fare; as if the Company were afraid that, having paid his money, he should not have his ride. When the train is ready, the first-class passengers are liberated, and everyone scrambles to his seat with as much agility as circumstances will admit; the second-class travellers follow; and the third are then allowed to deposit themselves in the vehicles provided for their reception.[8]

While this Gallic regimentation was anathema to 'Mr Bull', the style of the French conductors was regarded with wry amusement: 'Instead of the neatness and simple efficiency by which those functionaries are characterized in our own land, they wear a blue cotton blouse like the country people, to which is added a red belt, and a long, slouching broad-brimmed hat like the priests. As men of authority, they of course wear swords, and they wield red signal flags and horns, which give them the combined characteristics of the countryman, the soldier, the priest and the huntsman.'

As Thomas Brassey, William Mackenzie and a host of other British railway contractors left behind their elegantly engineered lines in France and other parts of Europe, so each nationality adopted and adapted the revolutionary form of transport in its own way. But it seemed not every European nation was really ready for railways. Frederick Williams was quite sure that they were not suitable for a country such as Spain, though in 1848 Joseph Locke had completed the first steam locomotive line there, eighteen miles running north from Barcelona – with half the funding coming from the London and South-West Railway Company. Of the Spanish, Williams opined: 'The people hate innovations, abhor being hurried, and in general find the ambling of a mule a sufficiently rapid means of transit.' Spain had not done much in the way of road- or canal-building, said Williams, for there was little call for transport from their stunted, local industries. As for the muleteer or *arraeiro*, Williams quotes a contemporary tourist guide:

> He, the *arraiero*, constitutes one of the most numerous and finest classes in Spain. He is the legitimate Manuel of the semi-oriental caravan system, and will never permit the bread to be taken out of his mouth by the Lutheran locomotive; deprived of the means of earning his livelihood, he, like the smuggler, will take to the road in another line, and both will become either robbers or patriots. Many, long, and lonely are the leagues which separate town from town in the wide deserts of thinly peopled Spain, nor will any preventive services be sufficient to guard the rail against the *guerrilla* [literally, 'little war'] that will then be waged.[9]

This turned out to be more prescient than fanciful. Brassey, once again the contractor, shipped to Catalonia his own navvies and other construction workers as well as the rails and rolling stock, all made in Britain. When they saw the line being laid down along the coast, the local fishermen launched a series of assaults, as they feared, quite reasonably, that it would interfere with their lucrative activities as smugglers and, on occasion, highwaymen. Unfamiliar with the robust railway navvy, the fishermen tried to organize protection rackets in which they would offer security against brigands. When this was brushed aside, they turned to sabotage, burning down one of the wooden bridges on the line. Undaunted, the navvies made good progress across coastal terrain that was generally easy to work. The final assault came when the line began to run: on one occasion the train was held up and all the passengers robbed.

By the mid-nineteenth century, steam locomotives were running over a wide area of Europe as the first lines, often only a few miles long, were opened. Brassey, Mackenzie and some other British contractors, notably Morton Peto, built wherever they could get a contract and often worked together to complete a line. The days when Brassey could move to live next to the site of his latest project were gone as his company now built lines around the world. All in all, his company was responsible in part at least for 1,550 miles of railway outside Britain: in the Italian Alps, Argentina, Brazil, Australia, Canada and India. Brassey survived near financial ruin in the great economic slump of the 1860s but died in 1870 a very rich man with a fortune estimated to be some £5 million.

Though Brassey, Mackenzie, Peto and the other major contractors built railways wherever they were called for, the costs of construction and the initial purpose of lines varied enormously, as did the economic impact of railways. In Britain, the steam railway was the creation of half a century or more of industrialization, a logical 'next step' in a country producing huge quantities of goods and great wealth. With all the rest of the world then on the verge of industrial 'take-off', the railway could be the catalyst which broke down old barriers, made the shifting of raw materials cheap enough to feed new industries and provided the essential transport system that any nation had to have if it were to break free from its past inertia.

Frederick Williams, in his 1852 account of the development of railways up to that time, provides a handy snapshot of their spread, and of how their future was imagined. While Spain still moved, for the most part, to the pace of the muleteer, the British and French were flying around at astonishing speed:

> Two daily expresses now leave London Bridge, and, on reaching Folkestone, the passengers, almost without a pause, step from the train into the steam-vessel, cross the Channel in about an hour and a half, and then, by *convoi à grande vitesse*, or express train, on the Great Northern of France, proceed to Paris, Brussels, and other chief points of attraction in various parts of the Continent. The time occupied en route is about as follows: London to Folkestone, 83 miles, 2 ½ hours; from Folkestone to Boulogne, 26 miles, 2 hours; from Boulogne to Paris, 170 miles, 6 ½ hours.[10]

In both Belgium and France, central government had become involved in the financing and designing of lines. As a rule, these were built more cheaply than in England, where the purchase of land and the cost of parliamentary representations were uniquely high. On the Continent, railways were laid down on routes which were not the most direct but were the easiest to engineer. There were none the less some amazing structures, such as the low bridge that crossed the Laguna Veneta into Venice with its 222 arches built on foundations of 80,000 larch-pole piles. And there were ambitious proposals for new lines everywhere, especially across the vast spaces of Russia – perhaps even a line from St Petersburg to Odessa, joining the Baltic and the Black Sea, a distance of 1,600 miles. At first, the Russians had been dependent on British rail technology, though getting equipment across the wilderness, especially in winter, required real bravado. To fulfil one order, Timothy Hackworth sent his teenage son to Russia with the parts for an engine. He found himself crossing an arctic landscape on a sledge, pursued at one point by a pack of wolves. The first railroads built in America had crossed wild country, and the experience of building them was clearly more relevant to the Russians than the British approach. A full report on the lines in the United States was made for the Tsar by an Austrian, F. von Gerstner, in 1842–3, while the first major line in Russia – between Moscow and St Petersburg – was begun in 1842.

Although by the middle of the nineteenth century steamships were crossing the Atlantic, the great age of the ocean liners was still a way off and plans to link distant parts of the world focused on railways. There was, for example, the great scheme to build a line 'from Calais to Calcutta'. Frederick Williams thought this quite feasible:

> ...the capitals of the eastern and western worlds may be brought
> into the distance of a seven days' journey! Instead of steam-ships,
> oceans, canals, rivers and camels, we are to have carriages and
> locomotives; and, by their aid, continents are to be traversed,
> mountain ranges crossed, and deserts to be tracked. Instead of
> harbours, there will be stations, instead of passing through straits

and seas, we shall fly over viaducts; instead of weaving a devious way among sandbanks and reefs, we shall be intersecting hills and whirling through tunnels.[11]

The Calais–Calcutta line would be 5,075 miles long, and would provide the traveller with a veritable panorama of exciting visions. Williams quotes a writer from the publication *The Eclectic Review*, who imagined 'rushing along an iron road, straight from west to east; of rattling at the heels of a locomotive through many countries in succession; of exchanging, in the course of one week, the bitter winds of England for the sultry calm of Bengal'.[12]

Within India, Williams was keen to point out, railways would be of immense value for moving around British troops who were currently allocated a single camel between two soldiers. But camels were slow, averaging only two miles an hour, expensive at £20 each and had a short working life. To move 30,000 troops would entail an expenditure of £300,000: how much more cost-effective and swifter to put them all on a new railway line and steam along at thirty miles an hour. Not only the defence of India, the serenity of which was perpetually threatened by 'hordes of semi-savages on its frontiers', but its commerce too, could be greatly enhanced by the building of railways.

Great lines were built right across America and eventually across Russia, and the steam railway became familiar in most parts of the world by the late nineteenth century. There was, however, one other region of Europe, not yet united to form a recognizable nation, in which the railways were destined to provide the vital breakthrough. Yet the man who did most to promote this new form of transport in his homeland endured a life of persecution and exile and came to a very sad end.

CHAPTER TEN

A PROPHET WITHOUT HONOUR

In the spring of 1817, a portly, bespectacled young man put up at an inn in the riverside town of Heilbronn in Württemberg, a region of what is now southern Germany. A few years earlier, Heilbronn had been a so-called imperial free city in what was then known, most misleadingly, as the Holy Roman Empire. The young man who had just arrived there had been born twenty-eight years earlier in another imperial free city, the little town of Reutlingen. Since that time, the outbreak of revolution in France in 1789 and the subsequent rise to power of Napoleon had swept away much of the semi-feudal world in which Heilbronn, Reutlingen and other cities of the Holy Roman Empire had existed for centuries. But the nation which in the century after 1817 was to become the world's third greatest industrial power remained economically backward. There was widespread discontent in Württemberg, and for the enterprising artisan the best hope for the future appeared to be emigration to the United States of America.

This was why the young government official Friedrich List had been sent to Heilbronn. The town was on the Neckar, a river which flowed into the great waterway of the Rhine – and the Rhine led directly to the ports of Holland from where ships regularly sailed for America. When List arrived at the quay in Heilbronn, he found more than six hundred bedraggled would-be emigrants. Not all of them would complete the journey, however; the authorities who had sent List to persuade them to stay feared that those who did not have the money to get to America would return home as paupers and become a burden on the state. List himself had hoped he might talk some of the emigrants out of leaving, for he was part of a movement campaigning to modernize Württemberg so that its people could benefit from the great advances in agriculture and industry that had been made in Britain, America and, latterly, in France. But he had little luck. His interviews revealed so many deep-seated grievances: the emigrants were impoverished by ancient tithes, by exorbitant local taxes which lined the pockets of a corrupt elite who employed dishonest, bullying and inefficient officials. Württemberg in those days still had a king whose court was attended by noblemen such as Herr von Weiler, whose herds of wild boar ravaged the countryside. Peasants were forced to work for landowners who still imposed feudal laws. Those from the town of Weinsberg complained that during the long years of war before Napoleon's defeat they constantly had troops billeted on them. One said memorably, if naively, 'We would rather be slaves in America than citizens in Weinsberg.'

List had also suffered from arbitrary and corrupt administration in his home town. In 1813 his elder brother Johannes died in an attempt to bypass the petty bureaucracy in Reutlingen. From time to time young men were conscripted into the army, though they could apply for exemption if they were over the age of twenty-five. Johannes was about to get married and applied to be excused military duty as he was over the age of compulsory service. When this was not forthcoming – it was neither granted nor refused – he set out on his horse for Stuttgart in the hope of obtaining his certificate of exemption there, but his horse stumbled and he was thrown. He died of his injuries two days later. Then, in 1815, List's mother died following an altercation with Reutlingen officials.

Born in 1789, List had spent his earliest days in a city relatively free of irksome laws. As a free city, Reutlingen was essentially self-governing: what it was 'free' of was interference from the wider administration of the Holy Roman Empire. The origins of this eccentric institution, of which the French philosopher Voltaire quipped that it was not Holy, nor Roman, nor an Empire, go back to the ninth century when Charlemagne was crowned emperor by the Pope in

Rome. Over the centuries, the territories that fell within the jurisdiction of various emperors – whose status would also be confirmed by their coronation in Rome – expanded enormously. Within them, there were many cities and principalities and bishoprics, all with so-called electors who had a say in choosing the emperor, whose appointment was not hereditary. Bit by bit, this originally papal and Catholic grouping underwent a series of transformations. With Martin Luther and the Protestant incursions, its Catholicism was challenged and in time the popes no longer had anything to do with the emperor. By the eighteenth century, France and the other nations which surrounded this dwindling medieval constellation of little states were whittling away at them. By the time List was born, the Empire was a huge anachronism and the French Revolution was about to set in motion a chain of events which would bring about its violent end. It was bound, anyway, to break down under the pressure from forces beyond its frontiers, notably the growing industrial power of Britain. But the way in which this came about, and the way in which it all affected the life of Friedrich List, is truly extraordinary.

One of the most prosperous of the free cities in the Holy Roman Empire was Frankfurt, which had arisen on the junction of trade routes through central Europe. By the eighteenth century, it was dominated by Lutheran merchants and artisans who were able to issue quite arbitrary laws and regulations. For centuries there had been within Frankfurt a single street called the Judenstrasse to which all Jews in the city were confined. This ghetto, and the regulations which confined Jews to it, represented repression on a quite unimaginable and barbaric scale. Officially, the maximum number of Jews allowed in Frankfurt was 500 but by the 1740s there were more than 3,000 people crammed into the housing of the Judenstrasse. At one entrance to the ghetto was an obscene mural, the Judensau, which was not the graffiti of an anti-Semitic group but the officially sanctioned representation of Frankfurt's opinion of the Jews. In it, several Jews are seen suckling from a sow, while one has his tongue out to eat the excrement which protrudes from her backside as the devil looks on.

Yet it was from this hideous enclave that a dynasty of financiers emerged who were to exert immense influence over both the development and fate of nineteenth-century Europe. To brighten their lives just a little, the owners of houses in the Judenstrasse gave them pretty or comical names: White Tulip, Tower, Golden Well, Crown of Roses, Saucepan, Elephant, Ship or Green Jar. One was called Red Shield (*Rothschild* in German) and had an emblem to match. On 23 February 1744, Mayer Amschel Rothschild was born here to a family which, like some other Frankfurt Jews, had made their money in trade. As a boy Mayer was forbidden to leave the Judenstrasse without a special pass and could visit none of the town's coffee houses or shops, but nevertheless his father was able to send him to a Jewish school. However, when he was twelve years old, both his parents died in one of the frequent epidemics that swept through Frankfurt. Mayer had two brothers and a sister still living in the Judenstrasse, but he was sent to work in a firm in Hanover owned by a man who had probably been a business associate of his father. This was Wolf Jacob Oppenheim, who had the lucrative position of court agent, handling the money of one of the wealthy electors of the Holy Roman Empire.

When he returned to the Judenstrasse in 1764, Mayer was already an experienced wheeler-dealer. His first business was in coins and medals which he acquired for the local dignitary, Prince William of Hesse-Kassel. Mayer continued to deal in these and in antiques, buying for his wealthy client and taking a cut for himself. His brother Kalman joined him in the business. In 1769 Mayer was officially made William's court agent and in 1770, when he was just twenty-six, he married Gutle, the sixteen-year-old daughter of another court agent, Wolf Salomon Schnapper, thereby acquiring a valuable dowry on his wedding day.

Mayer's first tranche of modest wealth came from the sale of all kinds of trinkets, coins and medals to aristocratic collectors by what we would now call mail order. As Mayer began to amass enough wealth to move into banking, his young wife bore him one child after another. Their first child was born in 1771 and for the next nineteen years Gutle was apparently pregnant, giving birth to perhaps nineteen children of whom ten survived beyond infancy. Of these, five sons would one day be amongst the most famous – or notorious, depending on your viewpoint – men in Europe. Amschel Mayer was born in 1773, Salomon in 1774, Nathan Mayer in 1777, Kalman or Carl in 1788 and

Jakob or James in 1792. The Rothschild daughters were never allowed to work in the family businesses.

In contrast with Britain, or even with France at the end of the eighteenth century, most German states were industrially backward. There were attempts to lure British artisans to a number of cities to build steam engines or establish the latest spinning equipment, but the wealth of the elite was not founded in manufacturing. One great source of riches, which came Mayer Rothschild's way indirectly, was the sale of young peasants as soldiers to foreign armies. The father of Elector William, for whom Mayer became in effect a kind of stockbroker, had made a fortune selling armies of his subjects to the English when they were fighting the American revolutionaries in the War between 1775 and 1783. Treated like livestock, these serfs earned money for their owner when they died in battle as there was a special rate of compensation.

Mayer's patron, William, was a shrewd investor of the family fortune, putting a great deal of it into bonds issued in London and lending to other princes and minor monarchs who were short of cash. The Rothschilds' first fortune was based partly on the commission Mayer received for the buying and selling of this potentate's investments and loans. After the outbreak of revolution in France, however, Frankfurt came under threat and was invaded by French troops in 1792. A bombardment destroyed a large part of the Judenstrasse and for a while the ghetto was opened up. Then Napoleon's armies began to move eastward in great sweeps, culminating in the victory over the Austrians at the Battle of Austerlitz in 1805. The imposition of the Code Napoleon, an entirely new set of laws, swept away much of the archaic legislation of the old Holy Roman Empire, and ancient states were amalgamated and rationalized as Napoleon sought to reward those who sided with him and punish those who opposed him. Officially, the Holy Roman Empire came to an end in 1806.

Meanwhile, the outpourings of consumer goods from the first industrial nation was having a serious impact in Frankfurt and other German cities. The trademark goods were the fine cotton textiles woven from the threads now mass-produced in the great spinning mills of Derbyshire and Lancashire. On quality and price they were far superior to anything produced in Frankfurt or the textile towns of the ailing Holy Roman Empire and Mayer Rothschild and other tradespeople from the Judenstrasse did a lively trade in them. To make the buying and shipping of goods more efficient, several Frankfurt dealers sent agents to act for them in England.

Around 1800, Mayer Rothschild followed suit, dispatching Nathan, then twenty-three, to Manchester. Nathan proved to be as astute a businessman as his father and made a success of the textile business. For much of the time he had to trade across the Channel when this was illegal, as war between England and France broke out in 1803 and continued until the final defeat of Napoleon at Waterloo. Nathan was in continual correspondence with his father, the family evolving their own codes and writing in the local dialect called Judendeutsch, a mixture of Hebrew and Frankfurt German that was written from right to left in Hebrew letters. (Yiddish was not the language of the Judenstrasse.) One by one, Nathan's brothers took up strategic positions, James in France, Salomon in Vienna and Carl in Naples. The eldest brother, Amschel, took over the Frankfurt business when their father died in 1812.

Nathan and James between them played a large part in the defeat of Napoleon, though they made their fortunes in a manner very different from that related in one of the most popular stories about them. In 1811 Nathan had abandoned the textile business in Manchester and moved to London, where he became established as a financier. Like his father's business, Nathan's relied on the transfer of sums of money, either legally or illegally, from those who wanted to lend it to those who needed hard cash. And nobody was in greater need of cash than the British forces pitted against Napoleon and his allies in Europe. Fighting in Spain and Portugal, the Duke of Wellington was continually embarrassed by a lack of money to pay his troops, who were liable to desert or pillage the countryside if left with empty pockets for too long.

Although British industry had made huge advances in the eighteenth century, and its naval cannons were probably the most reliable and most efficiently manned in Europe, there was no significant new weaponry available to Wellington or his allies. At sea, the American Robert Fulton's torpedoes and submarines had been deemed worthless and Trafalgar had been won in classic and traditional style. On land, things were much the same: the rockets developed by William Congreve which had been fired ineffectually during the British-American war of 1812 were to make another brief and unspectacular appearance at the Battle of Waterloo. In the wars in Spain, the new sharp-shooter brigades, equipped with rifles that possessed a greater range and accuracy than muskets, were deployed to good effect. But for the big set-piece battles, it was still the infantry formed up in a square who repelled a cavalry charge. Muskets were crude, but they were quicker to reload than the early rifles and still the favoured weapon at Waterloo.

The chief contribution to Britain's final defeat of the French was not weaponry as such but money. It has been estimated that the wars between 1793 and 1815 cost Britain well over £800 million. No other European country had the resources to combat the French so it fell to Britain to subsidize Napoleon's enemies, buying the weaponry they needed, providing money for their troops and shoring up their economies. Napoleon's attempts to isolate Britain by decreeing in 1806 what became known as the Continental System were largely a failure. Trade with Britain was outlawed but the borders were full of holes. Certainly the Rothschilds, principally Nathan and James, found it relatively easy to smuggle bullion through France into Spain to fund Wellington's campaigns. The Rothschilds, who enjoyed the cloak-and-dagger nature of these lucrative operations, adopting codenames such as 'Jerusalem' for London and 'Rabbi Moses' for transfers of funds, also shipped money to Russia and Prussia. They oiled the wheels of these transactions with backhanders for officials where this was thought necessary to secure the business, although in reality they had few rivals.

As international bankers, the Rothschilds developed their own courier services, sometimes using carrier pigeons for the latest news, and it is probably this aspect of their operations which gave rise to the myth that they profited by being the first to receive the news of Wellington's victory at Waterloo. The legend has it that Nathan fooled the City by selling shares when he heard of Napoleon's defeat so that everyone else would believe the French had been victorious. In a panic, other investors followed his lead and sold, driving down the price of stock. Nathan promptly bought it all up, knowing that, when the City realized the rumour of Napoleon's victory was false, bond and share prices would rise again, making Nathan a huge profit. The truth, however, is that Nathan did get advanced news of the victory but he did not use this inside information to fool the Stock Exchange. Instead, he immediately passed the news on to the British government. As it was, the end of the Napoleonic Wars took away a good deal of lucrative business from the Rothschilds but by that time they were fabulously wealthy anyway and ready for new challenges.

Whereas the Rothschild brothers, raised in a cramped room in Frankfurt's Judenstrasse, made a brilliant success of the Napoleonic period, Friedrich List, the son of a moderately successful tanner, had a tough time of it. On the death of his elder brother and then of his mother, he was obliged for a while to help run the family business in Reutlingen. After that, he was able to pursue his career as a civil servant, and he made great efforts to reform the corrupt and inefficient service from within, writing critical reports and articles. In 1817 he became a Professor of Public Administration at Tübingen University, advocating all the time the establishment of a better qualified and an honest civil service. List fell foul of the university authorities, partly because of his critical views, but chiefly because he agreed in 1818 to become secretary of a newly formed group calling themselves the Union of Merchants and campaigned to end the multitude of customs duties that inhibited trade between various regions of the former Holy Roman Empire.

List took up the campaign for a customs union or *Zollverein* in which all the duties and restrictions which prevented trade between regions – wine from the south, for example, being charged duty in the north – would be abolished. He made more than one attempt to stand for the local assembly at Württemberg. He was elected first in 1819 but disqualified, as he could not prove he was over the eligible age of thirty: his baptismal certificate did not state exactly when he was born. He finally got a seat on the assembly in December 1820 and continued to argue for the modernization of his region of southern Germany, beginning with the removal of local tariffs. That was not too contentious an issue, though little notice was taken of it. But List went further and put his name to a petition calling for the abolition of punitive taxes on goods and the introduction of some kind of wealth tax. This brought immediate response from the King of Württemberg – who despite the assembly remained a powerful figure – and less than two months after the start of his political career List was arrested for sedition.

The wheels of Württemberg law ground slowly, but finally List was convicted in his absence and in April 1822 sentenced to ten months' imprisonment in a fortress. He had time to make a run for it and, as he put it, like 'a thief in the night' made his escape to France. He possessed no passport and had to avoid border guards, hiring boats to cross the rivers. He was stopped by customs officials in France but they let him go and he set up home in Strasburg. By now, he had a reputation as a potentially dangerous liberal, and the authorities in Württemberg asked the mayor of Strasburg to keep an eye on List. In effect, he was on the run and was soon hounded out of the city.

In 1818 List had married a widow who had a young son but they saw little of each other as he was always on the move and found it hard to keep in touch. For a while he lived in Switzerland. A recollection of him in 1823 captures something of the wild indignation of the man. A friend, Wolfgang Menzel, had been in a party with List on a boat trip on the Vierwaldstatter See:

> As we crossed the lake, List recounted his experiences and burst into a storm of abuse against the Württemberg 'scribblers'. In his anger he rose up, clenched his fists, gnashed his teeth, and shouted: 'Those damned clerks!' He rocked the boat, stumbled and would have drowned had we not seized him. He was the most impetuous man whom I have ever met – still young, but already corpulent. Anyone who had seen him once would surely never forget that short squat frame crowned by a disproportionately large leonine head. His eyes sparkled, thunder played round his fine brow, and his lips were as fiery as the crater of Vesuvius.[1]

As it turned out, List was not safe even in Switzerland. He contemplated going to America and in 1824 paid a brief visit to England, staying chiefly in London. Later he would say that his interest in railways was aroused then, though what he saw in London at that time is not clear. The only line he could have visited would have been the horse-drawn Surrey Iron Railway. In the end he was persuaded by friends to return to Stuttgart, where he was offered work writing for the liberal newspaper *Neckar Zeitung*. Within a few days of his arrival at the beginning of August 1824, List was arrested and locked up in Württemberg's state prison, the Hohenasperg fortress. He remained there for five months of his ten-month sentence, arguing as always but enjoying certain freedoms: he was allowed to have his four-year-old son with him for a while. Uncertain what to do with List, the authorities finally came to an agreement with him that he would be released provided he left Württemberg for good. Australia was suggested, but he said he preferred the United States.

And so it was, only eight years after List had tried to persuade the disenchanted emigrants at Heilbronn to stay at home and not risk the long journey to America, he was on his way himself. But he did not hurry to cross the Atlantic and he never had any intention of settling for good in the United States. At first he thought he might be able to go no further than Strasburg, but the authorities waved him on as he had only a transit visa. He stayed for a while in Paris before, finally and reluctantly, taking a ship on 26 April 1825 from the French port of Le Havre bound for New York.

The United States was to be List's true university. It was here that he evolved the political ideas which one day he hoped to persuade his fatherland to adopt. There are political and economic theorists today who still regard List's analyses as superior to those of Karl Marx or Adam Smith. Whereas Marx's view was that industrialism in its capitalist form would inevitably lead to the same kind of social and economic structure wherever it spread, List's view was that industrialism took different forms in different countries. He was at odds with Adam Smith because he did not accept that trade tarrifs and protectionism was always bad: for nations just beginning to industrialize they were essential. List called his economic theory the 'American System'.

On his arrival there, List was shown around initially by the Marquis de Lafayette, whom he had met in Paris and who was a war hero in America, having fought with George Washington against the British. List settled in Reading, Pennsylvania where there was a German community, and was soon involved with railroad and canal schemes which were already underway. He joined the management of the Little Schuylkill River Navigation, Railroad and Canal Company as a means of earning a living. This was a scheme which was still hedging its bets between horse-drawn railroads, steam trains and inclined planes and was borrowing what it could of British technology under the influence of Moncure Robinson and others who had made the European engineering pilgrimage.

By his own admission, List had not thought much about the vital part transport played in the development of economies before he arrived in America. Nor had he really sorted out his ideas about the best way for a developing economy – as Germany's would have to be – to prosper. In the year he arrived in the United States, he found that a debate was taking place about that very issue, one which was to trouble any nation that wanted to challenge British industrial supremacy in the nineteenth century. Their own Revolution had been fought to free the colonists from the imperial yoke and the Americans were intent thereafter, as earlier chapters have made clear, to develop their own industries, borrowing whatever they could from Britain. However, there was disagreement over whether they should model themselves on British enterprise, which was initially funded entirely by private capital, or use government funds to get new industries underway and protect them from foreign competition while they were becoming established. John Quincy Adams, who was elected president shortly after List's arrival in America, was an advocate of this interventionist policy. His opponent, Andrew Jackson, despite his staunch opposition to Britain in the revolutionary war, was an ardent free trader.

List found himself emotionally drawn to Jackson, who was supported by the Pennsylvania Germans, though philosophically he was on the side of Adams and an economic policy in which government played a vital part as a promoter and protector of indigenous industry. List became a fierce opponent of Adam Smith, whom he regarded, not without reason, as someone who had failed to understand what was going on in his own country; not recognizing, even in 1776 when his *Wealth of Nations* was published, the importance of the steam engine, which was by then beginning to transform the British economy. For a short while, List tried farming in America, without success, but he did observe first-hand the rapid transformation that country was undergoing, writing:

Here you see rich and powerful states arise out of the wilderness. It was here that it first became clear to me how the economy of a people develops step by step. A process which required a succession of centuries in Europe unfolds here in front of our eyes – the transition from a condition of wilderness into animal husbandry, then into a developed agriculture, followed by manufacturing and commerce. Here you can observe how the landowner's income increases gradually, from nothing at all to considerable levels. Here the simple farmer understands the practical means for elevating agriculture and his income far better than the shrewd scholars in the Old World; he seeks to draw manufacturers and industries into his vicinity.[2]

Although he always intended to return to Europe, List applied for, and was granted, American citizenship in October 1830. This meant that he could now apply to be a representative of the United States in his own country or some other region of Europe. Through his friendship with Andrew Jackson, now President, List was made honorary American consul to Hamburg. But neither the free traders in the US Senate nor the burghers of Hamburg would ratify the appointment. Meanwhile, List had obtained a commission to go to Paris to discuss the issue of reparations between France and America, but this, again, turned out to be an abortive expedition.

List was back in America in 1831 and intent on becoming the American consul in Baden. While this was being discussed, the consul in Leipzig died and List was given the post of American consul in the Kingdom of Saxony. He was now in a position to get involved in one of his cherished projects, the building of a railway line between Leipzig and Dresden. This would go hand in hand with a freeing up of trade between at least some of the thirty-nine different states in Prussia and the Rhineland. In a petition before he was banished from Württemberg, List had written:

Thirty-eight customs boundaries cripple inland commerce, and produce much the same effect as ligatures which prevent the free circulation of the blood. The merchant trading between Hamburg and Austria or Berlin and Switzerland must traverse ten states, must learn ten customs tariffs, must pay ten successive transit dues. Anyone who is so unfortunate as to live on the boundary line between three or four states spends his days among hostile tax gatherers and custom house officials; he is a man without a country ... Only the remission of the internal customs, and the erection of a general tariff for the whole Federation, can restore national trade and industry and help the working classes.[3]

During 1833, Prussia managed to get agreement from a large part of the old Holy Roman Empire, including List's Württemberg, to join a customs union comprising fourteen states and 23.5 million people. At dawn on 1 January 1834 the wagons began to roll through open toll gates and within a few years the *Zollverein* was judged to be a tremendous success in promoting commerce and industry. But there was still a great debate about whether or not free trade was the best stimulus for the emerging German economy. List argued that for the few years of Napoleon's Continental System, native industries had benefited from protection from cheap British goods. Some textile manufacturers certainly had, but few counted the banning of trade with Britain a success and the free traders argued that the Continental System had been overall a disaster for manufacturers and industry.

By the time he had returned from America, where he had met the railroad engineer Moncure Robinson, List had become a huge enthusiast for railways. He sought to promote them wherever he went in Europe, travelling to Belgium and to Paris, where in 1837 he met King Louis Philippe and Thiers, the man who had rebuffed Charles Blacker Vignoles four years earlier. Thiers tried to entice List to France, offering him a government post at a handsome salary, but without success.

As everywhere else in the rapidly developing world, railway projects came in fits and starts, some projected and funded entirely with private capital, others with state loans, subsidies or straightforward government investment. In London, Nathan Rothschild expressed a distaste for the new form of travel, writing on one occasion that he would not make a meeting in Calais as 'railway travelling makes my head ache so terribly that I really can not make up my mind to a thirty hours' shaking'. But his brothers James in Paris and Salomon in Vienna were caught up in the excitement of the first phase of railway-building in Europe. The very first line in what might be called List territory was the short run from Nuremberg to Fürth in Bavaria, which was opened as a passenger railway at the very end of 1835 with a Robert Stephenson locomotive, the *Adler* or *Eagle*, providing the power. Salomon Rothschild was a promoter and financier for the first line built in Austro-Hungary, dubbed the Kaiser-Ferdinands Nordband, the first section of which was opened in 1837. The intention was that it would eventually run to the salt mines at Kracow but that section was never built. The first sections of the Dresden to Leipzig line were opened in 1839.

The fragmentation of Germany's administration meant that individual states took different views on whether public money should be put into railway-building. As in America, there was a mixture of schemes. Free traders were generally opposed to government intervention of this sort, whereas the List camp argued that to get things rolling and to keep British technology at arm's length, public finance was necessary, if only in the early stages of development. List argued for the creation of a national network of railway lines linking principal cities and industrial regions, but this was not possible. The Belgians, and a little later, the French, came the nearest to that ideal. Nevertheless, the piecemeal development of lines in the regions of the defunct Holy Roman Empire turned out to be more vigorous than in France. By 1850, Germany already had in operation 5,856 kilometres of railway compared with France's modest 2,996 kilometres.

Despite Nathan Rothschild's distaste for railway travel and railway speculation, the European branch of the family were important couriers of British capital which was liberally distributed around the Continent as City of London speculators continued to put their trust in railway shares, which could be enormously profitable. Towards the end of his troubled life, Friedrich List saw part of his vision for Germany fulfilled, with the first railway lines built and the *Zollverein* established over a wide area, but he never felt that he had accomplished much and continued to argue bitterly with his political opponents. One of List's most vociferous detractors was an Englishman who had settled in the north of Germany and rejoiced in the name of John Prince-Smith. He was born in London in 1809, the son of a barrister. At the age of eight, he went with his father to Demerara, a British colony on the northeast coast of South America. When he was eleven, he was sent to Eton, the most prestigious English public school. He had been there only two years when his father died and he had to leave and make his way in the world. At thirteen he was apprenticed to a City of London merchant house, after which he worked as a banker's clerk and part-time parliamentary reporter and journalist. It was as a journalist that he went to Hamburg in 1830, moving in 1831 to the Prussian port of Elbing to become a school teacher.

Elbing and the other Prussian ports had a good trade with Britain, shipping out corn and timber and bringing in manufactured goods. These Baltic ports lay outside the Prussian customs union, however, and therefore found that trade they should have enjoyed was carried away from them on the River Rhine. Prince-Smith learned of this and joined the Elbing Wednesday Club, a debating society and pressure group formed by merchants, all of whom were free traders and opposed to the barrier the *Zollverein* presented to those outside its borders. Like List, Prince-Smith became a prolific writer of pamphlets and by 1840 devoted all his time to free trade propaganda. Whereas List wanted to protect nascent industries from British competition with high import tariffs, Prince-Smith wanted the tariffs lifted to promote the trade of the Baltic ports. Both Prince-Smith and List professed a desire to see the lot of the working classes improve as they believed they undoubtedly had in industrial Britain. Yet they disagreed fiercely on how this would be best achieved. Prince-Smith by and large followed the philosophy of his namesake, Adam Smith, believing that any form of protection distorted the market for goods of all kinds and was ultimately inefficient. He disliked government spending because the money tended to go on arms and the military.

Over the years, right up until Germany's spectacular industrial take off after unification in 1871, the argument over free trade ebbed and flowed. In reality, the *Zollverein* underwent many adjustments during its existence and was both a protectionist measure in relation to those outside it, and a free trade measure for those within its boundaries. It was certainly an economic success, with revenue from duties nearly doubling between 1834 and 1845. The transport revolution brought about by the building of railways was, however, more significant than any other innovation in mid-nineteenth-century Germany. Very soon the lines linked formerly isolated coalfields with cities and manufacturing districts. This stimulated mining, and the demand for steam engines to pump out deep workings and to pull coal wagons and raise pit cages grew rapidly. Whereas there had been only 419 steam engines in Prussia in 1837, twelve years later there were 1,444. Some of these engines drove spinning mills on the English model, and a few the new power weaving looms which had taken over from the hand-loom weavers in Britain in the 1820s. Coke-smelting of iron began and very rapidly all the innovations of eighteenth-century Britain were introduced. The demand for iron was increased not only by the building of railways but the growth of steamship navigation on the Rhine and the Elbe. Germany was beginning to industrialize and to fulfil List's dream of a prosperous Württemberg.

But Friedrich List did not live to see his fatherland – which he once said he loved as a parent loves a 'sick child' – become a great force in the world. Not unlike William James, the English railway promoter, List was a sacrificial figure in industrial development and he came to an even sadder end. In 1846 he was working as a journalist, but he had virtually no income and was dependent on his wife's capital for survival. This was barely adequate to make ends meet. At the age of fifty-seven he showed signs of mental distress and, according to a friend, was full of 'veritable hare-brained literary schemes'. He began to complain of headaches and felt feverish. In November 1846 he took a trip to the Tyrol, where he hoped warmer weather would help him recover. He wrote to his wife that he would go via Innsbruck. When he reached the picturesque town of Kufstein in the northern Tyrol, he put up at an inn, asking for the cheapest room. He stayed in his little hotel room for two days, refusing to leave or to see a doctor. On the morning of 30 November, he left and did not return. He was not seen alive again. It was two days before his body was found in the Tyrolean countryside. List had shot himself in the head. When a search was made for his belongings, it was discovered that he had no luggage with him, which suggested he had planned to commit suicide. An inquest concluded that he had killed himself while 'suffering from such a degree of melancholia as to render him incapable of thinking clearly or of acting rationally'.[4]

It is tempting to suggest that List would have done much better to have stayed in the United States, where his talents were recognized, and he could perhaps have fulfilled his dream of steering a nascent economy towards some kind of maturity. But he was too passionately nationalistic for that and his ambition to rescue the 'sick' German economy proved to be his downfall. For others, however, America remained a land of opportunity and it was no particular concern of theirs if, in pursuing their own careers, they boosted the economy of a nation which might in time rival their own.

By the time of List's death, the United States was rapidly becoming a powerful industrial nation. But there remained huge checks on its further development. Canals had been cut and railways laid down. There were powder works such as those of du Pont and spinning mills for both wool and cotton. But remarkably, even in the 1830s, coal had not become a significant fuel in America. It was not that the United States did not have any: there were millions of tons of it. The problem was that, for certain vital industrial purposes, it was simply the wrong sort of coal. Despite enormous efforts, Americans failed to solve this problem and were driven to buy in the answer from Britain. Thus it was that a Welshman and his family, armed with an invaluable piece of Scottish know-how, laid the foundations for the growth of the American economy in the second half of the nineteenth century.

CHAPTER ELEVEN

A BLAST OF HOT AIR

In the first week of May 1839, a studious-looking man in his forties boarded a steamer at the port of Swansea and waved farewell to the valleys of Glamorgan where he had been born and had made a name for himself in the iron industry. With David Thomas were his wife, whose ambition had persuaded him to leave his homeland, and his three sons. The coastal steamer took them to Liverpool, where they were to embark for New York and a new life in America. There were no railways then between the Welsh coalfields and Liverpool, and to take a steamship across the Atlantic was still very much a novelty. The Thomases chose instead to sail on the clipper *Roscius*, which made a good crossing in twenty-three days, just four days behind the steamer *Great Western*, which had left Liverpool at the same time.

The family were confined to New Brighton on Staten Island for a month as David was laid low with a fever. It was early summer before he was able to travel with his son Samuel to Philadelphia to meet the American mine-owners who had enticed him across the Atlantic. Father and son then set out for the Lehigh Valley, where David Thomas was to work his magic on the Pennsylvanian coalfields. It was here that great beds of anthracite coal had been found and the Lehigh companies were intent on cutting canals and building railroads to ship this coal to towns and industrial regions.

At the time Thomas first set foot in America, the coal industry there was in its infancy. Timber still made up 80 per cent of the fuel used to heat homes, drive steam engines and to provide heat and power of various kinds in the United States. Anthracite coal provided just 14 per cent of the nation's fuel. The kind of coal Thomas had worked with for most of his life in Wales was the abundant British soft bituminous coal which had been mined for centuries. It was this coal that had first been used to make coke, a development which began the revolution in British iron-making as it freed the furnaces from reliance on charcoal. It had taken at least half a century for coke-produced pig iron to become common in England and another fifty years for a revolution to come about in the way pig iron was turned into wrought iron with the tensile strength necessary for railway tracks and bridges and girders of various kinds.

A first major breakthrough had been that made by a Lancastrian, Henry Cort, who came to iron-making through his work as a prize agent for the Royal Navy and marriage to the niece of an ironmonger, William Attwick, who supplied Portsmouth dockyards with anchors, chains and many other items to the tune of 200 tons a year. In 1783, Cort had patented a method of turning scrap iron – barrel hoops at first – into good-quality wrought iron by a method known as puddling and rolling. The scrap was melted down with raw coal and the end product, which was carefully evaluated by the navy, turned out to be as good as the bar iron formerly imported at great expense from Sweden and Russia. Though Cort had tried to retain his patent, he was bankrupted when it was discovered that his business partner, Adam Jellicoe, deputy paymaster of the Navy Pay Office, had illegally loaned Cort money. It was only after Jellicoe's death that this was revealed, along with the devastating news that Cort's patents had been given as surety and he was liable for Jellicoe's debts. Cort, the father of twelve children, died in 1800 at the age of sixty, ruined and destitute. But his method of producing wrought iron had spread rapidly and by the 1830s Britain was well on the way to making half the world's iron.

All the fuel for this iron was, by that time, soft bituminous coal. In Britain the seams of the much harder anthracite coal, known variously as 'splint coal' or 'stone coal', were hardly exploited. There were bands of ironstone, too, but these were worthless because they could not be used by the technology available at the time. The necessary breakthrough in the use of anthracite coal and low-grade ores came in the 1830s when James Neilson, the young manager of a gasworks in Glasgow, Scotland, had the inspiration to turn one of the traditional beliefs of ironmasters on its head. It had always been easier to smelt good-quality iron in winter than in summer and the reasonable assumption had been made that furnaces worked better at low ambient temperatures. Neilson discovered that the reverse was true and that much greater quantities of good-quality iron could be produced if the furnace was superheated by a blast of hot air. In 1828, in partnership with three others, one of whom was George Macintosh, inventor of waterproofing, Neilson took out a patent for the hot-blast furnace. It was improved over the next few years and it was this innovation that, ten years later, had David Thomas on his way to America.

The son of a Welsh farmer, Thomas was born in 1794 and brought up to a strict moral and religious code by a pious father, who was a church warden and overseer of the poor. Though the family had little money, Thomas was an only child and, when he showed promise at school, the funds were found to send him to a fee-paying college. At the age of seventeen, he went to work at Neath Abbey ironworks, which had two blast furnaces and made pumping engines for Cornwall and a range of mining machinery. After five years there learning his trade, which included erecting pumping engines in Cornwall, Thomas moved on to become superintendent of Ynyscedwyn ironworks, where he established himself as a highly skilled and knowledgeable ironmaster and mining engineer.

At more or less the same time as James Neilson in Glasgow was experimenting with his novel hot-blast furnace, David Thomas in Wales was trying to find a way to make use of the rich seams of anthracite coal and black band ironstone which lay together unexploited beneath the Ynyscedwyn ironworks. He was given encouragement by George Crane, who bought the works in 1823 on his retirement from a successful hardware business in Birmingham. But all Thomas's efforts to turn anthracite coal into coke were a failure. So too were the efforts of those on the other side of the Atlantic who were experimenting with smelting iron with Pennsylvania anthracite.

For Thomas and his boss, George Crane, the failure was frustrating but not fatal for their business. For their American counterparts, however, the impossibility of exploiting the rich anthracite seams and iron ore deposits for smelting was a serious impediment to the industrial development of the United States. There was then no deep mining of bituminous coal in America and all iron was still smelted with charcoal. And a huge amount of United States demand, especially with the rise of the railways, was supplied, at great expense, by Britain.

Some time after James Neilson had patented his hot-blast furnace, Thomas and Crane discussed the possibility that it might be just what was needed to make use of their anthracite coal and black band ore. In 1836, Thomas went to Glasgow, discussed the matter with Neilson, obtained a licence to employ the hot-blast system – a legal nicety a number of Neilson's Scottish competitors ignored – and set to work. Furnaces had to be completely redesigned, but within a year or so Thomas had them working and producing good-quality pig iron, using anthracite as fuel to smelt black band ore.

From 1837, the Ynyscedwyn ironworks went over to hot-blast furnace production entirely and the news of Thomas's success caused excitement in Pennsylvania soon after. It appears that the first American to learn about the new process was a man called Solomon White Roberts, who was in Wales buying iron rails for a Philadelphia company that supplied the new lines being laid on the east coast of the United States. He wrote to his uncle, Josiah White, who was a manager of the Lehigh Coal and Navigation Company which owned huge reserves of anthracite coal. In December the following year a manager of that company, Erskine Hazard, and his son arrived in Wales and knocked on Thomas's door. They inspected the furnaces, saw that they were ideal for their purposes and discussed with George Crane how they might take the technology back home. For reasons which are not clear, Crane suggested they take Thomas. Already well into his forties, Thomas was not keen to go and, according to his son Samuel, it was his wife who urged him to take the opportunity. He signed an agreement with a newly created firm called the Lehigh Crane Iron Company, after George Crane, who invested only his name in the venture.

Once David Thomas had recovered from his fever, he and his family duly set off in July 1839 from New Brighton to the Lehigh Valley, where they were to establish a brand-new home and a brand-new industry. They went part of the way by railroad, from New Jersey to New Brunswick. In his reminiscences, Samuel mentioned that the locomotive ran on strap-rails – lengths of timber with a strip of iron nailed on top. This was some indication to him and his father that the American iron industry was still in its infancy. These strap-rails were a serious hazard, for when the nails which held them down worked loose, the iron strip would whip up like a spring and smash through the floor of the fragile timber coach-style carriages. Americans called these rogue iron strips 'snake heads' and there were many tales of their destructive power. A conductor from the early days of the Buffalo and Niagara Falls Railway recalled one such incident. 'I remember a narrow escape a young lady had. She was reading a novel and quietly enjoying her ride, when suddenly and with a crash, the end of a rail tore up between her feet, went through her skirt, and fastened itself to the roof of the car! We had to cut the lady's dress in order to rescue her.'[1]

All there was for David Thomas to build on when they reached the Lehigh Valley was a site and a stream. A watermill had to be put up, to his specifications, to drive the bellows for the blast. Many of the component parts for the furnace had to be shipped out from Wales. Two cylinders were left behind because they would not go into the hold of the clipper and it took Thomas some time to find American ironmasters who could bore anything the size that they needed. While the ironworks were being constructed, a house was built for the family close by which became the nucleus of the town of Catasauqua.

David Thomas effectively created the foundations of an entirely new industry from scratch, and few other pioneers have managed as much. He had to find the materials to construct what was to be the largest furnace erected in the United States, and he had to open up new iron ore mines. The demands he made on American ironmasters stimulated them to produce a new range of cylinders, and as pig iron production increased hugely, so the dependence of America on timber, the supply of which was shrinking with the spread of agriculture, began to lessen. The first of Thomas's furnaces was 'blown in' at five in the afternoon on 3 July 1840: it had all taken him a day less than a year since his arrival in America, an astonishing feat. A freshet or flash flood briefly put the furnace out of action but it was soon back in production and had turned out 3,316 tons of pig iron by August 1842, when construction of a second furnace began.

Samuel Thomas, who was only thirteen when he first helped his father create the new ironworks, recalled that a local charcoal iron smelter had ridiculed them, saying he would 'eat' any iron they managed to smelt with anthracite. David invited him to a dinner cooked in the furnace by way of settling the wager amicably. More furnaces were built, Thomas was consulted on the construction of these by other ironmasters, and very rapidly the American iron industry took off. Until 1845, all the power of the Crane Iron Company was provided by watermills on the river. From that time on, after much discussion, the company switched to steam power.

By 1850, about half of America's pig iron was made in anthracite-fuelled, hot-blast furnaces, and about a quarter of all iron made was in the Lehigh region where Thomas had first established a furnace. The speed with which he and his fellow Welsh iron-workers who came out to join him were able to exploit the raw materials in Pennsylvania and to teach others to do the same was an indication of the increasing pace of industrialization. A century and a half of experience and experimentation had resulted in the knowledge Thomas took with him to America. It had begun with Abraham Darby's successful smelting of iron with coke at Coalbrookdale and developed through the use of steam engines to provide the blast, the innovations of Wilkinson, the efforts of Cort and others, the inspiration of Neilson and, finally, the flash of insight of David Thomas and George Crane.

Though it was Crane who was keen for Thomas to go to America, he himself did not prosper as he perhaps imagined he would. The two wrote to each other regularly, sometimes about business and sometimes with news of their families and social activities. Crane at one time seemed agitated about the amount of time he had to spend organizing shipments of equipment to America, not all of which reached their destination. He made a half-hearted attempt to enforce a patent when other ironmasters started to use the hot-blast furnace. In 1846 a despondent mood overcame him and he drank some liniment, thinking it was cough mixture, and died of poisoning.

David Thomas, however, did well for himself. In 1854, when he was sixty, he formed the Thomas Iron Company with his son Samuel as superintendent. The works were established at Hokendauqua, Pennsylvania, and became one of the most successful in America. Though virtually unknown in Britain outside his native South Wales, he became a celebrated figure in the United States and was awarded the sobriquet 'Papa' Thomas in his distinguished old age. He lived to the age of eighty-eight, dying in 1882.

What might be called the 'anthracite era' in American iron-making history lasted all of Thomas's lifetime and beyond and laid the foundations for the great Philadelphia steel industry. Later, abundant bituminous coal deposits were found in Pennsylvania and other States, and the American iron and steel industry was freed of its dependence on anthracite. As people and industry moved westwards across America from the 1850s onwards, extensive deposits of easily mined iron ore were discovered, much of it in the region of the Great Lakes, and with steam-driven river and rail transport this could be shipped to the newly worked bituminous coal fields. New techniques for forging iron and, above all, for the manufacture of steel that could draw on America's vast reserves of coal and ore soon made the United States by far and away the biggest producers in the world.

In Britain, the rise of the coke-smelted iron industry long predated the practical application of electricity to communications. However, in the United States, as the country began to catch up with European industrial advance, the establishment of the iron industry by David Thomas coincided with the introduction of the electric telegraph. It has long been a cherished article of faith among Americans that anything electric – whether the telegraph, the light bulb or wireless – was their invention. A case in point is the belief that the first message sent by electric telegraph was transmitted by a man called Morse in 1844. The message read 'What hath God wrought!' and such an apocalyptic statement suggested that nothing like this had ever been achieved before. Yet in reality the electric telegraph had by then a long and interesting history, one which had unfolded not in America but Europe.

CHAPTER TWELVE

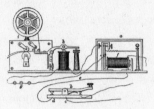

MORSE DECODED

On 15 April 1837, Samuel Finley Breese Morse, a well-known but not very successful painter who was struggling to make a living in New York after a sojourn in Europe, was enraged by an item printed in the city's *Observer* newspaper, published by his younger brothers. The article concerned two Frenchmen who were in the United States to sell their brilliant new form of telegraph communication which could transmit information across continents in a matter of minutes. It came as some relief to Professor Morse (an academic at New York University) that the French invention was merely a version of the hilltop telegraph relays that had existed in Europe for some time. Telescopes rather than the naked eye were used to read messages over long distances, provided, of course, the sun was up and the skies were clear.

However, hard on the heels of this piece of news came further items about electric telegraphs being developed in Europe. These once again aroused the indignation of Professor Morse, for he believed that he was the only man in history who had ever thought of such an apparatus. In his rooms at New York University were some bits of equipment he had been tinkering with for some time – five years, in fact. But it does not appear to have occurred to Morse that the discoveries of the properties of electricity and the ability to generate a current artificially had been made as long ago as the late eighteenth century.

When he had lived in London and later travelled in France and Italy, Morse's sole interest appeared to be in painting. He had high ambitions for his own work and he undoubtedly had talent, which was recognized and encouraged by his more successful contemporaries. Furthermore, in the considerable archive of Morse's letters and reminiscences, there appears to be hardly a single record of him ever having shown an interest in anything electrical. The only invention with which he was involved was that of a portable fire extinguisher devised with his brother when they were both teenagers. Yet in 1837 Morse had a burning conviction that he, and only he, had conceived of the idea of an electric telegraph. But how could he prove it?

There was absolutely no record in any journal, learned or otherwise, of the invention of a Morse telegraphy system, so he had no evidence to show exactly when the idea had occurred to him. Racking his brains, he concluded that the idea dated from his voyage back to America from France in October 1832 aboard the ship *Sully*. What he needed to do, therefore, was to make contact with the ship's captain and some of his fellow passengers who would surely recall the conversations they had with him in which he had outlined the possibility of creating an electrically driven telegraph. The history of invention is riddled with claims and counter-claims about who really thought of what first, but nothing can compare with the ludicrous audacity of Morse's letter to the captain of the *Sully* and the passengers he chose to support his claim. 'There is,' he wrote, 'a contest, it seems, for priority of invention of this Electric Telegraph between England, France, Germany and this country. I claim for myself and consequently for America, priority over all other countries in the invention of a mode of communicating intelligence by electricity.'

Morse was a man of strongly held and sometimes high prejudiced views. He was in favour of slavery in the South and was fiercely anti-Catholic. Above all, he was a great American patriot, keen that his country should be shown in the best possible light. But Morse was not in any way a scientist, nor was he a skilled instrument-maker or mechanically minded. Most significantly, as far as the electric telegraphy was concerned, he was profoundly ignorant of its history, which is the only possible explanation for his claim that he thought of it first. Morse appears to have convinced himself that, somehow or other, the idea he so unwisely bandied about in jovial company in the *Sully* in the middle of the Atlantic had been leaked back to Europe, where unscrupulous rivals had promptly stolen it. This is laughable. And yet, in the history of the electric telegraph, which was in a few years to revolutionize national and international communication, just one name stands out: Morse, the inventor, apparently, not only of the electric telegraph but of the Morse code in which letters and numbers are represented by patterns of dots and dashes, either printed out or picked up and decoded by the ear of a trained operator.

That Samuel F. B. Morse laboured long and hard, with the assistance of accomplices who possessed greater scientific and mechanical skills than his own, to create a working electric telegraph system that became widely used in America and Europe is not disputed. Nor is there any doubt that the dot-dash code proved to be the best of many different techniques for tapping out messages with telegraph equipment. However, whether Morse himself was solely responsible for it has long been a matter of contention and its true origin remains a mystery. This particular code was certainly not Morse's first method of signalling words and it did not emerge for some time after he had been striving to improve the equipment being developed for him. But how was it that, out of the blue and in mid-ocean, Morse the painter conceived of the electric telegraph?

When he wrote to William Pell, the captain of the *Sully*, Morse asked not only if he recalled talk of the telegraph but also if he had by chance mentioned it to anyone else. Pell's reply, dated 27 September 1837, was encouraging: 'I am happy to say I have a distinct remembrance of your suggesting, as a thought newly occurred to you, the possibility of a telegraphic communication being effected by electric wires. As the passage progressed, and your idea developed itself, it became frequently a subject of conversation. Difficulty after difficulty was suggested as obstacles to its operation, which your ingenuity still labored to remove, until your invention, passing from its first crude state through different grades of improvement, was, in seeming, matured to an available instrument, wanting only patronage to perfect it, and call it into reality.'[1]

Pell continued diplomatically:'I sincerely trust the circumstances may not deprive you of the reward due to the invention, which, whatever its source in Europe, is with you, I am convinced original.'[2] In other words, someone in Europe might well have thought of it before Morse but he, in his ignorance, was apparently innocent of plagiarism. The captain clearly did not believe that Morse's inspiration had somehow leaked from the *Sully*. After all, there were only twenty-six passengers aboard the ship that might have overheard Morse and most were Americans. The seven French farmers in steerage were unlikely spies and the four passengers Morse asked to recall his discussion of the telegraph all gave gratifying responses: the whole idea had clearly been discussed with some regularity on the voyage.

To stake his claim, Morse now began to advertise his invention in the American press. It is clear from the reception that he received that the United States was all agog for some proof that it no longer had to rely on importing new technology from Europe and could produce its own, indigenous inventions. At this stage in its history, the country could make no claims with regard to iron or steel or steam engines or railways or locomotives or mining or any of the heavy industrial innovations which were rapidly transforming it. But there was something about electricity which was brand-new and therefore especially suited to America. At any rate, a patriotic press was only too keen to back Morse as the true originator of the electric telegraph.

Unfortunately for Morse, the publicity he received alerted a passenger from the *Sully* whom he had chosen not to contact. This was Dr Charles Jackson, a young man with a Harvard degree, studying medicine and geology in Europe. By 1837, Jackson had his own chemistry laboratory in Boston and was the state geologist for Maine. He wrote to Morse to say that he rejoiced to learn of the success of 'our' electric telegraph and added, 'I suppose the reason why my name was not attached to the invention of the Electric Telegraph is that the editors simply did not know that the invention was our mutual discovery.'[3] Not a bit of it, Morse told Jackson. His memory – unlike that of Captain Pell and the other passengers – was at fault. In a correspondence of escalating anger, Jackson insisted that he had prompted the whole idea, recalling, in their conversations, a demonstration he had seen at the Sorbonne in Paris of an electric current sent around a room some four hundred times. It was he who had suggested that this might be used as a form of communication. And so the squabble continued, just one of a great many disputes Morse was to have with those who were ungentlemanly enough to claim that what he had thought of first they had in fact suggested to him.

Brushing Jackson's claims aside, Morse hastened to apply for a patent for his system and to get the apparatus that had been gathering dust in his rooms at New York University into some kind of working order. To do this, he had to consult someone who knew something about the science of electricity and found, close at hand, Professor Leonard Gale, who taught chemistry at the same university. Gale had read about the research of America's foremost scientist, Joseph Henry, and soon had Morse's crude equipment operating over longer distances than the inventor could have dreamed of by increasing the power of the batteries used and rewinding his electro-magnet. On 2 September 1837 Morse gave the first public demonstration of his telegraph in a room at New York University at which signals were sent and recorded over a distance of about a third of a mile of wire – although at this stage his so-called 'port-rule' apparatus did not register messages in dots and dashes but in a sequence of numbers which corresponded to whole words.

Meanwhile, in England the first working telegraphs were in operation after a long period of development across Europe. One of the earliest and most dramatic demonstrations of the way in which an electric current could travel from a battery around a circuit was made by the French scientist, the Abbé Nollet, in 1746. Using a Leyden jar, which had been made available a year earlier, to create a current, Nollet sent a shock through a circle of Carthusian monks who were linked together grasping iron wires. When the circle was joined, the monks were convulsed by the electric charge, proving, in a gratifyingly conspicuous manner, that the current had travelled through them. A year later, Sir William Watson in England demonstrated that electricity could be sent through water and earth and through 10,000 feet of wire, and Benjamin Franklin did the same in 1748. In 1753, an article in the *Scots Magazine* proposed a system of electrical telegraphy, the author signing himself simply 'C. M.'. This was thought to be Charles Marshall of Paisley near Glasgow in Scotland, for he was one of a number of experimenters who proposed codes for the recording of messages.

But the Leyden jar gave an uneven and unpredictable flow of electrical current, and it was the Italians Luigi Galvani and his pupil Alessandro Volta who evolved the battery, which provided a steady flow of current. Volta duly sent details of his invention to the Royal Society in England in 1800 and the subsequent availability of reliable batteries inaugurated both a new era of experimentation and the creation of the first viable electric telegraph systems. Beginning in 1809 with that of von Sommering in Munich, experimental systems of one kind or another were tried – in Denmark by Hans Oested and in England by Francis Ronalds.

The Ronalds telegraph, in which he transmitted signals through eight miles of wire in his London back garden in 1816, was probably the first working system that might have been put to commercial use. Ronalds made many advances in the insulation of wires and use of brass dials for recording messages. However, he made the mistake many had made before him in offering his invention to the British Admiralty. They took a look, decided that the existing semaphore system was perfectly adequate, despite the fact that it did not work in conditions of poor visibility, and turned him down. Ronalds gave up on telegraphy and took up metereology instead. He did record some of his discoveries in a written account, *Descriptions of an Electric Telegraph and other electrical apparatus*, which was published in 1823. Had Ronalds persisted for just a few more years into the railway age, he might have been the pioneer of the commercial telegraph, for it was the companies running locomotives between Liverpool and Manchester and London and Birmingham that became the first customers for the new invention.

As it was, the Ronalds telegraph did not lead directly to further developments in England and the baton was passed to the remarkable and warlike Baron Pavel Lwowitch Schilling of Candstadt, an attaché at the Russian embassy in Munich who had been thrilled to witness Sommering's demonstrations of the telegraph. With war looming between France and Russia in 1812, Schilling put his mind to using electric currents to explode gunpowder mines from a distance. He devised his own form of wire insulation with copper covered in a solution of India rubber and varnish so that he could lay his cables anywhere. In 1814, when Napoleon was driven into exile by the allies opposed to him, Schilling amused the Parisians by setting off gunpowder on the opposite side of the Seine with his electric exploder.

The baron was a busy diplomat but over the next few years he began to devise his own form of the electric telegraph, using a needle deflected by a current to indicate a code. It was a binomial system in which a movement back and forth once meant A, three times in one direction B, once in one direction and twice in the other C, and so on through the alphabet. This was a variant of the semaphore codes that had been in use since the seventeenth century. Schilling took his telegraph to China in 1830 and toured Europe with it in 1835. He experimented with overhead wires and wires buried in the ground. He demonstrated his telegraph in Russia, impressing Emperor Nicholas and a commission of inquiry, and he was all set to establish a link between Kronstadt and Moscow with a cable running at the bottom of the Gulf of Finland when in 1837 he died.

There were many other telegraph pioneers in Europe, among them Messrs Gauss and Weber in Göttingen, who used a telegraph to communicate between two observatories a mile and a quarter apart from 1833. One other important innovation was the substitution of battery power with a small electrical generator, the prototype of which had been made by the English scientist Michael Faraday in the 1820s. Altogether, there was a great variety of systems for sending and receiving messages in the 1830s. In some, the electric current excited movement in needles, the twitching of which indicated a code which could be translated by a trained operator into words. These telegraphs left no permanent record of the message sent: it had to be read at the time it was received. But very soon other methods for recording coded messages were devised.

An English inventor, Edward Davy, also came very close to developing something which would later become a standard form of electric telegraph. Born in 1806, Davy was the son of a Devonshire doctor and studied medicine himself at St Bartholomew's Hospital in London where he was apprenticed to the house surgeon. He qualified later as an apothecary or chemist and founded his own business in the Strand in London. Davy became a leading experimental chemist, inventing in 1835 a special cement for mending china and glass that he called Davy's Diamond Cement. This gave him some spare income to devote to his researches. Apparently without reference to any other systems, Davy devised his own telegraph with a multiplicity of wires and a complex keying system which he demonstrated publicly at the Belgrave Institute in London in 1837. He failed to obtain a patent as he had just been beaten to it by others, but he was able to patent a system for printing out messages on a roll of calico, or plain cotton cloth, impregnated with chemicals which reacted to contact with an electric current to leave a mark.

Davy soon became aware of the rival claims of the two men who in England were to put their names to the very first commercial telegraphy systems, William Cooke and Professor Charles Wheatstone. The Cooke-Wheatstone patent was registered in 1837 and the partners were very vigilant in protecting it, challenging any rival systems that appeared to match any part of their specification. In the face of this, Davy gave up. For reasons that his family and friends have never divulged, he emigrated to Australia in 1837 and never returned to England.

William Fothergill Cooke was born in west London in the same year as Edward Davy and he was also the son of a medical man, his father Dr William Cooke working as a surgeon and later Professor of Anatomy at Durham University in the north-east of England. Dr Cooke had at one time been a neighbour of Francis Ronalds at the time he was experimenting with his back-garden telegraph. According to a letter lodged with the Institute of Electrical Engineers, Dr Cooke remembered sending messages to and forth with the Ronalds telegraph. Whether or not William Cooke was aware of this as a boy or not, in later life he developed a desire to devise a telegraph of his own. After a classical education at Durham and Edinburgh universities, he had joined the East India Company Army at the age of nineteen and he served in it for eight years until 1833. He then began to earn his living making anatomical models and visited Heidelberg to learn something of techniques there. As it happened, while in Heidelberg he saw a demonstration of the Schilling needle telegraph and was fascinated by it.

It occurred to Cooke that this wonderful piece of apparatus was being used simply as a kind of scientific toy when it should be turned into a generally available and novel form of communication. However, like Morse, Cooke did not have the scientific training which might have given him a grasp of the possibilities of electrical communication. A major issue was always the limit there might be on the distance a current could be made to travel across country. And how would the cables be laid? In insulated pipes underground or strung up on poles? Before he knew how it might work, Cooke published a pamphlet outlining a plan for a national system of telegraphs. It would have many applications. It might be used, for example, '… in case of disturbance to transmit orders to the local authorities and, if necessary, to send troops to their support; whilst all dangerous excitement of the public might be avoided'. It could also provide businessmen with rapid information on the markets, enable the railways to avoid disastrous collisions and run more efficiently, and ensure families received prompt help in the event of some domestic crisis.

Cooke first pursued his idea commercially with an approach to the directors of the Liverpool to Manchester railway: a telegraph system might be useful in the tunnel into Liverpool station to control traffic. But he had devised a crude kind of instrument which did not impress anyone. He continued, nevertheless, to peddle his idea around and eventually was given an introduction to Professor Charles Wheatstone, who in 1834 had been appointed Professor of Experimental Philosophy at King's College, London. Wheatstone came from a family of musical instrument-makers and had become fascinated by the science of the transmission of sound. He had also experimented with early forms of electric light and studied the speed of electrical discharges. In 1836 Wheatstone was made a Fellow of the Royal Society and it was the secretary of that celebrated scientific body, Dr Peter Mark Roget, who introduced him to Cooke.

It turned out that Wheatstone had already devised his own form of electric telegraph and he and Cooke hammered out an agreement in which Cooke would be the main mover in promoting a system commercially while Wheatstone remained the brains in the background. On 10 June 1837, a few months before Morse's first demonstration of his telegraph in New York, the Cooke-Wheatstone patent was signed. It was for 'Improvements in Giving Signals and Sounding Alarms in Distant places by means of electric currents transmitted through Metallic Circuits'. This was immediately challenged by a system devised by William Alexander of Edinburgh. Alexander's telegraph required a separate wire for every letter of the alphabet and, although he gained widespread publicity for it, he withdrew his claim when he examined the Cooke-Wheatstone model more closely.

In Britain, the government took no interest in the telegraph. If Cooke and Wheatstone were to profit from their joint efforts, they would have to sell their system to private business. The most likely customers were the railways, where the speed of trains had made older forms of communication obsolete. Cooke worked hard to get orders, but found tremendous resistance, chiefly because of the cost. The form of telegraph he and Wheatstone devised, which remained in use for more than a century in some places, was the needle type, elegant-looking, with its dials in a kind of clock case, but decidedly less efficient in the long run than the printing telegraph that had always been Morse's favoured system.

It was on Isambard Kingdom Brunel's Great Western Railway between London and Bristol that the first commercial working telegraphy system was installed, employing Cooke and Wheatstone's equipment. This was before the railway line was complete. Initially, the 13.5-mile stretch of telegraph ran from the London terminus of Paddington to the station at West Drayton; it took a year to set up and went into use in July 1839. Cooke reckoned he lost money on the venture, but it proved the practicality of the telegraph as an adjunct to the railways and paved the way for many profitable schemes.

Meanwhile, in America Samuel Morse had taken steps to improve his version of the telegraph. As a young man, Morse had relied on his father, a clergyman and highly regarded geographer, to support him with allowances at college and when he travelled to Europe to pursue his career as a painter. He was forever writing home asking for more money as he felt he had to keep up appearances. The thought does not seem to have occurred to him, even when he was in his twenties, that he might support himself through his own efforts. And when the time came for him to do so, he found he was not very good at it. He tried to make a living painting portraits but the fees he received were never enough. In 1818, not long after he returned from his first trip to London, Morse, then twenty-seven, married a girl of nineteen he had met two years earlier while looking for portrait commissions in Concord, New Hampshire. With Lucretia Pickering Walker he had three children, but he lived away from her for much of the time, seeking his fortune with huge canvases he hoped would provide him with a living. He was, in fact, painting a portrait of the French general, Lafayette, when he received the news that Lucretia had died at the age of just twenty-five. Unable to support his children, he lodged them with members of his family and friends.

In 1837, Morse not only lacked the scientific knowledge to develop his telegraph, he also had neither funds nor any mechanical skills to draw on. His problems were, however, to be solved by the appearance at New York University – when he first demonstrated his crude system – of a former pupil called Alfred Vail. Then thirty years old, Vail was from a family of successful ironmasters with a foundry at Speedwell in New Jersey. Vail persuaded his father to back Morse's project and he was able then to sign an agreement for the development of the telegraph. In return for a quarter of the financial interest in the invention in the United States and half of that from abroad, Vail agreed to fund the development of an improved form of the apparatus and to pay for the cost of seeking patents both at home and abroad. In reality, Vail's father funded the whole thing despite his scepticism about the telegraph. Alfred's brother George helped with the technical side of development, as did others at the Speedwell Works.

Morse had already approached Congress to seek funding for the telegraph and promised to demonstrate his improved system fairly soon. Indeed, a Congressman, Francis O. J. Smith, became interested in the telegraph and persuaded Morse to take him on as a partner. New agreements were signed between Smith, Morse and Professor Leonard Gale, who had been scientific adviser to Morse at New York University. Smith had the money to fund a trip to Europe to see if they could get patents there and Vail produced a compact and portable version of the telegraph in time for the journey. As always, Vail was left behind to get on with improvements to the telegraph – something he did quietly and without any claims for himself. He had an agreement with Morse that whatever improvements were made would be attributed to both of them.

Morse and Smith were in London in time for Queen Victoria's Coronation in 1838 and enjoyed the spectacle. But they were cold-shouldered when they applied for a patent. The refusal was not on the grounds that their invention had already been patented the year before, but that Morse had published an account of it and thereby rendered any application invalid. At this time, Cooke and Wheatstone were having trouble selling their system, so it is no surprise that Morse did not make much progress in trying to sell his. The rivals actually met and Wheatstone invited Morse to have a look at the apparatus he had developed. Morse saw other models too, including Edward Davy's. He was reassured, or so he asserted at the time. Nothing was as simple and effective as his single-wire telegraph with a printer which embossed Vs on paper. His code was still the one in which numbers represented whole words. The dot and dash had not, apparently, yet emerged.

From England, Morse and Smith moved on to Paris. The telegraph there, such as it was, had been made a government monopoly. On his earlier visit to Paris as a young painter, Morse had been a fierce republican. Now he kowtowed to the king, Louis Philippe, or tried to. His promised audiences were continuously postponed. He discussed the possibility of the use of his telegraph on the Paris–St-Germain line, but nothing came of it. He was about to leave Paris empty-handed when the astonishing news broke that a Frenchman, Louis Daguerre, had managed to fix on a chemically sensitized plate an image from a *camera obscura*. Daguerre hoped his photographic images would help him in the creation of scenes for his *Diorama,* huge paintings displayed in Paris. Morse contacted Daguerre and went to see him. He was astonished by the images produced. When he arrived back in New York, Morse was more excited about the daguerreotype, as this early form of phonographic image was called, than his cherished telegraph. The one order for his equipment he thought he had acquired from Russia did not materialize. So Morse, the inventor of the telegraph, became Morse, the great improver of the daguerreotype. And in no time he was in dispute over what he had somehow discovered intuitively and what he had borrowed from someone else.

When Morse was setting up as a photographic portrait artist on his return to New York, Daguerre had dispatched to America a business associate and pupil called François Gouraud, who was lecturing and promoting the new invention. Naturally enough, Morse sought him out and spent some time learning from him the intricate processes involved in developing images. Then, in praising Daguerre to the skies in newspaper articles, Morse failed to mention his partner Gouraud and the kind of unseemly squabble that poisoned most of Morse's working life inevitably ensued. It hardly mattered in the long run, for the scheme for making money out of photographic portraits did not come off. By 1841, Morse, now fifty and white-haired, was back promoting his telegraph. A man with the name of Isaac Coffin appeared, offering to promote the Morse telegraph in Washington: a handsome vote from Congress for development could finally get the show on the road. Coffin was an experienced lobbyist who hoped to turn a profit if he won funding for Morse.

The old team of Alfred Vail, Francis Smith and Leonard Gale had been disbanded. Vail was married and living in Philadelphia, Gale was in New Orleans and Smith in Maine. So Morse sought financial backing for his telegraph on his own, obtaining permission to act for the old partnership and teaming up briefly with Samuel Colt, the inventor of the revolver pistol, to tap his expertise on laying cables under water – like Baron Schilling, Colt demonstrated blowing things up from a distance. In 1843, by a narrow majority, Morse got the vote from Congress he needed to go ahead. There was money to entice Vail back as the instrument-maker and operator and Leonard Gale as the scientist. The demonstration line would be over forty-four miles between Washington and Baltimore, following that section of the Baltimore to Ohio railroad. Morse decided the cable needed to be buried and hired a man with a horse-drawn ditch-digger to start work cutting the required trench. But burying cables proved to be far too cumbersome, and doubts were raised by Joseph Henry and others about the corrosion of wires underground. So Morse resorted to posts and had a seven-mile run of tree trunks spaced out for a trial transmission.

Vail, meanwhile, continued to work on the equipment and by now was absorbing all he could from the experiments being undertaken in Europe where various techniques of telegraphing were written up in journals. Exactly what he achieved without Morse's involvement has been a matter of contention ever since and there are those who argue that Vail devised the dots and dashes of the code later named after Morse. This would seem perfectly credible, although Vail not only failed to claim this idea as his own, he also stated on one or two occasions that it was indeed Morse's. He even suggested later in life that Morse had come up with the idea on the *Sully* – a notion which is extremely unlikely as he then had a quite different scheme for a code. The other possibility is that, while reviewing European systems Vail, or Vail and Morse together, borrowed and improved upon some of the codes that had already been used. In his book on the history of the American telegraph, Vail shows Schilling's 'big-signal', which involved a needle swinging between two points, while the code used by Gauss and Weber in the 1830s actually looks very like Morse.

Regardless of who conceived the idea of using dots and dashes, the system was certainly employed for the first and much-celebrated transmission of a Morse message in America. The dots and dashes may have been embossed rather than printed, but this was essentially the code which was going to be used in the United States for many years to come. Those who support the view that Vail devised it say that he also decided which letters should be represented by which combination of dots and dashes, beginning with dot-dash for A and so on and so forth. There appears to be no record of Morse himself making such a decision, and in this respect, the code's precise origin remains a mystery.

It was on 24 May 1844 that Morse set up his end of the telegraph, with its neat paper printer and key devised by Vail, in the chamber of the United States Supreme Court in Washington. Vail took up his post in Baltimore. The message they had agreed upon was 'What hath God wrought!', taken from Numbers 23:23 in the Old Testament; it had been suggested by the wife of the commissioner who had got the project underway in Congress. Morse tapped it out and Vail sent it back. The subtext of the message was a claim that this was the first time such a thing had ever been done. However, this was not strictly true, for something similar had long before been achieved in Europe, as we have seen, and, in a sense at least, also in America, where several years earlier Joseph Henry had demonstrated a kind of telegraph which rang a bell. What could not be denied, however, was that this was the first occasion on which Morse's complete system had been used.

None the less, Morse's dream had become reality. From 1844 onwards, telegraph companies were established in America and Morse and Vail owned shares in them. The first sale of the system abroad was to Austria, that Catholic remnant of the Holy Roman Empire which had previously been anathema to Morse. In 1845, Alfred Vail published his history of the American Electro-Magnetic Telegraph, omissions in which caused tremendous upset. In particular, there was absolutely no mention of Joseph Henry, who had not only made a working machine before Morse and Vail but had given his expert advice freely from the time Morse first contacted him in 1837 until the date of the book's publication. Henry complained to Morse, who said the oversight would be corrected in the next edition of the book, but when that came out there was still no mention of him. On a number of occasions when lawsuits were brought against Morse, Joseph Henry had been called to give evidence as an expert witness by his opponents, and that he had done so for no personal gain and out of a sense of justice was accepted by the leading scientific institutions of the day. But Morse attacked Henry in print regardless, accusing him of dishonesty.

Morse himself ended his days in a blaze of glory. He had remarried in 1848 to a woman called Sarah Elizabeth Griswold who was thirty years younger than him and whom he had known for some time. She had been deaf from the age of one, an affliction possibly caused by scarlet fever, and her speech was impaired. Morse learned sign language to talk to her. Now in his late fifties, he was making money as the shares he had in various companies bore fruit. He lived long enough to be involved in the enterprise of laying the first successful transatlantic cable in 1866, although he was in France at the time and his name was not directly associated with it. On his death in 1872, Morse was duly hailed by the American newspapers as the greatest inventor of his age, the most 'Illustrious American' and so on. He was, at least on his own side of the Atlantic, the 'Father of Telegraphy'. Morse code, it transpired, had one huge advantage over many other systems: although the system was designed to make a permanent record of messages on paper, the operators soon discovered that they could decipher the clicking of the machine by ear, and as skill in the use of the telegraph increased, the best operators could handle Morse code at fantastic speeds. When wireless telegraphy came to be developed, there was already in widespread use a code which could be picked up both on tape and with headphones and was easy to transmit.

The development of the electric telegraph ushered in a new era in industrial development. First, it was not simply an invention exported from one country to another: its creation was truly international. Second, its use was not dependent on the availability of raw materials such as coal and it required no heavy industry. It was, in fact, portable and it had huge importance beyond the simple sending of messages. On the railways, especially in the United States, it enabled single tracks to be run safely as warnings could be given of the position of trains. It was adopted rapidly by newspapers, *The Times* running telegraphed items from Europe after the first cable was laid under the Channel in 1850. It was even handy in big houses, where it could be used to alert the staff to rooms in which their services were required. Above all, there was nothing essentially British about it. In a sense, that was Morse's greatest triumph: he led much of the world to believe the telegraph was American.

The electric telegraph was coming into its own at a time when Britain was about to stage the greatest show of artistic and industrial effort in history: the Great Exhibition housed in the Crystal Palace in London's Hyde Park. It was impossible not to view the 100,000 or so exhibits gathered in from a large part of the world as a kind of league table of how all the also-rans were doing in relation to the industrial domination of Britain. Certainly, many nations invited to submit their products were wary of the whole, grandiose event, not least the Americans, whom the British still regarded as a junior offspring of their own, highly advanced civilization, referring often to the much younger United States affectionately, albeit a little disparagingly, as 'Brother Jonathan'.

CHAPTER THIRTEEN

THE PALACE OF WONDERS

There is but one opinion on the merits of this construction ... It is elegant, simple, imposing, and convenient; it is inundated with light, and easy of approach. Every contingency has been provided against: rain cannot penetrate, nor fire destroy. Steam was necessary to put in motion the numerous engines and machinery established in the mechanical division, for it was thought better to enable the public to see the machinery in motion; there are pipes which distribute steam where it is wanted, and vast boilers have been erected in an adjacent building, which afford an abundant and constant supply ... An electric telegraph is there to convey each moment to a central bureau all communications that may be desired ... When one reflects that all this has been conceived, adopted, moulded, cast, adjusted, placed, and covered with glass in the space of a few months, we fancy ourselves to be in fairy-land. The Crystal Palace would have been an impossibility elsewhere than in England.[1]

Such was the opinion of the Frenchman Michel Chevalier, a much-travelled enthusiast for industrial advance who was apt to lament his own country's failure to fulfil its potential. He had travelled as an envoy in America, where he befriended railway pioneers such as Moncure Robinson, he had been thrilled to ride on the Liverpool–Manchester line, and now in 1851 he was enthralled by the gigantic greenhouse in London's Hyde Park in which more than a hundred thousand exhibits from a very large part of the world were displayed. Chevalier's judgement that the Crystal Palace could not have been constructed anywhere else in the world was undoubtedly true.

One of the aspects of British life that struck Chevalier was that so much was made of iron rather than wood or brick. Whereas a hundred years earlier, in the 1750s, the iron industry was nothing exceptional in England and not very different from that in France, it had since grown into the foremost producer in the world. At the turn of the century, it had made 150,000 tons a year. That figure had risen to 258,000 tons in 1806, 581,000 tons in 1825, 1,000,000 tons in 1835 and 2,200,000 tons in 1847. By the time of the Great Exhibition, Britain was exporting something like 700,000 tons a year and its only imports were of high-quality Swedish wrought iron to be made into Sheffield cutlery and other fine steel goods.

All those innovations in iron-making – from the use of coke for smelting to the development of Henry Cort's method of producing wrought iron – had, along with the ready availability of the ores and the fuel needed to develop the industry, made iron in Britain not only abundant but cheap. At the time the Crystal Palace was put up, French iron cost twice as much as English iron. As Chevalier put it: 'A cheap market is a great magician. When a nation has obtained one, it possesses the lamp of Aladdin, by which, in the twinkling of an eye, it accomplishes miracles, and it is available for other purposes besides the erection of prodigies like the Crystal Palace.'[2] He quoted a leading chemist from the Ecole Polytechnique in Paris as proposing that the state of a nation's civilization could be gauged by its use of iron. In that respect, poor old France, gifted though her people were in so many respects, was way behind, still smelting iron with charcoal and turning out small quantities of an over-priced product. Indeed, the building which had housed the 1849 Paris Exhibition, the inspiration for Britain's international exhibition in Hyde Park, was a grim edifice. Chevalier described it as typical of French constructions of the time 'in lath and plaster, low, ill-ventilated, imperfectly lighted ... and

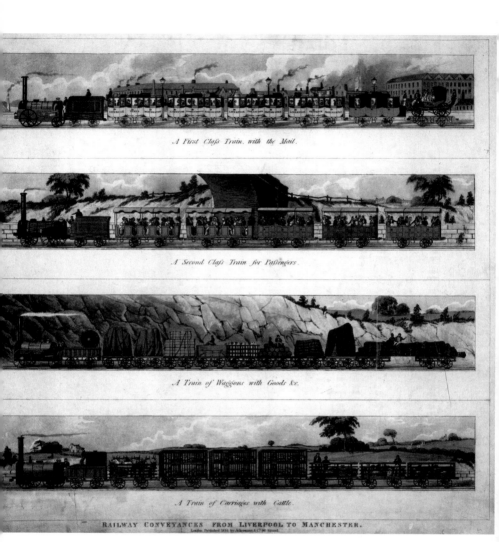

A First Class Train, with the Mail.

A Second Class Train for Passengers.

A Train of Waggons with Goods &c.

A Train of Carriages with Cattle.

RAILWAY CONVEYANCES FROM LIVERPOOL TO MANCHESTER.

Above: Four different engines haul four varieties of passenger and goods on the Manchester to Liverpool railway in this Ackerman lithograph of 1834. At the top the *Liverpool* pulls first-class carriages. Below the *Fury* hauls second-class carriages, the *North Star* goods wagons and the *Jupiter* livestock.

Above: A vivid evocation of South Sea whaling in 1835 when the industry was reaching its peak in America. Much of the world was lit with whale oil before the petroleum industry became established in the second half of the nineteenth century.

Right: A Japanese illustration which emphasizes the huge impact the American steamers made when they arrived in 1853 to persuade Japan to open up its harbours to foreign shipping.

Below: A Japanese illustration of the Battle of Chemulpo Bay, 8 February 1904, the first exchange of fire in the war between Japan and Russia. With a fleet mostly built in Britain, the Japanese inflicted a humiliating defeat on Russia the following year.

Left: A slightly fanciful illustration of the craze for 'high wheeling' in America, painted by the artist Hy Sandham in 1887 just before the introduction of inflatable tyres and the 'safety' bicycle. The cycle industry, with its races and constant change of vehicle design, laid the foundations for the motor industry, which was then in its infancy.

Below: A tinted photograph from 1888 of Johnnie Dunlop proudly astride the first ever bicycle fitted with inflatable tyres, the invention of his father, John Boyd Dunlop.

PLAYER'S CIGARETTES

THE FIRST PNEUMATIC-TYRED BICYCLE

Above: It took a little time for the motor car to become something more than a rich man's plaything that frightened the horses and kicked up dust storms on unmetalled roads. This French illustration of an English village from 1903 captures the atmosphere. France was much more enthusiastic about motoring in the early days.

Above: One of thousands of trade cards advertising meat extract produced in South America to a recipe devised by the German chemist Justus Liebig. It was made in the town of Fray Bentos on the Uruguay River from 1866 and later became Oxo.

very expensive in consequence of the necessity of being demolished after having served their purpose'.[3]

It was not, of course, just the low price of iron which gave rise to the Crystal Palace, as Chevalier well knew. The whole enterprise of the Great Exhibition was a superb display of the British way of going about organizing anything. Firstly, although the government set up a Royal Commission to oversee the arrangements for the building and the exhibition, it took no part itself and offered no money. The idea originated not with a government department but with the Royal Society for the Encouragement of Arts, Manufactures and Commerce, which had been founded in 1754 with the idea of promoting innovation in industry. This Society had had its ups and downs but by chance it provided the ideal vehicle for Queen Victoria's gauche consort Prince Albert to indulge his enthusiasm for science and culture. He was offered and gratefully accepted the Society's presidency and when a member, Henry Cole, just returned from the Paris Exhibition of 1849, put the idea of a British version to Albert, there was immediate enthusiasm for it. The French had not invited foreigners to their exhibitions. Albert, the internationalist, proposed that Britain should invite the rest of the world. Exactly how this might be achieved was left to the Royal Commission, which included in its ranks many of the most elevated men of industry – men such as Robert Stephenson, the head of the greatest locomotive manufacturing business in the world and engineer of the London–Birmingham Railway.

Any country wanting to exhibit in the Crystal Palace had to follow the rules laid down in London. They would be offered space in the hall but it was up to them to arrange and pay for shipment. To organize the choice and transport of the displays, each country should set up its own committee system. From the beginning there was a broad agreement that half the display area should be devoted to the products and manufactures of Britain and her colonies, and the other half to the rest of the world. It was decided that all this should be brought to a building to be erected in London's Hyde Park, a prospect which appalled the aristocratic and wealthy residents of Mayfair, Belgravia and Bayswater. A plot of nineteen acres was marked out, but a huge difficulty arose which threatened to put an end to the Exhibition altogether.

The commission would not accept any of the plans put forward for the building: not one of the 240 entries for the competition was thought entirely suitable. In desperation, the Commission put up its own plan, which caused further outrage as it meant covering a huge area of Hyde Park in bricks and mortar.

It was at this point, in 1850, that someone must have rubbed Monsieur Chevalier's Aladdin's lamp, for there emerged a genie who, in the twinkling of an eye, would accomplish a miracle. Joseph Paxton was then well known and highly regarded in horticultural circles, and he came up with a design for the Exhibition building when visiting London to discuss an issue with a Member of Parliament. Paxton was not, in fact, an architect but the head gardener for the Duke of Devonshire, the owner of several large tracts of land as well as the family seat at Chatsworth. The duke had met Paxton back in the 1820s and had taken him on, recognizing that this son of an agricultural labourer had exceptional gifts. Paxton's enthusiasm for plants inspired the duke, who became a keen horticulturist himself, and the two went on exploratory trips to Europe together. To house the duke's collection, Paxton learned to design greenhouses, developing his own ingenious structures to deal with the problems of condensation and decay.

The most exciting and exotic plant to arrive at Chatsworth was the giant South American water lily, given the name *Victoria Regia*. Its leaves, which could spread across the surface of a pond, grew to a span of six feet and were strong enough to take the weight of a child. The lilies were beautiful, but the plant did not always flower in Europe. Paxton managed to get one in bloom, and at the time he put his mind to the problem of the Great Exhibition building, he was constructing at Chatsworth the largest greenhouse he had yet devised to house the *Victoria Regia*. By his own account, given often in years to come in after-dinner speeches, Paxton adapted the Chatsworth greenhouse to produce the Crystal Palace. His first sketch was made on blotting paper while waiting for a train at the Midland Station, Derby.

Although, like many other successful men of his era, Paxton had humble origins, by 1850 he was very well connected. He was an enthusiast for railways, in which he had invested, knew Robert Stephenson well and had had dealings with a number of manufacturers through his business ventures and his construction of greenhouses. Paxton was introduced to Henry Cole, prime mover of the Exhibition, who encouraged him to pursue his idea for an iron and glass building. Very quickly, Paxton was able to discuss his idea and the practicalities of it with a coterie of brilliant engineers, all of whom had learned their skills in the construction of railways. On a train into London, he met Robert Stephenson, who admired the plans, made a few suggestions, and presented them to the Royal Commission. Isambard Kingdom Brunel had a look at the plans too. But most significant of all was a man famous in his day but largely forgotten by history: Charles Fox.

Fox was of that generation of engineers who grew up in the railway era, a near contemporary of Robert Stephenson, Isambard Kingdom Brunel and Joseph Paxton. He was born in 1810 in Derby, the son of a physician and was destined for a medical career at first when he was apprenticed to a brother who was a surgeon. Charles Fox, however, preferred engineering and got himself taken on in 1829 by John Ericsson and John Braithwaite when they were designing the *Novelty* for the Rainhill trials. From there he went to a Liverpool firm before working with Robert Stephenson on the London–Birmingham line. He designed a wrought-iron trussed roof for the London terminus at Euston Station and also devised a way of building skewed brick arches. Fox moved on to the Birmingham firm of Bramah, in which he became a partner. Fox and Bramah were joined by an ironmaster, John Henderson, and by 1845 the firm was renamed Fox, Henderson & Co. In the next few years, during the railway boom, they became the leading manufacturers and designers of cast- and wrought-iron structures.

It was therefore natural that Paxton should go immediately to Charles Fox in his London office to discuss the practicalities of building the Crystal Palace. Fox agreed to take it on at a very low fee provided the firm could keep the component parts. In fact, Paxton was already thinking in terms of moving the building to the outskirts of London to form the centrepiece of a pleasure garden. Fox, Henderson & Co not only supplied all the iron parts for the Crystal Palace – more than 2,000 pre-fabricated girders and nearly 400 roof trusses – but also supervised the whole operation. For periods during the construction Paxton was out of the country and had to leave Charles Fox in charge. The glass panels were all supplied by Chance Brothers & Co. of Smethwick, Birmingham.

The design of the Exhibition building had to be adjusted several times. Paxton's original sketch had a flat roof right across it, but this would have meant felling some fine elm trees. The elegant solution was, of course, to enclose them within a dome that would provide a splendid centrepiece for the Exhibition – no mean feat as the trees were 135 feet high. Furthermore, there was no steam-driven machinery for the lifting of the iron beams and trusses. All the work was done by horse-power and a simple three-legged hoist, while a special aerial runway was constructed for the glaziers fitting the higher panels. Paxton's ingenious means of preventing condensation and draining away surplus moisture was duly employed, with water running down the cast-iron pillars which held up the structure. The assembly of the parts drew fascinated crowds which had to be kept at bay, and after a while those who wanted a close view of the work going on were charged a fee. When the nineteen acres were covered, the interior of the building was reckoned at four times the volume of St Paul's cathedral. And yet it had been put together in only seven months, at a minimal cost.

The Crystal Palace represented a pinnacle of the achievements in engineering and manufacture over the first half of the nineteenth century and there was absolutely no doubt in the minds of visitors to the Great Exhibition that Britain led the world as the first industrial nation. It was not only the richest country in the world, financing projects everywhere from South America to India; its society was the first to be transformed by the forces of industrialism. London had a population of around 2.3 million in 1851 and the Census of that year showed that, after the rapid growth of industrial towns such as Manchester and Liverpool, more people in England now lived in urban areas than in the countryside. No other country in Europe was like this. Paris, which had rivalled London in size in 1750, had merely half its population in 1851 and the great majority of the French people still led rural lives. The same was true in the United States, where the largest city in 1850 was New York, with a population of just over 500,000. The second city was

Baltimore, with just under 170,000 citizens, about half the size of Manchester.

This picture was soon to be transformed. The growth of the United States through the acquisition of new lands was virtually complete by 1851: the year before California had become the thirty-first State of the Union. And the huge emigration from Europe to America, as well as a high rate of natural increase – that is, births over deaths – was quite spectacular in the second half of the nineteenth century. At the same time, the technology driving industrialism was evolving rapidly so that within a few years of its triumphant appearance in Hyde Park, the Crystal Palace itself, re-erected in South London, was a museum piece. Everything changed after 1851, and though Britain retained a lead for a while, it was clear to the more perceptive visitors to the Great Exhibition that this would not remain the case for much longer.

As Michel Chevalier strolled around the galleries at the exhibition, the thought occurred to him that the process of innovation had, as it were, gone global:

> The first idea of a machine or a manufacturing expedient shall be suggested in Paris or London. It receives its first improvement in some obscure village in Thuringia, and it takes a practical shape for first time at Manchester or Sheffield; then, by various transfigurations, not less curious than that of Vishnou, it reappears successively, always improved, in the atelier of Lyons or Zurich, or in those of Breslau or Verviers, Elberfield or Glasgow. Nor can we be certain that it will not be on the other side of the Atlantic at Lowell, or still further, at Pittsburg on the Ohio, that it will arrive at perfection.[4]

Chevalier gave as an example the first production of beet sugar in rural Germany, a process which was developed in Berlin and passed on to France, freeing much of Europe from dependence on West Indian cane sugar. Again, according to Chevalier if not British authorities, it was a Frenchman, Philippe Lebon, who first developed gas lighting; it was then taken to London and there turned into a commercial venture. And then there was the prize that Napoleon put up for anyone who could produce a very fine linen yarn which could rival cotton and thereby undermine British industry. A Frenchman, M. Philippe Henri de Girard, more or less succeeded around the time of Napoleon's first defeat in 1814. Girard took his technique to Warsaw, where he improved it. From Warsaw, the production of fine linen was taken up in the Yorkshire textile town of Leeds, where a Mr Marshall perfected it, establishing a successful business using a technique which had been developed to win a prize for undermining British industry.

The days of industrial espionage were not over, but the era in which it was necessary to entice skilled mechanics who kept the workings of machinery or a special technique in their heads was nearly done. By the mid-nineteenth century, there were a great many journals and encyclopaedia which gave details of how things worked. During the period of the Great Exhibition, which ran from May until October 1851, *The Times* carried articles by a Dionysius Lardner, an Irish popularizer of science and one-time Professor of Natural Philosophy at University College, London. Lardner reviewed a wide variety of mechanisms on display. The sort of detailed descriptions he indulged in were the very stuff of the nightmares Charles Dickens had about meeting someone who wanted to explain to him the workings of some invention or other. However, for the technically minded, there was enough information to enable them to put together a variety of the most up-to-date pieces of equipment, such as a 'carbon arc' electric lamp so bright it had to be viewed through coloured glass, or numerous versions of the electric telegraph as well as the latest steam engines. In the 1850s, there were a great many battles over patents at a time when published texts were making it more and more difficult to keep the details of an invention secret. But the greatest concern about the staging of such a huge international event was not industrial espionage but the imagined threat to public order.

The Great Exhibition was staged just three years after a wave of revolutions had swept through Europe, threatening the old social order and monarchies everywhere. Prince Albert received a sackful of alarmist correspondence from the King of Prussia, who very much hoped the rumours that Queen Victoria and her consort would escape from London during the months of the Exhibition were true. Certainly, none of Albert's German relatives would be risking their lives with a trip to Hyde Park. Albert, as one of the prime movers of the Exhibition, was hardly likely to miss it, however, and he felt it necessary to reply to the King of Prussia with a curt sarcasm:

> The rumour that the Court has been forced to make up its mind to desert London during the Exhibition is one of those many inventions concocted by the enemies of an artistic and cultural venture and of all progress in civilization, to frighten the public. From the very start they have shown remarkable persistence and ingenuity.
>
> Mathematicians have calculated that the Crystal Palace will blow down in the first strong gale, Engineers that the galleries would crash in and destroy the visitors; Political Economists have prophesied a scarcity of food in London owing to the vast concourse of people; Doctors that owing to so many races coming into contact with each other the Black Death of the Middle Ages would make its appearance as it did after the Crusades; Moralists that England would be infected by all the scourges of the civilised and uncivilised world; Theologians that this second Tower of Babel would draw upon it the vengeance of an offended God ...
>
> I can give no guarantee against these perils, nor am I in a position to assume responsibility for the possibly menaced lives of your Royal relatives. But I can promise that the protection from which Victoria and I benefit will be extended to their persons – for I presume we are also on the list of victims.[5]

The draw of the Exhibition in the end proved irresistible. A few French manufacturers pulled out, much to the annoyance of Michel Chevalier, but their compatriots provided the single largest foreign display. One by one, the countries of Europe organized themselves and found a way of delivering their exhibits. There was a small contribution from China, and something from Brazil, Chile, Mexico, Persia, Greece, Turkey, Egypt, Spain, Portugal and Madeira, Switzerland, Belgium, the Netherlands, Denmark, Sweden and Norway, Austria and Russia. There was nothing at all from Japan, although someone gathered together a few Japanese objects. Meanwhile, the Italian contribution came in three separate parts from Rome, Sardinia and Tuscany, and the German exhibits were presented by a host of provinces, grand duchies and towns: Hanover, Nuremberg, Hamburg and so on. (Even the states of the *Zollverein* managed to cooperate with their own display.) Exhibits from India and Australia were subsumed under the heading of British Dependencies.

In the foreign section, one of the largest areas had been allotted to the United States, which had responded to the invitation to lay before the world its many goods and manufactures with mixed feelings. Congress set up committees to gather in contributions from the various states and put at the disposal of exhibitors a naval frigate, the *St Lawrence*, to deliver them to England. But the decision about who was to exhibit was left to individual companies or people. In the summer of 1850 there was little interest shown in the American newspapers about the preparations going on in London. However, on 1 August 1850, the *New York Herald* carried an editorial which was a kind of rallying cry to chivvy Americans into putting on a decent show:

> This is the first opportunity we have had of fairly laying before the
> world our productions of art and it should not be passed lightly by.
> It is of more importance to us politically and commercially, than
> to any other nation. We are as yet unknown in the market of
> Europe except as producers of raw material. Now we can show
> them that we do not only produce cotton, iron, coal, copper and
> gold in greater abundances than any other nation, but that we can
> work them up into manufactures often equally, sometimes
> surpassing the oldest nations in a perfection and with a facility
> unknown to them.[6]

While Congress and most States seemed to agree with that view, they were not prepared to risk much money on it. When the *St Lawrence* arrived at Southampton in early March, the captain and crew were given a fine welcome by the city which laid on a banquet and offered to transfer all the exhibits from the port to London free of charge. However, it turned out, much to the embarrassment of the Americans, that they had no funds either to transport their exhibits from the railway station to Hyde Park or to set them up in the Crystal Palace. It was at this point that George Peabody intervened, making a loan of $15,000 and helping with the cost of mounting the exhibits. Then fifty-five years old, Peabody was an American who had made a fortune in the transatlantic trade in cotton and iron rails and in 1837 had settled in London, where he became a merchant banker. He never married but kept a mistress in Brighton with whom he had a daughter. In the capital, though, Peabody led the life of a bachelor and kept open house for all distinguished American visitors. He acted as a kind of unofficial ambassador for the American contingent at the Great Exhibition, hosting a series of dinners which brought together important individuals from both sides of the Atlantic. Without his help, it is quite likely the American show in the Crystal Palace would have been a disaster.

As it was, the space provided was not fully taken up and what was on display struck visitors, including an American, Horace Greeley, who sent back reports to the *New York Tribune*, as almost comical in its lack of lustre. Though he was pleased that there were some 'Yankee Notions' on display, such as a fine collection of daguerreotypes and some impressive ploughs, Greeley could not help noticing that American offerings lacked the dazzling quality of Austrian cloth embroidered with gold or a richly inlaid clock from Russia. Greeley had been against the United States sending such items as 'barrels of turpentine, hams etc' which represented America's 'accidental wealth'. He was anxious that his countrymen should not be perceived in Europe as mere suppliers of raw materials to be turned into fine goods in the factories of other nations. Yet there on the stands were samples of tobacco, steam-dried Indian corn, lard oil and beehives. Vermont sent a leaf.

At first, the American display drew a rather supercilious response from the British press, which tended to damn with faint praise. All newspapers, from *The Times* to the *Morning Chronicle*, remarked on how sparse was this corner of the Crystal Palace. There were some very useful things, such as lightweight carriages and a sleigh which looked very comfortable, and some impressive art such as Hiram Powers' statue *The Greek Slave*, which was a medal winner. 'Other nations rely upon their proficiency in the arts, or in manufactures, or in machinery, for producing effect,' intoned *The Times*. 'Not so America. She is proud of her agricultural implements, which Garrett, or Ransome and May (English manufacturers) would reject as worthless; she is proud of her machinery which would hardly fill one corner of our Exhibition, and upon the merits of which our civil engineers would not pronounce a very flattering opinion.'[7]

Punch, the satirical magazine which had come up with the nickname 'Crystal Palace', was the most critical:

> We could not help ... being struck by the glaring contrast between large pretension and little performance, as exemplified in the dreary and empty aspect of the large space claimed by and allotted to America. An enormous banner betokened the whole of the east end as devoted to the United States; but what was our astonishment, on arriving there, to find their contribution to the world's industry consists as yet of a few wine glasses, a square or two of soap, and a pair of salt-cellars! For a calculating people our friends the Americans are thus far terribly out in their calculations.[8]

Back in the United States, there was a general view in the newspapers that going to the Great Exhibition was a waste of time. It was all humbug, anyway, and they would have done better just to get on with being the most productive nation on earth instead of competing against the exotic goods of Europe. There was a stirring of the antagonism between the agricultural South of the slave plantations and the industrial North. The *Charleston Mercury* crowed at the failure of the latter to put on much of a show with its Yankee inventions. By August 1851, it seemed as if the half-hearted participation of America in Hyde Park had been a failure. Then everything changed.

What became known as the 'lock controversy' began on 23 July when Mr A. C. Hobbs, a New York agent of the lock-makers Day and Newell who were showing their 'Paratouptic Bank Lock' at the Exhibition, took up the challenge being advertised by leading London lock-makers, Bramah. 'The artist who can make an instrument that will pick or open this lock,' read the notice in their Piccadilly window display, 'will receive 200 guineas the moment it is produced.' Hobbs agreed to pit his lock-picking skills against Bramah and an elaborate test was arranged in which three referees ensured there was no trickery. The Bramah lock proved to be a tough nut for the American to crack. He began to fiddle with it on 24 July but did not open it until 23 August. Some of that time he was otherwise engaged, but according to the referees who granted him the award of 200 guineas, it took Hobbs fifty-one hours over sixteen days to open the lock. It was a condition that the lock should not be damaged in any way and Hobbs was able to lock and unlock it with the key to prove that it remained in mint condition. Though Hobbs did not quite abide by the rules, using four instruments instead of just one, Bramah none the less paid up.

Just before he challenged Bramah, Hobbs had opened a Chubb lock on the door of a strongroom in Westminster in just twenty-five minutes. Though he had several witnesses, Chubb were reluctant to accept that they had been humiliated in this way. However, *The Times* felt that Bramah, Chubb and the great British locksmiths had been humbled by Hobbs and might look to their patents rather than shrug off the defeat. Credit was given to Bramah for accepting the challenge, and the point was made that no burglar would be afforded sixteen days to pick a lock. But the achievement of Hobbs was regarded as a genuine American triumph. An attempt to pick the Day and Newell lock failed and the Bank of England ordered examples of it soon after. As *The Times* put it: 'We believed before the Exhibition opened that we had the best locks in the world, and among us, Bramah and Chubb were reckoned quite impregnable as Gibraltar ... The mechanical spirit, however, is never at rest ... Our Descendants on the other side of the water are even now and then administering upon this text and recently they have been "rubbing us up" with a severity which perhaps we merited for sneering at their shortcomings in the Exhibition.'[9]

While Hobbs was picking locks, there were other Americans who accepted the challenge to demonstrate the superiority of their inventions. In what was known as the Prairie Ground of the American display was an odd-looking machine which an English newspaper had described disparagingly as looking like 'a cross between an Astley's chariot, a treadmill and a flying machine'. This was the Cyrus McCormick reaper and, like a chariot at Astley's, the top

London venue for horse drama, it was a horse-drawn contraption. There was no way of knowing how it might perform while it sat in the Crystal Palace, but the challenge of a farmer in Essex was accepted at the end of July and the reaper taken out to be put through its paces. Present at the demonstration was one B. P. Johnson, Secretary of the New York State Agricultural Society, who sent back a thrilling report of McCormick's triumph which was published in the *Albany Evening Journal*:

> The Thursday of the trial was wet, and the corn at Mr Mechi's Essex farm was green and sodden. Johnson, who was one of the judges on the day, followed anxiously with others as the reaper set off into the soaking crop. After a while the machine was stopped and, according to Johnson, the farmer announced: 'Gentlemen, here is a triumph for the American reaping machine. It has, under all its disadvantages, done its work completely. Now let us, as Englishmen, show them that we appreciate this contribution to our implements for cheapening our agriculture; and let us give the Americans three hearty English cheers!'

McCormick's reaper, which went on to win a Great Medal at the Exhibition, was time-trialled and cut seventy-four yards of corn in seventy seconds, suggesting it could cut twenty acres in a day. This, again, greatly increased American credit at the Exhibition, though within the McCormick family a major row was brewing. Who had invented the reaper? Was it the father, Robert, who had struggled for twenty years trying to get a model which worked, or was it the son, Cyrus, who in 1831 supposedly solved all the problems with the reaper in six weeks and had it patented? Cyrus's brother and other family members claimed that the father had *given* Cyrus the machine in working order; Cyrus denied it. The battle was every bit as emotional as that between the Vail and Morse families over the true origin of the American electric telegraph, though the McCormicks managed to continue as manufacturers of farm machinery, in due course making one of the first horse-drawn combined harvesters.[10]

One of the strangest of the American exhibits, the full significance of which does not appear to have been understood by either the British or American press, was the India Rubber stand of the eccentric Connecticut inventor, Charles Goodyear. Goodyear dressed in rubber and had a rubber wall fronting his exhibit, which featured balloons six feet in diameter and all kinds of goods made out of a material that had been rendered eminently workable for clothing and shoes and many other objects by the process he called 'vulcanization'. Rubber, the sap from a tree, had been used since time immemorial by the indigenous people of Central and South America to shoe their feet. It was known in Europe from the time of Columbus but in its natural state was not much use as it easily went bad or mouldy. It changed its nature with temperature, becoming brittle in cold weather and sticky when it was warm, and it was for this reason that attempts to make wearable garments out of rubber had previously failed.

A number of people worked on the problem of rendering rubber – so called because one of its earliest uses was rubbing out pencil marks – more durable and usable. The Scottish chemist Charles Macintosh had found a way of softening rubber and had developed a technique of waterproofing goods which he then produced in a small factory in Glasgow before going into partnership with a Manchester textile firm. His treatment of rubber with naphtha, a waste product from gas works, was not entirely successful, however, because the rubber still reacted to changes in temperature. Macintosh died in 1843, whereupon the business was continued by an associate, Thomas Hancock, who applied the process Goodyear claimed to have invented – vulcanization – to the making of rubber goods and these became a huge success. Goodyear's chance discovery, after a great deal of experimentation which rendered him almost destitute, was that if you heated rubber and extracted the sulphur from it, you transformed it into a workable material no longer greatly affected by changes in air temperature. Hancock began producing a host of rubber goods including knapsacks and waterproof trousers for the military and for fishermen.

Goodyear was locked in a patent battle in England, where he claimed that Hancock had stolen his invention, while in America, another man claimed priority. But in 1851 it was acknowledged that he did credit to the Americans at the Great Exhibition along with Hobbs and McCormick. His name was adopted later in the century by a company formed to make rubber tyres for bicycles. At the time, however, Goodyear's new rubber world was not half as interesting to the British as the weapon displayed on another stall: Samuel Colt's 'repeating pistol'. This new-fangled weapon had had a chequered history before it went on show at the Crystal Palace, where its uses as a handy weapon to keep the native populations under control were quickly recognized by the British.

Colt himself was yet another inventor with a very unpredictable career: born in 1814 the son of a Hartford, Connecticut, textile manufacturer, he attended college but left at the age of fifteen, apparently under a cloud. He took to the sea, sailing to Calcutta and back before becoming a kind of showman with what became known as 'laughing gas'. This was nitrous oxide, discovered and popularized by the English chemist Humphry Davy, who noted that it was a painkiller and might be used as an anaesthetic, a suggestion that was left untested for a long time. Sniffing nitrous oxide produced a mad giggliness which had its adherents dancing around like happy drunks.

Rather like Morse on the *Sully*, Colt is reputed to have got his inspiration for the revolver while watching the turning of the capstan aboard ship. He is said to have carved a pistol of wood which was the prototype for the repeater he patented first in 1835. He began to manufacture these guns and sold a few to men heading out West, but the business was a failure and went bankrupt in 1842. Then, during the Mexican War of 1846, the US military put in a large order for them. Colt had none left, not even a model, but he was able to supply one thousand revolvers by going into partnership with the Eli Whitney works at Whitneyville. Shortly afterwards, he set up on his own again at Hartford and, with the help of others, established what was to become one of the largest arms manufacturing businesses in the world. After the impression made at the Crystal Palace, Colt set up a factory in England and was interviewed by a parliamentary committee, which visited Hartford and was impressed enough to buy Colt's machines and bring some of his workmen back to England.

At the time of the Great Exhibition, the *Maidstone Gazette*, an English newspaper which had a circulation in an area with a large cavalry depot, mused on the value of the efficient and fast-firing Colt revolver which could shoot six bullets in quick succession:

> Amongst the most humiliating circumstances in the recent war in the Cape was that of a horde of Kaffirs rushing on a small detachment of our troops, and wresting their muskets from their hands after the first discharge, before they could reload. Here the courage and energy of the savage were more than a match for the more disciplined soldier, who, after the first fire, was completely at the mercy of those who were not hit. The musket may be an admirable weapon for operating on close masses of men, but in the irregular impetuous rush of such warlike tribes as the Kaffirs, the Afghans, the American Indians and the New Zealanders, a different description of weapon is requisite, which will give the largest number of shots at a given time.[11]

So there were the lock, the vulcanized rubber, the reaper, the pistol and then, to cap it all, the New York yacht *America* beating all the English boats at Cowes Regatta on the Isle of Wight, to confirm what all Yankees knew, that their sailing ships were the fastest on the ocean. By the end of it all, in October 1851, *The Times* was prepared to concede: 'Great Britain has received more useful ideas and more ingenious inventions from the United States, through the exhibition, than from all other sources.' The *Observer* went further: 'Our cousins across the Atlantic cut many degrees closer to the ground than we do in seeking for markets. Their industrial system unfettered by ancient usage, and by the pomp and magnificence which our social institutions countenance, is essentially democratic in its tendencies. They produce for the masses, and for wholesale consumption ...With an immense command of raw produce they do not, like many other countries, skip over the wants of the many, and rush to supply the luxuries of the few.'

Eventually the Americans took home 159 medals from the Great Exhibition – an impressive tally which amounted to a win for one in every four of their exhibits. Even the magazine *Punch* had changed its tune, offering a 'Last Appendix' to the popular song 'Yankee Doodle':

> Yankee Doodle sent to town
> His goods for Exhibition;
> Everybody ran him down
> And laughed at his position;
> They thought him all the world behind
> A goney, muff or noodle.
> Laugh on, good people – never mind –
> Says quiet Yankee Doodle
>
> Chorus
>
> Your gunsmiths of their skill may crack
> But that again don't mention
> I guess that Colt's revolvers, whack
> Their very first invention.
> By Yankee Doodle, too, you're beat
> Downright in agriculture
> With his machine for reaping wheat,
> Chaw's up as by a vulture.[12]

There was one rather sad little codicil to the American success at the expense of some of the prouder nations of Europe, whose luxury goods dazzled at first but were seen in the end as archaic. Just as the Exhibition was about to close, a policeman was called to Charles Goodyear's stand, where a young Prussian interested in chemistry was seen making off with a map of the United States made of vulcanized rubber. He claimed he had been given it, whereas in fact he had been offered some other piece of rubber to take home. The Prussian got off with a fine and without the map.

It seemed, in the end, that American inventiveness was everywhere at the Exhibition. Even though there were six versions of the electric telegraph on display, Samuel Morse himself was not an exhibitor. Yet one of the offerings from the German city of Hanover was none other than a 'Morse-style' telegraph which had recently been installed there and represented one of the first sales of modern American equipment in Europe. Indeed, the Great Exhibition of 1851 turned out to be a watershed in the industrial revolution and the Crystal Palace was a fantastic monument to the first century of industrialization. But times were changing rapidly and new powers were arising in the world. America had made its mark, France was in its own way 'catching up', and very soon Germany would become significant. Russia, however, was to remain a lumbering giant, ever dependent on foreign ingenuity for whatever advances it made. Its close but isolated eastern neighbour, Japan, was not officially represented at all, though there were already plans afoot to unlock the mysteries of the empire which Herman Melville, the American author of *Moby Dick,* called 'that double-bolted land'.

CHAPTER FOURTEEN

'A VERY HANDSOME TAIL'

At much the same time as visitors to London wondered at the marvel of the Crystal Palace, a drama was unfolding on the other side of the world which would, in its way, play just as significant a part as the Great Exhibition in the global spread of industrialism. Early in 1851, three Japanese fishermen who had been shipwrecked ten years earlier were on their way back to their native land. This was no easy homecoming, for the men knew they would be treated by the Japanese authorities with deep suspicion. Any Japanese who visited the West, whether intentionally or by the accident of shipwreck, were regarded as traitors who were potentially contaminated by alien beliefs and values. For some two hundred years, the ruling Shogunate in Japan had enforced rigorously and often brutally a policy of excluding foreigners and those who had been in contact with them. This xenophobia was a legacy of the Japanese rejection of Jesuit missionaries, mostly from Portugal, in the seventeenth century. The missionaries and their converts were regarded as seditious, their beliefs as undermining the values of Japan's military rulers, and they were hunted down and killed or exiled.

Even in 1851, the Japanese Shogunate still held out against the growing pressure from Britain, Russia and America to open up their islands for trade. The three fishermen returning home were well aware of the risks they took, but they longed to see their friends and families again, and they had a tale to tell about the world outside of Japan. One of them, who was generally known to his American friends as John Manjiro or John Mung, had saved up enough money to buy himself and his friends a place on the American ship *Sarah Boyd*, which was sailing out of Bath, Maine, and heading for China. In his time away, Manjiro had become a competent seaman on American whalers: he was, in fact, one of the crew of the *Sarah Boyd*. The plan had been for Manjiro's two Japanese friends to be put off at the Ryukyu Islands and make their way back towards their homes in the south of the country while Manjiro would continue as far as China. However, when the captain of the *Sarah Boyd* witnessed Manjiro's intense excitement at the sight and smells of his homeland, he insisted that he leave the ship along with his companions. Manjiro gathered up his belongings, wrote letters to friends and then said his farewells, taking the oars of the little boat that would take the three men to the shore.

Although Manjiro rowed energetically, the three were tossed around in heavy seas so frightening that one of his companions collapsed in panic, fearing they might be shipwrecked once again. Happily, when they finally beached the boat, they were not badly treated by the islanders, although they were regarded with caution and handed on from one clan to another, always under guard. It took a whole year for Manjiro and his friends to reach the Shogunate in the capital of Edo (the old name for Tokyo). All along the way, they had been interrogated about their experiences and they now had to perform a ritual to prove that they had not been converted to Christianity: this involved stamping on a medallion depicting the Madonna and Child. As Manjiro related his adventures in the West, however, what he had to say was increasingly regarded by the authorities as valuable information rather than dangerous propaganda.

Attempts had been made in Japan to keep abreast of Western developments, chiefly through translations of Dutch texts brought in by traders, but Manjiro's revelations seemed scarcely credible to his interrogators. He had, for example, a world map drawn in 1846 which astonished the authorities: they had never seen anything so detailed, and as they could not understand the script, the young fisherman had to translate place names into Japanese. As for Manjiro himself, he had effectively been catapulted from an almost medieval world straight into the Victorian era and he did not find it easy to describe a modern democracy such as he had seen in the United States. The Japan he returned to was a scattered nation of two hundred and fifty clans whose chiefs paid homage each year to the ruling military elite, the Bafuku. To demonstrate their loyalty, the chiefs and their retinues of samurai had to travel once a year to Tokyo and stay there for a fixed period: it was a way of keeping an eye on clans who might get ideas above their station and attempt to undermine the Bafuku's authority. The Japanese emperors had been rendered powerless and lived under a kind of palatial house arrest, while the mass of the population were essentially serfs. Manjiro was from the lowest stratum of Japanese society, yet he was clearly a young man of considerable ability.

During the last period of his seventy-day interrogation, Manjiro worked with a young artist, Kawada Shoryo, who did his best to illustrate many of the scenes from Manjiro's adventures. Together they produced a four-volume travelogue which was given the enigmatic title, *A brief account of drifting towards the south-east* or *Hyoson Kirykau* in Japanese. Manjiro added his own subtitle in English, *The story of Five Japanese. A very Handsome Tail*, which was dated 25 October 1852.

This was his story. In the Japanese calendar it was the twelfth year of the Tempo, the Year of the Ox. In the Western calendar it was 1841. John Manjiro was just fourteen years old, the youngest of a crew of five fishermen whose small boat was blown off course hundreds of miles from their home and wrecked on an uninhabited volcanic island in the South Pacific. Though he and the older men were in despair and often cried about the hopelessness of their circumstances, they managed to survive on this little outcrop, which was known to mariners as Bird or Hurricane Island. They found a cave which they made their home, fashioning beds out of the salvaged wreckage of their boat. One of the fishermen had broken his leg and lay helpless in the cave, cared for by his brother, while the other three, and John Manjiro in particular, gathered what food they could. They created their own castaway recipe which they called 'stone roast', made with the pounded flesh of seabirds laid out to cook on rocks exposed to the sun. They fished and gathered what they could on the seashore and in this way they survived for four months. From time to time, they saw a ship in the distance but failed to attract the attention of the lookouts.

One day John Manjiro saw two boats heading towards the island and shouted excitedly, 'Rescuers! Rescuers! The rescue boats are coming.' Two of his friends, Toraemon and Goeman, came running. They tied Goeman's trousers to a broken sailyard and waved frantically. Seeing them, the crew of the boats waved back, some raising their hats in greeting. They invited the castaways to come out to them and Manjiro and his friends stripped off and swam to the boats. There was a crew of six men in each, some with long, ragged hair, others with skin blacker than they had ever seen before – like soot on a kettle was how Manjiro put it later – and curly hair. Though they had no knowledge of each other's language, Manjiro managed to gesture to the seamen that there were two more castaways on the island. These were taken aboard as well.

John Manjiro had a vivid memory of the boat and the men who had rescued him and his friends. He was impressed by the height and bearing of the *John Howland*'s captain, who was some six foot with swept-back black hair and imposing 'like a nobleman'. Brought up to fear authority, the Japanese fishermen knelt before William H. Whitfield, shaking with anxiety, but were quickly reassured that they would be well treated. The captain ordered a set of clothes to be found for each of them, and arranged a careful diet of herb soup and a little pork, waving away the boiled sweet potatoes the cook had prepared. As they began to recover their strength, the captain made sure they were given rice often as he guessed this would be their normal diet.

The *John Howland* itself also mightily impressed John Manjiro. As it sailed away from the island to continue its patrol of the Pacific in search of whales, the ship carried some 6,000 barrels that were to be filled with their oil. Two cannon and thirty bayonets (this was how Manjiro described the ship's guns) comprised its only defence against pirates. For fresh food, there were on board several cows and pigs, and there was some grain to make bread. As for Captain Whitfield himself, his wife had died shortly before he set out on this voyage and he had no children. Over six months, as the *John Howland* hunted whales, killing sixteen, John Manjiro, or John Mung as the crew liked to call him, became a favourite of the captain as he was quick to learn and keen to observe how these foreigners had become so proficient at killing and butchering whales in such large numbers.

It was not until they reached the Sandwich Islands (later renamed Hawaii) that Captain Whitfield took the five castaways ashore. He introduced them to an American doctor and missionary called Gerrit Parmele Judd, who had met castaways from Japan before and quickly understood that this was John Manjiro's country of origin. He also found the four older men places with families in Hawaii. Manjiro might have stayed there too had not Captain Whitfield asked his friends if he could take him to America, where he would be well cared for and might learn a trade. After some discussion, this was agreed and John Manjiro embarked on an adventure beyond his wildest imagination.

It was the early summer of 1843 before the *John Howland* dropped anchor back in New Bedford. In the two years they had been at sea, Manjiro had visited some of the most primitive communities that had survived far from any nineteenth-century influences: people living in palm-leaf huts or simple holes in the ground, surviving on coconuts and shellfish they gathered on the shore. Now, in New Bedford, he was to experience for the first time Western life at a level of sophistication that only the ruling elite in Japan might enjoy. There was at first nothing very strikingly technological that caught Manjiro's attention. In fact, New Bedford was not very different in appearance from the bustling Hawaiian capital of Honolulu. Manjiro was more taken with the beauty of its inhabitants, especially the women, their friendly, open manner and the pleasant climate.

Manjiro lodged with a variety of people in New Bedford and learned the cooperage trade so that he could make the barrels used to hold whale oil. He was sent to school to study arithmetic and European writing and cared for by Captain Whitfield's family and friends. The captain had married a second time and bought himself a farm which his wife managed, and Manjiro stayed there for a while, helping to look after the livestock. By 1846 Manjiro could speak and write English well enough to make himself understood and he was pleased to meet again a friend who had been a harpooner on the *John Howland*. This man, a New Yorker called Ira Davis, was now captain of his own whaler, the *Franklin*, and he asked Manjiro to join the crew.

On the *Franklin* Manjiro was at sea for nearly two years and had many adventures. He met again in Honolulu two of his fishermen friends: they had tried to return to Japan but had failed to get ashore as the American captain of their whaler did not want to risk a confrontation. Halfway through the voyage, Ira Davis began to behave in a strange manner and was finally judged insane by senior members of the crew. He was put off in Manila and Manjiro was promoted to first mate. In September 1849 Manjiro returned to New Bedford as a qualified seaman on a ship that had been away for more than three years and had a spectacular catch, according to Manjiro, of 500 whales, all of which had been expertly butchered and then boiled down into thousands of barrels of oil. Manjiro's share of the profits was $350, which he was pleased to show his benefactor, Captain Whitfield, who was himself back home from sea.

Manjiro had not long returned to New Bedford when news came of the gold finds in California and he decided to try his luck there so that he might earn enough money to pay his way back across the Pacific to Japan, for he was determined to go home to see his family again, whatever the risks. Captain Whitfield gave him his blessing and within a month of returning to New Bedford, Manjiro was aboard the *Stieglitz* out of Fairhaven, heading for Cape Horn, then up the west coast of South America towards San Francisco, which the ship reached in May. For the first time, Manjiro saw a paddle steamer and took a ride on it up to Sacramento. He had by now also seen some of the first steam railroads in America. Panning for gold was tougher than Manjiro had thought it would be, and dangerous too as there were protection racketeers preying on the panners. But he made more than $600 in seventy days and looked for a ship out of San Francisco which would take him to Hawaii, where he hoped to find two of his friends and persuade them to return to Japan with him.

Manjiro was duly reunited with Goeman and Toraemon, who had adopted the nickname 'Denzo', in Hawaii and hatched with them a plan to return to

Japan. He felt guilty about going home without first revisiting Captain Whitfield, and so wrote a letter in his spidery hand:

> I never forgot your benevolence of bringing me up from a small boy to manhood. I have done nothing for your kindness till now. Now I am going to return with Denzo and Goeman to my country. My wrong doing is not to be excused but I believe good will come out of this changing world, and that we will meet again. The gold and silver I left and also my clothing, please use for useful purposes. My books and stationery please divide among my friends. John Mung[1]

Had Manjiro been shipwrecked a few years earlier than 1841, the chances of his being rescued would have been slim indeed. To enforce their isolationist policy, the Japanese forbade the building of ocean-going ships. All their whaling, which had been carried on for centuries, was done inshore, as it had been at one time in Europe and on the east coast of North America. No Japanese ship would have sailed as far as the island on which Manjiro and his friends were stranded. But the number of American ships in the southern Pacific Ocean had been growing year by year.

The hunting of whales may have been an age-old practice, but the American whaling industry of the 1840s was on a spectacular scale, delivering to the ports of New England millions of barrels of oil a year as well as thousands of tons of baleen or whalebone. Tucked away on an inlet sheltered from the Atlantic by the island of Martha's Vineyard, the twin capitals of the industry were Fairhaven and New Bedford. There was a belief in America at the time that New Bedford was one of the richest, if not the richest, town in the world, so prosperous were the owners of the whaling fleet, the agents who administered the trade and the captains of the fleet that crossed the world in pursuit of the Leviathans of the sea. Herman Melville summed it up in *Moby Dick* : 'Nowhere in all America will you find more patrician-like houses, parks and gardens more opulent, than in New Bedford. Whence came they? ... Yes; all these brave houses and flowery gardens came from the Atlantic, Pacific, and Indian oceans. One and all, they were harpooned and dragged up hither from the bottom of the sea.'[2]

There were two kinds of whale that New Bedford's captains hunted. The most valuable was the sperm whale, for it contained an oil which could be ladled out by the barrel-load and burned cleanly and brightly in lamps. It was this oil that produced the glow of the earliest lighthouses and provided fine lubrication for the moving parts of metal machinery. Blubber from sperm whales, when melted down, was also of a very high grade, making the finest candles. And now and again these whales, through some kind of ailment, produced a peculiar substance called ambergris that was used in the perfume trade, not for its scent but to 'fix' the fragrance of distilled plants. Right whales, so called simply because they were slow enough for sailing ships to pursue and catch, were also a source of oil, but one of an inferior variety which stank when burned in lamps and provided a less refined lubrication. Whalebone was taken from the huge jaws of both species and was used much as plastic is today.

A whaling ship from New England of the kind described so graphically by Melville in *Moby Dick* was a model, in theory at least, of egalitarian enterprise in which every member of the crew, however humble, was entitled to a percentage of the profit of a voyage. A captain might be awarded one eighth, an ordinary seaman a 200th. The more successful a voyage, the more everybody on board would receive at the end of it, so they had common interest. Most whalers in the 1840s were at sea for at least two years before they returned with their cargo of oil, although often a voyage lasted twice that long. The crews were often a wildly cosmopolitan bunch of men, including Africans and South Pacific islanders such as Melville's fictional harpooner Queequeg. In fact, Melville remarked on the strange spectacle of probable cannibals chatting and smoking their pipes on the street corners of New Bedford.

The captains of New Bedford whalers, however, were for the most part devout, church-going Christians, men such as William Whitfield from Fairhaven, which faces New Bedford across the Acushnet river. Whitfield was by all accounts a fine, upstanding figure of a man: he was in his forties when his ship rescued Manjiro and he kept the then fashionable black beard around his jawbone trimmed and his upper lip clean-shaven. Like nearly all the whalers at that time, the *John Howland* headed south for Cape Horn at the treacherous tip of South America and into the rich grounds of the Pacific. In the eighteenth century, most whaling had been closer to home, but those earlier fleets had been badly damaged in the wars with Britain and whale stocks were low when the arrival of peace late in 1812 allowed the Yankee square-riggers to set sail once again.

To survive thousands of miles from their home port, the whaling ships had to discover Pacific havens where they might refit and restock with fresh water, food and the livestock they always carried. There were by the 1840s many steamships operating on the great American rivers such as the Hudson and the Mississippi, and one, the *Savannah*, had already crossed the Atlantic, powered for some of the way by steam, in 1815. But there was still no way in which whalers, if steam-powered, could have been replenished with coal on the Pacific Islands and they were therefore all sailing ships. A popular and busy port of call was Honolulu, capital of the Sandwich Islands, and some American missionaries and agents had become established there. They also handled the post between ships and the New England ports, operating as a sorting office.

The first whaling expeditions to the Pacific had been in part voyages of discovery, the sea mapped with every handy island marked as a place where there might be a natural harbour, fresh water and rich fishing grounds in the shallow waters. But Japan was one large archipelago where the whalers could not put in to refit or refuel. Stricken crews who sought succour on the Japanese coast were fired on or arrested and treated cruelly. Russian crews were treated in the same fashion, and when, on occasion, they attempted to return some shipwrecked Japanese fishermen to their homeland, they were driven away. It was one thing for Japan to remain aloof from the rest of the world; it was quite another for this nation to treat innocent foreigners as if they were criminals.

At the peak of Pacific whaling, New Bedford had 329 ships and crews totalling ten thousand men in an industry capitalized at around $12 million a year. Sooner or later, the United States was going to ask for a treaty with Japan which would give its shipwrecked seamen a degree of protection and might open up some trade with this populous, and potentially prosperous, part of the world. As well as the safety of the whaling fleet, there was, after

1848, the prospect of sailing direct from the West Coast of the United States to Japan, for in that year California was added to the Union at the close of the wars with Mexico. Indeed, steamships were now heading across the Pacific and these would require coaling stations. The spread of industrialism across the world had finally caught up with Japan.

An Englishman opening his freshly ironed copy of *The Times* on the morning of 26 March 1852 would have been intrigued by an editorial prompted by news from across the Atlantic that the Americans were preparing what they called 'an expedition against Japan'. For far too long, or so it seemed to *The Times* leader writer, the 'Empire of Japan' had 'remained a sealed book to the various nations of the civilised world'. And the newspaper was very much in favour of the expedition, backed by the United States government, to persuade the Japanese to open up their ports to trade with the newly industrializing nations of the West. Not long before, the British had broken down the disdainful isolationism of the Chinese emperor with a few rounds of cannon fire. No doubt the Japanese, though by reputation a militant nation, would not 'offer any effective resistance against the howitzers and rocket-tubes of the United States' Squadron'.[3]

Though Japan had not been officially represented at the Great Exhibition, it was not regarded by Britain or any of the industrializing Western nations as backward. *The Times* leader referred to Japan as a 'rich and populous' country, recalling that at one time it had exported timber, wheat, rice, cotton, silk and ambergris. That Japan was potentially a very wealthy nation that might benefit from trade made the intractable policy of its autocratic rulers, which forbade anything more than minimal contact with the West, especially frustrating. Accordingly, *The Times* leader proposed, 'It is a fair question how far any tribe or race of human beings possess the right of excluding the rest of mankind from all participation in the benefits to be derived from an extensive and beautiful region.'[4]

Exactly what the 'benefits' were that Japan had to offer, *The Times* did not make clear. But its tone suggested that, from the perspective of the industrialized world, and Britain and America in particular, there were raw materials and useful ports and trading posts to be had here. There was certainly no hint that this nation, which had few roads or wheeled vehicles and effectively remained in the Middle Ages, could rival the West as a manufacturer of anything other than luxuries such as silk garments and lacquered boxes. 'Japan not only refuses to hold commercial intercourse with the rest of the world ...'[5] the *New York Courier and Enquirer* complained in 1852, 'but she goes further, and, occupying as she does an enormous extent of sea-coast, she not only refuses to open her ports to foreign vessels in distress, but actually opens her batteries upon them when they approach within gunshot of her shores; and when driven upon them by stress of weather, she seizes upon, imprisons, exhibits in cages and actually murders the crews of such ill-fated vessels.'[6] As a result, American crews were compelled to put ashore miles from their hunting grounds: 'The single fact that at one time within the last year there were 121 American whalers lying in the harbours of the Sandwich Islands – far away from their cruising grounds, because they could not enter any harbour on the coast of Japan for repairs – shows not only the extent of our commerce in that region, but the claims of humanity itself for protection against the barbarians who thus cut off, as it were, the commerce of the Yellow Sea and the Sea of Ochotsk.'[7]

Taking with him a letter from Millard Fillmore, the President of the United States, Commodore Matthew Calbraith Perry set off from Chesapeake Bay on 24 November 1852 in the *Mississippi*, a sail-rigged steamer which had been his flagship in the Mexican war. Perry had waited for other ships taking part in the expedition to be refitted, but left without them, planning to meet up with the steamship *Susquehanna* and sloops-of-war *Vandalia* and *Macedonia* which were then already in the Far East. The voyage took them to the island of Madeira, around the Cape of Good Hope and on to Mauritius and then Singapore. Oceanic travel by steamship was still in its infancy and Perry had to send coal ships ahead so that he could be sure of supplies in the Pacific. By the time the Americans reached Japan, having stopped off at many places along the way, it was July 1853 and Perry had only four ships with which to impress the Shogunate: the steamship *Susquehanna*, which towed the sailing supply ship *Saratoga*, and the *Mississippi,* which towed the *Plymouth*. The *Susquehanna* led the way.

'As the squadron sailed up the coast, some eight or ten junks hove in sight, and two or three of them were observed soon to change their course and to turn back toward the shore, as if to announce the arrival of strangers,' wrote Francis L. Hawks in the official record of the expedition published in 1856.

> The morning seemed to confirm the reputed character of the Japanese climate for the atmosphere was so thick and hazy that the extent of view was unfortunately very much restricted, and it was not possible to get a distinct outline of the shore until the squadron came to anchor off the city of Uraga (now Yokohama). The steamer, in spite of the wind, moved on with all sails furled, at the rate of eight or nine knots, much to the astonishment of the crews of the Japanese fishing junks gathered along the shore or scattered over the surface of the mouth of the bay, who stood in their boats, and were evidently expressing the liveliest surprise at the sight of the first steamer ever beheld in Japanese waters.[8]

The Americans were heading into the wide bay at the end of which was Tokyo, the capital. Passing Yokohama, they prepared for action: 'As the ships neared the bay, signals were made from the Commodore, and instantly the decks were cleared for action, the guns placed in position and shotted, the ammunition arranged, the small arms made ready, sentinels and men at their posts, and, in short, all the preparations made, usual before meeting an enemy.'[9] After a while, the American ships came within two miles of land and were greeted by a flotilla of more than a dozen large boats heading in their direction. Imperiously, Perry pressed on, leaving the Japanese baffled by the progress of the steamers whose sails were still furled.

Commodore Perry's arm's-length approach to the Japanese was entirely understandable. In 1846, an earlier attempt had been made to establish a dialogue with the country's rulers and the American ships had been overrun by inquisitive crowds who then refused to allow the visitors to land. And there were a number of stories of ships being fired on. As his squadron moved towards Tokyo, Perry gave orders that nobody should be allowed to board any but his ship. A few cannon shots were noted from the hillsides along the bay but they were too far away to be troublesome. Then armed boats came out and began to surround the four American ships. 'They made several attempts to get alongside and on board of the *Saratoga*,' wrote Francis Hawks in his report compiled from the diaries and memories of Perry and others, '– their tow-lines, with which they made fast to any part of the ship, were unceremoniously cast off. They attempted to climb the chains, but the crew was ordered to prevent them, and the sight of pikes, cutlasses and pistols, checked them, and when they found that our officers and men were very much in earnest, they desisted in their attempts to board.'[10]

The Americans were impressed by the Japanese 'guard boats' which seemed to skim across the water at great speed and were built in a similar fashion to the great yacht *America* which had recently beaten all comers at Cowes. The crews, up to thirty in a boat, wore only a kind of loincloth and had tattoos on their backs which resembled coats of arms. A few were armed with swords. Perry treated them all with disdain. An attempt was made to deliver a message on parchment to the *Susquehanna* but this was turned away and it was finally handed over to the *Mississippi*: written in French, the document demanded that the Americans go away and informed them that they would anchor at their peril. The near-farcical nature of the proceedings was made more comical by the problem of language. The Americans had a Chinese interpreter who was supposed to translate from Japanese into English as well as a Dutch speaker. This was perhaps just as well, for as attempts were made to negotiate the terms of a meeting, one of the Japanese said, in perfect English, that he spoke Dutch. As it transpired, so did quite a number of Japanese: it was the only Western language they had learned, and they had done so through their long-established dealings with Dutch traders.

Once the Americans and Japanese had begun to communicate, there were endless discussions about how President Fillmore's letter might be delivered to a suitably highly placed official. Those educated Japanese who could converse in Dutch were liberally entertained on the *Susquehanna* and became very sociable after accepting the whisky and brandy on offer. The Americans were interested to learn that, when presented with a globe, the Japanese could identify Washington and New York, and correctly name England, France,

Denmark and some other European countries. All in all, they seemed better informed than the visitors had anticipated. This was no doubt due in part to the wealth of information brought back by Manjiro, whose world atlas they had probably studied. One of the shoguns, too, apparently had a subscription to the *Illustrated London News*, in which he had seen pictures of railroads. By far and away the best interpreter and diplomat would have been Manjiro, who had assured his masters that the Americans were a peaceable people. But those who thought he might have become too friendly with the visitors won the day and he was not introduced to Commodore Perry. Another Japanese castaway called Sampachi and known to the American sailors as Sam Patch was a guest of Perry's on the *Mississippi*, but his value as an interpreter was severely hampered by the fact that, as soon as he met a superior Japanese, he threw himself at their feet, an act of obeisance which both startled and disgusted his fellow crewmen. It took several days for arrangements to be made to deliver President Fillmore's letter, which is worth quoting in full as it expresses very well the reasons for America's desire to open up Japan to world trade.

GREAT AND GOOD FRIEND:

I send you this public letter by Commodore Matthew C. Perry, an officer of the highest rank in the navy of the United States, and commander of the squadron now visiting your imperial majesty's dominions.

I have directed Commodore Perry to assure your imperial majesty that I entertain the kindest feelings toward your majesty's person and government, and that I have no other object in sending him to Japan but to propose to your imperial majesty that the United States and Japan should live in friendship and have commercial intercourse with each other.

The Constitution and laws of the United States forbid all interference with the religious or political concerns of other nations. I have particularly charged Commodore Perry to abstain from every act which could possibly disturb the tranquility of your imperial majesty's dominions.

The United States of America reach from ocean to ocean, and our Territory of Oregon and State of California lie directly opposite to the dominions of your imperial majesty. Our steamships can go from California to Japan in eighteen days.

Our great State of California produces about sixty millions of dollars in gold every year, besides silver, quicksilver, precious stones, and many other valuable articles. Japan is also a rich and fertile country, and produces many very valuable articles. Your imperial majesty's subjects are skilled in many of the arts. I am desirous that our two countries should trade with each other, for the benefit both of Japan and the United States.

We know that the ancient laws of your imperial majesty's government do not allow of foreign trade, except with the Chinese and the Dutch – but as the state of the world changes and new governments are formed, it seems to be wise, from time to time, to make new laws. There was a time when the ancient laws of your imperial majesty's government were first made. About the same time America, which is sometimes called the New World, was first discovered and settled by the Europeans. For a long time there were but a few people, and they were poor. They have now become quite numerous; their commerce is very extensive; and they think that if your imperial majesty were so far to change the ancient laws [sic] as to allow a free trade between the two countries, it would be extremely beneficial to both.

If your imperial majesty is not satisfied that it would be safe altogether to abrogate the ancient laws which forbid foreign trade, they might be suspended for five or ten years, so as to try the experiment. If it does not prove as beneficial as was hoped, the ancient laws can be restored. The United States often limit their treaties with foreign States to a few years, and then renew them or not, as they please.

I have directed Commodore Perry to mention another thing to your imperial majesty. Many of our ships pass every year from

California to China; and great numbers of our people pursue the whale fishery near the shores of Japan. It sometimes happens, in stormy weather, that one of our ships is wrecked on your imperial majesty's shores. In all such cases we ask, and expect, that our unfortunate people should be treated with kindness, and that their property should be protected, till we can send a vessel and bring them away. We are very much in earnest in this.

Commodore Perry is also directed by me to represent to your imperial majesty that we understand there is a great abundance of coal and provisions in the Empire of Japan. Our steamships, in crossing the great ocean, burn a great deal of coal, and it is not convenient to bring it all the way from America. We wish that our steamships and other vessels should be allowed to stop in Japan and supply themselves with coal, provisions, and water. They will pay for them in money, or anything else your imperial majesty's subjects may prefer; and we request your imperial majesty to appoint a convenient port, in the southern part of the Empire, where our vessels may stop for this purpose. We are very desirous of this.

These are the only objects for which I have sent Commodore Perry, with a powerful squadron, to pay a visit to your imperial majesty's renowned city of Yedo [Tokyo]: friendship, commerce, a supply of coal and provisions, and protection for our shipwrecked people. We have directed Commodore Perry to beg your imperial majesty's acceptance of a few presents. They are of no great value in themselves; but some of them may serve as specimens of the articles manufactured in the United States, and they are intended as tokens of our sincere and respectful friendship.

May the Almighty have your imperial majesty in His great and holy keeping.

In witness whereof, I have caused the great seal of the United States to be hereunto affixed, and have subscribed the same with my name, at the city of Washington, in America, the seat of my government, on the thirteenth day of the month of November, in the year one thousand eight hundred and fifty-two.

[Seal attached.]

Your good friend,
MILLARD FILLMORE.
By the President:
EDWARD EVERETT,
Secretary of State.[11]

On this first visit, Commodore Perry had not brought many gifts. Along with the letter to the Emperor – whom he believed, incorrectly, was the ruler of Japan – he delivered a note which said there was much for the Japanese to consider and that he would return the following year. What the Japanese now called the 'Black Ships' steamed away, their decks bristling with arms in case they were attacked before they had reached the open sea. Perry promised that, when he returned, he would have a more impressive squadron than the one now leaving Tokyo Bay. All along, Perry made it quite clear that he would have no truck with any Japanese nonsense about his landing only at places they designated: he was not a mere tradesman content to be shown the side door into Japan. Besides, he knew very well that if a conflict broke out, the United States could subdue the recalcitrant easterners with its superior armoury.

The expedition did not return to America, but retraced its steps through the Lew Chew islands and spent time on the China coast. Here the American gifts for the second visit were delivered, brought apparently from France by a British mail steamer which left them at Canton, from where another British ship took them to Shanghai. Perry was in no great hurry to return to Japan until he heard that a French frigate had put to sea 'under sealed orders' received from Europe. At the same time there was a Russian frigate apparently preparing to make a return trip to Nagasaki and Perry suspected this might be a prelude to a rival attempt to sign a treaty with Japan. It was now December, when the seas around Japan were especially treacherous with alternating fogs and storms, but Perry decided he would have to leave as soon as possible and not wait for the spring as he had intended. And so he assembled his squadron, sending ahead three supply boats with which he would rendezvous in the Lew Chew islands. On 14 January 1854 his expedition left Hong Kong. Along with the steamers *Susquehanna* and *Mississippi* were the *Powhatan* and the store ships *Lexington* and *Southampton*.

While Perry was away in China, he received news from the Dutch that the old emperor had died. When he arrived once again in Tokyo Bay, the fact that there was a new ruler was used by the Japanese as an excuse for further procrastination. However, they had more or less made up their minds that they would have to make some concessions to the Americans. Perry was an imposing figure, nicknamed by the crews he worked with as 'Old Bruin' for his booming voice, and this second squadron was considerably more daunting than the first. Perry played the game of ritual as well as he could, marching ashore with a military band and the promised gifts from the American people. The Japanese were the ideal audience – one that, for the time being at least, might be led to believe that *everything* exciting and modern had been invented in America. Asked who had invented the steamboat, Perry's men replied, naturally, that it had been an American named Fulton. And, of course, they had invented the electric telegraph, a demonstration of which astonished the Japanese, although the official account's claim that the operators even managed to send a Morse message in Japanese beggars belief.

There were other sensations. The Colt revolver impressed the Japanese as much as it had everyone else. So did the taking of a daguerreotype, for which the Japanese, keen to show the President of the United States just how beautiful their women were, assembled a gorgeous cast. A rumour even took flight that anyone having their picture taken would die within three years, such was the fear of this extraordinary invention. But the biggest excitement surrounded the American-built quarter-size locomotive and carriages which were set to run on a circular track about a mile across, like some giant Christmas toy. Perry remarked, when he showed off the train, that he felt like a cross between 'Santa Claus and a conjurer'.

This was the first steam-driven engine of any kind to be seen in Japan and it marked the beginning of the transformation of that society which would in an astonishingly short period of time bring it into the industrialized world. Perry prised from his hosts an agreement that they would treat any shipwrecked crews of whaling ships with respect and that a port would be opened up for trade and the coaling of steamers: a more elaborate treaty could wait. Inevitably, though, it was not long before the British and Russians were making their own agreements with the Japanese and the first missions were setting off from Japan to discover just what had been going on elsewhere in the world over the past two centuries. Manjiro himself was honoured with a place on the first such adventure in 1860. Ten years later, he was a member of a mission which monitored the war between Prussia and France in 1870. They travelled via New York and so Manjiro was able to take a train to meet the man who had rescued him all those years ago. Captain Whitfield was then sixty-five, as devout as ever, and considered it an act of providence that Manjiro had been brought back to him.

The lasting image of what in the West has been called the 'opening up of Japan' must come from the official report compiled by Francis Hawks in which he describes the excitement engendered by the 'Lilliputian locomotive':

> All the parts of the mechanism were perfect, and the car was a most tasteful specimen of workmanship, but so small that it could hardly carry a child of six years of age. The Japanese, however, were not to be cheated out of a ride, and, as they were unable to reduce themselves to the capacity of the inside of the carriage, they betook themselves to the roof. It was a spectacle not a little ludicrous to behold, a dignified mandarin whirling around the circular road at the rate of twenty miles an hour, with his loose robes flying in the wind. As he clung with a desperate hold to the edge of the roof, grinning with intense interest, and his huddled body shook convulsively with a kind of laughing timidity, while the car spun rapidly around the circle, you might have supposed the movement, somehow or other, was dependent rather upon the enormous exertions of the uneasy mandarin than upon the power of the little puffing locomotive, which was so easily performing its work.[12]

Although there were clearly benefits to be had from a trade treaty with Japan, it had been the hunting of whales for their oil, and the welfare of the crews of whaling ships, that had been the driving force behind the American approach to Japan. But even as Commodore Perry and his entourage watched with amusement the excitement of their distinguished Japanese hosts whirling around atop a model of the world's most advanced means of transportation, new industrial discoveries in both Britain and North America were being made that would render the whaling ship a thing of the past.

CHAPTER FIFTEEN

THE PETROLEUM PIONEERS

Although whale oil had many uses, it was most valued as a luminant. Sperm-whale oil was the best, as we have seen, burning with a bright light and little smell or smoke. In 1850, however, it was fetching $2 to $2.50 a barrel, which meant that it was expensive and only available to better-off households. Oil from the right whale was less than half the price yet still dear. There were cheaper artificial alternatives, some of which had appeared on the market as early as the 1820s, but for one reason or another they had not been taken up with any great enthusiasm, especially in the home.

Primitive gas lighting systems had been devised at the end of the eighteenth century by William Murdoch in England, working for Boulton & Watt, and Philippe Lebon in France. Murdoch heated coal in a kettle and siphoned the resulting gas off in a gun barrel to light his home in Cornwall, and he lit part of Boulton & Watt's Birmingham factory in the same way. Lebon burned wood chippings in a glass bowl and lit the gas that was given off, calling his invention a *thermolampe*. A demonstration in 1801 by Lebon in which part of the Hotel Seignaly in Paris was lit with his system was seen by Watt's son, also called James, who urged his father and Boulton to develop gas lighting, but they did nothing. A maverick German called Frederick Winzer tried to buy a *thermolampe* from Lebon but could not persuade him to sell. Lebon, meanwhile, was murdered in Paris's Champs Elysées in 1804 in mysterious circumstances while Winzer went on to Britain with his own version of the Lebon lamp. He anglicized his name to Windsor and set about giving demonstrations and attempting to raise money to form a gas company. But scientists, including Sir Humphry Davy, ridiculed him, not because gas did not burn – everyone knew it did – but because a means had not yet been found to store and distribute it. Davy actually suggested, sarcastically, that the dome of St Paul's might do as a gas holder.

Many objections were raised against piped gas, among them the contention that it would destroy the whaling industry and therefore the reserves of fine seamen who might be pressed into naval action in times of war. Windsor returned to Paris a disappointed man, but others, including a former employee of Boulton & Watt, pursued the idea of a gas lighting company and, after a presentation to a parliamentary committee, won the day. The Gas Light and Coke Company was the first such, founded in London in 1810 to the fury of William Murdoch, who felt his idea had been stolen. By 1819, nearly all the large towns in Britain had gas lighting both in the streets and in factories.

However, the introduction of piped gas lighting did not do away with the demand for domestic oil lamps. Compared with a 'fish-tail' gas flame from a wall appliance fitted by a gas company, decorative oil lamps with finely designed glass shades were much more attractive. A favourite was the invention in the eighteenth century by the Frenchman François Pierre Ami Argand of a lamp which had a hollow, cylindrical holder for the wick that allowed a flow of air to the flame to reduce smoking. It remained popular well into the nineteenth century. Argand was one of those unfortunates who was hoodwinked by associates and had his invention pirated to such an extent he made no money and died in 1803 a bankrupt. His lamps, although designed to burn whale or vegetable oils, were easily adapted to use artificial fuels and they became a feature of the Victorian drawing room in the age of gas lighting.

When stocks of right and sperm whales fell rapidly in the mid-nineteenth century as they were hunted to near-extinction, the price of whale oil inevitably rose sharply, providing an impetus to find alternatives for lighting. Coal gas works provided one new luminant with the by-product benzene. There were also resins from pitch pine which yielded oils, and camphene, derived from turpentine, also served, even if it was inclined to smoke a good deal. None, however, could compare with either whale oils or the best vegetable oils. As it was, the problem of finding a substitute for these was to be solved almost simultaneously by two men working, quite independently, on either side of the Atlantic. Though the Scot James Young is often credited with being the first to derive a commercial luminant from a particular form of coal, earning him the sobriquet 'Paraffin' Young, precedence should really go to a man who has been almost lost to history. Dr Abraham Gesner, born in 1797 in Cornwallis, Nova Scotia, is arguably the founder of the modern oil industry for it was he who first discovered how to break down and refine raw tars and coals by a process that was later widely adopted.

Gesner's great grandfather had emigrated to New York in 1710 and the family were settled there until the War of Independence in 1776 when Abraham's father, Henry, joined the loyalist King's Orange Raiders, who were stationed in Nova Scotia at the end of the conflict. As Nova Scotia was to remain a British colony, Henry and his brother, who had joined the same corps, were given grants of land. Henry Gesner was given 400 acres in the Cornwallis Valley, settling there in 1786. Abraham was one of twelve children brought up in that rugged landscape and given a basic schooling. Nothing is really known about his early life, though his son recalled that Abraham had been involved in the sale of horses from Nova Scotia and New Brunswick to the West Indies. He had been shipwrecked twice while horse-trading and had failed to make any money. Hardly an eligible bachelor, Gesner was nevertheless accepted by Harriet Webster, the daughter of a Dr Isaac Webster of Kentville, Nova Scotia. Despite being already twenty-seven years old, Dr Webster arranged for Abraham to train as a doctor in London and he studied at Guy's Hospital and Bart's and qualified in 1827. Crucially, one of the subjects he studied was chemistry.

Back in Nova Scotia, Gesner set up as a country doctor, doing his rounds on horseback. He lived in an area rich in crystalline rocks and began to take an interest in geology and to build up a collection of stones. In 1836 he brought out his own book on the geology of Nova Scotia, and began to fancy himself a prospector for coal and iron ores. In 1838 he was made Provincial

Geologist of the Province of New Brunswick and moved to the town of St John. Prospecting began to take up much of his time as he explored the rivers and woods with Indian guides, always on the lookout for minerals that might be of value. Unfortunately, too much faith was put in his judgement as to the significance of his finds, and when prospectors were disappointed that there was no real treasure, they turned on him and he was dismissed from his post as official geologist. He went back to the family home at Cornwallis and continued to practise as a doctor.

Gesner continued his interest in geology and the commercial potential of local rocks. At some point – it is not clear when – he experimented with a piece of bitumen from what was called the 'Pitch Lake' of Trinidad. He had visited this huge deposit of black gunge that was used for caulking ships and waterproofing when he was a horse-trader and he also knew of the 'tar springs' of Barbados. Long after, he probably acquired some Trinidad pitch from a ship which had called at a port in Nova Scotia. Gesner distilled this pitch and obtained a luminant oil he called kerosene. The Greek word for wax is *keros* and that for oil, *elain*: Gesner's luminant was to have been called *keroselain* but this was changed to sound more like the already familiar 'camphene'. As it was too difficult to transport Trinidad pitch to Nova Scotia, Gesner searched for a similar tar which could be sourced locally and he was lucky enough to find it in New Brunswick.

In 1852, after the death of his father, Gesner moved with his family to Halifax. He had not attempted to exploit the local bitumen and might never have pursued his interest in luminants had he not met Thomas Cochrane, tenth Earl of Dundonald, who made his headquarters in Halifax as Admiral of the British North America and West India Station. In Scotland, Cochrane's father had tried to make money distilling coal tar to make lamp oil but had failed, losing the family fortune to this and other worthless enterprises. Thomas inherited no money, only an ambition to retrieve the family fortune. He joined the navy and saw a good deal of action, commanding a ship in the war of 1812 with the United States. He was elected to Parliament but became embroiled in a scam in which relatives of his tried to make a fortune on the stock market in 1814 with a false rumour about the death of Napoleon that produced a sudden rise in the price of shares they held. Unfairly it seems, Thomas Cochrane was convicted of taking part in the scam and was stripped of all his medals and jailed. On his release, he travelled the world as a kind of freelance naval commander, taking charge of the Chilean and Brazilian navies at various times. He was eventually cleared of corruption, but by the time he was stationed in Halifax, he was already seventy-five. In his old age, however, he had returned to his father's interest in turning pitch or coal into a variety of useful products and had bought up the land around the Pitch Lake of Trinidad. When he met up with Abraham Gesner, the two could not believe their luck.

Gesner and Cochrane worked together to take out patents and to discuss the possibility of setting up a company to exploit both the Trinidad pitch and a very similar coal-like mineral that could be mined in Albert County, New Brunswick. Cochrane went back to England in 1851 when his term of office in Canada had expired and also took out patents there for the exploitation of Trinidad pitch or 'natural asphalt'. At that time he had not considered the distillation of this tar into an oil for lighting. Gesner tried to secure the mining rights to the Albert County deposits of coal-like asphalt but was defeated in the courts by a rival claimant. Undaunted, he moved to New York, where he set up a company with Cochrane in March 1853 to turn the rock he called Albertite into a wide range of sought-after products. In addition to kerosene for lighting, the company would make various forms of insulating and waterproofing material, asphalt paving, railway grease and so on. The patents for the Asphalt Mining and Kerosene Gas Company were granted in 1854 and in them three different grades of kerosene were defined. Kerosene C was the best quality, and with further distillation and cleaning, became a clear lighting fuel with little smell and good, steady burning properties.

Although the Asphalt Mining and Kerosene Gas Company was profitable, Gesner did not own it but was in effect its chief chemist. After a while he became a practising doctor again in New York before returning in 1863 to Halifax, where he had been offered the chair of Natural History at Dalhousie University. Sadly, he died on 29 April 1864 at the age of sixty-seven before he could take up the professorial post. Gesner's lack of financial success appears to have been due partly to a lack of business acumen but also to bad luck. Although he had almost certainly discovered how to turn pitch or asphalt into lighting fuel before anybody else, his patent was filed too late. His New York company had been pipped at the post by a Scotsman, James Young, who was able to charge it for a licence to use his method of producing what in England was known as paraffin.

James Young was very much a man of his time. The son of a carpenter, he was born in Glasgow, Scotland, in 1811 and first worked for his father. At Anderson's University the Professor of Chemistry, Thomas Graham, gave evening classes which Young attended. By the time he was twenty, Young was able to give up carpentry to work as Graham's laboratory assistant. He had, in effect, won a place in the impressive world of Glasgow's scientific intelligentsia, which included David Livingstone, later to earn fame as a missionary and explorer, and Lyon Playfair, one of the most gifted and enterprising scientists of his day. Playfair studied in Germany with the leading chemist Justus von Liebig (see Chapter 21) and was befriended by Prince Albert, with whom he could converse in German. He was in charge of the giving of prizes at the Great Exhibition of 1851 and, as an expert on coal and fossil fuels, he headed the Geological Survey of Britain. It was Playfair who set Young on the trail of oil shale and a personal fortune, some of which Young would invest in his old friend David Livingstone's African expeditions.

Thomas Graham was given the chair of chemistry at University College, London, and Young joined him there in 1837 as a laboratory assistant, working for a time alongside Playfair. Soon after, Playfair went off to study with Baron Liebig in Germany while Young joined the firm of James Muspratt and Sons, manufacturers of alkalis – a horribly polluting industry which none the less supplied an ingredient essential to the making of glass, soap and artificial dyes. There was at this time a kind of European brotherhood of chemists who shared information and recommended their most talented students to each other. Liebig himself had studied in France with chemists such as Gay-Lussac and was a friend of James Muspratt, whose sons had studied in Germany and with Graham. Young took the Muspratt job as it gave him a better income than the university and he had just become a family man, having married in 1838.

In 1844, Young moved on to another chemical firm, Tennant, Clow & Co., based at Ardwick, Manchester, where he was allowed to act as a consultant while earning a salary. Here he flourished, producing a cheap indigo dye and some other patent chemical processes as well as establishing himself as a figure among the Manchester Liberals – he was a founder of the *Manchester Examiner* newspaper. It was while he was working in Manchester that he heard from Playfair, who was by now in London and head of the Geological Survey, that he knew of a source of naphtha or natural petroleum. It was on the Derbyshire estate of Playfair's brother-in-law, James Oates, and Young would be free to set up a company to exploit it. This was Young's first enterprise with oil and he concluded, erroneously, that the Derbyshire oil, which lay above a coal seam, was somehow derived from the coal by condensation. Yet it was precisely this misapprehension that led him on to his next, and major project, for he began experimenting with an artificial way of producing the same effect. When in due course he discovered he could distil certain kinds of coal, or oil shale, to produce petroleum, he quickly patented the system and bought up the rights to the entire supply of the best sources of oil shale at Bathgate near Edinburgh. At first he produced lubricants, but another chance discovery led him to realize that his paraffin – the term had been coined by a German chemist in the 1830s – was also suitable for lighting.

One of Young's rivals in Scotland was George Miller, whose company thrived in the coal-oil business for a number of years before it was put out of business by Young in an action for breach of his patent. Miller heard about a lubricant which had been developed in America from the waste from gas works and given the name 'coup oil'. It had been produced by the Massachusetts-based United States Chemical Manufacturing Company as a lubricant, but, like many of these early coal-derived products, it produced a horrible smell. George Miller & Company were not put off, however, and asked for a sample as they would consider manufacturing it under licence. Luther Atwood and Josepha Merrill from the American company went to Glasgow and began to experiment with local coal and oil shale. One of the uses Miller had for the oil shale was in the dissolving of rubber to make it liquid enough to impregnate cloth for waterproof clothing. This oil shale came from the Bathgate deposits controlled by Young. Atwood, by chance, found that in distilling this Bathgate shale a second time he obtained a clear liquid which burned brilliantly in certain kinds of oil lamp. When Young saw as much on a visit to Miller's offices, he immediately realized the commercial potential and cut off Miller's supply of oil shale so that he could exploit it himself. This was the foundation of Young's fortune, for it would lead to the use of coal and oil shale and, eventually, to crude petroleum as the fuel that lit millions of lamps.

Young himself retired in 1870 and spent much of his time before his death in 1883 farming three estates and cruising on his own steam yacht. He had been fortunate, though, making his money in the years before the Scottish oil industry faced competition from America. In 1866 Young's Paraffin Light and Mineral Oil Company employed 1,500 workers and was one of some 120 oil firms in Scotland. But the oil boom there was not to last much beyond the late 1860s – what finally destroyed it was the discovery that beneath the land there were great pools of naturally occurring oil which could be siphoned off into barrels and refined by the very same processes which had been developed to produce kerosene and paraffin.

From time immemorial, petroleum oil had been gathered where it seeped from the surface of the land. It was so abundant in some parts of the world that it had been used for centuries for lighting and lubrication, as medicine and even in the pitch for waterproofing roofs. But it was not traded over any distance, except as a medicine. In America, a Pittsburgh chemist, Samuel Keir, began in 1843 to market crude petroleum as a panacea for all ills, making claims such as 'There's nothing like it for burns', 'Chronic Cough Cured' and 'Rheumatism yields to the power of Petroleum'. Keir and others had came across 'rock oil' while prospecting for salt water. For many years, the oily substance that rose up with the saline deposits was regarded as an unfortunate pollutant and was simply drained away. All Keir did was to let the contaminated salt water stand in a metal tub and wait for the oil to settle on top. He then creamed it off and bottled it. Keir's Allegheny-bottled rock oil was novel only in so far as it had been derived from a salt well. It was no different essentially to the petroleum oils that had been sold as medicine for many years, often under the name of Seneca oil. None the less, in January 1852, Keir devised a witty means of advertising his patent medicine. It was in the form of a mock banknote with the value 400 at each corner, a reference to the fact that this wonderful cure-all had been found 'about four hundred feet below the earth's surface'. There was also an illustration on the note of a wooden drilling derrick, which was eerily evocative of an industry that would soon completely transform the economy of the United States and of much of the world.

While Samuel Keir devised new methods of marketing his rock oil, a lumber company in Titusville, Pennsylvania, by the name of Brewer and Watson continued to enjoy a steady natural supply of oil on its land. The black fluid came from a spring on what was known as Oil Creek and was used to lubricate machinery and sometimes to light up open areas where the dense smoke given off along with the flame was tolerable. Francis B. Brewer, the son of one of the founders of the company, was a doctor and when practising in Vermont he had with him a five-gallon barrel of 'creek oil' given to him by his father: he thought it a useful medicine. In 1851, however, Francis returned to Titusville to work in his father's business and two years later he leased the oil spring to a J. D. Angier of Titusville whose responsibility it was to keep it running.

Brewer had studied at Dartmouth College and when visiting former friends there he took along a sample of the Titusville oil. A professor of chemistry at Dartmouth, O. P. Hubbard, thought the oil would be valuable if it could be found in greater quantities and Brewer left a sample with his uncle, who taught medicine at Dartmouth. This sample came to the notice of another Dartmouth graduate, George H. Bissell, who was then just starting out as a lawyer in New York. Along with a partner, J. G. Eveleth, Bissell already had an interest in industrial enterprises, selling stock for clients, and he was struck by the similarity between what Americans called coal oil and Brewer's bottle of medicinal petroleum. Intrigued, he put up the expenses for a cousin of Brewer's, Albert Crosby, to take a trip to Titusville and make an assessment of the possible exploitation of the oil spring.

Crosby reported back that the spring was a valuable resource and that his cousin Brewer was prepared to sell Bissell and Eveleth a hundred acres of farmland for $5,000 and the rights to extract oil over 12,000 acres if they set up a joint-stock company with capital of $250,000, one fifth to be assigned to the Brewer and Watson lumber company. This, however, was more than the two partners could manage on their own. They sought the advice of James M. Townsend, president of the New Haven Savings Bank, who found backers prepared to risk their capital if an expert report proved favourable to the project. Townsend chose Luther Atwood, the discoverer of coup oil, and Benjamin Silliman, who had just taken over from his father as only the second Professor of Chemistry at Yale University. It was Silliman's report that would be crucial, and he took his time, announcing in April 1855 that he had completed it but refusing to release the results until his fee of $526.08 had been paid. He had, in fact, been thorough, analysing the oil and speculating on its various possible uses. Silliman thought half of it could be distilled into kerosene, imagining, wrongly as it turned out, that this would be a simple matter of boiling it with water. He also thought a gas for illumination could be made from Titusville oil. Silliman's report revealed that he was no expert on oil, for he failed to understand its uses as a lubricant and was apparently unaware of the developments in Scotland, where James Young had begun to make paraffin wax candles as well as lamp fuel. And yet he was perceptive and enthusiastic enough to encourage investors and, despite his own limited knowledge of the processes of distillation, he guessed correctly that in future it would be possible to break crude oil down into many different and commercially valuable substances.

In the United States, the responsibilities put on stockholders for joint-stock ventures varied from one state to another. Connecticut was lenient and for that reason Bissell and his partner Eveleth registered their new venture there as the Pennsylvania Rock Oil Company of Connecticut. Twelve thousand shares at $12.50 each were issued to bring in $300,000 of capital. Quite how this company was to turn a profit remains a mystery and it is hardly surprising that it suffered a series of setbacks which very nearly put an end to its ambitions altogether. Would-be investors came and went, nothing much happened and the company's financial problems landed back in the lap of James Townsend, the banker who had been approached to raise the money in the first place.

Terms for exploiting the oil were renegotiated. J. D. Angier, who had been quietly draining off a few gallons a day with the already established 'trenching' operation, was signed off. At some point – it is not known when or whose inspiration it was – the idea arose that they might actually drill for oil. (A popular story, sadly never confirmed by the man in question, is that Bissell got the idea from Keir's mock banknote flyer showing the salt-well derrick.) What is certain, though, is that there were still some outstanding legal matters regarding the ownership of land in Titusville – Brewer's wife and another woman had not signed the conveyance papers when they should have done – and that Townsend looked for someone to sort them out. The individual he settled on was an out-of-work conductor from the New Haven Railroad, Edwin L. Drake. Recently widowed and with a small child, Drake had been ill for some time when Townsend proposed he earn a few dollars by going to Titusville to tie up loose ends. Drake arrived in December 1857 after a journey through Syracuse, New York and Erie. The last forty miles to Titusville had to be by road: whatever industry was to be established here would have to function without a railway.

Before Drake left, Townsend had given him the spurious rank of 'Colonel' to lend him a little gravitas. Exactly what Drake envisaged on his visit to Titusville is not clear: nothing was recorded at the time. But he later claimed that it was his idea to drill for oil. This is not impossible, merely unlikely. At any event, he returned to New Haven full of enthusiasm for the project. Some fleet corporate footwork brought the land into the ownership of Townsend's new Seneca Oil Company of Connecticut. Drake had got himself the job of prospecting for oil, and moved to Titusville in May 1858 at a salary of $1,000 a year. He began in atrocious conditions and was not getting more than ten gallons of oil a day by June. He was still digging with picks and shovels at this stage, but it was clear this method was not going to produce results and so Drake decided to travel to Samuel Keir country in search of an experienced salt driller. He had no luck that year, perhaps because he had heard that drillers were hard-drinking men and he wanted a teetotaller. As it was, the man he thought he had hired did not turn up. Nevertheless, Drake proceeded to build housing for a steam engine and a wooden derrick to hold drilling equipment.

It was spring 1859 before Drake found a salt-well driller willing to come to Titusville, one William 'Uncle Billy' Smith from the evocatively named township of Saline, near Tarentum, Pennsylvania, a centre of salt works. Smith turned out to be a bargain, a skilled blacksmith who brought with him his fifteen-year-old son as an assistant. Together, they could turn out all the drilling tools needed. But the drilling proved difficult, as the surface soil was quicksand and the bore hole continually flooded. Smith then devised a drill of malleable iron which began to cut through the rock, and when he hitched it up to a steam engine, they were cutting down about three feet a day. Salt wells had been bored to a depth of a thousand feet, so this was nothing. And it produced nothing. By midsummer 1859, the investors in New Haven were pulling out and only Townsend was left. He, too, finally decided this was a failed enterprise and a letter was posted with the money for Drake to pay off himself, Smith and any others who were owed wages.

That letter was still in the post when on Sunday, 28 August 1859, Uncle Billy Smith found a slick of oil on the surface of the water in the well which was then just over seventy feet deep. The phenomenon was familiar enough to any salt driller, who would have regarded the oil as a pollutant which had to be removed. In this case, though, it was what they were looking for. It was not exactly a gusher, but soon oil was pumping out at eight to ten gallons a day and the problem was finding tubs to hold it. Drake might have become a very rich man, but he did not understand what he had begun. He also had a good deal of bad luck: his derrick and oil storage tanks caught fire that autumn. In any case, he had no idea how to market his oil. With the profits he had made, he sold up and moved to New York, where he lost most of his money in speculation. The world's first commercial oil well did him no good at all, for Drake died broken and impoverished in 1880.

But the idea that oil was not just a medicine or a handy local machine lubricant but something worth a lot of money had somehow seeped into the consciousness of American prospectors, for they arrived in Titusville like men panning for gold. Leases were sold, derricks appeared everywhere, and minds were turned to the problem of storing and shipping a viscous, highly inflammable raw material to the markets that needed it. The oil had to be refined and an entirely new industrial structure devised. As it was, within ten years the American production of kerosene had not only heralded the end of the Scottish oil shale industry, but had also stimulated a huge rival source of production thousands of miles away, on the shores of the bleak and brackish Caspian Sea.

Here was the Land of Eternal Fire which lay around the ancient trading city of Baku (in Azerbaijan), where for centuries East had met West. Parsees, religious refugees who had left Persia at the time of the Islamic invasions, settled here as well as in India and built their temples. Baku bubbled with surface oil and gases, and there was a long-established trade in which the oil was carted in barrels to Persia. Much of it was used locally, enabling, for example, the Parsees to maintain perpetual flames in their Zoroastrian temples. The commercial potential of the Baku oilfields had been recognized by the Russians, who parcelled out the land in contracts lasting only a few years. By the mid-nineteenth century, there were well over a hundred oil 'pits' in the area, producing around 5,500 gallons of oil a year. As in America, the oil was used for lighting as well as a lubricant and for various other industrial processes, such as treating leather. But the Baku oilfields remained incredibly primitive in their operations. Whereas the Americans had already laid the first successful oil pipelines in the mid-1860s, ten years later Baku oil was still being poured into wooden barrels and loaded on to the backs of camels or mules. Only two wells had been sunk, with the rest of the oil being won from hand-dug pits.

It was early in 1873 that Robert Nobel chanced upon the region of Baku. He was then forty-four years old, one of three brothers whose father had moved from Sweden to Russia in search of a fortune and ended up bankrupt and penniless. Old Immanuel Nobel was one of those eccentric inventors who produced one brilliant idea after another, occasionally had a success but was somehow doomed to ultimate failure. Born in 1801, he went to sea as a teenager, then studied at Stockholm's Academy of Art before attending mechanical school. Among his inventions was an inflatable rubber back-pack for the army – he had a penchant for new military equipment. Next he came up with the idea of a marine mine, not unlike Robert Fulton's contraptions of the same period, but perhaps more sophisticated. In 1837 he had failed to interest his home country in his new weapon when he met a Russian-Finnish official who suggested he might have better luck abroad. Close to bankruptcy, Immanuel Nobel felt he had no option but to go to Finland. For a year he developed his mines there but then moved on to Russia, settling in St Petersburg. At that time, and for most of the nineteenth century, Russia encouraged foreigners to set up industries as it seemed quite incapable of generating much in the way of indigenous enterprise. The Baku oilfields were another case in point.

Immanuel had left his wife and young boys in Sweden while he tried to establish himself as a supplier of mines to the Russian military. In 1842 he sent for his wife and Robert, then thirteen, Ludwig, eleven, and the sickly Alfred, who was nine. All had had some schooling in Sweden. In Russia they had private tutors, all three learning Russian, German, French and English as well as engineering. Alfred also had a chemistry tutor and went on to create a new explosive from nitro-glycerine which he called dynamite, and to astonish and anger his family (he never married) by leaving his fortune to a Swedish committee which created the Nobel Prizes for various fields of endeavour.

At first, the Nobels prospered in Russia. The market for mines was limited, but Immanuel established other businesses. With his sons he manufactured machine engines and iron wheels and prospered during the conflict between Russia and Turkey which became known as the Crimean War of 1854–5. When Britain, France and Austria took Turkey's side in the war, Russia banned all imports from those countries, giving the Nobels an advantage as domestic producers. Britain's military showing in the Crimea was regarded as a national disgrace, but the impact in Russia, the ultimate loser, was even greater. The demand for weapons fell away and Immanuel's business declined until he was finally declared bankrupt in 1859 and returned to Sweden. Ludwig took over his father's factory and managed to keep it going, while Robert pursued a variety of other enterprises, and Alfred began his experiments with explosives.

In time, Ludwig entered the business of making breech-loading rifles for the Russian army. Robert had returned to work with him and travelled from

St Petersburg via Paris to Baku, where he met up with Alfred to look for a well-priced supply of walnut to make rifle stocks. Baku was remote and none of the brothers had been there before. On board the ship which took him on the last leg of his journey across the Caspian Sea, Robert began to hear stories about Baku oil. He had at one time sold kerosene in Russia and knew there was a market there. The captain of the ship was a Dutchman called De Boer who, like a number of foreigners, had acquired land in Baku. As it happened, he wanted to sell. Robert took one look at Baku and decided to take a gamble. His brother had given him 25,000 roubles to spend on walnut. He used the money to buy De Boer's land instead.

Robert set out, single-handedly at first, to make a go of his oil wells. Like Alfred, he had learned chemistry, and very quickly produced a much finer kerosene than the local Baku sludge. He brought in expertise from Sweden and sent to America for drillers. The region turned out to be fantastically rich in oil, with one gusher – or fountain, as the Russians called them – exploding after another. In 1876, Ludwig finally went with his son to see Baku for himself. He realized there was a potential fortune to be made and set about creating an oil enterprise, borrowing everything he could from America. One thing clearly had to change straight away: the oil could no longer be carried by camel trains in wooden barrels. Ludwig duly established the first pipelines in Russia after studying their dimensions in Pennsylvania, although the pipes themselves, almost inevitably, came not from a Russian ironworks but from Glasgow. Vested interests resented the loss of the camel trains, however, and the pipelines had to be protected by Cossack patrols and lookout towers.

Once he had borrowed what he could from existing technology, Ludwig began to devise a novel means of moving oil about. He wanted to do away with wooden barrels and to move in bulk both his kerosene and the sludge left after distillation which could be used as fuel. To this end, he devised the first successful oil tankers. The Americans had tried something similar but their attempts to transport oil across the Atlantic had been a failure. In any case, the United States still had plenty of timber for barrels, whereas in Russia wood for cooperage was very expensive and added greatly to the cost of kerosene. When shipowners in Russia refused to convert their vessels to carry oil,

Ludwig had his tankers designed and built in Sweden. The first he called *Zoroaster* after the prophet of the Parsee followers, whose temple flames still burned in Baku until the 1880s. Two more ships, the *Buddha* and the *Nordenskjold*, were put into service after the *Zoroaster* proved a success in 1878. To reach Baku from Sweden, it had made an incredible trip across the Baltic, through two lakes, the Ladoga and Onega, along two Russian canals, down the Volga and then across the Caspian. By 1880, as his business grew to one of the largest in the world, Ludwig was having tankers built in which the entire hold could be filled with oil. There were, of course, tragic accidents: the *Nordenskjold* exploded when a gust of wind made it list, pulling loose a supply pipe, and half the crew perished.

The loss of the *Nordenskjold* was a setback, but the oil tanker rapidly became a familiar sight on the Caspian as more oil firms were established on the Nobel model, most of them funded and run by non-Russians. In 1879 Robert Nobel retired from the business because of ill-health, leaving Ludwig, with his technical and organizing genius, to make their Baku oil company the most technically advanced in the world. America had the lead in refining techniques in the 1870s, for the Titusville strike had spawned a huge industry, and so Ludwig sent a Swedish engineer, Alfred Tornquist, to study them at first-hand. Tornquist spent three years in the United States and returned with a thorough knowledge of all the techniques then in use. There were some patented, however, which had not been put into practice, and it was these that gave Ludwig and Tornquist the idea for creating a plant for 'continuous distillation' of the crude oil pumped up from the wells.

A large oil lake was formed with a layer of pitch on top to reduce evaporation and from this lake the oil flowed down a gentle slope into a series of tanks where it was progressively cleared of impurities and then heated at different temperatures until finally it produced a highly refined kerosene ideal for illumination. Once it was established in 1882, this Nobel process made the company far and away the biggest producer of Russian kerosene and oil by-products: it had, in fact, something like 50 per cent of the market. Ludwig also had a railway built from Baku to the Black Sea and oil storage tanks built all over Russia as well as in Sweden and Finland. By the turn of the century, there were only two big oil producers in the world – Russia and the United States. In 1899 Russia actually produced more crude oil than America, but much less of it was exported. The United States still had the lead in the production of kerosene and also a huge export market.

American exports of both crude and refined oil were sent across the Atlantic in the 1870s and 1880s in barrels or cans stowed in the holds of sailing ships. Norwegian shipowners built four sailing ships with specially designed oil tanks for bulk transport and these began to take crude oil from Philadelphia to Europe in 1879. Whereas oil in barrels or cans made for a relatively stable cargo, large oil tanks in the holds of a ship presented new technical challenges which had to be overcome: the oil was liable to expand or contract in volume at different atmospheric temperatures, and the resulting movement of large quantities of liquid could destabilize the ship transporting it.

Meanwhile, Nobel had a cargo vessel, the *Ferguson*, converted in 1885 to carry oil from Batoum, the terminus of the railway from Baku, to Antwerp, and then the *Sviet*, which arrived in London in 1885 with half a million tons of Russian oil after a voyage through the treacherous Bay of Biscay. The first really modern steam-driven tanker was ordered by a German and built by the British firm of W. G. Armstrong, Mitchell & Company. This was the *Gluckauf*, which carried its first cargo of American kerosene from New York to Bremen in Germany in the autumn of 1886.

It was less than forty years since 'Paraffin' Young had obtained his patent for refining Bathgate oil shale, and barely thirty years since he had gone into the lamp oil business, and now there was established a vast international trade and industry. The production of illuminating and lubricating oils that replaced animal and vegetable oils lowered the price of lighting across a large part of the world. Abraham Gesner lived long enough to see the rise of a new industry he had helped to create. In 1861 he published a book entitled *A Practical Treatise on Coal, Petroleum and Other Distilled Oils* and wrote with genuine modesty: 'The progress of discovery in this case, as in others, has been slow and gradual. It has been carried on by the labors, not of one mind, but of many, so as to render it difficult to discover to whom the greatest credit is due.'[1] Advances in the science of chemistry were certainly important, for it is unlikely that either Gesner or Young would have experimented as they did without some understanding of the nature of materials and how one substance could yield others with many useful properties. But chance still played a big part in discovery. This was certainly true of the momentous advance which led to the transformation of an essentially wooden world into one constructed out of relatively cheap yet immensely strong metal. The man who began this revolution, working at the same time as Gesner and Young, liked to boast that he made the breakthrough because he was completely ignorant of the iron and steel industry. He had, in fact, begun his astonishingly inventive career making fake gold.

CHAPTER SIXTEEN

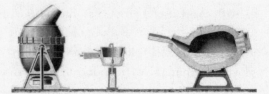

THE STEEL REVOLUTION

In his autobiography, Henry Bessemer, whose name has long been associated with the making of steel, tells a story of how, while on holiday in Germany in the 1840s, he was arrested in the town of Fürth near Nuremberg and accused of industrial espionage. When Bessemer appeared in court, he was startled to be told that he had been observed bribing a Fürth workman to steal the secret of making false gold, a bronze decorative paint. Asked what he had to say in his defence, Bessemer was able to argue that he was an unlikely industrial spy because a few years earlier he had invented machinery which could turn out as much bronze powder in a day as eighty German workmen labouring with archaic methods of manufacture. In fact, Bessemer thought it likely the trumped-up charge had only been made because the Fürth workmen knew who he was and that he had stolen much of their trade.

The case against Bessemer was dismissed, but he was warned to leave Germany. He was then a supremely confident young man, just thirty years old, and he refused. It was only when the close attention paid to him by the authorities became irksome that he returned home to be reunited with his wife and children, who had been holidaying by the English seaside. Once back in London, however, Bessemer could savour his most recent triumph. In his own, very secret laboratory he had invented a steam-driven press for extracting juice from West Indian sugar cane. This had just won him the Gold Medal from the Society of Arts and Manufactures, an award that had been presented to him by no less a personage than the Society's president, Prince Albert, at a special ceremony.

The name Bessemer is French Huguenot, and so it is fair to assume Henry's ancestors left France in the seventeenth century as part of the exodus of Protestants no longer given religious protection. His father, Anthony Bessemer, had been born in London but been taken by his parents to the Netherlands, where he studied engineering. He became an engraver and moved to France, where he became a member of the Academie Royale des Sciences and worked for the Royal Mint. Anthony fled France during the Revolution, but with enough money to acquire a small estate at Charlton in Hertfordshire where Henry was born and spent his childhood. He had only an elementary education but spent a good deal of his time in his father's workshop. When he was seventeen years old, his father moved to London and Henry went with him. Here he began a career of what was to prove quite astonishing inventiveness. One of his first innovations was a device which would prevent the fraudulent removal of official stamps from old deeds and their attachment to new ones, to evade the payment of duty. Bessemer devised a die-stamp which perforated stamps with many small holes, making their counterfeiting virtually impossible. The Government Stamp Office, which calculated it was losing £100,000 a year (about £5 million in today's money) to fraud, accepted Bessemer's invention and offered him the post of Superintendent of the Office at a good salary. But he soon realized that it was simpler merely to date each stamp; the Stamp Office agreed and withdrew the offer of the job.

Some time in the early 1830s, Bessemer's sister, who still lived in the village of Charlton, asked Henry if he could design in gold an inscription for the cover of a collection of her paintings: *Studies of Flowers from Nature by Miss Bessemer*. He took his sister's book with him to London and bought from a local chemist some 'gold powder' which struck him as extremely expensive. He wondered why it was so costly and treated a little of it with sulphuric acid to discover if it contained any gold at all. It did not. He asked chemists and art suppliers why it was so expensive. Nobody knew. All that they could say was that it was manufactured somewhere near Nuremberg. Henry guessed that it was really some kind of brass and that, if he could only discover how it was made and then mass-produce it, he would make a fortune.

The making of false gold powder had changed so little over the centuries that Henry was able to discover the secret of its manufacture by referring to a twelfth-century encyclopedia compiled by a German monk, Theophilus. From it, he learned that brass was pounded to a leaf, then ground with a pestle and mortar, with honey added to prevent 'clumping'. This goo was then washed repeatedly to get rid of the honey. It was an incredibly slow, laborious process, which was why the resulting fake gold was so expensive. Henry set out to see if he could mechanize the process. It took him a while to mimic the Nuremberg powder, and he finally found the secret with a microscope which revealed the necessary shape of the particles. He invented a steel-roller system to produce leaf and a tumbler to create the right shape of particles. A sample immediately brought an offer of £500 a year for the machinery once it was developed for commercial use. But Henry refused to sell and instead established, at some cost, his own gold-paint powder manufactory.

Bessemer decided he would make greater profits for longer if he did not patent his invention because even if legal protection proved effective it would only last for fourteen years. So he set about creating his factory in such a way that nobody would be able to discover, or imitate, the process. The heavy machines required were each ordered from different manufacturers in Glasgow, Manchester, Liverpool and London: none knew how the machine they made was harnessed to the others. All this plant was housed in a windowless building secured with Chubb locks and the secret of the process was divulged only to Bessemer's brothers-in-law, Richard and William Allen. It was to be kept for forty years, during which time the price of fake gold paint plummeted and Henry made huge profits as it was only his factory which could make it cheaply in bulk.

In due course, Bessemer purchased the lease on a fine house in Highgate, then on the rural fringes of London, and would travel to and from his factory in his own carriage. But what was to prove rather more significant than his becoming a member of the carriage-owning classes was that he now had enough money to finance his own research projects without seeking funds from partners or backers. Bessemer's gold paint may have made him a fortune but it did not win him international fame. The invention which did – and it was just one of more than a hundred that he patented – again had him meddling in a technology that, to begin with, he knew nothing about. In later life, he would say that his ignorance gave him an advantage over expert metallurgists as he was prepared to try techniques they would have rejected on first principles. In fact it was to take a considerable amount of expertise to make a success of Bessemer's basic innovation – the production of what became known as 'mild steel'.

When, in 1854, British forces became embroiled in the war between Russia and Turkey, Bessemer put his mind to producing a more accurate weapon than the smooth-bore musket and cannon. The Crimean War exposed Britain's army as hopelessly out of touch. Commanded by Lord Raglan, who had last seen action in 1815 at the battle of Waterloo, where he had lost an arm, it was poorly led, ill equipped and badly organized and it performed disastrously. Yet there were aspects of the two-year campaign which were a credit to the nation. When the road from the British base at Balaclava to the besieged citadel of Sevastopol became virtually impassable, the contractors Thomas Brassey and Morton Peto and their British navvies went into action and in a few weeks built a railway to carry siege guns and supplies, the navvies even carrying pistols to defend themselves. Florence Nightingale reorganized the appalling conditions for the wounded taken to Scutari, and the famous chef from the Reform Club, Alexis Soyer, went out to teach the troops how to cook, devising a field stove that was still in use a century or more later. In those days there was a great deal of freelance activity around a battlefield, with food being supplied by the British sutlers or the French *vivandiers*: the West Indian nurse and provider of provisions, Mary Seacole, also made a name for herself and became a national heroine for a while.

Besser's own contribution to this patriotic effort was, however, brushed aside by the War Department. His idea was straightforward enough. It was well known that 'rifled' guns, which gave a twist to the bullet when it was fired, were more accurate over longer distances than smooth-bore guns. It was the spin of the elongated projectile which gave it its steadiness in the air. Rifles had long been used as hunting pieces and they saw service with rifle brigades during the Napoleonic Wars. However, as we have seen, the rifle took longer to reload than the musket and was not suitable for squares of infantry standing to repel a cavalry charge. Most guns were therefore still smooth-bore. Bessemer devised a way of 'charging' a bullet in such a way that it would spin out of a smooth-bore musket, giving it greater range and accuracy. He even had a little model built to show how it worked.

When the War Department declared they were not interested, Bessemer built a mortar to prove that the system would work. He fired projectiles into his own grounds at Highgate, aiming them steeply into the air. He marked each shot so that he could check how far different designs would travel. Then, in 1854, while visiting friends in Paris, he mentioned his project to a number of French officers who were about to set off for the Crimea. They were intrigued and got him an audience with Prince Napoleon. The French duly gave him a blank cheque to develop his spinning bullets and he was asked to demonstrate them on a firing range at Vincennes just before Christmas of the same year.

In his autobiography, Bessemer gives an account of the subsequent moment of revelation which led him to a study of metallurgy:

A bright blazing fire of logs on the low hearth looked so inviting that we all instinctively gathered round it, and under the happy influence of a steaming cup of good mulled claret, there was much noisy talking and gesticulation. During one of our more quiet intervals, Commandant Minié remarked that it was quite true that the shot revolved with sufficient rapidity, and went point forward through the targets; and that, he said, was very satisfactory as far as it went. But he entirely mistrusted their present guns, and he did not consider it safe in practice to fire a 30-lb shot from a 12-pounder cast-iron gun. The real question, he said, was: Could any guns be made to stand such heavy projectiles? This simple observation was the spark which has kindled one of the greatest industrial revolutions that the present century has to record, for it instantly forced on my attention the real difficulty of the situation, viz.: How were we to make a gun that would be strong enough to throw with safety these heavy elongated projectiles? I well remember how, on my lonely journey back to Paris that cold December night, I inwardly resolved, if possible, to complete the work so satisfactorily begun, by producing a superior description of cast-iron that would stand the heavy strains which the increased weight of the projectiles rendered necessary.[1]

Although he was not an ironmaster, Bessemer was familiar with the way in which cast iron, wrought iron and steel were produced. At the time he began his experiments with a furnace he designed himself, steel, the highest quality metal, was used only for such things as springs, various tools and cutlery. Turning iron into steel was an ancient art, known to both the Chinese and the Japanese, for steel made the best knives and swords. But it took several weeks to produce and it could only be made in small quantities because of the special conditions required to heat the molten metal. In England, the finest steel was made by a method devised by a watchmaker, Benjamin Huntsman, in which wrought iron imported from Sweden was heated in crucibles made of special clays which could withstand intense heat and which did not introduce impurities into the iron. Huntsman perfected his crucible or 'cast' steel process around 1750 and was the first person to produce steel in blocks or ingots. Huntsman borrowed technologies from both brass-founders and glass-makers and he did not patent his process – which was perhaps why his technique remained a secret for a very long time.

Napoleon Bonaparte, forever frustrated by the industrial lead Britain had gained over France, offered a prize of four thousand francs for the first ironmaster in his Empire who could find the secret of English steel. One of those who tried and failed, bringing ruination on his once wealthy family, was Friedrich Krupp, a tragic figure who lived and worked in the walled city of Essen in the region of the Ruhr. In 1826 Friedrich's little foundry, with its five smelters and two forgers, was bequeathed to his widow and its running was taken on by his son Alfred, who was then only fourteen. Alfred was determined to revive the family fortunes and was obsessed with the notion of finally cracking the problem that had ruined his father – production of steel as good as that imported from England.

A tall, gangling figure, Alfred Krupp was an intensely neurotic, hard-working and brilliant industrialist. Yet it is a wonder he survived the early years as he experimented day and night in his efforts to discover how to make fine steel. The little River Berne, which provided power for his bellows and forge hammers, frustrated him on many occasions when it became either a trickle or a flood. In the end, he managed to buy an inefficient and leaky steam engine to drive his hammer. The first genuine crucible of Krupp steel was not produced until 1830, when the ailing foundry was given a life-saving injection of family money. This was the same year that Bessemer began work on the production of gold paint: it is strange that he would be the one to revolutionize steel production and not Alfred Krupp, who had spent four years experimenting in his Essen works. What Krupp did discover – an invention properly attributed to his brother, Hermann – was how to turn out forks and spoons by running metal sheets through patterned rollers. This was a really lucrative business and the turning point in the Krupp fortunes.

In 1838, Alfred set off on a quest to visit other parts of Europe, and England in particular. As an industrialist, he was acutely conscious of the backwardness of his native Prussia and he had in mind to undertake some latterday industrial espionage when he crossed the Channel. Paris had not interested him at all – it was far too frivolous. His mecca was the British Midlands and, in particular, Sheffield, the home of crucible steel. Intensely secretive, Alfred had a passport made out in the name of A. Crup, and in a fit of Anglophilia, changed his name permanently from Alfried to Alfred. He had a travelling companion, Friedrich Heinrich Solling, and the two of them tried to make out that they were Prussian aristocrats on a kind of cultural tour: Alfred even took to wearing swan-neck spurs. But such feeble attempts at deception belonged to another time, and 'the Baron', as he became known, was the butt of many a whispered joke. All in all, he spent five months in England and was shown around most of the works he visited. Nevertheless everyone knew who he was and why he was there.

It is not clear whether Alfred did learn any industrial secrets in England, yet he was greatly appreciative of the hospitality he received. One thing he did discover, though, was that you needed different kinds of iron for different kinds of steel and his search for the right kind of ore was to prove lengthy and problematic. Even so, by the 1840s his Essen works was producing genuine crucible steel and by the time of the Great Exhibition in London in 1851 he was able to put on display the largest single ingot of steel ever seen. It weighed 4,300 pounds and was a wonder of the Crystal Palace, winning him a gold medal. To make an ingot of pure steel that large had required an amazing piece of choreography in the works, with the contents of many crucibles being poured together into a single mould with split-second timing. Alfred also put on show one of his steel cannons which, in twenty years' time, were to decide the fate of much of Europe.

Bessemer, who had had his own impressive display at the Great Exhibition, one that included his cane sugar-refining machines, might have been impressed with Krupp's monster ingot, but it did not answer the task he had set himself. Steel in such quantity was a rarity, and the metal was prohibitively expensive. If he was to make tougher guns which could fire his spinning bullet, he needed to find a way of mimicking the qualities of steel with something which cost a good deal less. At the time, and for long afterwards, there was a dispute about what exactly distinguished fine wrought iron from steel. Was it the carbon content of the metal or the way it was forged?

Bessemer's revolutionary means of producing a form of steel which could be made directly from pig iron, without any of the laborious process of first transforming it into wrought iron, was tantamount to a miracle in metal-working. In fact, when many ironmasters first heard of Bessemer's so-called 'converter', which produced good steel from molten pig iron simply by blowing cold air across it, they were incredulous. Bessemer gave some demonstrations of his process and then established a steel works in Sheffield once he had lodged his patent. He invited ironmasters to come to the works and to take out a licence to produce Bessemer steel, if they wished. A number of ironmasters did so, with Bessemer licensing one in each of the major producing regions. They built their converters, set them to blow, and looked at the product. It was brittle, 'rotten' as they called it, and useless. Recalling this catastrophe in his autobiography, Bessemer wrote:

> The ordinary pig iron used for bar-iron making was found to contain so much phosphorus as to render it wholly unfit for making iron by my process. This startling fact came on me suddenly, like a bolt from the blue; its effect was absolutely overwhelming. The transition from what appeared to be a crowning success to one of utter failure well nigh paralysed all my energies. Day by day fresh reports of failures arrived; the cry was taken up in the press; every paper had its letters from correspondents, and its leaders, denouncing the whole scheme as the dream of a wild enthusiast, such as no sensible man could for a moment have entertained. I well remember one paper, after rating me in pretty strong terms, spoke of my invention as 'a brilliant meteor that had flitted across the metallurgical horizon for a short space, only to die out in a train of sparks, and then vanish into total darkness'.[2]

The story of how this problem was overcome is long, tortuous and full of controversy. One possible solution was to look for non-phosphoric ores, but they turned out to be relatively rare in Europe and in the wrong places. The French imported ore from Algeria, moving their steel works to the Mediterranean coast for ease of transport. Alfred Krupp was the first German steel-maker to try Bessemer's system: he had heard about it from his London agent, Alfred Longsdon, who was the brother of Robert Longsdon, a partner of Bessemer's from the gold paint days. But by the time Krupp had his first converters working, the problem with phosphoric ores had been revealed; it was a huge disappointment, since much of the pig iron he had formerly used was of no use in the converters, and he had to purchase Spanish mines which produced suitable ores to ensure his supply. Only Britain and the United States, where the Bessemer system was adopted in the 1860s, had good supplies of non-phosphoric ores.

An alternative to the Bessemer converter was devised by two French ironmaster brothers, Pierre and Emile Martin, together with the German brothers, Werner and William Siemens, and was generally known as the Siemens–Martin process. It involved the highly economical reuse of furnace heat and, though it was slower than Bessemer's converter, it was more controllable and could produce a better quality steel. But phosphoric ores were not suitable for either of these revolutionary methods of producing steel and so the search continued for some way of overcoming this problem.

Nevertheless, the era of bulk steel production had begun, and in Prussia Alfred Krupp became far and away the largest supplier. He had tried to obtain a Prussian patent for the Bessemer converter but no interest was shown so he agreed to keep the process secret, disguising the building in which the furnaces were housed with a false name. It was discovered early on that steel produced by the Bessemer system was ideal for railway tracks and anyone producing these made a fortune. Krupp, like his British counterparts, exported enormous quantities to America which, in the late 1860s, had a railway boom. He had also devised a way of casting iron wheels for locomotives in a single mould so there were no joins, and this too earned him a great deal of money. But Krupp had one particularly ambitious dream which he had revealed at the Crystal Palace in 1851. He believed that breech-loading steel cannon would outperform the brass cannon then favoured by the military. He constantly offered to develop these and supply them to the Prussian army for virtually nothing, or even for free. But his efforts were frustrated by the conservatism of the German state's military leaders.

The first conflict in which Krupp's cannon saw action was the so-called Seven Weeks' War in which Prussia crushed its former ally, Austria, in 1866. This was a significant step on the road to German unification, which itself would lay the foundations for the spectacular rise of industry in that country towards the end of the century. Krupp's steel cannon did not perform that well in 1866: there were technical problems with the loading mechanism. But by the time of the outbreak of war between Prussia and France in 1870, they were vastly superior to anything that could be pitched against them. Their range, accuracy and speed of fire overwhelmed the French and brought Prussia a swift and quite unexpected victory.

Krupp waited anxiously for news from the battlefield of the performance of his artillery, and when he was told what devastating weapons he had produced he wrote to an English friend with the wonderfully German phrase: 'Now look what have done our army!'[3] When Napoleon III surrendered at Sedan, the Prussian army moved in on Paris, the heavily fortified French capital, and laid siege to it. The French government moved south to the Loire and made a temporary headquarters at Tours and later at Poitiers. They hoped to keep in touch with the besieged Parisians via the electric telegraph, but when the Prussians succeeding in surrounding Paris on 18 September, they cut the overhead cables. Nine days later, they found the cable in the Seine and cut that too. In desperation, the French attempted to get both governmental and personal messages into Paris by placing them in zinc balls which were floated on the river. However, these *boules de Moulin* were instantly spotted and then fished out by the Prussians. Not a single message eluded their nets.

It was virtually impossible to enter or leave Paris by either road or river. However, there was one means of escape which promised some chance of success – the gas or hot-air balloon. Hundreds of balloons were hastily made and launched when the weather was favourable – or thought to be so: one ended up in Norway. Sometimes letters were sent out by balloon, but there was no way of controlling where they landed. Finally, with all other links either unusable or unreliable, the French resorted to the homing pigeon.

Against orders, a number of these birds had been taken down to Tours from their Parisian lofts before the siege and they were now employed to establish a limited postal service into the city. The birds were released with messages clipped to their legs and flew straight home. Inevitably, they suffered casualties: some were brought down by the Prussians and others by the starving French out in the countryside. Then in Paris itself a pigeon-fanciers' club called L'Esperance offered its birds for what was to become the most celebrated pigeon post in history. They were brought out of Paris in manned balloons which carried outward messages and taken first to Tours and later to Poitiers when the Prussian advance continued. Despite the disorientation of their journey, the pigeons set off for the rooftops of Paris as soon as they were released. Sometimes they were taken on trains as close to the city as it was safe to go in order to shorten their journey and make it less hazardous.

Where modern technology had failed, the oldest known means of long-distance communication triumphed. It was aided, too, by an astonishing innovation: micro-photography. During the siege of Paris extensive messages were written out, photographed and reduced to tiny 'chips' which could then be read either by magnifying glass or projection on to a wall. In this way both private and official letters were sent and received, not just between Paris and the 'free French' but from other countries as well, including Britain. *The Times* reported on 19 November 1870: 'It is said that the pigeon post is gone off, with sheets of photographed messages reduced to an invisible size, which in Paris are to be magnified, written out and transmitted to their addresses. They are limited to private affairs, politics and news of military operations being strictly excluded. But the Prussians, it is said, with their usual diabolical cunning and ingenuity, have set hawks and falcons flying round Paris to strike down the feathered messengers that bear under their wings healing for anxious souls.' At the time of the siege of the city, which ended in February 1871, Charles Darwin was working on the text of the *Descent of Man* and it is said that some of his manuscript, which was being translated into both French and German, was smuggled into Paris through the Prussian lines.

When Alfred Krupp heard of the balloons and their cargoes of pigeons, he devised what must have been the world's first anti-aircraft gun. Whether or not it was effective is not known, for there are no records of it being used. But Krupp steel cannon were now in demand worldwide, and Alfred was always the businessman, prepared to supply anybody, even an enemy such as France, if the orders came in. In the meantime, as part of the war reparations, Bismarck, the Chancellor of the newly unified Germany, demanded that France concede the region of Alsace-Lorraine, a potentially important industrial area which contained huge reserves of phosphoric iron ore.

Some of the greatest minds in metallurgy sought to solve the phosphorus problem, but they were outdone by a young man whose background was far removed from industry. Sidney Gilchrist Thomas was born in 1850, the son of a Welshman who had moved to London to work for the Inland Revenue.

He was brought up in the district of Canonbury in Islington, north London, home to many a Dickensian clerk, and attended Dulwich College as a day boy from the age of nine. Though he took a great interest in science at school and would have liked to make this his career, at seventeen he had to go out to work to support his mother following the death of his father. He worked as a schoolmaster in Essex before taking a junior clerkship at Marlborough Street police court in 1867. He moved shortly afterwards to the Thames Court, where he stayed until 1879. While he worked, he attended night school at Birkbeck College, where he studied law and chemistry. One of the great teachers at Birkbeck was George Chaloner, who told Thomas's class that anyone who could solve the problem of phosphoric ores in the Bessemer converter would make a fortune. Thomas was then just twenty and he set out to find the solution which had eluded so many others.

To learn all he could about iron- and steel-making, Thomas took exams at the Royal College of Mines, visited laboratories, toured iron-making districts during his holidays and carried out a number of experiments at home. He came to the conclusion that what was needed was a furnace lined with material which would 'fix' the phosphorus. With help from Percy C. Gilchrist, a cousin who worked in a Welsh foundry, Thomas proved his method was practical and took out his first patent in 1877. The key to the problem was the lining of the converter. If crushed dolomite was used in the sudden flare of transition from pig iron to steel with the blast of air, the phosphorus was absorbed. Bessemer himself was to realize that, by chance, he had used non-phosphoric ore in his first experimental converter without realizing how significant this was. What became known as the Thomas-Gilchrist adaptation of the Bessemer converter was greeted with some scepticism at first, but after a demonstration in 1879 at an ironworks in Middlesbrough in the north-east of England it was accepted. Old Alfred Krupp, by then worn out and frail and also the owner of extensive non-phosphoric Spanish ore deposits, rejected an innovation which had suddenly made the ores of Lorraine immensely sought after. But his son introduced the system, and soon it swept the world, rapidly putting an end to the production of wrought iron and bringing on the age of steel.

For a while, British steel-makers enjoyed a boom as demand in America for all kinds of steel products rapidly increased. But after the 1870s, American steel production took off using both the Bessemer and Siemens–Martin systems and Thomas–Gilchrist converters. By the end of the century, many steel fortunes had been made in the United States, including that of Andrew Carnegie. After twelve years working as a manager with the Pennsylvania Railroad, Carnegie went into partnership with two others to explore the possibility of going into steel production. In 1872 he visited England and viewed the Bessemer system. He then hired in the best men he could find in America and set up a steelworks near Pittsburgh, Pennsylvania, which began to turn out steel rails and other railroad hardware in 1875. No fewer than thirteen towns in the United States were either called Bessemer or incorporated his name and a number of locomotives were named after him. Bessemer himself won many medals for his steel process and was knighted in 1879, by which time he had made a second fortune out of licensing the converters.

In 1881, Sidney Gilchrist Thomas paid a visit to the United States, where he was greeted with great enthusiasm and feted for the invaluable contribution he had made to the steel industry. The following year, he established his own steel works. Like Bessemer, he was showered with awards, including the Society of Arts gold medal. Sadly, at the height of his triumph he became sickly, perhaps through overwork. He set off on a world tour in 1883 and the next year spent some time in Algiers in North Africa. Thomas had never married but had stayed close to his Scottish mother and younger sister, both of whom he met up with in Paris for a holiday in early 1885. But by then his health was deteriorating fast and he died of emphysema on 1 February of that year and was buried in the French capital. He was only thirty-five. Sir Henry Bessemer was to live rather longer, dying in 1898 at the age of eighty-five.

The coming of the age of steel and the founding of the oil industry amounted to a second industrial revolution. From the 1870s onwards, German industrialism gathered pace as its scientists and technicians embraced the new chemical and electrical industries. The United States was rapidly becoming the world's most advanced industrial nation. France moved more slowly, and

Russia still lagged behind despite the development of its oil industry by the Nobels and their like. Other European countries, including Italy and Spain, had made little real progress. Britain was being overtaken yet remained immensely wealthy and powerful, and the industrial society it had created had now taken hold across a large part of the world. And Japan? The land of shoguns and samurai was still barely on the industrial map.

CHAPTER SEVENTEEN

OF SCOTS AND SAMURAI

When Commodore Perry had sailed away from Tokyo Bay in 1854, he had left the Japanese in turmoil. The American show of force, along with what they had learned from returning castaways such as Manjiro, had convinced the ruling military Tokugawa junta, the Bafuku, that they would have to make concessions and open their 'double-bolted' door a little to trade and diplomacy. Treaty ports were opened and the traders started moving in. At the same time, a movement arose in Japan which both opposed the concessions made by the Bafuku and rallied support for the idea of returning the Mikado or Emperor to power and expelling the American and European invaders. This cry was taken up by many of the young samurai, particularly those in the powerful Satsuma and Choshu clans, whose territory was a long way from the Bafuku stronghold at Tokyo.

A Choshu teacher, Yoshida Shoin, believed that it was necessary to learn how the West had become so powerful in order for Japan to acquire the military strength to resist invasion. Just twenty-four years old when the American expedition appeared for a second time in Toyko Bay, Shoin and a friend tried in great secrecy to get Commodore Perry to take them to America. Perry turned them down and they were caught by the Japanese and put in a cage in Tokyo, a humiliating form of imprisonment. Shoin was horrified when the Bafuku signed the first treaty with the Americans and began to plan the overthrow of the Shogunate and the reinstatement of the Emperor. His battle cry became 'Honour the Emperor, Expel the Barbarians' and he urged his young followers to learn from the West so they might defeat the Bafuku and rekindle Japanese imperial pride.

Distrust of the Bafuku led members of the Satsuma and Choshu clans to seek to arm themselves illegally. It was not clear whether they wanted guns and steamboats to repel the barbarians or to overthrow their own rulers. In either event, their sedition was not to be tolerated and in 1859 Yoshida Shoin was beheaded for his political activities. What the rebels needed, though, was some Western contact from whom they could obtain modern weapons, and a group of Choshu samurai found their saviour in a Scotsman called Thomas Blake Glover.

Glover had arrived in the southern port of Nagasaki in the late summer of 1859. He was just twenty-one and a clerk with the Scottish company of Jardine Matheson. Some ambitious firms had jumped the gun to set up in business the year before the trade treaties came into effect, and Jardine Matheson was among them: its first office had already been established by its representative, Ross MacKenzie, when Glover reached Japan. Life for the small expatriate community in Nagasaki, one of the three ports in which some trade with the West had been sanctioned by the Shogunate, was exotic, tedious and extremely dangerous by turns. MacKenzie found there were quick profits to be made at first, exporting seaweed to China, where it was a culinary delicacy, and silk to Europe for the finest and most fashionable clothes. However, as rival merchants moved in and trade was restricted by the Japanese, business became more humdrum; Glover himself dealt mostly in the export of tea, silk and rice. Quite soon, however, the British contingent in Nagasaki had formed a club and created for themselves a characteristic enclave in which they met for drinks at the end of the day. Most of the time they stayed out of trouble, haggling with petty officials, groping towards some understanding of the language and enjoying the favours of the pretty girls for which Nagasaki was well known.

Under the treaties which were forced upon the Bafuku, the British had established diplomatic posts in Yokohama and Tokyo. The presence of these

Westerners was resented and there were a number of incidents in which the British were assaulted. The worst was in Tokyo in 1861 when the British legation was attacked at night by sword-wielding samurai, two of whom were shot dead by the British Consul from Nagasaki, George Morrison, who happened to be visiting Tokyo at the time. These attacks provoked the classic British response – gunboat diplomacy. Ominously, ships of the Royal Navy now began to cruise in Japanese waters.

Meanwhile, Thomas Glover had settled in and by the time he was twenty-four he was the leading member of Nagasaki's little expatriate community. He had acquired a 'wife' – the marriage ceremony was more a negotiation than a lifetime commitment – and had had a child by her. A house was built for him in what was an approximation of Western style and he became a figure familiar to the two leading clans of southern Japan, the Satsumas and the Choshu. Some of the clans began to buy British steamships, against the strict orders of the Bafuku in Tokyo, and it became clear to Glover that civil war was brewing and he had no doubt whose side he was on. If trade were to thrive, then the 'modernizers' would have to win. And when the tension in Japan was reaching its height, Glover became directly involved in a daring scheme to open up the country to Western influences.

It had all come to a head in 1862 when a party of British merchants and diplomats out on a riding trip from Yokohama found themselves approaching a party of the Satsuma clan in procession from Tokyo to Kyoto. When the British refused to give way, the Satsuma samurai attacked them and in the ensuing fracas a merchant, Charles Lennox Richardson, was killed. The British demanded an apology and financial compensation for Richardson's death. The Satsuma refused. With the deadlock came a period of high tension, and out-and-out war was only averted when the Satsuma began to back down.

In the summer of 1863, when relations between Britain and Japan were still strained, Glover was approached by some young Choshu samurai, acolytes of Yoshida Shoin whom he knew personally, and asked if he could help them escape to the West. Their plan was not to live in exile but to learn what they could about Western technology and industry and then to return to Japan armed with these new skills and knowledge in the belief that the old order would not endure much longer. At considerable risk to himself, Glover agreed to help them. The trading network established by Jardine Matheson provided the means to smuggle the samurai out of Japan. The five – Ito Hirobumi, Inoue Kaoru, Inoue Masaru, Endo Kinzuke and Yamao Yozo – had their hair cut in the Western style and were dressed up as British sailors. Although one of them knew some English, as a group they would mumble a kind of gibberish in an attempt to conceal their identity. While they waited for a ship to take them to Shanghai, the Choshu Five hid in the home of a Jardine Matheson agent in Yokohama, a port which was then not much more than a fishing village.

The plan was that once they reached Shanghai, the five would be found passenger berths on a ship to London. But due to a misunderstanding, two of them, Inoue Kaoru and Ito Hirobumi, were enrolled as novice seamen and had to endure a tough passage to England as lowly crew mates on the steamer *Pegasus*. At the very outset, however, it was not entirely clear why they were travelling to Europe. Was it their eventual intention to overthrow the Bafuku or to repel the Western invaders, or perhaps even to attempt both? Ito Hirobumi certainly believed when they set out that they would learn about foreign navies, particularly that of the British, and arm themselves so they could drive away the invaders. He was fiercely proud of Japan and in 1863 had composed this little verse:

Be assured – it is for the Emperor's realm
That I embark on this journey
Shamed though I am in my manly pride.[1]

Ito had been a disciple of Yoshida Shoin's. It was even rumoured that he had been in a party which had been involved in an attack on the British legation on the outskirts of Tokyo. It is not clear if Glover knew this or not when he helped Ito and his friends to escape. Perhaps he was confident that once Ito reached England, he would realize that resistance was hopeless and his dream of acquiring Western technology to defeat the 'invaders' was just that, a fantasy. As it was, when Ito and the other young samurai reached Shanghai, they could only look on in amazement at the fleets of steamers in the harbour there and were converted to the cause: clearly, Japan's only option was to modernize and industrialize, otherwise she would remain no more than just another supplier of raw materials to the West. It was, after all, this same fear which a century earlier had galvanized the newly independent United States to develop its own industries.

After their arrival in Southampton, the Choshu samurai were met by Hugh Matheson of Jardine Matheson, who took them to University College, London. At the time, this was the only non-denominational university in England so there was no bar to their enrolment. The Professor of Chemistry, Alexander Williamson, looked after them and four of the five would attend his classes for analytical chemistry after he had applied for special permission for them to register.

With their smart suits and Western haircuts, and looking for all the world like a pop group, the five young men settled into lodgings near University College and set about learning the language. But they had not long been in London when they read in *The Times* of the tensions back in Japan and of the battle of Kagoshima. Long after the event, on 29 October 1863, a report taken from the English language *Japan Commercial News* of 26 August and another from 'Our Occasional Correspondent' told the story. On 11 August, a flotilla of British ships under the command of Vice-Admiral Kuper, in the flagship *Euryalus*, had entered the wide and beautiful bay of Kagoshima and moored off the town with a view to obtaining reparations from the Satsuma clan for acts of violence towards the British. Kuper noticed that there were moored in the bay three steamers belonging to the Satsumas: they might well have been acquired by Glover, who provided the clan with anything they wanted. As Kuper anticipated that the Satsuma would be tough negotiators, he decided to 'capture' these steamers and had them towed away from their moorings by his own ships.

The response to this was a volley from the defensive batteries set up at the end of the bay where the town was situated, the flagship getting the worst of it. Her captain and a commander were killed and the ship damaged. In response, Kuper resorted to a show of force: he had the captured Satsuma steamers set alight and then gave Kagoshima itself a pasting. The batteries were soon abandoned and both the town itself and many of the junks moored in the harbour were set ablaze. There was no way of knowing what the Japanese casualties were, but some estimated them at 1,500 killed or severely injured. Twelve British seamen were killed outright or mortally wounded, and perhaps twenty suffered some kind of injury. The shocking news of the brutal suppression of the Satsuma town was followed by even more worrying reports that the five's own clan, the Choshu, were firing on British and American ships as they passed through the Straits of Shimonoseki on their way from Yokohama to Shanghai.

Inoue Kaoru and Ito Hirobumi had been to Aberdeen, where they had been shown around shipyards by relatives of Glover and, once again, looked after by Jardine Matheson. What they had seen was daunting: powerful, armoured vessels that could subdue any Japanese force with ease. The two samurai had intended to stay much longer in Britain, but by the spring of 1864 they felt they should return to Japan to warn their own people of the futility of their resistance against the Europeans and Americans. The other three samurai stayed on, one continuing to study chemistry at Glasgow University.

When Ito and Inoue reached Japan in the middle of July 1864, the stand-off with the Choshu, who had been blockading the Straits of Shimonoseki for about a year, had come to a head. A combined fleet of British, French, Dutch and American warships was on its way to force the Choshu to cease hostilities. The British Representative in Japan, Sir Rutherford Alcock, noted the return of the errant samurai and suggested that they take a message to their *daimyo* or prince telling him to lift the blockade or face an assault. Ernest Satow, the English translator, wrote out Alcock's message in Japanese and noted, as he handed it to Ito and Inoue, that they had about a 70 per cent chance of having their heads chopped off when they delivered it. Two British warships dropped the anxious samurai off at an island on the morning of 27 July, informing them that they would return on 7 August. In fact the British collected the pair a day earlier, only to learn that the Choshu militants were prevaricating. It was hopeless, and Ito and Inoue themselves suggested that the only way out of the impasse was to depose the Shogun and reinstate the Emperor, who would negotiate new treaties.

On 5 September 1864 the international armada opened fire, rapidly crushing Choshu resistance. Not only did the clan have to pay reparations for its attacks on the British, it was also forced to fund the expedition that had subdued it at a cost of around £270,000 (more than £13 million in today's money). All the more progressive young samurai now realized that they would have to join forces to overthrow their rulers and embrace Western industrialism. The following year, a party of nineteen Satsuma samurai and officials were spirited out of the country with the help of Glover and his associates. Two of them kept diaries in which they described their first taste of ice cream in Hong Kong and their amazement at a train journey along the route of the Suez canal. One, Arinori Mori, wrote: 'More than half our number had been leading instigators of anti-foreign sentiment, but when they stepped ashore at Malta in the Mediterranean and saw for the first time the enlightened progress and the mighty power of Europe, they awoke at once.'[2]

The Satsuma party were accompanied by an escort, Ryle Holme, all the way to London via Southampton: he telegraphed ahead so that Thomas Glover's brother Jim was there to meet them, a use of the telegraph which amazed the Japanese. While they were staying at a hotel in London, the Satsuma Nineteen met up with the three members of the Choshu Five who had remained in England and their friendship was mirrored by the beginnings of an alliance between the two clans in Japan. While the renegade samurai settled in to experience British life, some staying with the Glover family in Aberdeen and others studying at University College, London, plans were being laid back in Japan for the overthrow of the Bafuku, and it was Thomas Glover who supplied many of the weapons for the rebel Satsuma and Choshu forces who eventually triumphed.

The year 1868 saw the fall of the Bafuku, the restoration of the fifteen-year-old Emperor, the renaming of Yedo as Tokyo and the true beginning of Japan's adoption of modern technology. For Thomas Glover, the victory he had helped win as a gun-runner was very nearly an economic catastrophe, for much of his main business dried up. However, in time he became a consultant for the Mitsubishi shipbuilding company and lived a comfortable life in Glover House, the residence that had been built for him in 1863. On his death in 1911, Glover was feted. A wreath was sent by one of the Choshu Five, Inoue Kaoru, who was by then one of the leading politicians in modern Japan. In fact, all five of the plucky samurai who had risked death to go to the West became political leaders of the new Japan. Ito Hirobumi was for a time prime minister and had become the colonial governor of Korea, which had been annexed by Japan as it established an empire, although in 1910 he was assassinated by a Korean nationalist. Similarly, most of the Satsuma entourage became important figures in Japan's modernization.

Once the new Japanese regime had decided on a course of industrialism and trade with the West, virtually all the engineering skill had to be brought in from abroad, and much of the British contribution in the early days was made by Scotsmen. Nobody did more to transform the country than Richard Henry Brunton, who arrived in 1868 and stayed for eight years, working on a staggering range of projects. Brunton was born in Aberdeenshire in 1841 to a modestly prosperous family, who sent him to private schools and engaged tutors to further his education. He joined a firm of civil engineers in Scotland before moving to London, where he worked for a firm involved in building the London and South-Western Railway. He had applied unsuccessfully for a post in British India when he noticed an advertisement for an engineer to construct lighthouses in Japan.

Part of the treaty agreement which the British minister Sir Harry Parkes had negotiated in Japan was for the once hostile coast to be made safer for shipping. Orders had been put in for lighthouses, but there was no proper scheme and eventually the Scottish firm Stevensons were asked for their advice. They put up the advertisement that young Brunton saw and he got the job with approval from the Board of Trade in February 1868. He was twenty-four and had never had anything to do with lighthouses, but after a crash course organized by the Stevensons he reached Yokohama on 8 August 1868.

In an account Brunton left of his first impressions of Japan – a document that remained unpublished until 1991, nearly a century after it was written – he expressed his horror at the primitive nature of the living conditions he encountered in Yokohama, where Parkes had asked him to help lay out a settlement for foreigners. The wooden houses he found badly constructed and uncomfortable, the only heating in winter being provided by a central brazier or *kotatasu*. As for sanitation, 'At the back of the houses there are generally two carefully protected casks sunk in the earth forming cesspools. Human excreta, used for manuring the paddy or wet rice fields, are regarded as being of great value.'[3]

Requested by Parkes to build some better roads, Brunton reported: 'Hard and dry roads were not thought of in old Japan. There was no horse traction, and only a little wheeled traffic with push carts. Both man and horse wore sandals made of straw. Human beings used wooden clogs which raised their feet an inch or two above the ground and protected them from the mud.' It was none the less part of an agreement signed by the Japanese in 1866 that the foreign quarter of Yokohama should be laid with stone-chip roads along the lines recommended in England by Macadam in the early 1800s. Brunton at first could find no stone that was easily transportable to Yokohama. As there were no horse-drawn vehicles in Japan and the roads which criss-crossed the interior and the coast were narrow and passable only with pack-horses, Brunton had to look along the coast. He found what he needed at Shamoda and a fleet of junks brought the stone to Yokohama. The broken rock had to be rolled to compact it, a job that could be done with horse- or steam-power in Europe. Brunton's only solution in Yokohama was to have a large piece of quarry stone weighing four or five tons rounded off. This was then hauled up and down the new roads for a year by teams of twenty or thirty labourers.

Brunton believed the Japanese were far too excited about building railways and owning steamships and that they should first have built themselves a decent road network. Rather like Britain in the early eighteenth century, Japan had an efficient coasting trade and transport of bulk goods was nearly always by sea. The junks, designed only for inland waters, were flat-bottomed and could sail in shallow water so there was little need for scouring out the estuaries of the rivers. Brunton, who appeared to be able to turn his hand to any engineering problem, argued long and hard for a means to sweep away dangerous sand bars from the mouths or rivers and to build flood defences. In the meantime, every construction in Japan, from the building of lighthouses to the construction of railways, was made more difficult by the frequent threat of earthquakes.

In these early years, Brunton had to improvise, making use of anything he could get his hands on. The first iron bridge in the world had spanned the River Severn in Shropshire in 1779, the work of the Darbys of Coalbrookdale and John 'Iron Mad' Wilkinson.

Nearly a century later, Brunton was asked by the governor of Yokohama, Terashima Munenori, if he could build the first iron bridge in Japan. Terashima had spent two years in England from 1865 to 1867 and so must have seen iron structures everywhere. Certainly, something more substantial was needed than the typical Japanese bridge, which Brunton described thus: 'The piers were formed by two trees with the bark on. These were driven into the ground as far as native appliances would allow. The space between these was then spanned by two other three trunks, selected as having the necessary bend which gives Japanese bridges their arched form. On top of these, wooden planks were laid crossways. A rough handrail completed the structure. Such bridges were in need of constant repair.'[4]

Terashima had no money to import iron from Britain or to bring in any artisans. Brunton, however, found an Englishman in Yokohama with some experience as a blacksmith. Old iron plate was found in Hong Kong. A punching and shearing machine was borrowed from an engineering works and Japanese workmen were taught how to join iron plates together with rivets. Crowds turned out to watch the building of Japan's first iron bridge which would carry the traffic from Yokohama to Tokyo. Exactly what it looked like, Brunton does not say, but the impression is that it resembled one of the iron girder railway bridges he had engineered in England. The bridge was a great success, though, despite some loose riveting at the centre, and for a while it was a wonder of Meiji Japan.

Brunton had originally been employed solely to build lighthouses. He toured the coast a number of times in a variety of steamers and with some difficulty managed to get the buildings put up where he wanted them, bringing in some workers from Britain. There was a near-calamity when a ship transporting the lighting and reflecting equipment was lost at sea. Brunton's response was typical – to acquire headlights designed for American locomotives and install them in some of the lighthouses. Japan had ample supplies of petroleum, which was produced in pits similar to those used in Russia before American drilling techniques were introduced, but Brunton could not get it refined into lighthouse fuel and had to import oil for the lamps.

On one of his exploratory tours of the islands, Brunton was taken to Kagoshima, now rebuilt after the British bombardment of 1863. Even then, after the Meiji restoration, it was not clear what sort of reception a British engineer would get from the proud Satsuma prince. Brunton's guide, Inoue, went ashore first to gauge the mood and returned to say that they were welcome to visit and would be entertained at a banquet, although his hosts were sorry that they had no wine. But Brunton had ample supplies of alcohol aboard his ship and his party took ashore six bottles each of champagne and of sherry.

Before the banquet, Brunton was given a tour of the new industries established by the Satsuma. These included a huge cotton factory with machinery imported from Oldham in Lancashire by Thomas Glover. He was also shown, among other things, the arsenal where cannon were being cast, a boat-building yard and a glass-blowing facility. The banquet itself was laid out for twenty people in a large room adjoining the cotton factory and Brunton noted, as he took his place, that the crockery was imported from Staffordshire, home of the celebrated Wedgwood pottery, and that the Western-style cutlery – entirely novel for the Japanese, who ate with chopsticks – was made in Sheffield. The food, however, was 'in Parisian style', starting with soup and ending with pastry. No sooner had Brunton and his fellow guests finished the ample meal and wiped their mouths approvingly than the whole banquet was served all over again. They managed the second round but had to risk giving offence as the third sitting began. Brunton nudged Inoue, who quietly informed the chefs that the guests had eaten quite enough. When Brunton in turn entertained his Japanese hosts in Yokohama, they tasted pork and lamb for the first time as in Japan there were neither pigs nor sheep.

Though there was a great enthusiasm for railways among Japanese modernizers, it was some time before the authorities worked out how they might be financed. Jumping the gun as always, Thomas Glover had imported a steam engine from Shanghai in 1865 and ran it on a narrow 2' 6" track at Nagasaki. On occasion Glover drove the British-built locomotive he called *The Iron Duke*, but it was a mere novelty which he later shipped to Osaka for further demonstrations. Japan presented special problems for the pioneer railway-builders. The bridges used by the pack-horse trains were easily replaced whenever they were washed away by floods, but they were very flimsy. Railway bridges had to carry considerable weight and, according to British engineers, needed to be built of stone, or at least with stone piers. Then there were the dangers of earthquakes and, in certain regions, of heavy snowfalls which could create drifts of up to eight feet. Above all, Japan is mountainous, the most difficult terrain for the engineer. The highlands rise to between seven and ten thousand feet, and Mount Fuji, which towers over Tokyo, is over twelve thousand feet high.

The first proper line was laid over twenty miles from Yokohama to Tokyo, a government-funded project engineered by the ubiquitous Brunton. At the ceremonial opening of the line in September 1872, the young Emperor said: 'We express our great satisfaction for the undeviating obedience to our will for the introduction of railways, and the overcoming of all opposition and difficulties, and consequent completion of the work we witness today.'[5] Two grandsons of the locomotive pioneer Richard Trevithick became notable railway-builders in Japan, they themselves being the sons of Francis Trevithick, a locomotive engineer on the London and North-Western Railway. The first of the grandsons to arrive was called Francis like his father: he had been hired by the Japanese in 1877 and went on to write the definitive history of the early railways in the country.

For the first ten years, almost everything, from the track to the locomotives, was brought in from abroad, mostly from Britain, although engines were later imported from France, Germany and America. From the very beginning, the government supervised the building of the railways. Many were publicly run and even the private companies, which had charters lasting between twenty and ninety-nine years, were, in Francis Trevithick's view, feather-bedded. Whereas in England railway companies carried the cost of all the survey work, the engineering and the laying of the lines, in Japan this was all taken care of by the State Railway Bureau. Then the government guaranteed investors an 8 per cent return on investment and the right to plan railways in some of the most densely populated and therefore profitable parts of the country. This state backing for railways meant that they were constructed quickly: by 1887 Francis Trevithick thought the clamour for more lines had become 'almost a mania'. Seventeen companies had by then proposals for routes which would total 1,375 miles, the privately run lines outstripping those run by the government.

This was all achieved without the Japanese building a single locomotive for themselves. They had works turning out rolling stock at Shinbashi and Kobe, which first Francis and then his older brother Richard looked after. Indeed, it was Richard who in 1893 succeeded in building the first working steam locomotive in Japan. Not all of it was made at the Kobe works as some pieces had to be imported. But it was the beginning of Japan's independence from imported engines. 'History repeats itself,' wrote Francis Trevithick in 1894, recalling the treatment his grandfather had to endure a century earlier. 'Richard Trevithick senior was branded with folly and madness by the late James Watt for bringing into use the high-pressure engine, and even now is not known to the general public as the builder and inventor of the first locomotive; so will Richard Trevithick of Kobe never be known in Japan by the Japanese as the designer and builder of the first locomotive, the credit being given to a Japanese who has very little mechanical knowledge.'[6]

For his part, Richard Brunton was equally familiar with the Japanese tendency to bask in reflected glory or claim credit for innovations borrowed from abroad. More often, though, he was scathing of Japanese attempts to crew steamships with their own mariners, whose inexperience of such fast and powerful vessels meant that they were constantly running them aground or into each other in the first years of their operation. In his diaries Brunton was often critical of his hosts. He railed against corruption amongst officials, their pig-headed refusal to acknowledge the superiority of Western technology and occasional aggression. But he clearly warmed to the Japanese and he happened to be back in London in 1872 when one of the touring Japanese embassies called as it made its way around the world. Aware that little was known of these Oriental guests, Brunton wrote a letter to *The Times* in advance of their arrival in which he encouraged the British to take an interest in what was a rapidly industrializing nation.

Brunton heaped praise upon a country of beautiful scenery and rich mineral reserves which was making 'noble efforts ... to raise herself to the level of highly civilised nations'.[7] English was being taught in all the schools and English habits were being adopted by the better classes, while he thought about 550 young Japanese men were studying abroad: thirty to forty in Germany, forty to fifty in France, 200 in America and 250 in Britain. At the same time, English engineers were working everywhere in Japan and British academics were heading departments in Japanese universities. The embassy about to arrive in London was composed of the most distinguished politicians, said Brunton, and they had been given a suitably warm welcome in the United States, where Congress had voted $50,000 for their entertainment. 'I have no desire that this country should emulate the "loud" and fussy hospitality of America,'[8] Brunton wrote. What he hoped, however, was that the Japanese would be greeted with respect and courtesy. He certainly greeted them in a very friendly matter before returning, once more, to his work on Japan's lighthouses.

By the 1890s, Japan had begun to establish its own industries, especially ship-building, an area in which Thomas Glover, who had been so instrumental in initiating the country's transformation, remained a consultant. Its modernization had been paid for largely out of the proceeds from the export of silk and a variety of minerals. After fierce resistance to the West, it was rapidly becoming one of the most powerful nations in the world and, as if wishing to emulate Britain in this respect as well, was now in search of an overseas empire. Yet this would inevitably bring Japan into conflict with that giant of a neighbour, Russia, which was now also finally beginning to modernize. And Japan was industrializing rapidly at a time when, in the Western world, another revolution had begun on the roads, one which would see the replacement of the horse by the petrol engine.

CHAPTER EIGHTEEN

HORSEPOWER

At the time Japan was adopting the very latest technologies made available by Britain and other European countries, there was one source of motive power it was able to do without. This was the draught horse, which pulled all the passenger transport and goods vehicles in every major city in the world and, on both sides of the Atlantic, hauled the plough and the harvesting machines in the countryside. When the railways took away long-distance traffic from the stagecoach, the roads connecting towns tended to fall into disrepair. But within towns and in any region close to a railway station or a port, horse-drawn road transport was not only essential, it was increasing in the last half of the nineteenth century at a tremendous rate. In fact, such was the demand for horses that if some way had not been found to replace them as the main source of motive power within cities, the progress of industrialism might well have ground to a halt. The saviour turned out to be the motor car, but it took a huge international effort to bring this novel form of transport into existence, for the idea of a petrol-powered vehicle aroused immense opposition. As one American gainsayer put it during the pioneer days of motoring, nobody would want to travel around 'sitting on top of an explosion'.

Borrowing a concept from economic historians, the historian F. M. L. Thompson, author of two monographs entitled *Nineteenth-Century Horse Sense* and *Victorian England: the horse-drawn society*, invented what he called the 'counterfactual horse'. A counterfactual study asks of history the question, what might have happened if things had been different, and Thompson imagines what early twentieth-century life would have been like without the internal combustion engine. As he puts it, a railway station was 'like a stranded whale' if there was no road transport to take passengers and goods to and from a train to their various destinations. Railway companies themselves all kept huge numbers of horses, as did the bus and tram companies. These animals all had to be fed and stabled and they took up an enormous amount of space, both on the roads and when they were rested. London's new British Library is built on the site of a multistorey horse park next to St Pancras Station.

Professor Thompson provides some startling figures. At the end of the nineteenth century, there were about 3.5 million horses in Britain, one for every ten people, and in the United States there were around thirty million, one horse for every four people. Horses were not manufactured, of course, nor were they mass-produced in studs: only a few elite military stables went in for highly specialized breeding. Instead, four-legged 'engines' were produced by a man going on tour with a stallion who would 'cover' mares thought to be in season, collecting a fee as he went. There was a certain skill to the job of getting horses to mate and it could be a nervy business. One of the last of the English stallion-walkers, interviewed a few years ago, gave this description: 'You'd push the mare's tail aside, and tie it back with small pieces of string. The stallion would then mount her, and you'd guide the penis into her. When he was finished, you had a bucket of water and you always washed his penis straight away. The mare then went away and you hoped that was the end of it. But because you travelled the route regularly, if after three weeks the farmer thought she'd come into season again, you'd go back. And if she wasn't interested in the stallion, then she'd probably taken.'[1]

The success rate of the stallion-walkers was impressive, but in the last decades of the nineteenth century the price of horses began to rise dramatically. Keeping a horse and carriage in a big city such as London became more and more expensive: as well as the cost of the horse there were the stabling and the wages of the groom and the cost of feed. And there was the fuel. Britain's road transport required fifteen million acres of farmland to supply an annual demand for hay and oats. In the United States it is thought about a third of all cultivated farm land – 88 million acres – was needed to provide horse feed. At the same time there were 20,000 steam locomotives in Britain and 60,000 in the United States. Each of these locomotives could do the work of about a hundred horses and had therefore vastly increased the quantity of goods and people transported around over long distances.

Finally, before we wave goodbye to the 'counterfactual horse', mention has to be made of some of the less pleasant aspects of the four-legged motor. Each horse produced about seven tons of manure a year, very handy in the farming regions but a real problem in towns. In London in the 1850s, a Board of Health report reckoned that in the Westminster and City districts alone the horses there deposited 200,000 tons of manure. The journalist Henry Mayhew, who loved statistics, produced a much lower figure of 52,000 tons, but he was only counting the droppings for the six hours a horse was on the streets.

Mayhew also gave a vivid description of the knacker's yard where the worn-out horses were taken to be thrown into huge vats: every part of them would be recycled in one way or another. When he was writing in the mid-nineteenth century, Mayhew estimated there were 37,000 horses sent to the knacker's yard in London alone each year. In the 1890s, the figure was 26,000. The bulk of the horse flesh was sold as food for cats and dogs, the meat put on wooden skewers and touted around the streets in horse-drawn or hand-pushed carts. In the 1890s, some seventy tons of horsemeat were sold each week: writing earlier in the century, Charles Dickens, in one of his flights of fancy, imagined that if you had saved all the wooden skewers, you could have built a naval vessel, the *Royal Skewer*, to frighten Britain's enemies. As well as meat, there were hoofs to be sent off to the glue-makers, bones for fertilizer and hides for the leather trade. This colourful and pungent world of horse transport employed thousands of blacksmiths and farriers as well as stallion-walkers and carters, yet it must surely have been reaching its limits by 1900.

As it was, the slow evolution of the motor vehicle really had nothing much to do with the idea of replacing the horse. For a long while, in fact, the horse got in the way because any mechanical vehicles that appeared on the road tended to frighten these sensitive creatures and threaten the livelihood and interests of those who bred them, cared for them and regarded them as an indispensable part of life. In particular, the earliest steam wagons had a dragon-like demeanour which could be alarming and it was to rein in these monsters that the Locomotive Acts were passed in England in the 1860s. The first of these, in 1861, fixed a prohibitive toll payment on steamers using the turnpike roads and set speed limits of ten miles per hour in the countryside and five miles per hour in town.

Then in 1865 came the notorious Red Flag Act which not only reduced the speed limit to four miles per hour out of town and two miles per hour in town but required that at least three people should be in charge of a steam wagon and that 'one of such persons, while such Locomotive is in motion, shall precede such Locomotive on foot by not less than sixty yards and shall carry a red flag constantly displayed, and shall warn drivers of horses and riders of the approach of such Locomotive and shall signal the driver thereof when it is necessary to stop and shall assist horses, and carriages drawn by horses, passing the same'.[2] This Act, with the slight amendment in 1878 that the flag was no longer necessary and that the person preceding a vehicle need be only twenty yards ahead of it, was not repealed until 1896.

Nevertheless, steam-powered road vehicles were developed in America and in Europe and ran on English roads throughout the nineteenth century. In fact, by the turn of the century they were hardly distinguishable in appearance from petrol-driven cars, their boilers heated by some liquid fuel such as paraffin (kerosene). But it was not the steamer that led directly to the development of the motor car. The origins of what the French called the *automobile* lay in the convergence of two quite different strands of invention.

First, there was the bicycle. The hobbyhorse, or what the French called the *velocifère*, first appeared in the late eighteenth century and riding around on them became a craze among young gallants and society ladies. There were simply two wheels, front and back, attached to a wooden frame. The rider pushed himself or herself along with feet on the ground. There was no front steering and to change direction the rider had to hoist the heavy frame up and redirect it, a habit which caused a spate of hernias amongst male enthusiasts. The first innovation is attributed to Pierre Michaux, a Parisian mechanic who had the idea of putting crank arms on the front wheel that could be turned with the rider's feet. Much doubt was cast on the ability of anyone to maintain their balance on such a machine, but it was soon shown to be possible and another craze resulted. At this stage, there were no chains, no gears and only solid tyres. To achieve speed, while providing some suspension, ht edriving wheels were made larger and larger with the rider on a saddle high off the road. Such machines proved popular for both touring and racing. They were turned out in a variety of forms, sometimes with the small wheel in front, sometimes behind; they went under the generic name of 'ordinaries' and were later nicknamed penny-farthings, after the English coinage. The English engineers James Starley and William Hillman patented the first all-metal model in 1870 and these high-wheelers remained in fashion until the 1890s. They were improved piecemeal by a variety of technicians as 'high-wheeling' gained in popularity across Europe and in America, where many cycling clubs had been established.

Cyclists were regarded by horsemen as a nuisance, especially when they were overtaken by a band of whirring enthusiasts who could, on the right stretch of road, reach quite impressive speeds. For the cyclists themselves, the big drawback of the high-wheeler was the danger of taking a 'header', as happened often enough when, for example, they hit a pot-hole in the road or turned the hidden corner of a country lane and ran into a flock of sheep. They could also be charged by the police – in England anyway – for 'riding furiously'.

Though the cyclist could not replace the draught horse in hauling heavy loads, the bicycle was a rival attraction to horse riding. Cartoons of the 1870s and 1880s had cavalry mounted on penny-farthings and gentlemen peddling their escorts around parks, the man on the bicycle taking the place of a pony. This was fantasy, of course, but as the design of the bicycle evolved it became a real alternative to the horse for those with sufficient energy in their legs. Penny-farthings came in many shapes and sizes and some enterprising manufacturers began to join two of them together. James Starley had the bright notion of putting two seats between the paired frames and advertising the result as the romantic 'Honeymoon Sociable' in which the lady pedalled in front and the man behind. When he rode one of these tandems with his son on a demonstration near Birmingham, both of them ended up in a ditch because the son had pedalled harder than the father on a corner at the bottom of a hill. The accident gave Starley the idea of having each wheel run on its own independent axle, a solution which effectively solved the problem that on a curve an outside wheel travels further than the inside wheel.

Manufacturers on both sides of the Atlantic now offered a quite bewildering variety of two-, three- and four-wheeled designs, and an international fraternity of cyclists organized meets and races. Many of the names in Europe later associated with motor cars began with bicycle manufacture: Rover, Humber and Hillman in England, for example, and Peugeot and Renault in France. In so many ways, the huge bicycle industry of the late nineteenth century set the pattern for the future. New models were launched on an annual basis, and all kinds of accessories advertised for them. The trade in bicycles was truly global, and manufacturers competed in races, vying with each other for the best cyclists just as car manufacturers sign up racing drivers today. There was a renewed interest in the urban and rural roads which had been neglected since the coming of the railways, and the more socially elevated wheelmen formed pressure groups to demand these routes were improved.

The modern bicycle, with its two wheels of a similar size, a diamond frame and central pedals turning a chain which drove the back wheel, emerged around 1884. A great many inventive minds were at work in the field, but an Englishman, Harry J. Lawson, who was later involved in the motor industry, is usually credited with the idea of the chain-driven back wheel, while James Starley certainly produced one of the first so-called 'safety' bicycles of modern appearance. They were safer because the rider was not atop a huge wheel, but they were not popular until a way was discovered of cushioning the ride on wheels smaller than the penny-farthing's.

An inflatable rubber tyre had been patented as early as 1846 by a Scot, Robert William Thomson, and demonstrated in Regent's Park, London, in 1849. But it hardly caused a sensation, and Thomson gave up on it except for use on his own carriage. The fact that it had already been patented was completely forgotten forty years later, when it was invented all over again, and the man who devised this revolutionary and highly significant improvement to road transport was neither an industrialist nor an inveterate inventor but a successful veterinary surgeon. John Boyd Dunlop was born in Scotland in 1840, the son of a farmer. He qualified as a veterinary surgeon at a young age and set up a practice in Edinburgh before moving to Belfast. By the time he was in his forties, according to his own brief autobiography, Dunlop had the largest veterinary practice in Ireland, which was not then partitioned. He had a number of carriages, employed a dozen 'horse shoers' and had made good money from his patent animal medicines. In fact, he was not in the best of health and was considering retiring when the idea for the pneumatic rubber tyre came to him. As Dunlop himself wrote, this was surprising in some respects: he had never ridden a bicycle and there were no rubber or cycle manufacturers of any size in Belfast. However, he had long contemplated devising some form of suspension for carriages, such as springy steel wheels, and he had some knowledge of working with sheets of rubber in his veterinary practice: exactly what he had been devising with rubber he does not say, but it might have possibly had something to do with horses.

The inspiration for the inflatable rubber tyre came from his son Johnnie, who had a tricycle which he rode to and from school and with which he would race other boys in the People's Park in Belfast. Horse-drawn tram lines criss-crossed the cobbled streets of the city and Johnnie complained that these slowed him down. The problem intrigued his father, who began a series of experiments. First, he made himself a bicycle wheel with looped American elm wood and attached to it a tyre which he fashioned from rubber sheets that could be bought from a wholesaler. The crude tyre was attached to the wheel with linen cloth and then blown up with his son's football pump. He then conducted a test in which he rolled a solid rubber wheel across his yard to see how far it would go before it twirled to a halt. Next he pushed his new-fangled pneumatic wheel and found that it went further than the wheel with a solid rubber tyre. He repeated the test many times and had some of his workmen do the same. There was no doubt the inflatable tyre ran faster and further. His son Johnnie became very excited and urged his father to make inflatable tyres for his tricycle so that he could outstrip his friends in their park races.

On the night of 28 February 1888, Johnnie set out on to the streets of Belfast with his tricycle fitted with pneumatic tyres on its back wheels: the front wheel remained solid as it took most of the impact on the rough roads. An eclipse of the moon plunged the city streets into darkness and the trial run was delayed, but after a further run Dunlop was sufficiently encouraged to persevere. He abandoned the old tricycle and ordered a new one without wheels from the Belfast dealers he knew well, Messrs Edlin and Sinclair. He made his own wheels again, using American elm, rubber sheets and linen cloth. When Mr Edlin asked Dunlop when he wanted wheels for the new tricycle, he was told he did not need them as he had them already to his own specification. Like everyone else in these early days, Edlin and his partner were sceptical about pneumatic tyres. However, both of them rode out on the new wheels and found them not only more comfortable but much faster than solid rubber tyres. An advertisement soon appeared in the newspapers: 'Look out for the New Pneumatic Safety. Vibration Impossible. Sole makers – W. Eldin & Co, Garfield Street, Belfast.'

These crude pneumatic tyres looked rather odd and later versions, often not as well made as the original, were known variously as the 'mummy' or the 'pudding' because of their bulging appearance. And there was no immediate enthusiasm from the huge cycling fraternity on either side of the Atlantic. On 19 December 1888 the magazine *Irish Cyclist* had a bit of fun with the whole idea: 'We note the advent of a pneumatic – News room attic – bah – a new Pneumatic Safety. Pneumatic! Something to do with air, isn't it? Quite right too, we like to see new ideas well ventilated. Happy thought, we hear of draught horses. Perhaps the pneumatic may be a draught bicycle.'[3] Such sneers were commonplace for a while, but the cycling fraternity changed its tune when riders with the new Dunlop tyres began to win races, out-pedalling contestants who were regarded as more proficient. Even Harvey du Cros, the president of the Irish Cyclists' Association, was knocking on John Dunlop's door after his sons had been beaten by riders using the new tyres. Dunlop was persuaded to form a business partnership which involved taking over a cycle agency in Dublin. In 1889 the Pneumatic Tyre and Booth's Cycle Agency was formed, with Dunlop a major shareholder. Patents were applied for and granted.

A London patent agent duly discovered that the claim to originality was invalidated by the long-forgotten specification of the Scot Robert William Thomson, yet there were other aspects of the wheels which could be patented and eventually the Dunlop Rubber Company was formed: it was named in honour of John Dunlop but he had no involvement with it. He did not, in fact, maintain his financial stake in pneumatic tyres and made little or no money out of them. At his death in 1921 it seemed that he had left a rather meagre estate, although in her introduction to his autobiography, Dunlop's daughter Jean pointed out that her father had very successful investments in Australia and lived comfortably on them before leaving a legacy not recorded in England.

At the time John Dunlop was producing his first tyres, a French family which had factories near Clermont-Ferrand in the Auvergne region of central France chanced into the same line of business. The business had been founded by the brothers Edouard and André Daubrée in the 1820s to refine sugar from locally grown beet. Edouard, who had served as an army officer and sugar agent in Paris, married an Englishwoman, Elizabeth Pugh Parker, who was related to Charles Macintosh, the manufacturer of waterproof clothing. She and Edouard settled in 1830 in a country property about ten miles from Clermont. Here they borrowed money to build a second sugar refinery and Elizabeth, with her family interest in rubber, set up a small business with a workforce of local women, making rubber balls. A cousin of Daubrée, Aristide Barbier, who had fallen on hard times, joined the business and it proved modestly successful, making a number of rubber goods and machinery for sugar refineries. When both Daubrée and Barbier died within a short time of each other in 1863, the firm, which then employed nearly 400 workers, was passed on to Jules Michelin, who had married one of Barbier's daughters.

Michelin handed the business on to Daubrée's son, who in turn handed it on to a lawyer. By 1886, however, the company had fallen into near bankruptcy and Michelin's two sons, André, the elder, and Edouard, were called in to run it. Both had had more interest in painting than manufacturing, though André had two small metal-working practices in Paris. Edouard arrived in Clermont-Ferrand in the spring of 1888 and began to learn from the workforce about the manufacture of rubber. The brothers had their first success with rubber brake pads for horse-drawn coaches.

The story may be apocryphal, but this was apparently the genesis of the Michelin fortune. André, who was based in Paris, had seen a Dunlop pneumatic tyre and written to Edouard: 'These stick-on pneumatics of Dunlop's – great fat sausages – frightful. Everyone agrees they'll wreck the bicycle. No future in them.'[4] After glancing at André's letter, Edouard was at the door of their little factory when he saw an ox cart coming up the hill towards him. Walking beside the cart was an Englishman and in it was his bicycle, whose Dunlop tyres had burst. Edouard himself had no experience of making rubber goods but his workmen were able to mend the tyres and the grateful Englishman responded with a generous payment. They watched him sail down the hill, whereupon one of the tyres burst again. Edouard, however, was not so deflated. On the contrary, he decided that Michelin would make tyres for France.

A big disadvantage of the early Dunlop tyres was that they were glued to the wheel. It was recognized early on that what was needed was a detachable tyre which could be mended easily and quickly. Du Cros and his workforce in Dublin had produced such a tyre by 1891, as had the Michelin brothers, Eduoard apparently taking charge of the design. Dunlop and Michelin appear to have worked to different but similar patent specifications. The two makes of pneumatic tyres were tested as early as September 1891 in a bicycle race from Paris to Brest in Brittany and back. Riding for Michelin was the champion Charles Terront, while Dunlop had the favourite, Jiel-Laval. Of the 210 riders who started the race, no fewer than fifty-seven had pneumatic tyres. Terront won for Michelin, apparently pedalling for seventy-one hours without sleep.

With pneumatic tyres fitted to the new safety bicycles, cyclists achieved quite remarkable feats. In the spring of 1890 C. A. Smith pedalled from

London and Brighton and back in less than seven hours. He followed the route of the Brighton stagecoach and beat the best time it had ever made of seven hours and fifty minutes, achieved in 1888 with no less than sixteen changes of horses. Cyclists began to make journeys no horseman could ever have contemplated. In 1895 the intrepid Robert Louis Jefferson, Fellow of the Royal Geographical Society and a leading member of Catford Cycling Club in South London, set himself a personal endurance test. He announced that he would attempt to cycle from London to Moscow and back in less than fifty days. Mobbed by well-wishers and accompanied by English pacemen, he left Kennington Oval on 20 April 1895 and headed for the coast, where he took a boat across the southern North Sea to Holland. He travelled light: mackintosh cape, leggings, maps, nuts, bolts, ball bearings, cyclometer, a box of a patent medicine called Homocea, which the maker claimed would cure anything from a bout of flu to bruises, chilblains and eczema, and several handkerchiefs. He also packed a 'plentiful supply of Bovril', a can of White's Electrine Oil and a revolver.

For most of his journey he was met by local cycling enthusiasts who showed him the way. His only real setback was at the Russian border, where his passport was tossed unceremoniously across a guard room and he nearly lost his bicycle to some impoverished Polish Jews whom he felt were not upholding the standards of those of the 'Yiddish creed' in London. He had to knock one poor chap out with a blow to the chin to retrieve his Imperial Rover bicycle, a top-of-the-range model from Starley of Coventry. He was also chased by a dog which was harnessed to small cart in an impoverished region close to the Russian border; dog and cart crashed before they could catch him.

Jefferson reached Moscow in precisely twenty-three days and one hour, his cyclometer readings showing he had covered a distance of 2,120 miles. He was given an appropriately enthusiastic welcome by fellow riders in Moscow, who toasted him with champagne and pinned a gold brooch to his jacket. He left Moscow for the return journey on 16 May and was back in London twenty-three hours and fifty-four minutes inside the fifty days he had allowed for the round trip. Jefferson wrote in his account *Awheel to Moscow and Back*:

My cyclometer showed the distance as 4,281 miles, and this had been accomplished in forty-nine days six minutes, constituting absolutely the longest consecutive ride ever done in a given time … I lost two stone in weight, two and a half inches around the chest and four and a half inches around the stomach … It will readily be granted that black bread, sour milk and *vodki*, however toothsome they might be, are certainly not fattening. The reception I received at the hands of my brother wheelmen was deeply gratifying. Naturally there were one or two carping critics who could see no good purpose in the ride – but let that pass.[5]

Long-distance cycling was popular in both North America and Europe in the 1890s, but few people had the stamina of Jefferson and the more sedate cyclists puffing about on a variety of tricycles and four-wheelers were bound to welcome a measure of automotive help. The problem was, of course, devising an engine neat and light enough to fit to a tricycle or a horseless equivalent of the carriage. There were steam-powered broughams, such as that made by Mr H. Mackenzie of Scole in Norfolk, England, which ran smoothly and quietly on solid rubber tyres at ten to twelve miles per hour. In the 1890s there was quite a range of electric, battery-powered carriages which were handy for nipping around London where the early electricity generating stations could be relied upon to recharge batteries. It was then, however, that gas- and petrol-fuelled motor vehicles began to appear on the roads, and though they were not at first able to outpace the top cyclists, within a few years they had developed immense power and swept all other road vehicles aside, including the horse-drawn buses and trams, taxi cabs and private carriages.

Though the earliest motor vehicles adopted much of the bicycle's technology for their structure, their engines were novel. If the early experiments of the luckless Frenchman Denis Papin, in which he drove a piston with gunpowder, are discounted, then the forerunner of the internal combustion engine was that devised by the Belgian Etienne Lenoir. Born in 1822, Lenoir experimented with electricity, especially electro-plating, and set up business in Paris. In the 1850s there were various attempts to build a gas engine, and Lenoir succeeded in doing so in 1860. The fuel was not gasoline (petroleum) but illuminating gas, which was ignited electrically to drive a piston. The Lenoir gas engine looked rather like a smaller, compact version of a Watt steam engine and was used in much the same way to drive stationary machinery. It was especially useful in small workshops. Lenoir did fit one to a road vehicle and another to a boat, but his engine was used only for factory work; it required too much attention to be any use on the road.

The Lenoir engine received a great deal of publicity, however, and inspired others to find a way of making it more practical. As is so often the case with invention, the man who made the breakthrough had no background in engineering nor any means to develop an engine independently. Nikolaus August Otto was born on 6 June 1832 in the village of Holzhausen auf der Heide which stands high above the River Rhine on a plateau surrounded by fir forests. His father Philipp Wilhelm Otto was the postmaster and an innkeeper in the village but he died while August was still a baby. As the family needed whatever income they could get, the boy had to leave school early and find himself a trade. He worked first in a grocery store in a nearby town, then as a clerk in Frankfurt before moving on to Cologne, where a brother found him a job as a travelling salesman.

It was while he was taking the mail coaches around Cologne, bringing in orders from the villages for all kinds of goods and delivering them, that Otto began to think about engines. He knew about Lenoir as he had taken an interest in mechanical things as a boy. And in Cologne he had befriended a man called Michael Zons who had a machine shop. The Lenoir engine ran on gas, so the engine either had to be near a permanent supply or connected to a canister whose contents would not last for very long. Otto conceived instead of an engine running on petrol vapour mixed with air. He made a sketch, showed it to Zons and together they built a crude apparatus with alcohol as its fuel. Otto then applied for a patent which stipulated that he had enivsaged an engine that would 'propel vehicles serviceably and easily along country roads, as well as prove useful for the purposes of small industry'.[6]

Otto's patent application was turned down on the grounds that others had had much the same idea before him. But Otto and Zons did not give up. They built a replica Lenoir engine and were thrilled to see it work. Otto spent all his spare time puzzling over improvements and arrived at the idea of a four-stroke cycle for a gas or petrol engine. He had become engaged to a girl, Anna Gossi, he had met at a carnival while on his travels and wrote to her in 1862 excitedly, saying that he thought he had made a breakthrough. She was anxious to be married and so was he, but he did not have the financial wherewithal. In the autumn of 1862, however, he decided to take a gamble, leaving his job as a salesman, working full time in the Zons workshop and then taking a trip to London. It was the year of another World's Fair – they were in vogue at the time – a huge international exhibition staged in South Kensington, which was as ambitious, if not nearly as successful, as the Great Exhibition of 1851.

August Otto went in search of rivals to his four-stroke engine, but there was nothing to worry him and he determined to put his design into production. When he returned to the workshop in Cologne, however, he realized he still could not make his engine work efficiently. After contemplating the problem for some time, he had the idea of using the atmospheric principle of the engines built by one of his heroes, James Watt. So it was back to the old Newcomen engine, but with a different fuel, gas. By the time he arrived at the idea of atmospheric pressure providing some of the drive, Otto was very nearly broke. His small inheritance was gone and he would not have been able to continue had he not met a young and wealthy engineer called Eugene Langen. The son of a successful sugar refiner and banker, Langen had some technical training and already had his own business. Fired with enthusiasm about the new engine, he provided the money in March 1864 to create N. A. Otto & Company, engine-builders.

Lofts were rented in an old warehouse and Otto went to work with the help of machinists who worked for local locksmiths. The engines he devised were extremely noisy but they worked, and a local locksmith was the first to buy one. But Otto and Langen found that the engines were not really saleable in their early form for the same reason the Lenoir engines had not been more successful: they were too difficult to run and required some expertise to maintain. Langen became more involved and, after three years' experimentation, they had a better engine with a vertical cylinder and a piston which turned a cog wheel as it moved up and down. It was still an odd-looking contraption but Otto and Langen were confident enough to exhibit at the next great international exhibition held in Paris in 1867. Once it was put together and set running in the exhibition hall, their engine could not be missed for it made a terrible noise. None the less, it was confidentially advertised as a 'Gas Engine ... offering industry a one to three horsepower motor, cheaper to operate than a steam engine'.

At first, the committee awarding prizes at the exhibition ignored the Otto-Langen engine. All around were versions of the Lenoir engine whirring away, powering pumps and turning small machines. The German engine seemed, if anything, a retrograde piece of engineering. But Professor Franz Reuleaux of Berlin University, who a few years before had turned down Langen's offer to become involved in the firm, was on the committee. He argued that the Otto-Langen engine should be given a fair test and compared with the Lenoir. This was arranged and it performed extremely well, using only a third of the fuel consumed by the Lenoir engine. Otto and Langen triumphed, winning the gold medal, which they received at a grand ceremony attended by Napoleon III.

The orders rolled in and Otto and Langen had difficulty keeping pace with them. By 1868, they were selling their engines to Russia and America as well as other European countries. The next year, they moved from Cologne to a larger site at Deutz on the right bank of the Rhine. They sold eighty-seven engines in 1869, 118 in 1870 and 197 in 1871, and they began to turn a profit. In 1869, a British firm of engineers, the Crossley Brothers of Manchester, began to manufacture Otto-Langen engines under licence. The new gas-engine business became established at the same time as Prussia defeated France in 1871 and the unification of Germany was completed. By 1872, the firm had to expand again to fulfil orders and new partners were taken on and a new company formed: Gasmotoren-Fabrik Deutz AG. A new manager was also taken on, an experienced engineer who knew all about the Lenoir engine and had studied in London: his name was Gottlieb Daimler and he joined the firm in July 1872.

Daimler was not then interested in developing any kind of motor car, though in time he was to be its most influential promoter internationally. He was born in 1834 in the small town of Schorndorf in Württemberg where his father had a baker's shop and wine bar. Daimler had some schooling up to the age of fourteen, when he was apprenticed to a gunsmith. He proved a skilled craftsman and, after four years learning his trade, he was awarded a place at the School for Advanced Training in the Industrial Arts in Stuttgart and an older cousin encouraged him to go there to develop his engineering skills. Students worked in a factory during the day and studied in the evenings and at weekends. At the age of nineteen, Daimler moved on to a firm near Strasbourg which built railway carriages, goods vans, bridge sections and other kinds of machinery. This proved another tough training regime, with long working days that began at five in the morning and included instruction away from the factory floor. While he was there, the firm began to build steam locomotives and Daimler became foreman at the age of just twenty-two.

A year later, he won a scholarship to the Stuttgart Polytechnic Institute and was given study leave. He had little money to live on and stayed with the family of a butcher who was a friend of his father's. Here Daimler learned chemistry, physics, mathematics, engineering, economics and English, cramming a four-year course into two years. In 1859, he returned to the firm in Stuttgart, as he was obliged to do, but his heart was no longer in steam locomotives. He stayed on for two years then obtained permission to leave. The next phase of Daimler's career is not well documented, but he did travel to Paris and was apparently interested in the Lenoir engine which was being manufactured there commercially as well as under licence in Hamburg. In Paris, Daimler called on a man called Perin who had a small woodworking factory, but he found it of little interest even though this same firm would later play a large part in his life.

From Paris, Daimler went on to England. He went first to Leeds, where he was greatly impressed by the industrial bustle and vigour and for a while he worked in the engine shop of a firm called Smith, Peacock and Tannet. Then he moved on to Manchester, where he worked for Roberts and Company, makers of everything mechanical from weaving mills to sheet-metal shears for shipbuilders. There does not appear to have been even a modicum of secrecy or reluctance to show Daimler whatever he wanted to see, and on this whistlestop tour he also visited the precision toolmakers Whitworth in Coventry. William Whitworth, the company's founder, had been apprenticed to Henry Maudslay, the maker, along with Marc Brunel, of the British navy's pulley blocks.

The high point of Daimler's trip was his visit to the 1862 World's Fair in London, an event that once again impressed him with its array of inventions. At that time he knew nothing of August Otto, who had, of course, also made the trip to London to see if there were any rivals to the engine he was developing. When Daimler returned to Germany, he took a job running an unusual engineering works which had charitable origins. The Bruderhaus factory produced machines for paper mills, weighbridges and farm implements, a proportion of its profits going to support orphans and others. Indeed, it was in Bismarck's Germany that the concept of the welfare state was first established with the intention of heading off the threat of socialism. Britain duly adopted the idea before the First World War, influenced by reformers such as William Beveridge and Winston Churchill, who was then still a Liberal.

Daimler stayed at the Bruderhaus works from 1867 to 1869. It was not an especially good time for him professionally as his managerial ambitions were often frustrated. But he did marry Emma Kurz, a chemist's daughter, and befriend a much younger man, Wilhelm Maybach, with whom he was to work during the most creative years of his life. Born in 1846, Maybach had been taken in by the Bruderhaus when he was orphaned at the age of ten. He lived by its strict regime and took an apprenticeship as well as evening classes where he learned physics and free-hand technical drawing. Maybach and a friend also learned English and French from another employee. Daimler recognized Maybach's gift as a draughtsman and innovator and gave him a job in the design office of the Bruderhaus. When Daimler moved on to manage another works, he returned to take Maybach with him. And in 1872, when Langen poached Daimler to run the Deutz firm making Otto engines, Daimler persuaded him to take on Maybach as chief designer.

Daimler and Maybach worked on the Otto engines from 1872 until 1881. The firm was very successful, but in the end there was a clash of personalities between Daimler and Otto and, as the financial backer and senior manager, Langen had to intervene. Daimler went on a trip to Russia to explore the possibility of opening up a factory in St Petersburg, but on his return he decided he did not want to move there. His contract was not renewed and he left to set up on his own. Daimler was now forty-eight and exhausted by the relentless schedule he had set himself. In 1882 he moved with his wife and five children to Cannstatt, where he had a beautiful villa with a large garden. Here he established his own workshop, a tiny unit in contrast to the firm he had left which now employed 300 men and turned out 600 Otto engines a year.

It was in Cannstatt that Daimler began work on the engines that would be the foundation of the motor car industry. Maybach joined him and together they set out to produce a petrol engine that had an efficient and quick-starting ignition and a power-to-weight ratio which would make it ideally suited to propelling road vehicles and boats. Daimler thought not only in terms of the private car but of goods wagons as well. By 1885 they had produced a one horsepower engine that worked at 650 revolutions per minute. Daimler ordered a coach from a firm in Stuttgart, saying it was a present for his wife to deflect any interest there might be in it from rivals. They fitted the new engine to the coach and drove it around the gardens. The following year, Daimler fitted the engine into a boat and launched it on the Neckar river, where its propulsion puzzled onlookers: aware that people were still fearful of petrol, he hung wires from the boat so that it would appear to be electrically driven.

At more or less the same time as Daimler and Maybach were perfecting a two-cylinder engine and arriving at something like a model of the modern motor car, another German inventor, working quite independently, had produced a motor tricycle. Karl Benz was a child of the Germany Friedrich List had worked so hard to bring about before his descent into depression and suicide. Karl's father, Hanns Georg Benz, had come from a family of blacksmiths, craftsmen in an old tradition whose world was opened up by the customs union and then the coming of the railways. Hanns Benz had an ambition to work on the railroads as an engineer, although he had no formal training. First, he became a mechanic and foreman of a sugar factory, then he applied to the imposingly named High Commission of Roads and Waterworks of the Grand Duchy of Baden in Karlsruhe for a job as a steam-train driver. He was offered a trial period in the workshops and told to report to the Grand Ducal Railways station in Heidelberg. By the autumn of 1843, he was appointed engineer for the Karlsruhe Railway and his wife Josephine gave birth to their son Karl on 25 November 1844. Two years later, Hanns died of pneumonia.

Though Karl's mother had to keep herself and him on a small state pension, she managed to get her son into the Lyceum in Karlsruhe, which had a good record in teaching natural sciences. From there, he won a scholarship to the polytechnic school, where he was a pupil of the inspirational Ferdinand Redtenbacher, who taught both the theory and practice of mechanical engineering and had his own workshop. This was where Karl was told that the next key invention in the development of industrialism would be a small, powerful engine. When he graduated, Karl found a job as an engineer with a factory in Karlsruhe which made, amongst other things, steam engines: it was the same works that Gottlieb Daimler was to manage three years later. In 1866, he went on to work for a firm in Mannheim that made highly specialized weighing machines and, after two years there, moved on to an ironworks and an engine shop in Pforzheim. He was working there in 1870 when his mother died.

In 1871, Karl managed to escape military service in the war with France. He had met the girl he was to marry, Bertha Ringer, who was the daughter of a builder and contractor, and she persuaded her father to put up the money for the first Benz enterprise. He bought a plot of land in Mannheim and set up a machine shop. To make ends meet, he tried his hand at offering for sale all manner of tools, but it was hard-going. By 1877 he was close to bankruptcy and was saved from the debtor's prison only by a sympathetic bank which recognized that the value of the land he had bought for his workshop had risen. For Benz it was now all or nothing, and he decided he had to come up with *the* great invention, a new kind of engine. He was familiar with the Otto engine, of course, and the fact that Otto had just taken out his four-cycle patent. This meant that Benz had to work with the two-cycle engine if he was to avoid patent infringement. With an iron will, and the support of his young wife, Benz went to work and had a functioning two-cycle engine by New Year's Eve of 1879.

For a while it seemed as if Benz was going to suffer the same fate as Otto and end up just making engines for factory work. He found a backer who offered to fund the business and a company was set up with a considerable investment from a number of shareholders. This firm, Gasmotorenfabrik Mannheim, survived for a number of years, but Benz himself left it as he wanted to pursue his own dream and was not content to make a living as an engine-maker. He found new backers and another firm was founded in 1883, Benz & Cie. This was successful and had to expand as there was a growing demand for engines. As far as the business partners of Benz were concerned, the firm was flourishing and there was no need to get involved with anything as futuristic as motor-car manufacture. Benz was determined, though, and once again went looking for new backers who allowed him to develop his plans for a motor vehicle. He was granted a patent in 1886 for a vehicle with a 'gas engine drive' which was defined as an engine 'whose gas fuel derives from volatile substances to be processed by an apparatus included as part of the mechanism'.

Benz and, on one memorable occasion, his wife and sons, began to take the motor he created out on the road and there were the first reports of his invention in the press. In 1888, a Munich newspaper ran the following story:

> Seldom, if ever, have passers-by in the streets of our city seen a more startling sight on a Saturday afternoon when a one-horse chaise came from the Sendlingerstrasse over Sendlingertorplatz and down Herzog Wilhelmstrasse at a good clip without any horse … a gentleman sitting under a surrey top, riding on three wheels – one in front and two behind – speeding on his way towards the centre of town … the astonishment was general and widespread.[7]

Though Benz's motorized tricycle attracted a good deal of attention, he was disappointed that there was no immediate demand for the new vehicle. It turned out that the Germans, brilliant though they were at technological innovation, had no great yearning for the motor car and continued to covet their horses. And, in truth, the Benz trio-car had plenty of room for improvement, as Benz was told in no uncertain terms when he tried to interest a Mr Kugler, the postmaster in the Rhineland town of Speyer, in his invention. Kugler's thoughtful response can be found in the Benz archive and is edited here:

> 1. The steering mechanism in your smaller three-wheel vehicle is inside the chaise ... in your new four-wheeler model could you not have a sort of coachman's seat up front so that the enclosed room could be all at the disposal of the passengers?

> 2. Could you not put under the driver's seat, or in the rear, two closable compartments, a large one and a small one, where letters and money for postal transfers could be safely kept?

> 3. Why are there no controls for going backwards? The fact that you cannot go backwards is really something to puzzle at.

> 4. Should you not employ a more powerful engine so that swampy sections of the road and deep snow could easily be traversed?

> If you are able to include these improvements in your car, indispensable for a safe and sure road performance, then I am positive that your ingenious and most practical invention will be crowned with a great success. I am not only thinking of its usefulness to the postal services, but I am utterly convinced that it would be most excellent for a country doctor. Not every doctor in a small village has box stalls, horses, and a farm to maintain them, yet some kind of a cart is essential for a doctor who has to make calls in a number of places distant from each other. How often is a doctor called on during the night, and how else is he meant to get

where he has to go? Before he has roused the sleep-drunk peasant out of his bed and got him to put the bridle and harness on the horse, a lot of valuable time has been lost …

There is another thing about your vehicle: it comes to a stop and turns off and that's it. It doesn't need any feed, or any groom, no blacksmith … [there is] no danger of having a horse shy, it just moves along as if a ghostly hand were pushing it, and one stroke of the brakes and it stops.[8]

Benz took heed and developed four-wheeler cars. Despite little interest being shown in the model he exhibited at the 1889 World's Fair in Paris, where Daimler was also looking for buyers for his own version of the motor car, Benz went ahead and began to manufacture cars for sale. With a new business partner, in 1894 he put on the market a light vehicle they called the Velo, short for velocipede, a name they thought might attract cycling enthusiasts. The other Benz models were the Viktoria and the Vis-à-Vis. He also built some charabancs, one of which began to run a service between the towns of Siegen, Netpen and Deutz. By 1895, the Benz factory had delivered 135 cars, ninety-seven of them to France, which was by some way the best customer. Over the next few years, this firm became for a while the most important maker of automobiles in the world, exporting them to Cape Town, Mexico, Buenos Aires, Singapore, Moscow and St Petersburg as well as to Paris and London.

Meanwhile, Daimler and Maybach were not far behind, and their international influence was perhaps even greater than that of Benz. Their first breakthrough came following a meeting with a Frenchman, Emile Levassor. Levassor had worked in Belgium with an engineering firm which had been founded by an Englishman, John Cockerill, and made steam locomotives amongst other machines; he also knew an engineer and patent agent called Edouard Sarazin, who represented Otto-Langen. When Sarazin was asked to find someone to manufacture the Otto engine in France, he naturally thought of Levassor, who had by now moved there to work with the machine-makers Perin and Panhard. The latter began to make Otto engines under licence in 1875 and when, four years later, the German company decided to establish its own factory in Paris, they lost a lucrative business. However, when Daimler left the Otto and Langen company to set up on his own, Sarazin got back in touch with him and offered to become his French agent. Perin and Panhard agreed to make Daimler engines simply to establish the French patent.

In 1888, while Levassor was working on the Daimler engines for Perin and Panhard, the company was sent a kit of a Benz Velo in packing cases by a Parisian engineer who had thought it might interest them. They eventually assembled the vehicle but could not get it to work until Benz himself arrived to show them how it was done. Levassor, however, was not terribly impressed, as the Daimler engines seemed more powerful. Meanwhile, Edouard Sarazin had died and in his last days had urged his wife to continue to pursue Daimler as he believed he was on to something. Accordingly, in 1887 Sarazin's widow, along with Levassor, visited Daimler in Cannstatt to negotiate an agreement to become his representative in Paris. This done, she had driven a Daimler car back home and, shortly after, married Emile Levassor. At first, Levassor expressed no interest in motor cars: instead, he put Daimler in touch with the Peugeot brothers, who made bicycles, to develop a French vehicle.

The first competitive road tests for 'horseless carriages' were held in France, which, for a few years before the First World War, became the major manufacturer and exporter of automobiles. France won its head start partly by default, for German authorities proved to be antagonistic towards the new machines and imposed bans and very restrictive speed limits. Though Americans quickly embraced the motor car and were soon the world's foremost producers, they were held back by an absurd patent granted to one George B. Selden, who claimed all the US rights to any vehicle powered by any form of internal combustion engine. Selden had constructed a vehicle of sorts in 1877 and in 1879 filed for a patent for his one-cylinder engine and its application to a four-wheeled vehicle. As a spoiling measure, Selden filed amendments over sixteen years preventing other applicants from submitting rival claims and finally obtained his patent in 1895. He then sold this on to a William Whitney, whom he partnered in producing electric cars. As the

American auto industry got going, any manufacturer had to pay Selden and Whitney a licence fee. Henry Ford, who had established his own company in 1903, and three other manufacturers contested the Selden–Whitney patent claim. After an eight-year legal battle, they lost in a judgment passed in 1911. Ford appealed and finally won on the grounds that his engines were not derived from Selden's but from those of Nikolaus August Otto, who thereafter became a hero of Ford's.

In the meantime, Gottlieb Daimler had engaged William Steinway, the famous piano-maker, as an ad hoc agent for his engines, advertising them as suitable for 'Street Railroad Cars, Pleasure Boats, Carriages, Quadricycles and Fire Engines'. In 1888, shortly before Steinway had become involved, Daimler had produced the world's first motorized fire engine, and when the World's Fair was staged in Chicago in 1893, Steinway persuaded him to make a trip to the United States to promote his engines and vehicles. Daimler had recently remarried after the death of his first wife and so the trip would also serve as a honeymoon. Though Daimler himself was feted, the take-up of motor car manufacture while he was there was still held back by the Selden patent and not much came of it.

In England, a Daimler Motor Company was established in 1896 to manufacture cars in the traditional home of the bicycle, Coventry, where Daimler had paid homage to British inventiveness as a young man. After intense lobbying, the stringent law on the speed of motor vehicles on the roads was revised in the same year and so the production not only of Daimler cars but many other home-grown models could start in earnest. Almost immediately, the car replaced the bicycle as the favoured form of transport for the well-to-do. The first motor buses appeared on the streets of London in 1903, when there were just thirteen of them among 3,623 horse buses. By 1913, however, there were only 142 horse buses left while there were already 3,522 motor buses on the streets. The London cabs went the same way, with just under 2,000 horse-drawn hansoms and broughams left in 1913 as against 8,000 motor taxis. It was the beginning of the end for the horse, although during the First World War hundreds of thousands were to be shipped across to France, where a great many of them perished.

Although each played a huge part in the creation of the motor car industry, Gottlieb Daimler and Karl Benz never met. Just after Daimler died in March 1900, his agent in the south of France, where motor racing was popular on the steep mountain roads behind the coast at Nice, ordered a new and more powerful car from the company. The agent, Emil Jellinek, was a leading light among the glitterati of the Côte d'Azure and he wanted a car that was both powerful and safe and could compete against the French models being produced by the Panhard and Levassor company. Maybach duly designed an impressive 35-horsepower car and Jellinek ordered thirty-five of them in return for an exclusive licence to market them in America, France, Belgium and Austria–Hungary. He named them Mercedes after his eleven-year-old daughter, though in some countries they were known as the 'New Daimler', and the name was retained. Karl Benz died in 1929 in his eighty-fifth year, but not before the firm he founded had merged in 1926 with Daimler, a union which would create that most celebrated of motor car manufacturers, Mercedes-Benz.

Within only a few years of the making of the first commercial models, it became clear that the United States was the natural home of the motor car. The petroleum industry was already well established there and the fuel for the new transport readily available. By contrast, Japan had adopted the bicycle and would ignore the motor car in the years leading up to the First World War. The roads there were bad and besides, Japan had a much greater priority: the creation of a modern merchant marine and a powerful navy. In the meantime, Britain, the country which had supplied the industrial blueprint America and Japan were now following in their very different ways, was suffering a serious crisis of confidence. The signs had been there for some time, but by the last decade of the nineteenth century they were undeniable. At the Great Exhibition of 1851, the brash Americans had been patronized as parvenus. Now, in the new age of oil, steel and electricity, they were major rivals competing for business on the global stage.

CHAPTER NINETEEN

THE WIZARD OF MENLO PARK

Like many of his countrymen, the English novelist and futurist H. G. Wells believed that Britain had fallen behind its industrial rivals by the early years of the twentieth century. He was an advocate of the National Efficiency movement, whose members were concerned about the poor health of the British working classes and regarded with envy the scientific advances of the Germans and manufacturing vigour of the United States. The huge effort required to defeat the Boers in South Africa in the war of 1899 to 1902 had certainly been sobering. 'The modern Boer,' wrote Arthur Conan Doyle, the creator of Sherlock Holmes, 'is the most formidable antagonist who ever crossed the path of the Imperial Britain ... Napoleon and all his veterans never treated us so roughly as these hard-bitten farmers with their ancient theology and their inconveniently modern rifles.'[1] Those rifles were Mausers and they were German-made.

In his novel *Mr Britling Sees it Through* (1916), Wells tells the story of an American who visits England for the first time with the aim of persuading Mr Britling, an eccentric English intellectual of the Edwardian era, to give a lecture tour in the United States. The American is charmed by the quaintness of old England: the local railway station where Britling meets him is festooned in prize-winning sweet peas. Britling arrives in suitably tattered clothing and ushers his guest into the passenger seat of a brand-new American-built motor car he has acquired and is just learning to drive. After a few near misses on the road out to Britling's country home, the car skids into a hedge of dogrose and honeysuckle. Unable to move until help arrives, Britling delivers a Wellsian monologue on the sorry state of the country:

> Our manufacturing class was, of course, originally an insurgent class ... it had the craftsman's natural enterprise and radicalism. As soon as it prospered and sent its boys to Oxford, it was lost. Our manufacturing class was assimilated in no time to the conservative classes, whose education has always had a mandarin quality ... very little of it, and very old and choice. Machine haters. Science haters. Rule of thumbites to the bone. So are current socialists. They've filled the country with the idea that the automobile ought to be made entirely by the hands of traditional craftsmen, quite individually, out of beaten copper, wrought iron and seasoned oak. All this electric starter business and this electric lighting outfit I have here is perfectly hateful to the English mind ... It isn't that we are simply backward in these things, we are antagonistic. The British mind has never really tolerated electricity; at least not the sort of electricity that runs through wires. Too slippery and glib for it. Associates it with Italians and fluency generally, with Volta, Galvani, Marconi and so on ...[2]

What rankled with those who felt Britain was slipping behind was the fact that the nation which had pioneered industrialism was no longer in the vanguard. It was not, for example, that there were no motor-car makers in Britain: familiar brand names – Humber, Hillman and Rover – were already becoming established, while Henry Royce and Charles Rolls had joined forces to produce cars in 1904. But Mr Britling's automobile was an artefact that had its origins not in northern coal mines or blazing Midlands forges but in an international technology in which German ingenuity had been developed in France and then exported to America before reaching England.

Britain had led the world in the first half of the nineteenth century, but now, at least in the mind of Wells and the promoters of National Efficiency, the latest technology in the early 1900s was inherently foreign. The notion Wells had that the British thought of electricity as essentially 'Italian' was, of course, ludicrous. Volta and Galvani were certainly Italian. So was Marconi, although his mother was Anglo-Irish, he spoke perfect English and he developed his wireless telegraphy in England with an English company. There was also Sebastian Ziani de Ferranti, whose family could trace their ancestry back to the Doges of Venice but who was born in London, went to school in Hampstead and set up in business in Liverpool doing portrait photography with his father-in-law, the painter William Scott. Ferranti duly went on to establish himself as a maker of electrical installations but the only really Italian thing about him was his ancestry.

Nevertheless, the sense was there in the early 1900s that Britain was being invaded by industrial rivals, most notably the Americans, who were crossing the Atlantic on huge ocean liners, nearly all of them British-built, with the intention of buying up large slices of the mother country's industry. In 1901, for instance, the flamboyant James Buchanan Duke – known as 'Buck' Duke – of the American Tobacco Company, arrived in Liverpool, walked straight from the dock to Ogden's, the British tobacco firm, and bought it up. Outraged, British companies fought back with the slogan: 'Don't be gulled by Yankee bluff, Support John Bull with every puff!' A number of the smaller British firms amalgamated to form the Imperial Tobacco Company and came to an agreement with Duke on a division of world markets.

Another American invader was the lavishly moustachioed Charles Tyson Yerkes, whose business plan, so he casually remarked, was to 'buy up some old junk, fix it up a little and offload it on some other poor fellow'.[3] He had made money building the elevated railway in Chicago but had fallen foul of the law. At the time, American city transport was being revolutionized by the introduction of electric tramways which had first been developed in Germany by the Siemens Company. London's first electric underground, a short run from Stockwell to the Bank in the City, had started operating in 1890 and then an international consortium had raised the money for the Central Line, which was opened in 1900 and ran east–west through the centre of the capital. American financiers fought over the right to fund London's transport and the

Yerkes consortium won. The District Line, which had been steam-driven, was electrified and then the first sections of the famous Piccadilly, Bakerloo and Northern Lines were dug out and established, largely with American technology. Yankee terminology such as 'northbound' and 'southbound' were introduced to British railway companies that had always run 'up' and 'down' trains. American interests were involved, too, in replacing the horse trams with electric trams: the London County Council bought from the American George Westinghouse an entire system which had been exhibited in the Agricultural Hall, Islington, in 1900.

But the most audacious campaign of American technological and economic invasion was waged by Thomas Alva Edison, perhaps the first inventor to become an international star in the age of mass communications. In fact, Edison became such a legendary figure, and was such a favourite of the American newspapers, that his true contribution to modern industrialism is extremely difficult to fathom. Always ready with a quote, it was Edison who said that genius was '99 per cent perspiration and 1 per cent inspiration', which was not a bad way of describing his own dogged approach to technological discovery. The American newspapers liked to call him 'The Wizard of Menlo Park', a sobriquet coined by a reporter after a visit to Edison's rustic workshops in New Jersey. He was lionized too in Britain and in Europe, and he and his financial backers worked hard to create the impression that it was America where the real breakthroughs were being made.

Thomas Edison was born in Milan, Ohio, on 11 February 1847, the seventh and last child of Nancy and Sam Edison. Nancy had been a schoolteacher while Sam had made a living with a sawmill when the small town of Milan had enjoyed a brief economic boom producing grain which was then shipped on a canal cut down to the Huron River and out to Lake Erie, bound for New York. Both Sam and Nancy were Canadian and would no doubt have stayed north of the border had Sam not joined aan armed revolt in 1837 which made him a fugitive. His grandfather had fled New Jersey as a defeated royalist in the American War of Independence, finding a sanctuary in Nova Scotia and then in Upper Canada. In 1837, Sam himself became a hunted man and had to run for two days through the woods to escape the pursuing king's men.

So many unverifiable stories are told about the childhood of Edison – all of them fables of his precocious genius – that they are best discounted. It seems certain that he contracted scarlet fever at some time because he suffered impaired hearing from childhood. He did not have much in the way of formal schooling, though his mother must have provided him with some instruction. The first great trauma in his life was when, in 1853, the Lake Erie coastal railway was opened, bypassing Milan and destroying the sawmill business his father had established. Their modest prosperity lost, the Edisons had to start all over again, moving to Port Huron on Lake Michigan. Although it is impossible to be sure of anything in the legend of Edison's life, it seems likely that the family fell on hard times and that was the reason Thomas went to work at the age of twelve. The railroad had come to Port Huron and his father got him a job selling newspapers and snacks to the passengers on the three-hour run to Detroit.

As Edison later told the story, he spent a good deal of time between trains reading in the Detroit Public Library, perusing everything from a translation of Victor Hugo's *Les Miserables* to Isaac Newton's *Principia Mathematica*. He could not get on with science at all, at least not Newtonian physics. He is reported as saying: 'It gave me a distaste for mathematics from which I have never recovered.'[4] Those who worked with Edison certainly discovered that he was hopeless at maths and was not very good at drawing or draughtsmanship either. He was a great deal better at fashioning simple bits of machinery, but others who worked for him were much more skilled. What Edison *was* good at was thinking up things that needed to be invented and getting financiers to back him while he worked out how things were done or, more often, hired the person who was likely to discover the solution to a particular problem.

Of all the stories of the exploits of the young Edison on the railroad, there is one which is perhaps true and did really set him on the road to success. He saw the young son of the stationmaster at Mount Clemens was in danger of falling in front of a train and rescued him, and for this the stationmaster rewarded him with an intensive course of training as a telegraph operator. At that time, 1862, this was an excellent apprenticeship for an ambitious young boy, with the Morse system spreading across the country, and the demand for telegraphy heightened by the continuing conflict of the Civil War. Once he was proficient as a Morse operator, Edison became an itinerant telegraph boy, travelling widely for five years and ending up in the South in Louisville, Kentucky, in 1866. He planned to join a group of 'rebels' escaping to Brazil, but was warned off at the last minute. That might have been the end of him, for many of those who did go to South America died in a plague of yellow fever, a mosquito-borne disease that induced severe jaundice and had a high fatality rate.

As it was, Edison returned to Port Huron in the autumn of 1867 worn out and penniless. His family was falling apart as they had lost their home which had been requisitioned by the military and Sam Edison was earning very little money. Nancy, his mother, was close to a complete breakdown. After a short stay, Edison went east to Boston, where a friend told him there was a job with the Western Union. Here Edison continued his self-education as he returned to the drudgery of telegraph work. He read *Experimental Researches* by Michael Faraday, the English scientist who had risen to eminence from a humble background, and dreamed of emulating him.

Edison really had no idea in his early days what it was that he wanted to invent. He tinkered with telegraphy systems, always trying to figure out how to improve existing mechanisms: he experimented with ways of passing two signals simultaneously down a single telegraph wire, as well as with ticker-tape printers and a vote recorder for political chambers. But he got nowhere. In 1869, after a disastrous demonstration in Boston of an automatic vote-recording system which failed to work, Edison headed for New York. Telegraphers then formed a kind of fraternity, and he was taken in by Franklin L. Pope, who knew of him from Boston. Pope was experimenting with a company which produced up-to-the-minute information on gold prices. Edison camped in his office and his big breakthrough came at the height of frantic dealing in gold in 1869 when the indicator, a device that displayed prices on a board in the Gold Room of the New York Stock Exchange, broke down. There was panic and Dr Laws, the indicator's inventor, was desperate for his machinery to be repaired. Edison, noticing a few loose bits and pieces, came to the rescue. It was like a scene from a Hollywood movie: Edison was placed on the payroll, his friend Pope, who had had enough of the histrionics of Dr Laws, left and Edison took his job.

Very soon, while working on improvements to the gold indicator, Edison found himself in the midst of a huge financial scandal concerning an attempt to corner the market in gold. When it was all over, Laws sold out to Western Union, Edison's former employers, and decided to move on. Pope had gone freelance, looking for work as an electrical engineer, and Edison joined him. With their partner J. L. Ashley, the publisher of *The Telegrapher*, offering to provide free advertising space, Pope, Edison and Company promoted its services to anyone who might wish to buy them. It was a bold and original gesture. Pope lived in Elizabeth, New Jersey, and Edison was his lodger. They rented an old shop which became Edison's laboratory. Here he produced an improved 'gold printer' which he and Pope rented out to rivals of Western Union. Just as they had hoped, within six months they were bought out for what then seemed the small fortune of $15,000. Straight away, Edison was telegraphing home, offering his parents money.

Now established as an inventor, Edison began his lifelong habit of taking out patents, more often than not for some improvement to an existing piece of machinery. Western Union then employed their own 'inventors' and Edison was finally headhunted by them. He was asked to find a way to stop share-printing machines suddenly going haywire, and when he did so, the financiers at Western Union were mightily impressed. Edison had not named his fee when he began work for the company, and when he was asked what he wanted by General Lefferts, head of its Gold & Stock Telegraph Division, he said he would like to be made an offer. He was staggered by the amount, which he recalled later was $40,000. Records suggest it was $30,000. Either way, it was a sudden and quite unexpected fortune.

Western Union had obtained Edison's first patents, and when he set up in business to make stock ticker-machines, the company gave him a business associate, William Unger. Edison hired his own men, advertising for clockmakers and machinists 'with light fingers'. Among those to join him in his first enterprise established in Newark was a young Englishman, Charles Batchelor, who had learned his trade in textiles and had gone to America to install some machinery in a spinning mill. When Batchelor called on him, Edison was immediately impressed by his skill as a draughtsman and his handling of machinery. Batchelor was to stay with Edison for many years. Very quickly, the Edison works became cosmopolitan, drawing on a variety of skills which had been honed in European industry. There was John Kruesi, a Swiss clockmaker, and Sigmund Bergmann, a German mechanic who spoke no English when he arrived but whose workmanship, as Edison said, spoke for itself. Bergmann and another German, Sigmund Schuckert, returned home after working for Edison and went on to found a major electrical company in Berlin.

In 1871, Edison was only twenty-four, yet he was in charge of up to fifty workers. There was no returning now to his family. His mother had died on 9 April that year and Edison had attended her funeral in Michigan. His father, at sixty-seven, took up with a seventeen-year-old dairy maid whom he eventually married. The Edisons were long-lived: Thomas recalled visiting his grandfather when the old man was 102 and still chewing and spitting tobacco. They were certainly a tough family, noted for their stamina. Edison himself had a reputation for working day and night, not caring at all about his appearance – he was often said to be 'dressed like a tramp'. Yet he attracted the interest of financiers and businessmen keen to turn a profit from some new or improved piece of machinery, and he duly succeeded in obtaining funding from a group of businessmen who wanted him to improve on an automatic Morse sender and printer for which they had the patent rights. He worked on this for two years and was eventually bought out by the financier Jay Gould.

On Christmas Day 1871, Edison married Mary Sitwell, a Sunday school teacher. Such is the accretion of conflicting stories about Edison's life that there is no way of knowing how he met his wife: was it when he demonstrated telegraphy at her school, or while sheltering in a doorway from a sudden shower? One account says she worked for him in Newark. Up until his marriage, Edison had lived in lodgings. Now he bought a house, and within a year he had become a father, nicknaming his first child Dot and his second Dash. An established 'inventor' and master of the automatic telegraph, Edison was asked in 1873 to make his first trip abroad. His financial backers thought the English Post Office might be willing to buy Edison patents and he took the boat to Liverpool in April. After he had demonstrated his system between London and Liverpool, he was asked if it might work over much longer distances. A new telegraph line running for 2,200 miles was planned to link Britain with Brazil. The cable was stored in Greenwich and Edison attempted to send a Morse signal along the whole length of it. He failed: a single dot emerged as a smear twenty-seven feet long.

After his return from England with nothing to show for the six-week excursion, Edison was engaged in a number of schemes, all of which involved litigation of one kind or another between competing companies. His most significant work was in devising a form of quadruplex telegraph which could handle four signals at once in a single wire. But Edison was not making any money. In fact he was losing it, having spent his first small fortune on his Newark works. At a time when he was facing destitution, the financier Jay Gould reappeared with a cheque from the Atlantic and Pacific Telegraph Company for $30,000 to buy Edison out and get him away from the rival Western Union. Even though he now had the money to keep going, Edison soon became caught up in the endless legal wrangling between Gould and his great rival Vanderbilt at Western Union.

It was in 1876 that Edison made his escape from Newark, closed down his various businesses and asked his father to look out for a plot of land in New Jersey where he might build himself a research laboratory. The place old Sam Edison chose was Menlo Park and he stayed on to direct the building of the wood-shingle structure. Now Edison was a freelance technician and would take work from anyone. Soon he was being paid a retainer of $500 a month by, of all people, Western Union to work on a kind of primitive telephone that had been devised by Alexander Graham Bell and Elisha Gray. Edison was in his element and wrote to Frank Royce, a patent lawyer: 'Brand-new laboratory ... at Menlo Park, Western Div., Globe, Planet Earth, Middlesex Country, four miles from Rahway, the prettiest spot in New Jersey, on the Penna. Railway, on a High Hill. Will show you around, go strawberrying.'[5]

In reality, Edison and his team at Menlo Park had little time for fruit-picking. All of them recalled working long hours, often through the night, in their efforts to fulfil Edison's dream of inventing *something* that would make his fortune and fame. It has been said of him that he was 'the first great scientific inventor who clearly conceived of invention as subordinate to commerce'. In other words, there was no point in making something that nobody really wanted. This hardly distinguishes Edison from men such as James Watt, Matthew Boulton, John Wilkinson or Henry Bessemer. Historically, inventors have tended to be interested in making money, even if many of them have failed to do so. Edison himself nearly went under several times. And, by an odd twist of fate, the one invention that made him truly celebrated, not only in America but around the world, turned out to be a commercial dead duck.

While working on improvements to Bell's telephone system, Edison and his team chanced upon the discovery that they could record and play back the spoken word. Originally, Edison had conceived of a machine that would be rather like a modern answerphone, in that a spoken message would be recorded. There had been yet another huge legal battle over patent rights. Western Union claimed precedence for Edison's telephone transmitter while the Bell company replied with a counter-claim for patents acquired from Emile Berliner, a German emigré who was a self-taught engineer hired by the Bell Telephone Company. The battle was fought in England as well as the United States. In 1879, the young George Bernard Shaw was hired to demonstrate the wonders of the Edison phone, which at that time had a chalk disc receiver that was incredibly noisy. In the introduction to *The Irrational Knot*, a novel based on his experiences with Edison's team, Shaw wrote:

> These deluded and romantic men gave me a glimpse of the skilled proletariat of the United States; and their language was frightful even to an Irishman. They worked with a ferocious energy out of all proportion to the result achieved ... They utterly despised the artfully slow British workman who did as little for his wages as he possibly could ... They adored Mr Edison as the greatest man of all time in every possible department of science, art and philosophy, and execrated Mr Graham Bell, the inventor of a rival telephone,

as his Satanic adversary ... They were free-souled creatures, excellent company; with an air of making slow old England hum which never left them even when, as often happened, they were wrestling with difficulties of their own making; or struggling in no-thoroughfares from which they had to be retrieved like strayed sheep by Englishmen without the imagination to go wrong.[6]

It was while the great telephone contest was in full swing that Edison first realized that he could make a 'talking machine'. The first public announcement came in *Scientific American* in November 1877. Typically, Edison was predicting that he would have a workable machine within a year: he was forever telling the world he was just about to invent something. In fact, he had his so-called 'phonograph' working within a month. It was an incredibly simple piece of equipment in which sound activated a needle which formed indentations in a cylinder covered in tin foil and, when the cylinder was revolved mechanically and played back, there was the voice. Edison himself recorded, to the astonishment of Kruesi and his other mechanics, the nursery rhyme 'Mary had a little lamb'. In December 1877 Edison demonstrated his phonograph to the staff of *Scientific American* and models were sent to England where they were put on show by William Preece, Chief Engineer of the Post Office. The talking machine was considered to be the wonder of the age and his rustic research laboratory attracted pilgrims from all over America. The uses of the phonograph appeared to be boundless: it could take dictation and do away with stenographers; the blind could listen to books; it could be used to teach elocution; it could play music; it could be used to record dialect for historical records. In the long run, of course, that is indeed what happened. But Edison's prototype, once the wonder of it had palled, was just too crude. The venture capitalists moved in and an Edison Phonograph Company was set up. But the quality of sound the machine offered remained so poor that Edison himself lost interest, abandoning for ten years what he always said was his favourite invention.

The lionizing of Edison and his phonograph wore him down. In 1878 he was still just thirty-one and yet he had begun to look drawn and harassed. It was then that his extraordinary career took another unexpected turn. On 23 July 1878 there was an eclipse of the sun. George Barker, a professor at the University of Pennsylvania, was in a party travelling to the Rockies to make observations. He knew Edison had a device called a tasimeter for measuring small changes in temperature and thought he might want to try it out at the eclipse: the trip would give Edison both a chance to relax and to meet many eminent scientists. Edison duly went along and, while out in Wyoming, he and Barker discussed many applications of electricity, including its use for lighting, something to which Edison had not turned his mind. When they returned, Barker arranged for Edison to visit a firm called Wallace & Sons in Connecticut which had a brass and copper foundry and had made a powerful electrical generator or telemachon. They were experimenting with carbon-arc lighting systems and looking at the possibility of sending electrical currents over long distances.

When Edison made the trip to Wallace & Sons in September, a reporter from the *New York Sun* was allowed to tag along. His description of Edison's reaction to the demonstration of arc lighting is perhaps not as far-fetched as we might imagine:

> Edison was enraptured. He fairly gloated over it. Then power was applied to the telemachon, and eight electric lights were kept ablaze at one time, each being equal to 4000 candles, the subdivision of electric lights being a thing unknown to science. This filled up Mr. Edison's cup of joy. He ran from the instrument to the lights and from the lights back to the instrument. He sprawled over the table with the simplicity of a child, and made all kinds of calculations. He calculated the power of the instrument and of the lights, the probable loss of power in transmission, the amount of coal the instrument could save in a day, a week, a month a year, and the result of such saving on manufacturing.[7]

Edison had a vision of the world lit by his electrical lighting system. His model for a public supply of electricity for lighting was the existing gas network in which a central supply was fed to streets and individual houses. The brilliant carbon arc lamps would be too bright for homes and uneconomic: what was needed was some new version of the incandescent light bulb which had been made experimentally for more than thirty years. But the light bulb was only one, albeit crucial, element in a system that would require generators, switches, sockets and meters: in short, an electrical equivalent of the gas network. Edison was determined, though: he ordered one of Wallace's powerful telemachon generators and before long he had financial backing and was announcing to the world that he was on the verge of another great breakthrough.

By the time Edison came to work on it, electric lighting was not entirely novel in Europe. There had been several attempts to make an efficient light bulb to replace the existing arc lights. The most popular of these were Jablochkoff lamps. Paul Jablochkoff had started out as a telegraph engineer in his native Russia and had risen to become director of telegraphs between Moscow and Kursk. In 1875, when he was twenty-eight, Jablochkoff set off for America in the hope of visiting the Centennial Exhibition being staged in Philadelphia in 1876 to mark the hundredth anniversary of the outbreak of the War of Independence. He got no further than Paris, where he met the French engineer Louis Breguet, who invited him to use his laboratory. Here he devised a much improved version of the carbon arc lamp. Two carbon rods were set up vertically in parallel and electricity passing through them created a bright light which was enclosed in a glass sphere rather like that of an oil lamp. Known as Jablochkoff Candles, these lamps were marketed by a French company, La Société Générale Eléctrique, which had been founded as early as 1853 to exploit a machine that had been developed to obtain oxygen and hydrogen from water by electrolysis. An English Professor, F. H. Holmes, had adapted the generator to provide the power for arc lamps which were installed in two lighthouses in 1857 and 1858. Another French firm, the Compagnie de l'Alliance, also produced systems for lighthouses in both France and England.

The brilliant illumination provided by arc lamps was also suitable for large open public spaces. In Europe, France led the way: the Gare du Nord and the Grand Magasins du Louvre in Paris were lit by 1877 and Jablochkoff Candles began to appear all over the city. In July 1878, the English publication *The Electrician* was complaining that although Paris got brighter each night, not a single electric light had appeared in London. It was in the autumn of that year that the arc lamps finally made their debut in the British capital, lighting some commercial showrooms and part of the Thames Embankment. The Société Générale Eléctrique did a brisk business in London, lighting Billingsgate Fish Market in November 1878. There was no legislation in existence to authorize the laying of cables in public streets, but Holborn Viaduct, which lay on the borders of the City of London and Westminster, offered a suitable test site. The viaduct had been built in 1869 for horse traffic and carried a road rather than a railway line. This was lit towards the end of 1878, the cables being strung under the bridge, but the experiment was brought to an end in May 1879 because electric lighting proved to be so much more expensive than gas. England could, however, claim some firsts. In 1878, *The Electrician* carried this report:

> The intense interest aroused by the application of the electric light to novel uses was strikingly apparent on Monday night in Sheffield when nearly 30,000 people gathered at Bramall Lane ground to witness a football match played under that light. The match, which was played by two teams belonging to the Sheffield Football Association, commenced at half past seven o'clock. The electric light was thrown from four lamps, thirty feet from the ground, the players being seen as clearly as noonday. The brilliancy of the light, however, dazzled the players, and sometimes caused strange blunders ...[8]

In 1881, the town of Godalming in Surrey accepted a tender from a firm called Calder & Barrett to replace its gas lighting, the contract for which had expired, with electric light. The agreement was that the cost should be equivalent to that of gas, certainly no more. The River Wey was to provide the power by millwheel to turn a Siemens alternator which would generate the electricity. Rights to water power had to be negotiated with the local tannery, which accepted free lighting in payment. For its time, this scheme was very advanced, for in addition to the arc lights which would illuminate the main public areas of the town, there were about thirty incandescent lamps, the invention of Joseph Swan. A modest and retiring man, Swan was born in 1828 in Sunderland, County Durham, to parents of Scottish descent. His father had been comfortably off but his various business ventures failed and Joseph was apprenticed to a chemist at the age of fourteen. He continued to work as a chemist, moving to Newcastle-upon-Tyne and setting up in partnership with John Mawson. Swan was given the freedom to experiment in a laboratory the two men established above the shop and he became interested in photography, inventing a number of new processes. Largely self-taught, Swan read a great deal and came across accounts of the invention of incandescent lights. What was needed, however, was a material that would burn and glow when an electric current was sent through it, without giving off smoke and blackening the glass around it.

One of the products for which Swan and Mawson were well known was their patented collodion, a kind of cellulose-based glue that was applied to wounds to protect them as they healed. Experiments with this led Swan to use a celluloid filament for his light bulbs. It was possible to get a clear light only if oxygen was excluded from the glass bulb, yet once an efficient vacuum pump had been devised, it was relatively easy to manufacture these bulbs. Swan's bulbs were usable by 1879, although his partner John Mawson did not live to see this breakthrough: he died in an accident in 1867, being blown up as he was supervising the disposal of nitro-glycerine that had been dumped on the town's moor.

The use of Swan lamps in Godalming in 1881 was the first practical use of the modern light bulb. It attracted some international interest and the scheme was written up favourably in a German technical publication. But there were teething problems. It was found that one millwheel did not provide enough power for the generator. A second was harnessed to it but then, when the River Wey flooded, neither wheel worked efficiently. A steam traction engine had to be brought in to provide emergency power. The firm founded by William Siemens – by this time the Siemens brothers were established in Germany, Russia and Britain – took over the scheme but they could not make it pay. The anticipated demand from individual households for the new light failed to materialize, no doubt because the Swan lamps gave off a rather dull glow compared with that provided by gas. In 1884, the generator on the River Wey ceased to turn and Godalming went back to gas.

In 1881, when the Godalming experiment began, the first international exhibition devoted to electrical equipment and inventions was held in Paris. A little later than Swan, but working on the same principles, the frenetic experimenters of Menlo Park had produced not only their version of the incandescent lamp but something approaching an entire electrical system designed to fulfil Edison's dream of lighting up cities from a central generating station. The Paris Exhibition was the ideal stage on which Edison could outshine his European rivals. A team of keen young men, including Charles Batchelor, was sent across the Atlantic, along with Edison's own Jumbo generator adapted from the one he had received from Wallace. Simultaneously, a publicity team went into action, planting stories in the French newspapers about the brilliant display of electricity from America.

The judges were asked to compare four different versions of the incandescent bulb: those of Swan and Edison, that developed by another Englishman, St George Lane Fox-Pitt, and another by the colourful American, Hiram Maxim. There was little to choose between the bulbs themselves, but only the Edison camp understood the value of good public relations, allegedly even bribing influential journalists to give their invention a favourable write-up. Maxim had been well ahead of Edison in America, becoming in 1878 the chief engineer to the United States Electric Lighting Company after a career which had taken him from carriage-maker at the age of fourteen on to engineering works, gas lighting companies and then to the pioneer electric light firm in America. But he sold out to Edison in 1881 and moved to London, where he later designed a machine-gun which would be developed into the weapon that proved so murderous on the Western Front in the First World War. Despite a very murky private life – he appears to have been a bigamist with a penchant for young girls – Maxim was knighted in England in 1901, by which time he had made a fortune from the arms trade. He described himself as a 'chronic inventor', and while convalescing in Nice in the south of France in 1902, he even devised an inhaler to ease the discomfort of those with breathing difficulties.

Edison, meanwhile, pursued the electric light business doggedly. While his team was wooing the French, and the following year the English, he set up his own electricity station at Pearl Street in New York. In London, the Edison men obtained permission to have another crack at lighting Holborn Viaduct, this time with incandescent bulbs. It is often claimed that this was the first public lighting system in the world using incandescent bulbs, although Godalming has a stronger claim. The Holborn scheme went into operation from February 1882 and continued for four years until, once again, it proved to be uneconomic and was shut down. Any electricity operator in Britain from 1882 onwards had to contend with an ill-conceived Electric Lighting Act which discouraged private investment in any schemes. The Act was influenced by the policies of Joseph Chamberlain, then President of the Board of Trade in the government, who in local Birmingham politics had encouraged what was called 'gas and water socialism' – the taking over of 'natural monopolies' by public authorities. Among the pioneer electric lighting schemes in Britain were those run by local authorities in Brighton, Sussex and Newcastle-upon-Tyne. In London's Mayfair, a private scheme to light the Grosvenor Art Gallery soon had wires connected to private houses, but this was a very wealthy part of town. As it was, the Lighting Act effectively barred Edison from any progress. He failed, too, to make any progress in Paris, for an economic slump undermined confidence and there was little investment money available. What Edison's financiers did manage to do was to come to agreements with some of his rival patent-holders. In 1883, the Swan and Edison companies were amalgamated with a capital of £1 million, and it was not long before the Ediswan light bulb became a household name.

America proved to be more receptive than Britain to electricity not because – as H. G. Wells would have had it – the old country thought the new power to be too glib and Italian, but because the gas industry, the great rival to electricity, was less developed there. In coal-fired Britain, huge gas-holders were a feature of the urban landscape, whereas in America gas was produced on a smaller scale and was confined to larger towns, while many areas were still lit with oil lamps. The European country to develop electrical plants most enthusiastically at the end of the nineteenth century was Germany. It was here that the Edison system was adopted and adapted and the huge firm AEG was founded, and here, too, that the first electric trams were run.

There were many battles to be fought over electricity supply, one of the most bitter between Edison, who favoured 'direct current', and the American George Westinghouse, who advocated 'alternating current'. For long-distance transmission, Westinghouse was right but he and his supporters had to endure the spoiling tactics of Edison's men, who were determined to convince the public that AC was too dangerous. (Stray dogs and other animals were even captured and publicly electrocuted – by the Englishman Charles Batchelor, among others.) Yet Edison remained the quintessential American hero, not so much for his rags-to-riches story as for his legendary rise from ignorance to genius. He had more than one thousand patents to his name when he died in 1931 but, other than the phonograph, it remains uncertain which inventions he was personally responsible for. What is undeniable, however, is that Edison – and those like him – confirmed America's emergence as the world's industrial leader. And with economic power came international influence. In the early years of the twentieth century it was the United States which was called upon to broker a peace between two other industrial powers: Russia and Japan.

CHAPTER TWENTY

THE TERROR OF THE TORPEDO

On the night of 8 February 1904, Japanese torpedo boats launched a surprise attack on Russian warships in their base at Port Arthur, Manchuria. The Russo-Japanese War had begun and the world's major powers looked on uneasily. Even the British were anxious, despite the fact that they had signed a treaty of alliance with Japan in 1902. They had every right to be, as this conflict would establish Japan as a major naval power in the Pacific; and it would also have repercussions much closer to home.

In the afternoon of Sunday, 23 October 1904, two fishing trawlers limped back to Hull on the north-east coast of England, their flags flying at half-mast. Those who came to greet them were at first puzzled, then horrified. The boats, the *Mino* and the *Moulmein*, were riddled with shell holes. On board they carried the bodies of Henry Smith, the skipper of another of the Hull Gamecock fleet, the *Crane*, and his boatswain William Arthur Leggett. There were a further six men wounded. It was a wonder that there were no more casualties, for the Hull trawlermen had been attacked at night by a huge armada of Russian ships, whose nervous crews had opened fire as they passed through the fishing grounds of the Dogger Bank. Astonishingly, the Russians had thought they were being attacked by Japanese torpedo boats. It was true they were on their way to confront the now powerful Japanese navy in a last-ditch attempt to win the war that had finally broken out between Japan and Russia earlier in the year. But

Above: When the American expedition to Japan paid its second visit in 1854, it brought gifts from the industrial world, including a quarter-scale working model steam engine with carriages and a circular track. Some onlookers got astride the miniature carriages for an exciting ride.

Above: A portrait of the five samurai who risked their lives in 1863 by leaving Japan to discover the secrets of Western technology. Back row from left: Endo Kinsuke, Masaru Inoue, Hirobumi Ito. Front row from left: Karoru Inoue and Yozo Yanao.

Above: Justus Liebig (1803–1873), the German chemist who studied in Paris then trained British and American chemists in his laboratory at Giessen in Germany.

Above: Henry Bessemer (1813–1898), who became world-famous for his discovery of a cheap and rapid way of making steel. He was knighted in 1879.

Above: An engraving of Thomas Alva Edison (1847–1931), the American telegraph operator turned inventor, with his most celebrated creation, the phonograph.

Above: Pictured in 1875, Robert Whitehead (1823–1905) the Lancashire engineer who developed the first effective torpedoes while working for the Austrians in Fiume on the Adriatic.

Above left: This is generally regarded as the world's first motorcycle, built by Gottlieb Daimler and Wilhelm Maybach in 1885 in a back garden workshop in Cannstatt.

Above right: John Boyd Dunlop (1840–1921), a Scottish vet with a practice in Belfast, Northern Ireland, had never ridden a bicycle when, in 1887, he invented an inflatable rubber tyre.

Above: Before the invention of the petrol engine, nearly all the road traffic in the world's great cities was, like this London bus, horse-drawn, making a huge demand on farmland for feed and creating a mountain of manure.

Left: Vice-Admiral Petrovich Rozhestvensky, the ill-fated commander of the Russian Armada which in 1904 set out on a journey halfway round the world to confront the Japanese Navy in the Yellow Sea. He was badly wounded in the Battle of Tsushima in 1905 and his fleet was annihilated.

Above: The war between Russia and Japan was brought to an end with the signing of the Treaty of Portsmouth in New Hampshire on 5 September 1905, the peace brokered by President Theodore Roosevelt, pictured in the centre of this postcard. Flanking Roosevelt are the Tsar and the Mikado with negotiators below them.

Above: Huge quantities of khaki dye were needed for the uniforms of British soldiers such as these recruits training in August 1914. There was just one problem: the main supplier had been Germany, which dominated the world chemical industry. British suppliers were quickly signed up.

they were months away from hostile waters, and to mistake a crew of Yorkshire fishermen for Japanese sailors was tantamount to madness.

The Russian fleet, which comprised a total of forty-eight vessels, including battleships, destroyers, cruisers, supply ships, torpedo boats and a motley collection of superannuated craft, steamed on into the English Channel without stopping, when day came, to inspect the damage they had caused or to offer assistance to the stricken trawlermen. British naval officers arrived in Hull by train and what they learnt was soon reported in *The Times* and other newspapers under headlines such as 'Dogger Bank Outrage'. Alongside the fleet of trawlers was a mission ship, the *Joseph and Sarah Mile,* which had picked up one of the survivors of the *Crane* and it was this man who gave the first and most vivid account of that terrible night:

> We had just hauled and shot [the nets] away again and were in the fish pound cleaning the fish and passing jokes about the war vessels, which we could see quite plain, and heard their firing, when suddenly something hit us. The third hand said, 'Skipper, our fish-boxes are on fire; I'm going below out of this,' and walked forward, the skipper, who was on the bridge, laughing at him for being frightened. We were hit again forward, and someone called out and said, 'The bosun is shot.' I went forward to look, and found the boatswain bleeding and a hole through our bulwarks, and the fore companionway knocked away. I went to tell the skipper. Before I got aft, a shot went through the engine-casing, and I began to feel frightened. I could see that the skipper was not on the bridge. I went aft, passed the chief, who was bleeding, gave him my neckcloth to stop the blood, went right aft and saw the skipper lying on the grating. I said, 'Oh, my God, he is shot!' I picked him up and saw that his head was battered to pieces. I dropped him, rushed down the forecastle, and saw the boatswain lying on the floor, with his head battered in.
>
> Another shot came and hit us, I didn't know where. All hands were shouting out they were shot. I jumped on the bridge to blow

the whistle, but that and the steampipe were knocked away. I tried to alter the wheel, but the wheel-gear was smashed. I then found we were sinking. I went to the boat, cut the grips, plugged her up, and put the painter on the winch to heave her aft, but found some of the winch smashed. Then something hit me on the back. I saw the GULL launch her boat. I dragged the skipper forward and got the third hand up on the deck and went for the chief. He was unconscious. By this time the GULL's boat came alongside and we put in the skipper and bosun, and got in ourselves – how, I don't know.

When the boy came to me and said, 'Where is my father?' that was a pill I could not swallow. For the life of me I could not tell the boy what had happened to his father.

The searchlights made everything like day. The fireman, while he was in the engine-room, saw the warship that was firing on us – saw her through the hole they made in the ship's side. They made a target of us. They meant doing for us. They needed no lights to see what we were. The searchlights told them plain enough.[1]

While British naval vessels shadowed the Russian force as it headed down through the English Channel, urgent diplomatic negotiations were begun. The Russian commander, Admiral Zinovi Petrovich Rozhdestvenski, insisted that torpedo boats had been sighted and that one had been sunk. None the less he had realized that his crews, most of whom he despised, were firing on fishermen who were desperately holding up their catch to indicate that they were neither combatants nor, for that matter, Japanese. As *The Times* had thundered:

For twenty minutes, we are told, the Russians poured shrapnel on the helpless fishing boats. They then steamed off without waiting to ascertain what was the character or nationality of the craft on which they had directed, without warning, this deadly fire, and without making the slightest effort to rescue the crews of the boats they had sunk ... It is almost inconceivable that any men calling themselves seamen, however frightened they might be, could spend twenty minutes bombarding a fleet of fishing boats without discovering the nature of their target ... The only surmise we can make with our present knowledge of the facts is that the Russians were themselves the victims of a disgraceful panic. The telegram from our Copenhagen Correspondent shows that they were in a state of extraordinary nervousness as they passed through the Danish waters. All sorts of cock-and-bull stories about the preparations made by Japanese spies for blowing the Baltic fleet sky-high ...[2]

For a few tense days, war between Britain and Russia seemed a possibility. The Russian Baltic Fleet had been directed to the Far East by the Tsar, Nicholas II, to confront and defeat the Japanese, who were now challenging Russia for control of the disputed territories of Manchuria and Korea. The industrialization of Japan, encouraged by Britain and assisted by the other leading European nations, had created an entirely new force in the Pacific. Young samurai who had witnessed the reduction of the Satsuma clan's defences at Kagoshima in August 1863 were now military leaders: indeed, the commander of the Japanese fleet was Admiral Heihachiro Togo, who had been born into the clan in 1847. Although a mere sixteen years old when the British had bombarded Kagoshima, Togo had been present, wearing his samurai regalia as he rolled stone shot towards the antique gun he was serving in one of the forts, and he must never have forgotten the humiliation of trying to fight modern warships with such obsolete weaponry.

Togo's subsequent experience was proof of the extraordinarily close ties between Japan and Britain during the last decades of the nineteenth century. From the time of the Choshu Five, the Japanese had been learning as much as they could about Western industry and military technology, and after the Emperor had been restored, this no longer needed to be done in secret. In 1871, after Togo had seen action in the civil war which led to the overthrow of the Bafuku, he travelled to Britain to learn seamanship and to train as a

British naval officer. Along with a group of fellow samurai, he first spent a few days in London, the scale of which astonished him. Then members of the group were sent to boarding-houses in different ports, Togo rooming in Plymouth. Adapting to English food and customs was not easy: Togo developed a fierce appetite, dunking chunks of bread into his tea to satisfy it. British cadets, not too sure of their geography, dubbed him and other Japanese trainees 'Johnny Chinaman'. Togo first trained on HMS *Worcester* and later sailed the world in HMS *Hampshire*, visiting Australia. On his return to London, Togo suffered a serious problem with his eyes, which was treated successfully by Harley Street doctors. Later, he attended the Royal Naval College at Greenwich and visited a shipyard on the Thames where warships were being built for the Imperial Japanese Navy. Following his return to Japan in 1878, Togo was able to observe naval battles between the French and Chinese over disputed territory in Formosa before he saw further action, this time during the Sino-Japanese War of 1894–5.

After their defeat of the Chinese, the Japanese had been persuaded by Britain and France to relinquish a Chinese fishing port known locally as Lushun but in Europe as Port Arthur, after a British naval officer who had refitted there in 1860 during the second of the Opium Wars. The idea was that Port Arthur should remain neutral, but the Russians effectively annexed it, regarding it as a special prize because it remained open all the year while their Pacific naval base at Vladivostock was frozen in for the winter months. There was a dispute, too, over territory in Manchuria, where the final sections of a branch of the Great Siberian Railway had been built. The construction of the section into Vladivostock was also seen by the Japanese as a provocation. When diplomatic negotiations over Port Arthur appeared to be achieving nothing, the Japanese decided to strike and send in their torpedo boats.

The Russians dispatched their most celebrated naval commander, the much-decorated Stepan Makarov, to command the First Pacific Squadron based at Port Arthur. Makarov had seen action in the naval engagements in which Russia defeated Turkey in 1877–8 and had latterly become an expert on torpedoes and mines. Ironically, his flagship, the battleship *Petropavlovsk*, was sunk by a mine on 12 April 1904 and the admiral went down with her, some say after his head had been sliced off by a piece of flying metal. A month later, the Japanese themselves lost two battleships to mines, but by the end of June the harbour at Port Arthur had come within range of their guns. On 10 August, the new Russian naval commander, Admiral Wilgelm Vitgeft, attempted to break out but his squadron was pursued and then intercepted by Togo: Vitgeft was killed during the ensuing battle of the Yellow Sea when two shells hit the bridge of his flagship, the *Tsesarevich*. The Russians were once again compelled to return to Port Arthur, and it would not be until October that Rozhdestvenski's Baltic Fleet would leave on its marathon 18,000-mile voyage to reinforce Russia's naval forces in the Pacific.

Part of the Russian Pacific Squadron was in Vladivostock, yet it was not in any position to challenge the Japanese fleet. In theory, the Russians were superior, a vast and potentially powerful nation with the third largest fleet in the world. However, while Togo's officers had been trained in Britain, the United States and France and understood the very latest in naval technology and theory, Russia's naval high command remained largely inexperienced and corrupt. In 1904, Russia had a hundred admirals, compared with sixty-nine in Britain, which had by far and away the biggest and most powerful navy, fifty-three in France and nine in Germany. Appointments in the Russian navy were based as much on social prestige as ability.

The Russians had at least built most of their battleships in their own shipyards, even if they had done so to often eccentric French specifications. In contrast, most of the Japanese fleet had been bought in: the naval yards at Kure and Yokosuka would not start building capital ships until 1905 and 1906 respectively. Togo's flagship, the *Mikasa*, was herself only the latest of a series of pre-dreadnought battleships ordered from shipyards in Britain. In all, Japan had six British-made battleships, while of its eight armoured cruisers, four were British, two Italian, one German and one French. Of its twenty-four destroyers, sixteen were British-made and eight were Japanese. And Togo had in his fleet no fewer than sixty-three torpedo boats, twenty-six of them German, ten British, seventeen French and ten Japanese. This was the sizeable and capable force that awaited the Russian armada which had made such a disastrous start to its epic voyage, very nearly precipitating a war with Britain.

Rozhdestvenski stood little chance of success, even if his ships did manage to complete their epic voyage along coasts, through seas and across oceans of which their officers and crews had no experience or knowledge whatsoever.

There were other, almost insuperable problems facing the Russian admiral. Russia had not taken part in the imperial scramble for Africa in the last two decades of the nineteenth century, and so his fleet would find no friendly ports of call as it steamed all the way down the West African coast, around the Cape of Good Hope and then up to Madagascar, before crossing the Indian Ocean to Singapore and proceeding on to the waters of the Yellow Sea. There was a quicker route through the Suez canal, but this was controlled by the British, and as they were nominally allies of the Japanese, Rozhdestvenski did not want to risk being trapped there.

More importantly, there was the question of coal. The steam-powered Russian warships consumed vast quantities of it, some 3,000 tons a day when the fleet was cruising and anything up to 10,000 tons when it was moving at speed. And where were they going to get it? The very best steamer coal was mined in South Wales and Britain had supplied the Japanese with large stocks of it. But they would give the Russians none, and besides, the Japanese had warned that they would sink any boats supplying the Russians with coal. As for the French, they were reluctant to become involved and did not want the Russian fleet stopping off at their African colonial outposts. Neither did any other neutral country. A few freelance traders might have perhaps turned a profit supplying the Russians, but it was only an offer of assistance from Kaiser Wilhelm II of Germany, Tsar Nicholas's bellicose and eccentric cousin, that would enable them to set sail: sixty colliers of the Hamburg-Amerika line would rendezvous with the Russian fleet in neutral ports or transfer coal to it at sea. Of course, the Japanese might appear on the horizon at any time or, even worse, from under the sea with their torpedoes or submarines.

Rozhdestvenski duly managed to re-coal at the Spanish port of Vigo, where the British demanded an explanation for the attack on the Hull fishermen. There was still a real danger of war between Britain and Russia and urgent diplomatic negotiations continued as Rozhdestvenski headed off south towards Tangier. Eventually the Russians apologized and paid reparations, but the young Tsar remained indignant about British demands. At Tangier, the fleet was divided. The older, slower ships, which would have had difficulty making it around the Cape, would after all take the Suez canal route with instructions to rendezvous at an island off Madagascar, which was a French colony. As the squadrons prepared to go their separate ways, the anchor of one of the ships caught on and then hauled up the telegraph cable that had been laid to link Africa and Europe. Exasperated, the Russian commander ordered that it be cut: fortunately for him perhaps, the cable was not British but French.

In the weeks that followed, Rozhdestvenski's ships made their way down the west coast of Africa. The Russians explored inland now and again and over time they acquired a menagerie of exotic animals including a boa constrictor which apparently developed a taste for vodka. At Dakar in Senegal, the French made a feeble effort to shoo them away, but Rozhdestvenski felt he had to load as much coal here as possible from the German colliers. Even as the French shore batteries threatened to open fire, Russian officers and men went to work in temperatures of 120°F and 100 per cent humidity. When the bunkers were full, still more coal was stacked on decks and even in officers' cabins. It was all too much for some, and among those who died was Ivan Nelidov, the son of the Russian ambassador to Paris, whose mother had contributed towards the funding of the hospital ship to which he was taken. A French steamer would carry his body back to Russia.

The progress of the Russian squadrons was closely monitored by both the British and Japanese. Indeed, on more than one occasion, the alarm bugles blew when someone imagined they had spotted a Japanese torpedo boat. In some of Rozhdestvenski's ships, the seamen began to plot a mutiny and revolutionary tracts were circulated. Inevitably, romances blossomed with the nurses on the hospital ship *Orel*: the matron, Natalia Sivers, was the apple of Rozhdestvenski's eye, even though he had a wife and daughter back in Russia as well as a lover in the form of the now widowed wife of Admiral Makarov, who had been blown up by a mine off Port Arthur.

The Russians survived fierce storms as they sailed around the Cape and then struggled on to Madagascar, where they were to rendezvous with the ships that had passed through the Suez Canal. Then a telegraph arrived instructing Rozhdestvenski to wait for a further squadron of largely obsolete vessels from the Baltic. He ignored it, however, electing to let these ships catch up with him later. Eventually, by May 1905 the Russians had steamed up past Singapore and were finally approaching the seas around Japan. Theirs had been a remarkable achievement, but while the Japanese had had ample time to prepare themselves for a battle that would take place in their own home waters, the Russians were now far from home and exhausted after thousands of miles at sea, and their ships, decks and cabins black with coal dust, were badly in need of refit and repair. Rozhdestvenski himself was something of a gunnery specialist, but he was not optimistic about his men's abilities in this regard. All in all, the omens were not good: the death on 25 May of one of Rozhdestvenski's senior commanders, von Felkerzam, had to be kept secret for fear it would have an adverse effect on morale. And now more than ever, the Russian fleet was gripped with anxiety about the possibility of a torpedo attack.

Of all the innovations in naval weaponry since the last great sea battle at Trafalgar a century before, the torpedo was the most feared. The earliest torpedoes, like those demonstrated by the American Robert Fulton just before Trafalgar, had been pushed and steered along the surface. Subsequently, a great variety of designs were experimented with in the American Civil War, but none was self-propelled and all were more or less visible as they headed for their target. However, in the 1880s a quite new and revolutionary torpedo, the forerunner of the modern weapon, was devised by Robert Whitehead, an Englishman who could have had no idea that his ingenious device would, quite literally, terrorize the world's most powerful navies or lead, indirectly, to the unwarranted attack on the Hull fishing fleet. Furthermore, the almost parallel invention of the submarine, evolved from models devised by a British ordained minister, George William Littler Garrett, would lead by 1914 to the deployment of that most deadly tormentor of surface shipping, the German *Unterseeboot* or U-boat.

In 1897, the First Naval Lord, Sir Frederick Richards, was to say of Whitehead: 'No man ever did his country a worse service ... the millions which his invention has taxed this country up to the present would have built a large fleet.'[3] In his lifetime, however, Whitehead was fairly festooned with awards in recognition for his invention, yet he received no accolades in his native Britain for he had, in effect, produced a weapon which threatened the very naval supremacy of his own country. Whitehead's story is perhaps one of the most extraordinary in the history of invention and it is also a telling illustration of how rapid the spread of industrialism had become by the last decades of the nineteenth century.

Whitehead's father had a bleaching and textile finishing works at Bolton-le-Moors in Lancashire where Robert was born on 3 January 1823. His mother, Ellen, was from the Swift family, which had a considerable business making steam engines, hydraulic presses, gas light apparatus and mill machinery. Ellen's brother, William Swift, was an engineer and Whitehead's 'favourite uncle'. Whitehead went to Bolton grammar school until the age of fourteen and then attended a private school where he was taught Latin, Greek, history, geography, drawing, arithmetic and book-keeping. After two years in this institution, he was apprenticed to Richard Ormerod & Son, an engineering workshop in Manchester where his uncle William was manager. Very soon Whitehead was acquiring both practical experience and scientific training. By day he would be bolting girders in the roof of the new London Road railway station in Manchester and in the evening taking two-hour classes at the Mechanics' Institute where, for a fee, he studied mechanical drawing and pattern designing and some theoretical aspects of engineering. Meanwhile, his father had moved into the brewing business, for which Ormerod & Son built a variety of steam engines. By the time he was in his early twenties, Whitehead was an experienced and skilled draughtsman who could design a whole variety of engines and other equipment. In March 1846 he married Frances Maria Johnson, whose family were also in the dyeing business. It was around this time that Whitehead was enticed abroad, and it was his uncle, William Swift, who led the way.

In the mid-nineteenth century, the knowledge and expertise of British engineers was still highly valued and sought after on the Continent. The father and son team of Aaron and Charles Manby had, for example, built the world's first all-iron steamship, which they demonstrated on the Thames in London in 1822 and sailed across the Channel to Rouen on the Seine and then up to Paris. Both father and son were involved in engineering enterprises in Paris and at Le Creusot, where they helped revive the ironworks that had been established with the Wilkinsons' expertise in the eighteenth century but had fallen into disuse. Another Englishman who eventually found his fortune in France was Philip Taylor, whose father made a living writing hymns and whose mother was an essayist. Born in 1786, Taylor was brought up in Norwich, Norfolk, and was first apprenticed to a surgeon. Taylor found the brutality of the profession at that time unbearable and went into business with one of his brothers who was a chemist. He made a machine for cutting the parts for pillboxes and began an amazing career of invention. At one time he patented a method of making gas for lighting from oil, an innovation which was used for a time at Covent Garden Opera House and the Imperial Library in St Petersburg.

A friend of Marc Isambard Brunel, Taylor was a director of the Thames Tunnel Company and was one of those who helped bail Brunel out in 1821 when the great inventor went bankrupt and found himself in the debtor's prison. Shortly after that, Taylor had opened an ironworks in South Wales and also had a chemical works, but both failed and he ended up in Paris, where he tried to sell the French king, Louis Philippe, a scheme for bringing water to the city by gravity in a long pipe running from the Marne. When that scheme failed, he founded an engineering firm in Paris and then, when his wife became ill, he moved south to Marseilles. Here he first had a flour-milling business and then, along with two of his sons, an engineering works. Finally, in 1845, he bought a ship-building yard near Toulon at a place called La Seyne. This was soon employing some two thousand men and Taylor, by then a distinguished figure known affectionately by his workforce as 'Papa', went back to England to look for men who might manage the yard. At Ormerod & Son he found William Swift, who was attracted by a generous salary. William wrote enthusiastically to his nephew Robert about the working conditions in France, and Whitehead joined him some time in 1846.

Whitehead did not stay long with Taylor's firm, however, and at some point in 1847 he moved to Milan, where cotton-spinning had become established alongside the traditional silk-spinning industry. Here he set up as a consulting engineer and designed machines for the weaving industry and patented a device for winding silk from a cocoon. He had not been long in Milan when the social upheavals of 1848 erupted across much of Europe. The Milanese themselves rebelled against Austrian rule and there was fighting in the streets. This was a difficult time for Whitehead and his young wife, for their first child died in infancy and they were marooned in a town whose future appeared uncertain. But the Austrians, although repelled for a time, returned and proposed improvements for northern Italy. The grandest scheme was for draining the Lombardy marshes and Whitehead was given the job of designing the pumping engines.

From Milan, the Whiteheads might have returned to England, but they were encouraged by Robert's elder brother to seek work on the Adriatic coast with the ship-building firms being established there. Robert began work with Austria-Lloyd in Trieste then moved on to the leading marine engineers in the Adriatic, a firm called Stabilimento Strudhoff. At the age of twenty-six, he was appointed technical director and began to design and supervise the building of marine steam engines, mostly for the Austrian navy. After a few years, Whitehead had made his name and in 1856 he was head-hunted by a group of financiers who had set up a new firm, Stabilimento Tecnico Fiumano, down the coast from Trieste at Fiume (now Rijeka in Croatia and still a major ship-building centre). Here he had great freedom to work on engine designs and organize his own research.

The conflict between Austria, which was attempting to keep control of Venice and the northern regions of what is now Italy, and the Italians, who were intent on unification, led to an arms race in which Whitehead became involved. He worked for the Austrians and in 1865 his Fiume shipyard produced the frigate *Erzherzog Ferdinand Max* for their navy. With her armour plate and screw propellers, this ship represented the very latest in naval technology: the French had only launched the first true ironclad, the *Gloire*, in 1858, and the British their response, the *Warrior*, in 1860. Indeed, the first major engagement between ironclads took place in 1866 when the Austrian and Italian navies met at Lissa in the Adriatic. At the time, ramming was the favoured method of attack and Whitehead had provided much of the Austrian ships' equipment, including their all-important steam engines, which performed exceptionally well, and he was congratulated after the Austrian victory. It was to prove a short-lived triumph, however, for Austria was soon defeated in a brief war with Prussia and was forced to cede Venice to Italy.

It was in such an atmosphere of conflict and technological innovation that Whitehead first came across a retired Austrian naval officer called Giovanni de Luppis. He did so in 1864, some years after de Luppis had begun experimenting, in an amateurish way, with a small boat that could be packed with explosives and aimed at enemy ships – a device which was in essence not unlike the torpedo Robert Fulton had demonstrated in 1805. De Luppis had got the idea from another Austrian officer and tried to improve on it: he thought it might be especially useful for breaking a blockade. He called his invention *Der Kustenbrander* or coastal fireship. A clockwork motor turned a screw propeller at the rear end of the torpedo and steering was by means of ropes attached to it and manipulated by a man on the shore. If it succeeded in hitting the target, *Der Kustenbrander's* explosives would be detonated with a percussion cap.

When Whitehead was asked to take a look at the device, he realized that it would take only a few well-aimed shots from the deck of a ship to blow up something which did, after all, run on the surface and at a rather low speed. De Luppis was disappointed: the English engineer thought there was no future in it. But the idea that such a weapon might be made effective stuck in Whitehead's mind and he began to work on the problem, setting up a little workshop in a hut within the grounds of the factory in Fiume. His twelve-year-old son John worked in secret with him. At the time he began working on his own torpedo, Whitehead was already a popular figure in Austria and a favourite of the Emperor Franz Josef and so he was able to obtain funding. In shape, his first model was rather like a dolphin, 11' 7" long from tip to tail and with a narrow body which at its bulkiest point had a diameter of just fourteen inches. It was made from wrought-iron boiler plates and on the rear end there were fins and a propeller. The inner workings were not, of course, visible and Whitehead, like a number of inventors before him, chose not to take out a patent as this would reveal too much of the device's specifications and enable others to replicate them. As it was, the torpedo was propelled by a canister of compressed air which was released steadily through a valve, but it was not this that Whitehead regarded as 'The Secret' but a balance chamber which held the torpedo at a steady depth under water. It was therefore an invisible weapon – a mine with a motor.

The first trials took place in 1866 and Whitehead steadily improved the speed and accuracy of the torpedo, winning many orders. The keenest buyers were generally the smaller nations, who saw in the Whitehead 'fish' torpedo, as it became known, a weapon which might defeat a much better-equipped enemy. Whitehead himself proved to be a shrewd businessman and a good salesman, travelling widely in the 1870s and demonstrating his invention in Scandinavia and other European countries. The Royal Navy watched developments closely, asked for demonstrations and in 1872 became one of the many countries to pay Whitehead a handsome sum for the right to produce the torpedo, which was duly developed and improved at the Royal Arsenal in Woolwich.

Inevitably, there were rival designs but the constant improvements made by both Whitehead and those working on his torpedo under licence kept it ahead of the competition. In 1872 Whitehead bought out the Fiume factory in partnership with his son-in-law, Count George Hoyos, who had excellent connections, and they built themselves villas adjoining Stabilimento Tecnico Fiumano. John Whitehead, Robert's eldest son, later became the manager. Though his headquarters remained in Fiume, in 1885 Whitehead purchased a large country estate called Paddockhurst, in Worth, Berkshire, and in 1891 an English branch of his torpedo works was established near Weymouth in Dorset.

Throughout his life, Whitehead insisted he was a peace-loving man and liked to believe that the torpedo might be a deterrent to war. On his death in November 1905 at the age of eighty-two, *The Times* assessed the impact of the torpedo, echoing the judgement of Sir Frederick Richards:

There is no department of naval construction, armament, tactics or warfare on the sea in general and the preparation for it which has not been profoundly affected by the advent of the locomotive torpedo. In construction, it has successively developed the torpedo-boat, the catcher, the destroyer and the submarine. In armament, it has stimulated the production of the quick-firing gun with all its developments. On the defensive side, it has evolved the net-defence, the use of the searchlight in war, and the subdivision of a modern warship into a multitude of water-tight compartments. In tactics, the torpedo has compelled modern actions at sea to be opened at ranges at which the torpedo is powerless, thus giving an impulse to the appliances for securing the rapidity and accuracy of fire of the heaviest guns at very long ranges. In strategy, it has modified the methods of naval blockade and thrown grave doubts on its efficacy as against an enterprising and determined enemy. In general preparation for war, it has led to the maintenance of boom defences and the construction of immense and costly works for the defence of naval anchorages, such as the breakwaters at Portland and Gibraltar, and the harbour of refuge at Dover. These are all developments actually palpable and in operation at the present moment. But they are certainly not yet the end. Even if the torpedo is approaching its maturity with a range of 4,000 yards and 36 knots, the submarine is probably still in its infancy. There are those who hold that the submarine will before long be capable of reciprocally denying narrow waterways to both of two belligerents, and should that anticipation be fulfilled, the importance of some existing naval bases may be diminished. All this we owe to the invention of the locomotive torpedo.[4]

After Whitehead's death, and that of other engineers involved with the Fiume factory, it was put up for sale. The British Admiralty was quick to encourage two major English companies, Vickers and Armstrong, Whitworth to buy it up, which they did in 1906, paying £400,000 for 184 shares each, leaving 367 shares with Whitehead's beneficiaries. At the time, the Royal Navy was opposed to the development of submarines, but Vickers, in partnership with a New York company, began building them at Fiume. It was here, in 1908, that a young officer from the Austro-Hungarian Navy, Georg Ritter von Trapp, was sent to study submarine design. The launch of one of the early U-boats was performed by Agathe, the daughter of John Whitehead, Robert's son. She met and fell in love with Georg. He commanded a torpedo boat and then the submarine *U-5*.

Defeat in the First World War left Georg without a commission. Then, in 1922, Agathe died of diphtheria at the age of thirty-two, leaving five young children to be cared for. Georg found them a governess called Maria Augusta Kutschera, a nun who had once nursed the children when they were ill. Maria Augusta taught the children to sing and won the heart of Georg, who proposed marriage. Renouncing her vows as a nun, Maria became the matriarchal head of a large family, with her five stepchildren and three of her own after her marriage. When von Trapp lost the family fortune in the financial crash of 1932, Maria had the children literally sing for their supper. Under the name of the von Trapp family singers, they toured Austria until they fell foul of the Nazis when Hitler annexed their country in 1938. They fled to America, where they established a farm in Vermont and where Maria finally wrote their story, one which in time became the spectacularly successful musical and film, *The Sound of Music*. Five of the famous family singers were the great-grandchildren of the man who invented the torpedo.

Back in May 1905, however, the torpedo had still not proved its value and there was naturally much speculation as to what part it might play in any large-scale engagement between the Japanese and Russian fleets. With sixty-three vessels carrying torpedoes, the Japanese were certainly optimistic about the weapon. There was one other innovation, too, which Togo made use of and Rozhdestvenski spurned: wireless telegraphy. This novelty had been made a commercial success by the young Anglo-Italian Guglielmo Marconi, whose company was now equipping Atlantic liners with Morse transmitters and receivers, effectively ending the isolation of ships at sea. Shore stations could talk to vessels several hundred miles away, and ships could pass messages to and from each other. It is not clear how or when the Japanese acquired a Marconi system – it is possible it was pirated after a demonstration Marconi had given at the Italian naval base at La Spezia – yet the Japanese ships were able to send wireless messages over several miles. The Russians were fitted with a different, less reliable, wireless system and Rozhdestvenski decided not to use it at all.

In the early hours of 27 May 1905, the Japanese patrol ship *Shinano Maru* sighted the Russian fleet as it steamed up through the Straits of Tsushima towards Vladivostock, its only possible destination now that Port Arthur had fallen into Japanese hands. Togo ordered a flag signal to be hoisted in the *Mikasa*. Echoing Nelson's before Trafalgar, it read, 'The fate of the Empire rests upon this one battle; let every man do his utmost.' For his part, Rozhdestvenski kept straight ahead, refusing to use his wireless to jam the Japanese transmissions or to communicate with his own ships.

In the first, and decisive, hour of the battle, Rozhdestvenski's flagship, the battleship *Kniav Suvarov*, was hit repeatedly and he suffered a series of injuries which left him half-delirious. The Russian crews fought bravely but soon the armada was in disarray. The battle continued on into the night, with the Japanese torpedo boats moving in packs, like hunting dogs, and firing at almost point-blank range even as the Russian searchlights played on them. One or two were sunk by Russian fire, but it was clear by the morning of 28 May that the Russian fleet had been annihilated in what has been called the most decisive naval defeat in history. Only three Russian ships limped through to Vladivostock. Others fled back to Manila. Some battleships sank with all hands. The grim statistics, when they were finally revealed, were scarcely believable. The Japanese sank twenty-one ships, captured seven and disarmed six. Rozhdestvenski's fleet suffered casualties of 4,380 dead and 5,917 injured. Togo lost three torpedo boats, with 117 dead and 583 injured. The Russian admiral was taken to Japan, where the injured were cared for in a Buddhist monastery: Togo visited him and expressed his sympathy. However, the crushing defeat of the Russian fleet did not end the war with Japan. Fighting continued on land in Manchuria and, though it was clear that in the end Japan would triumph, Russia was reluctant to concede.

It was the intervention of the American president, Theodore Roosevelt, in June 1905 which brought the two warring sides to the negotiating table, a diplomatic triumph which would win him the Nobel Peace Prize in 1906. Though the Japanese navy had suffered very few casualties at Tsushima, in the war on land and other sea battles Japan's total losses were greater than her opponent's – 47,387 killed and 173,425 wounded, compared with Russia's 25,331 killed and 146,032 wounded. The peace treaty between the two countries was finally signed at Portsmouth, New Hampshire, on 5 September 1905 and, as *The Times* reported during the negotiations, 'Japan has vindicated her full right to be treated as equal of the other Great Powers, not merely in the arts of war and of diplomacy, but in civilisation.'[5]

Following his release by the Japanese, Rozhdestvenski returned to St Petersburg on the Trans-Siberian railway to be hailed as a hero by the Russian peasantry and to face a trial along with his surviving fellow officers. Although he insisted to the courts that the humiliating defeat at Tsushima was his responsibility alone, his admission of guilt was not accepted and he was acquitted while other officers involved in the battle were convicted and condemned to death, their sentences later commuted to ten years in jail. The war had not been popular in Russia and in 1905 there were serious riots and mounted Cossack troops had to be brought in to deal with demonstrations – a portent of the Revolution of 1917. As for Togo, the victor of Tsushima was fortunate not to have been on board his flagship in Sasebo when, on the night of 11/12 September 1905, the *Mikasa* sank at her moorings after an explosion which killed some 250 of her crew and wounded many more. The cause of the blast remains a mystery. It may have been an accident, the result, perhaps, of ammunition being mishandled in a magazine. But it could equally have been a deliberate – and characteristically Japanese – act of protest against what many in the country saw as a dishonourable peace: Japan had been granted neither all the territory it sought nor the financial reparations. (The *Mikasa* herself was later raised and repaired, and today she is a national monument, the only surviving battleship of her kind.)

The signing of the Portsmouth treaty came a month short of a century since Nelson's defeat of the French and Spanish navies at Trafalgar. Then, in

October 1805, only Britain could have been described as an industrial nation. In a mere one hundred years, however, a large part of the northern hemisphere had been transformed by the forces unleashed by industrialism, and the Kaiser's Germany, although only unified in 1871, had undergone an economic miracle almost as extraordinary as that of Japan. The secret of its success was science, and chemistry in particular. Even as late as the 1870s, nobody in Europe, including the Germans themselves, had anticipated the meteoric rise of the chemical industry. It happened in just two decades and it was the foundation of Germany's wealth at the outbreak of war in 1914.

CHAPTER TWENTY-ONE

THE SYNTHETIC WORLD

On 18 August 1914, just four days after Britain's declaration of war against Germany, a committee of scientists and manufacturers met in London to discuss the urgent need for supplies of what had become an essential material. Thousands of volunteers were signing up at army recruiting centres all over the country and they would have to be kitted out in uniforms dyed the standard colour, khaki. By the outbreak of the Great War, modern smokeless firearms, accurate over great distances, had rendered the dashing red of the British soldier's tunic obsolete: it was no longer feasible to intimidate an enemy with a colourful display of strength. Khaki was first adopted in India – the word is Urdu for 'dust' or 'mud-coloured' – and had become standard by 1914. When first made in the 1850s, the fabric for the khaki uniform was dyed with plant extracts; in fact, nearly all fabric dyes were derived from natural products before the mid-nineteenth century. But by 1914 the development of synthetic colourants had revolutionized the dyeing and textile printing industries which were dominated by the giant firms of just one country – Germany. And it was from Germany that Britain acquired its synthetic khaki dyes before 1914, which was why, at the outbreak of war, there was an immediate crisis in equipping the newly volunteered troops.

The 1914 committee convened to find a solution to the problem included some celebrated names in the world of synthetic dyes. There was W. H. Perkin, the son of William Perkin, who had discovered and manufactured the first widely used synthetic dye back in the 1850s, and Herbert Levinstein, the son of Ivan Levinstein, one of a community of German Jews who had played a prominent part in the textile-dyeing business in Britain. Indeed, it was the Levinsteins' firm which claimed it could make all the khaki dye that was needed for the war effort. By May 1915, it had produced 600,000 pounds of the green-brown dye from coal tar products and a further 400,000 pounds was available by the autumn of that year. This was enough dyestuff to kit out nine million men in their brand-new khaki uniforms.

Though the immediate crisis over khaki was quickly solved, the realization that Britain had somehow become dependent on Germany for a whole range of chemical products and that the country had fallen badly behind in the development of this most modern and lucrative of industries caused a great deal of soul-searching. There was also a concern that the same intermediary derivates from coal tar used to make dyes could be turned into modern explosives such as TNT. Yet there was really no fundamental technical reason why Germany should have come to dominate chemical production. Not that long before, even in the 1870s, Britain appeared to be in a very strong position in this field. Up to that time, Germans had been taking up scientific and manufacturing posts in Britain and there was a largely amicable and mutually beneficial working relationship between the two countries. By 1913, however, the dominance of Germany had become quite startling, especially where synthetic dyestuffs were concerned. The British textile industry, still the world leader, was a huge consumer of dyestuffs: it used 23,000 tons in 1913, compared with Germany's 20,000 and France's 9,000. But only Germany consumed much less than it manufactured, with a massive production of 135,000 tons compared with Britain's 5,000.

The making of bright colours for textiles and other goods such as leatherwear was only one branch of the chemical industry. Developments in the chemistry of synthetic dyes had led to other discoveries. For example, in the late nineteenth century some of the first synthetic drugs appeared on pharmacists' shelves: aspirin was one. There was the manufacture of explosives for both mining and the military. And there were the so-called 'heavy chemical' industries producing huge quantities of the basic materials of modern industry: sulphuric acid and soda. The very rapid development of these industries in the second half of the nineteenth century amounted to the creation of an entirely new concept of industrialism. At the heart of this lay the successful substitution of natural products – whether in textile dyes, food colouring, perfumes, fertilizers for farmers or medicines – with synthetic equivalents made, for the most part, from the otherwise worthless and polluting by-products of the coal gas- and coke-producing industry.

In particular, the noxious coal tar which was left as a residue in the manufacture of gas for heating and lighting provided chemists with a raw material from which they began to derive an astonishing range of materials. Once it was understood that the basic chemical building blocks of hydrocarbons and phenols derived from coal could be transformed systematically into a vast number of novel products, the possibility of freeing the world from its reliance on natural raw materials appeared to be immensely exciting and potentially very profitable. And the industrial revolutionaries who strove to create this brave new synthetic world were themselves a very new breed who combined scientific understanding with the entrepreneurial ambitions of the manufacturer. Their predecessors, the great innovators of the eighteenth century such as Josiah Wedgwood or Matthew Boulton, had also had a great interest in science, but the discipline of chemistry had remained rudimentary. Understanding of the nature of gases and the relationship between chemistry and electrical forces had been taken forward by Humphry Davy and Michael Faraday in England and chemists such as Gay-Lussac in France. In fact, in the first half of the nineteenth century France was regarded as the leading nation with regard to chemical theory. The founding of the new science of what became known as 'organic chemistry' was truly international, however, and its most prominent promoter was a German called Justus Liebig who, after an inauspicious start to his academic career, became one of the most famous European scientists of his day and an immensely popular and influential figure in Britain.

Liebig was born in 1803, the second son of a merchant in the town of Darmstadt, which was then situated in the Grand Duchy of Hessen-Darmstadt on the Rhine. His father, Johann, was a self-taught chemist who made up such useful items as boot polish and acquired a local celebrity when he lit his workshop with gas made from heated bones. Liebig's mother was illegitimate and brought up by a foster family. It is quite possible she was Jewish: certainly, efforts were made by the Nazis in the 1930s to show that she was not, so that her famous son Liebig could be claimed as a true Aryan. There was nothing easy or settled about Justus von Liebig's childhood. Darmstadt inevitably suffered the vagaries of fortune during and after the Napoleonic Wars, even though the Grand Duke Ludwig I was pro-French, the independence of his territory having been granted by Napoleon. The Liebig family had its share of troubles too. Justus's elder brother Louis disappointed the father by failing to become a pharmacist and spurning the chance to inherit the family business. He died young. Four of Justus's sisters died in infancy and a younger brother died at the age of five. However, two younger brothers, Georg and Karl, and a younger sister, Elizabeth, survived.

The region was one of poor farmers, yet Liebig's father was able to send him to a school which had a good reputation for teaching the classic subjects. He first attended this 'gymnasium' at the age of eight when the average age of the class was ten. The school records show that he finished near the bottom of the class when he was twelve, and Liebig himself dismissed this early part of his education as practically useless. He recalled later in life that the whole class and his teacher laughed when he said he wanted to be a chemist. There is some doubt about the veracity of this anecdote, but Liebig liked to make the point that traditional teaching had not been much use to him. His version was that he left the gymnasium at the age of fourteen because it was a waste of his time. His biographers think it more likely his father could no longer pay the fees because the economy of Hessen-Darmstadt was deliberately wrecked after 1815 in recriminations for the Grand Duke's support for the French during the Napoleonic occupation.

At fourteen, Justus was apprenticed to a pharmacist, living away from home in the town of Heppenheim to the south of Darmstadt. He was there only a few months. Here again, Liebig's recollection of events – that he was hopeless at pharmacy and was dismissed – is not backed up by the evidence.

Correspondence between his father and the pharmacist make it clear money was again the problem: the apprentice fee was too much for the family's modest budget. Why Liebig should have been so keen to dramatize his youth is a puzzle, though it is possible that, once he was famous and elevated to the aristocracy as Justus von Liebig, he wanted to disguise the relative poverty of his youth.

Liebig returned home, where he worked sometimes in his father's makeshift laboratory and read a great deal from books borrowed from Grand Duke Ludwig's library, whose contents were made available to his subjects. He believed that his attempts to repeat experiments he had read about in books was the beginning of his education in chemistry. From his late teens, he appears to have lived a kind of charmed life. He had no formal qualifications, was to a considerable extent self-taught and did not have the connections to get into his local university at Giessen. In any case, chemistry was only taught there as a part of the medical curriculum and was not taken that seriously. It seems that it was through his father that Justus met a leading German chemist, K. W. G. Kastner, a professor at the University of Bonn. Johann Liebig probably bought chemicals from Kastner, who would have called on him from time to time at Darmstadt. Kastner was clearly impressed with the teenage Justus, whose interest in chemical experimentation was evident and who had done some real research into the composition of what were known as fulminates, explosive substances used in fireworks. Kastner not only arranged for a paper by Liebig to be published in a prestigious journal; he also took him on as his personal assistant. Soon the seventeen-year-old Liebig was writing home enthusiastically about the experiments he was conducting with his mentor. One letter, dated 20 February 1821, read in part:

> Together with Kastner I have prepared the new metal, cadmium, from the Silesian zinc, also iodine from the sodium salt of hydroiodine acid, cinnebar and the blue molybid acid, tin oxide, which is known as Richter's Blue Carmin. To produce the blue carmin from indigo, one needs the addition of alum earth ... One now gets many earthen vessels from London which are covered

with a beautiful metallic glaze of platinum and which are not attacked by any acid, even vitriol oil. It is used for coffee things, candlesticks, and so forth ... If experiments would give good results, one could make enormous sums of money because such utensils are in great demand ...[1]

From the very beginning of his career as a chemist, Liebig was concerned to make practical use of any discoveries that he might arrive at. He was dismissive of unscientific pharmacy and woolly philosophizing. At one time, he imagined working with his father to create a new chemical business. However, when Kastner was appointed Professor of Chemistry at the prestigious University of Erlangen, Liebig went with him. Here he studied physics, botany and technology and under his patron's tuition began to analyse objects such as fossils in an attempt to unravel their true chemical nature.

At this time, as Liebig was fond of emphasizing in later life, there was not much in German universities that resembled an experimental laboratory. He dismissed the facilities available in most places as mere 'kitchens' with, by implication, the chemist as a kind of chef preparing useful concoctions. Though it was not intended, the analogy of the kitchen and the laboratory appears in retrospect to be quite apt, for a community of brilliant chemists arose in the nineteenth century in much the same way as the leading chefs of the modern restaurant revolution learned by apprenticeship to one another. In 1822, Liebig still had no formal qualifications and practically no income: he relied on his father for support. Yet the patronage of Kastner was enough to launch him on a career which made him one of the most influential figures of the nineteenth century and the founder of an entirely new industry in which his native Germany was to excel.

Serious though he was in his studies, Liebig was still a young man. At Erlangen, he fell in with a group of students who drank great quantities of beer while cocking a snook at authority. Liebig himself was involved in a skirmish in which he knocked the cocked hat off a local dignitary and became embroiled in a 'town and gown' fight between students and local youths. For a while, the students were expelled from the town, returning when the authorities realized they could not do without the income they provided – quite a number were from very wealthy families. Yet this was not the end of the matter for Liebig, who was accused of plotting against authority and summoned to appear before the magistrates. Had he been found guilty, he could have been expelled without a degree and exiled – some rebel students had even been forced to emigrate to America.

Liebig somehow avoided prosecution and survived a passionate love affair with an aristocratic lush and poet, August Graf von Platen, who was seven years his senior and wrote a series of 'Liebig Sonnets' in praise of Justus and their relationship. At the end of the academic year, Liebig escaped the dangers of Erlangen and went home. Here he waited anxiously for news of an application made by Kastner to the Grand Duke for a grant which would enable him to study in Paris. As it was, the French sympathies of Hessen-Darmstadt which had caused so much trouble after 1815 now stood Liebig in good stead. In May 1822 he was told he had the stipend.

In November 1822 Liebig began his studies in Paris, attending lectures which were then given to huge audiences of students, up to 400 at a time, by a brilliant group of French scientists who had been inspired by the informal but hugely influential Society of Arcueil, established by Claude Louis Berthollet in his home, just south of Paris. A legacy of Napoleon was the placing of the study of physics, chemistry and mathematics at the core of the French curriculum and by the 1820s the leading lights in Paris, men such as Joseph-Louis Gay-Lussac, were famous throughout Europe. Liebig was able therefore to learn from the very best: Jean-Baptiste Biot, who specialized in optics, Louis Jacques Thénard, a chemist and pharmacist, and Pierre Louis Dulong, a professor of chemistry, all of whom emerged from the Arcueil group. He wrote to a friend back in Erlangen: 'Science is no longer an old nag which one has to saddle so that one can ride on it. It is a winged horse – the more I try to reach it, the more it flees from me … I thought I had worked hard in Darmstadt, but in Paris the daily song [sic] is from seven in the morning until midnight or later, and I enjoy it.[2]

It is evident that Liebig was no ordinary student, though he still lacked any formal qualifications. All the lectures were in French, which he had to learn quickly, but he took the trouble to study English as well. He attended classes in mathematics as he realized he needed to be able to use it for experimentation. He went to lectures on industrial chemistry given by Nicolas Clément, a factory owner who instilled in Liebig an interest in the practical application of scientific discoveries, while the chemist Thénard recognized this pupil's exceptional talents and arranged for Liebig to have research space in a private laboratory. The cost of all this – his board and lodging and lecture and research fees – was borne by his modest grant and money from his father. In his laboratory, Liebig went back to his study of explosives and produced a paper which the great Gay-Lussac delivered while Liebig performed the demonstrations that accompanied the text. This so impressed the naturalist Alexander von Humboldt that he persuaded Gay-Lussac to take Liebig on as an assistant for a while. This was the pinnacle of Liebig's Paris education. He wrote many years later: 'Never shall I forget the hours passed in the laboratory of Gay-Lussac. When we had finished a successful analysis … he would say to me, "Now you must dance with me just as Thenard and I always danced together when we had discovered something new." And then we would dance!'[3]

Although he wrote from Paris to his former lover Platen, there is no suggestion that Liebig continued to have homosexual affairs and his dancing with Gay-Lussac was apparently the innocent celebration of two contented chemists. Their collaboration did not last long, however, for von Humboldt requested that Liebig be offered a post in Germany. Once Kastner had solved the problem of Liebig's lack of qualifications by buying him a doctorate, the fee being paid by his father, Liebig was made Extraordinary Professor of Chemistry at the University of Giessen. This was not, on the face of it, a very promising post, for Giessen was a small town of just 5,500 people which relied on a few hundred students for its livelihood. There was just a single university building, the library opened for just one hour on four days of the week, and the professors generally taught in their own homes. They made an income by charging tuition fees to top up a stipend they received from the local exchequer. Furthermore, the teaching of chemistry was not regarded in the Hessen district as something the authorities should be concerned with. As Liebig was told: 'It is the State's task to train civil servants, not apothecaries, soap-makers, beer brewers, dyers and vinegar distillers.'

Liebig's laboratory, housed in a newly built but disused barracks at Giessen, was a private venture which would succeed or fail depending on the number and calibre of the students who were attracted there. To prosper, Liebig had to outshine an incumbent professor of chemistry called Wilhelm Zimmermann, who had also studied in Paris but had fallen behind in his understanding of the subject. He duly did so, whereupon Zimmerman took to drink, then threw himself into the river and drowned. Liebig's teaching methods were unique: he made full use of his laboratory's facilities and he constantly emphasized the need to understand chemical reactions and processes and to apply this knowledge to industrial purposes. As a result, Giessen drew in students from all over Europe and some from America. There were just a few foreign acolytes – six were from France, and two from Britain – between 1830 and 1835, when Liebig was still establishing himself and pharmacy was still a more popular subject than chemistry. Between 1836 and 1845, however, the numbers arriving from Britain rose steadily until they were by far the majority: fifty-six students in all who would return to their home country with a new enthusiasm for experimental chemistry. France began to fall behind with just seventeen students, while Switzerland had twenty-two. In the early 1840s, the first of many pupils arrived from the United States.

As soon as he was earning a modest but steady income at Giessen, Liebig courted the daughter of a local official, Henriette Moldenauer, and they were married in May 1826 when she was just nineteen and he twenty-three. Though always a volatile character, given to outbursts of anger when his theories were challenged, he settled down to married life at Giessen with a family which provided him with stability, while his international fame drew him abroad. The first English student at Giessen was Charles Henry, just a year younger than Liebig and the son of the chemist William Henry, whose family fortune was founded in the manufacture in Manchester of Milk of Magnesia, a stomach settler which was very popular in Britain. Charles urged Liebig to visit England, where his teaching was becoming well known. As more English pupils arrived, Liebig was persuaded to address the British Association for the Advancement of Science.

In the autumn of 1837, Liebig crossed the North Sea and was met at Hull docks by Thomas Thomson, the son of a professor of chemistry at Glasgow. They went by stagecoach across the Pennine hills, to be greeted in Manchester by Charles Henry. Here Liebig became aware of the enormous wealth generated by the otherwise grim industrial regions of the country. He wrote to his wife:

> The district between Leeds and Manchester is one big smoking chimney … I was rather taken aback by the massive elegance of a rich English household … My room is provided with a number of things which only an Englishman is accustomed to use; four kinds of washbasin, one for the head and face, one for the teeth, one for the hands, and a bidet. In the evening, Henry had friends for dinner, which was dreadfully boring for me; the servants came in black tailcoats, knee breeches and stockings, white gloves, three slaves [black servants] behind us; in short, it was princely, but for me very dreary. I will say nothing about the food, still less of the dozen or so wines, ices, Spanish Frische, black and white grapes …[4]

The food was far too rich for Liebig and the conversation the duller because his English was still not that good. But he continued his travels, crossing the Irish Sea to Dublin, where he was reunited with some of his former Giessen students. He then visited Scotland, where Thomas Graham was Professor of Chemistry at Anderson's University in Glasgow at which James 'Paraffin' Young had studied. Liebig visited factories and a huge calico printing works that employed 1,500 people. From Glasgow, Liebig took the boat back to Liverpool, where his paper entitled, pungently, *On the decomposing products of uric acid*, was delivered by Michael Faraday and judged a huge success. In all, Liebig spent eight days in Liverpool, taking his first railway ride on the newly opened line to Birmingham. He visited Charles Macintosh's waterproof wear factory before taking the stagecoach to London (the railway from Birmingham to London was not opened until the following year, 1838).

Liebig's first visit to Britain was a sensational success. While the Royal Society voted him a Foreign Fellow and Copley medallist, Liebig was wide-eyed at the wealth of this industrial nation or, at any rate, of its prosperous middle classes. But even so, at a time when his native Germany had barely begun to industrialize at all, he discerned a failing which would later inhibit Britain's development. 'England is not the land of science, only widespread dilettantism presides here,' he wrote. 'Chemists are ashamed to call themselves chemists because the apothecaries (who are despised) have appropriated this name.'[5] The term 'chemist' remains to this day ambiguous in English, referring to a qualified retailer of medicines as well as to those working in industry on the creation of new substances.

In 1825, the young American Moncure Robinson, who had visited Europe, remarked on the superiority of French scientists and engineers when it came to theory, but their backwardness compared with the British in practical mechanics. At that stage of industrialization, it appeared that the British had the advantage. However, Liebig, making much the same observation about fifteen years later, perceived the weakness in the British attitude to science generally, despite its galaxy of gifted men such as Faraday, writing:

> What struck me most in England was the perception that only those works which have a practical tendency awake attention and command respect, while purely scientific works which possess greater merit are almost unknown. And yet the latter are the proper and true source from which the others flow. Practice alone can never lead to the discovery of a truth or principle. In Germany it is quite the contrary. Here in the eyes of scientific men, no value, or at least but a trifling one, is placed on the practical results. The enrichment of science alone is worthy of attention. I do not mean to say that this is better, for both nations the golden medium would certainly be a real good fortune.[6]

On the practical side of things, Liebig's first great interest was in the chemistry of plants and animals and he and his fellow chemists identified and specified the body fats, carbohydrates and proteins. Liebig did a great deal of work on what it is that promotes growth in plants, and the first publication which made him internationally famous was *Chemistry in its Applications to*

Agriculture and Physiology (1840; translated into English by Lyon Playfair). Not all his science proved to be correct: he believed, for example, that plants could get all the nitrogen they needed for growth from the air. But his promotion of artificial fertilizers was of great interest to landowners and farmers in Britain and America, both countries where his book was available in English, translated by one of his Giessen pupils, the leading scientist Lyon Playfair, the same Playfair who had encouraged James 'Paraffin' Young to investigate the commercial possibilities of shale oil. But most significantly for the future, at Giessen Liebig and his young team began in the 1830s to study the chemical constitution of the natural dye indigo as well as other natural products. Coal tar waste, when analysed, proved to contain an oil identical to one found in indigo, and Liebig's most brilliant assistant, August Wilhelm von Hofmann, gave this oil the name aniline.

Liebig, with all his works translated into English, recognized the importance of making an impact in Britain. In 1844, he had another wonderfully successful visit when a dinner in his honour was given in the Trades Hall in Glasgow, an event covered by the leading medical journal, *The Lancet*, in a special supplement. Lionized now, Liebig met the Prime Minister, Sir Robert Peel, and when plans were discussed for the creation in England of some kind of teaching institution like that at Giessen, Liebig was naturally approached to take charge. He was also considered as a possible Professor of Chemistry at King's College London. But he stayed in Germany, where he was about to be ennobled as Justus von Liebig and had acquired a small estate which soon became known as Liebig Heights.

It was still very much the official view in Britain that manufacturing industry could take care of its own research work and educational system and that, if a college of chemistry were needed, businessmen could pay for it themselves. Sir Robert Peel, whose family fortune was based in part on calico printing, argued the case with Liebig, who did not believe commercial interests would ever make real discoveries in science. In the end, Prince Albert, keen on science himself and thrilled that a fellow German was such a brilliant international figure, joined in a public subscription which raised £5,000 to found a Royal College of Chemistry. A number of chemists were approached to take charge and inevitably it was a favoured student of Liebig's who got the job. This was twenty-seven-year-old August Wilhelm von Hofmann, who had discovered aniline in 1837. Hofmann's father was an architect who had designed an extension to Liebig's laboratory at Giessen, and August had proved to be a star pupil there. Prince Albert was influential in getting him the post, his affection for the young man the greater because August actually lived in the house in which Albert had been brought up in Germany.

The Royal College of Chemistry opened in 1845, first in London's Hanover Square before it moved to premises on Oxford Street a year later. Hofmann quickly established teaching along the lines of that at Giessen and soon had a keen band of students working with him. One of these, Thomas Hall, went on to teach chemistry at the City of London school, where he came across an exceptional pupil by the name of William Perkin. Born in the Shadwell district of East London in 1838, Perkin was the son of a reasonably prosperous builder. He began his education at a private college before going to the City of London school at the age of thirteen. At that time he had already taken an interest in chemicals and had managed to take his own photograph. When Thomas Hall recognized that Perkin had a sound grasp of chemistry, he recommended that he go straight to the Royal College to study with Hofmann. Perkin's father was not pleased that his fifteen-year-old son, whom he hoped would train as an architect, might be spirited away into a career the future of which was not at all clear. However, after several meetings with Hofmann, he relented and allowed William to take a place at the Royal College.

The institution that young Perkin joined was, under the tutelage of Hofmann, a distillation of at least half a century of chemical investigation in which the mysteries of the constituent parts of basic substances were being gradually revealed. The dream of the alchemists of old had been to find a way to transform base metals into gold. Now, chemists such as Hofmann believed that, through experimentation and close observation of the results which were recorded as formulae, it would be possible to turn an otherwise useless substance into something useful and saleable. Along with Liebig and some English investors, he had become involved in a scheme to turn a waste product of the refining of quinine from the bark of the Peruvian cinchona tree into a much cheaper but just as effective substitute for this medicine, which was in great demand around the world as an antidote to malaria. For a variety of reasons, the scheme had been a commercial failure, but the principle was there: to find a way to manufacture with chemical knowledge a silk purse out of a sow's ear and you could make a fortune.

Hofmann did not emphasize the commercial aspect of chemistry to his pupils, though he acted as a paid consultant for many firms and was not aloof about money-making. It was commonplace for them to be given individual tasks in the laboratory, often repeating experiments that Hofmann had made. Perkin later recalled that Hofmann would sometimes take hold of a solution a student had made, add a dash of some other chemical and hold up a beautiful crystalline structure exclaiming: 'Gentlemen, new bodies are floating in the air!'[7] After Perkin had been studying at the Royal College for three years, Hofmann suggested to him a way in which quinine might be synthesized from one of the derivatives of coal tar. One approach was to analyse a natural substance such as the bark of the cinchona tree and try to replicate its chemical constitution using other substances, principally derivatives of coal gas tar. As it turned out, the secret of quinine's chemistry was not decoded until 1944 and the natural product remains the main source of the drug.

Commercially, however, the most promising possibility was the synthesizing of the dyes used by the textile industry to colour cloth made from silk, wool, linen and cotton. This had already been done to some extent as naturally occurring materials such as lichens or uric acid had been modified chemically to produce useable dyestuffs. One of these, murexide or Roman Purple, was first synthesized by an English doctor and chemist called William Prout using the uric acid in the excrement of a boa constrictor, a star attraction at London Zoo, which in 1832 had been transferred to the Regent's Park site from the Tower of London. The production of this purple on a commercial scale was made possible with the first imports of Peruvian guano, the accumulated droppings of millions of seabirds. Used mainly as a fertilizer, guano also contained uric acid, and firms in Manchester and the French city of Mulhouse (which was German from 1870 to 1914) used it to make murexide.

The discovery that a colour could be synthesized did not by any means make it a commercial proposition. For the dyestuffs industry there were well-established sources of basic raw materials, notably two plant species: madder and indigo. Tree barks, saffron, cochineal from the female beetles living on cacti in Central America, and a variety of other natural sources of colouring were well known: they were cultivated and in steady supply. For the dyer, a colourant had to be not only inexpensive but of a quality that was bright and that would hold its lustre when exposed to light for long periods and frequently washed. Making dyes fast was an ancient and always time-consuming art. Each fabric had different qualities and had to be treated in different ways: a colourant that might hold fast in silk did not do so in cotton. Fixatives called 'mordants' had to be applied to most textiles. Breaking into the dyestuffs market was therefore not a simple matter of finding a way of making a synthetic version of a natural dye. At mid-century, though murexide and some other chemically treated colourants were in use, they were not regarded as of great interest industrially. Certainly there was little made of them at the Great Exhibition in 1851. The story of how William Perkin discovered and exploited a new dye and by broad agreement founded the modern dyestuff industry is thus all the more remarkable.

Perkin's family home in Shadwell was known locally as King David's Castle and there was room there for him to fashion a makeshift laboratory that he could use in the evenings and when the Royal College was shut in the holidays. A fellow student, Arthur Church, who also possessed a homespun laboratory, sometimes worked with him. While trying to fulfil the task Hofmann had set him of synthesizing quinine, Perkin produced a substance that was a kind of reddish powder and then a black gunk. He then substituted aniline, the colouring agent of indigo (*anil* is the Arabic for indigo) which Hofmann had shown to be an oil that could be derived from coal tar. This produced a very dark liquid. Intrigued, Perkin experimented further and found that he had produced a brilliant purple colour. He initially called it Tyrian Purple after the dye made from juice extracted from Mediterranean molluscs. With the help of his brother, Thomas, he made a few batches of the dye, improving it each time.

It was not at all unusual for chemists at this time to produce weird and wonderful colours in the laboratory. They were admired, a paper on them was published, and then they were poured down the sink. It would take months of experimentation to discover if they were of any use as commercial dyestuffs and that was not the purpose of the Royal College. Hofmann certainly did not think so and, knowing as much, Perkin kept his discovery to himself. He dyed a piece of silk with his purple, then a piece of cotton, and it seemed to take and to be fast. To get an expert opinion, Perkin sent samples of coloured material to the company of Pullar of Perth in Scotland that he had heard was a leading textile dyer. He received a reasonably encouraging reply from Robert Pullar: 'If your discovery does not make the goods too expensive, it is decidedly one of the most valuable that has come out for a long time. This colour is one that is wanted in all classes of goods and could not be obtained fast on silks, and only at great expense on cotton yarns. I enclose patterns of the best lilac we have on cotton. It is done by only one house in the United Kingdom, Andrews of Manchester, and they get any price they wish for it, but even if it is not quite fast ... and does not stand the test that yours does, and fades by exposure to air.'[8]

What excited the interest of Robert Pullar, an ambitious twenty-eight-year-old, was that Perkin appeared to have discovered an entirely new colour. It was not that it was a synthetic substitute for dyers' plants: there was no shortage of supply of madder or indigo. But the textile industry was governed by fashion and anything new could have a tremendous value, if only for a few years. The problem with the dye Perkins had produced was that it was not at all clear that it could be used in quantity as a commercial dye. What mordant was required to make it fast? And would it work on cotton, by then the most significant fabric in the textile industry? If not, would any manufacturer risk their capital trying to develop it?

Nevertheless, Perkin took the plunge. To the astonished and angry Hofmann he announced that he was leaving the Royal College in order to establish a business producing this new dye. Much as Liebig and Hofmann wanted to make chemistry relevant to the industrial world, there was still a feeling that commercial ventures were, as Perkin himself put it, *infra dig.*, beneath one's dignity. Perkin was then only eighteen and had already upset his father by spurning a career as an architect. However, after an East End silk dyer, Thomas Keith, had endorsed the wonderful colour the new dye produced, Perkin's father took a huge risk, putting his lifetime's savings into the building of a dye factory. Shortly after, the elder brother, Thomas, left his architectural studies to join them.

The site the Perkin family found was on the other side of London from their East End home, a piece of land alongside the Grand Union canal at Greenford Green in Middlesex. It was here that they made history, inventing all the equipment required to transform coal tar into a synthetic dye that dyers were prepared to buy. At first, they could dye only silk, but after experiments they made themselves and those of the Pullars in Scotland a mordant was found for fixing the dye to cotton cloth, the textile which was the source of much of Britain's wealth. As it happened, both the lilac of murexide and a French purple derived from lichen had become fashionable, and it was lucky for Perkin that the first colour he had produced was in demand. In 1859, as sales took off and the family fortune was made, in England the dye was renamed mauve, after the French word for the purple-flowered mallow plant.

The production of new colours derived from coal tar followed swiftly, all of them known as the aniline dyes, synthetic substitutes for the indigo plant. Although August Hofmann had been fiercely opposed to Perkin leaving the Royal College to become a manufacturer, he was soon lauded as the scientific discoverer of the aniline dyes, and for the work he had carried out himself as a consultant for various dyers. Along with others, Perkin himself went on to discover that it was also possible to synthesize the essential ingredient of the dye plant madder, and a whole new range of dyes was created. These were the alizarin dyes, a term derived probably from the Arabic word for juice and one by which the madder plant was known. After 1869, when Perkin's production of alizarin dyes began, the growing of madder – a staple of southern France around the town of Aix – declined and the synthetic dyes took over. Indeed, the last decades of the nineteenth century witnessed the death of a huge international trade in both madder and indigo, many British planters in India losing the source of their fortunes.

Until around 1870, Britain, with France not that far behind, held the lead in the production of both aniline and alizarin dyes, with Perkin & Sons the most important manufacturer. Writing of alizarin towards the end of the century, Perkin recalled: 'Before the end of the year 1869 we had produced one ton of this colouring matter in the form of paste; in 1870, forty tons; in 1871, 220 tons; and so on in increasing quantities year by year. As we had been successful in producing artificial alizarin, others did not run much risk in following our lead; yet up to the end of 1870 the Greenford Green works were the only ones producing artificial alizarin. German manufacturers then began to make it, first in small and then in increasing quantities, but until the end of 1873 there was scarcely any competition with our colouring matter in this country.'[9]

For a while a rival British company, Simpson, Maule & Nicholson, who retained August Hofmann as their consultant, was one of the two largest producers of coal-tar intermediaries and dyes in the world, the other being Renard in Paris. Then, everything changed. With a rapidity that was scarcely believable, the dyestuffs industry in Britain began to shrink and to lose out to its German rivals. Writing in the journal of the Society of Dyers and Colourists in November 1914, William Perkin's son Frederick had absolutely no doubt why this had happened: 'The neglect of scientific research during the next decade (the 1880s) was the reason why the coal-tar colour trade, established as it was in this country, gradually got forced out by German competition.'[10]

William Perkin had sold up the Greenford Green works and business in 1874, when he was just thirty-six. Defending his father's decision, which had been criticized as 'unpatriotic' in some newspapers, Frederick pointed out that for the firm to expand it had to have a steady supply of trained chemists for the discovery of new dyes and the cheapest way of manufacturing them. Any firm that failed to recruit new blood would go out of business. The only suitably qualified chemists they could find in any number came from Germany, where the teaching of sciences promoted by Liebig had continued in leaps and bounds. In 1864, Hofmann had returned to Germany in the absence of any patronage in England after Prince Albert, his champion, had died prematurely in 1861. Liebig himself was still a hugely popular figure in England – like Hofmann, he was the guest of Queen Victoria – and a sought-after adviser on everything from fertilizers to sewage disposal. He died of pneumonia just before his seventieth birthday in April 1873 as the German chemical miracle that he had made possible was about to astonish Britain and the rest of the world.

Frederick Perkin made the point that the German chemists his company employed were good value, but added that they nearly all returned to their homeland once they had finished their stint in England. Whereas in Germany chemists were highly valued, and dyestuff manufacturers encouraged, in Britain the dominant government policy of laissez–faire left firms such as Perkin & Sons unprotected. The patent law, for example, was disastrous. English patents were ignored in Germany, which had no enforceable laws before 1877. German companies, on the other hand, could take out patents in Britain and enforce them without producing any dyestuffs at all. Yet the British manufacturers themselves were guilty of complacency, as Frederick Perkin was prepared to concede. Colourists in the textile business were very conservative: they did not want to be saddled with some new dye that proved to be faulty. The way in which dyes were applied could be crucial for their success and the maker had to show the dyer how to use them. The German companies trained up chemists as salesmen and sent them around the world to show how dyes were best applied, whereas the British tended, rather lamely, to warn purchasers not to be gulled by inferior foreign goods.

Everything was stacked against the British dyestuffs industry and in favour of Germany. There, alcohol, an essential ingredient in the manufacturing process, was cheap; in Britain, it was dear because of duty. There, the banks were prepared to fund and invest in chemical firms; in Britain, companies had to find their own capital. There, very large sums were invested in research; in Britain, dyestuff manufacturers had to skimp and scrape. Eventually, British governments did not believe that the best interests of industry and the country were served by any kind of intervention. 'Free trade' was the slogan, and if this meant it was more economic to import German dyestuffs than make its own, then that was the best policy for Britain. As W. J. Reader put it in his history of Imperial Chemical Industries (ICI), the giant British company formed after the 1914–18 war: 'The dyestuffs industry in Great Britain before 1914 had commonly been regarded as a servant, starved and neglected, of the textile industries, those imposing, but already somewhat antiquated, pillars of British industrial strength.'[11]

The dyestuffs industry was not the only product of the new approach to chemistry. Liebig had developed a meat extract which gave rise to other products such as Oxo cubes and Bovril and also artificial colouring for the food industry, despite one or two scares concerning the poisonous nature of the synthetic dyes involved. Then, in the very last years of the nineteenth century, German chemists began the successful production of synthetic forms of traditional drugs, notably the painkiller aspirin, which was derived from the baked bark of willow trees. The large chemical firms, as they grew, were able to produce a huge range of synthetic products, derived chiefly from coal tar. These included perfumes, soaps and the chemicals for the rapidly expanding photographic industry. A growing army of chemists was involved in devising new substances or discovering more efficient ways of producing a chemical that was in demand. The research laboratory was now asserting itself as the powerhouse of industry and by far the largest and most sophisticated laboratories were those of the German chemical giants. In contrast to Edison's Menlo Park or Bessemer's premises, the German research departments were dedicated to science-based discoveries, well-equipped and staffed with lawyers to ensure their patents were safeguarded.

The phenomenal growth of these chemical giants can be illustrated with just one example: the rise of BASF or Badische Anilin-und-Soda Fabrik. Formed in 1865, BASF was a partnership between a dynamic entrepreneur, Friedrich Engelhorn, a former gold worker who had been a promoter of the Mannheim gas works, and Carl and August Clemm, nephews of the founder of a Mannheim chemical firm. The company was set up in a hamlet, Ludwigshafen, on the west bank of the Rhine after an earlier chemical factory had been banished from Mannheim because of the pollution it had caused. At first, BASF's manufacturing of fuschine dye was not a great success. However, in 1868 the partners were able to employ Heinrich Caro, a chemist who was only thirty-eight but had a very wide experience in the textile and dyeing industries. Caro had studied in Germany and worked for a calico-dyeing firm there before moving to Manchester in England, where he had spent two years learning the trade before returning to Germany as a representative of the British firm, Roberts, Dale and Company.

Shortly after he was appointed chief chemist by Badische, as the company was generally known, Caro and two other chemists discovered how to synthesise alizarin at the same time as Perkin in England. It was a popular dye they were able to manufacture in great quantities: fifteen tons in 1871, 750 tons in 1877 and 2,000 tons annually in 1902. Badische also made the first German dye to be patented, methylene blue. In the 1870s, it acquired other firms as it expanded, including a well-known dyestuff merchants which provided the sales expertise. Year by year, the company grew. In 1870 it had 520 employees and a site covering just fifteen hectares; by 1885 there were 2,330 employees and the factories covered nearly sixty hectares; by 1900 there were 6,711 employees on a site of 155.8 hectares. The development of new dyes, new ways of making existing dyes and the discovery of a host of new and saleable chemicals turned BASF into one of the largest companies in the world.

The collapse of the German economy after defeat in 1918 for a while devastated the dyestuffs industry. A great many of its patents and secrets were commandeered by the Americans, who used them and the expertise developed by the Germans to establish its own industry, which grew rapidly from 1918. Yet it was the reviving chemical industry which got the German economy moving again between the world wars and enabled it to become once again a major and, as it turned out, dangerous power.

Since the mid-eighteenth century the driving force for innovation and the exploitation of new technologies had come from Britain. Its artisans, engineers, surveyors and entrepreneurs had been sought the world over for their expertise. Much of the industrial foundation of other countries – their spinning mills and ironworks and steam engines and railway lines – had been laid down by Britain or achieved with know-how borrowed from it. Even in the 1870s, Britain's position looked unassailable in Europe, though it was clearly being challenged in the new and gigantic market economy of the United States. Germany was still economically backward, as was Russia, and France had barely made any advances on Britain's technological lead. Japan, of course, had only just begun on the road to industrialization.

It might be said that Britain, over-confident in the second half of the nineteenth century, sowed the seeds of its own relative decline by its enthusiasm for free trade and its largesse in offering the rest of the world its technical knowledge and providing the United States, France, Germany and, most tellingly, Japan with the wherewithal to become competitors. The story of the spread of industrialism had begun in a different mood altogether – one of jealously guarded secrets, bolted factory gates and a ban on skilled men leaving the country with even a bag of tools.

POSTSCRIPT

All the individuals whose lives and achievements are chronicled in this book made a significant contribution to the spread of industrialism from its foundations in eighteenth-century Britain up until 1914. Most of them were inspired not by any patriotic or altruistic motives but rather by their desire for fame and fortune or, at the very least, a decent living. The young Japanese samurai who risked their lives to learn the secrets of Western technology are, arguably, exceptions to this rule, though they would not have distinguished between their own interests and what they saw as their patriotic duty.

The way in which the pursuit of self-interest by many thousands of entrepreneurs, engineers, surveyors and far-sighted politicians gave rise to a new kind of industrial society bears out to a considerable extent the principle most lucidly put forward by Adam Smith in his *An Inquiry into the Nature and Causes of the Wealth of Nations*, first published in 1776:

> Every individual is continually exerting himself to find out the most advantageous employment for whatever capital he can command. It is his own advantage, indeed, and not that of the society, which he has in view. But the study of his own advantage naturally, or rather necessarily, leads him to prefer that employment which is most advantageous to the society ... He generally, indeed, neither intends to promote the public interest, nor knows how much he is

promoting it. By preferring the support of domestic to that of foreign industry, he intends only his own security; and by directing that industry in such a manner as its produce may be of the greatest value, he intends only his own gain, and he is in this, as in many other cases, led by *an invisible hand* [my italics] to promote an end which was no part of his intention.[1]

There was never any political movement driving the spread of industrialism: it happened much in the way described by Adam Smith. However, exhaustive as his inquiry into the wealth of nations was, Smith failed to appreciate the huge impact the technological changes that had begun to transform Britain into the first industrial nation would have. Though he continued to revise his great work until close to his death in 1790, he did not foresee the significance of the steam engine, despite the fact that James Watt was an acquaintance, as was John Roebuck, who had been a co-founder of the Carron Iron Foundry in Scotland and funded Watt's experiments for a time.

In the *Wealth of Nations* there is just one reference to 'fire-engines' and clearly Smith had in mind those designed by Savery and Newcomen rather than any later versions. It is not the replacement of horse- or water-power with mechanical power that interests him; he refers only to a boy devising a self-acting system for the engine to save himself the trouble of turning a lever on and off all the time. It is certainly an apocryphal story and hardly the most significant aspect of a piece of coal-fired machinery which had revolutionized coal-mining by the 1770s.

There were other momentous innovations in Smith's lifetime which he failed to consider significant enough to mention in the *Wealth of Nations*. Whereas in 1764 the Frenchman Gabriel Jars from Lyons had made a pilgrimage to the Carron works in Scotland to see how iron was smelted with coke rather than charcoal – a vital breakthrough for eighteenth-century industry – Smith seems to have been quite unaware of its significance. As for the textile industry, he had not spotted the increasing importance of cotton and cites the spinning wheel as an innovation – something it certainly had been, albeit in an era much earlier than his own.

Smith was not alone in his ignorance of the latest technologies which were to be so significant in the years after his death. Samuel Johnson, whom Smith would meet many times in London, has absolutely nothing to say about steam engines in his celebrated dictionary, not even in the 1773 edition, the last one he personally revised. An engineer is defined as a military man specializing in explosives, including the petard, that primitive and unreliable kind of mine which often blew up the engineer himself – hence the expression 'hoist by his own petard'. There is nothing about mills or factories or horse-drawn railways and the word 'industry' is defined as 'Diligence; assiduity; habitual or actual labouriousness'. A manufacturer is defined as 'a workman; an artificer'.

It would appear that those foreign spies who were anxious to entice away British artisans were much more alert to innovation than Smith and the philosophers or intellectuals who were his contemporaries. Smith, anyway, believed that it was a mistake for the French to attempt to compete with British manufacturing industry and that they would be much better off sticking to what they were good at: making wine and growing corn. He thought the same about the American colonies which had begun that revolt which was to lead to independence from Britain in the year *Wealth of Nations* was published. Smith had considerable sympathy with the American revolutionaries as he was opposed to the kind of trading and manufacturing restrictions Britain had imposed on them. However, as with the French, Smith thought the Americans would be foolhardy to set up their own manufacturing industry. Far better to barter their agricultural produce for British-made goods:

> It has been the principal cause of the rapid progress of our American colonies towards wealth and greatness that almost their whole capitals have hitherto been employed in agriculture. They have no manufactures, those household and courser [sic] manufactures excepted which necessarily accompany the progress of agriculture, and which are the work of the women and children in every private family ... Were the Americans, either by combination or by any other sort of violence, to stop the importation of European manufactures, and, by thus giving a

monopoly to such of their own countrymen as could manufacture the like goods, divert any considerable part of their capital into this employment, they would retard instead of accelerate the further increase in the value of their annual produce, and would obstruct instead of promote the progress of their country towards real wealth and greatness.[2]

The revolutionaries seeking to break with Britain did not take the same view, and one wonders what exchanges of opinion there were between Benjamin Franklin, the oldest signatory of the Declaration of Independence in 1776, and Smith on the occasions when the two met. It has been said that Franklin actually read and commented on drafts of the *Wealth of Nations* but there is no proof of this and Franklin's own papers are disappointingly silent on the subject. Whatever Franklin's view, the leaders of the American Revolution did not agree with Adam Smith that there was no point in developing their own manufacturing industry. For them, political freedom was founded in economic and commercial independence and they were determined to be beholden to nobody. Once they had thrown off the imperial yoke in 1783, the Americans, then confined to the thirteen states inland from the eastern seaboard, made strenuous efforts to import the very latest technology from Britain and Europe.

No sooner had the United States begun its programme of canal-cutting with hired expertise from Britain than events in Europe were to radically alter its position in the world. A huge area of North America, to the west of the United States and then known loosely as Louisiana, came up for sale. It included what is today all of Arkansas, Missouri, Iowa, Oklahoma, Kansas and Nebraska, as well as Minnesota south of Mississippi River, most of North and South Dakota, north-eastern New Mexico, northern Texas, parts of Montana, Wyoming and Colorado east of the Continental Divide, and Louisiana on both sides of the Mississippi River, including the city of New Orleans. With parts of Alaska and Saskatchewan added, it amounted to nearly a quarter of the land area of what, by the mid-nineteenth century, was to become the modern United States.

Desperate for cash to fight the British and their allies, Napoleon had to persuade a reluctant American president, Thomas Jefferson, and his representatives in Paris to accept a deal in which the entire area comprising 530 million acres was bought for $15 million at three cents and acre. The resulting Louisiana Purchase of 1803 opened up a vast sub-tropical region, with New Orleans as its capital, in which cotton could be grown and which would supply nearly all the raw cotton wool that British spinning mills needed. With cotton, the relationship between the agricultural American South and manufacturing Britain was much as Adam Smith envisaged it. But the North developed differently, and when the Civil War came, it was the industrial North which triumphed.

It was industrial Britain, too, which had the wealth to fund not only its own army and navy but the troops of its allies as well in the wars with Napoleon. Defeat of the French at Trafalgar in 1805 and Waterloo in 1815 not only gave Britain a free run in the development of its industries while Europe either submitted to the ravages of Napoleonic invasion or recovered from them, it also made abundantly clear to any country wanting to challenge British supremacy that it, too, would have to industrialize. Napoleon himself had understood this well enough and tried to encourage the development of French industry, but there was too much to do in too little time.

Indeed, by the early nineteenth century it was evident that industrialism gave rise not only to wealth but also to military might, and that nations which remained economically 'backward' were vulnerable: they were liable to be defeated on the battlefield and, ultimately, to become subservient to a foreign power. This was sufficient reason to galvanize Britain's former American colonies and its European rivals into action, and it was undoubtedly why Japan was persuaded to industrialize so rapidly. None the less, it was certainly not in the interests of the ruling elite of any nation or kingdom to simply accept the new social order that came with industrialism, for these elites were already wealthy and they would have to surrender a large measure of political power to a new class of merchants, manufacturers and entrepreneurs. And there was this to consider too: Britain might have become wealthy as the model of the new industrial society, but it was also, at least in its most productive regions, hideously ugly – 'one big smoking chimney' was how the German chemist Justus Liebig described the region between Leeds and Manchester on his first visit to England in 1837.

It cannot be assumed, therefore, that those nations which did industrialize to a considerable extent before 1914 were wholeheartedly enthusiastic about joining the club of major manufacturing nations. France was equivocal for a long time and the German states of the former Holy Roman Empire were divided. In every country there were those for and those against competing industrially with Britain and, ultimately, with each other. It was no easy matter for the promoters of the industrial cause – men such as Friedrich List in Germany or Michel Chevalier in France – to persuade their fellow countrymen that they would all benefit from abandoning local customs duties and taxes.

List was an especially tragic figure, for his enforced exile in the United States from 1826 onwards opened his eyes to an economic system infinitely more vigorous than that of his native Württemberg, and his attempts to modernize his homeland led to frustration and, eventually, his own suicide. It was List who understood that, in order to protect its infant industry from the powerful rivalry of Britain, the United States had to adopt a protectionist policy, banning cheap imports for a time. In that he took issue with Adam Smith, long dead by then, of course, and blissfully unaware that the country he imagined would be best off as a nation of farmers was well on its way to becoming an industrial giant. It was, incidentally, Smith, rather than Napoleon, who disparagingly called England a 'nation of shopkeepers' because it regarded its colonial subjects simply as captive customers for its goods.

What List hoped for was a powerful Germany which would ally itself with Britain, for he foresaw the emergence of the United States and Russia as future superpowers. However, he took issue with Smith, whose writings he greatly admired, on one vital issue: he did not believe that the interest of nations was the same as that of individuals. Whereas Smith imagined Britain had gained a commercial lead *despite* all the protectionist legislation it enforced on imports and exports, List believed that they were crucial to its success. The free trade philosophy advocated by Smith and later by successive British governments was short-sighted, aimed at securing a short-term advantage during the brief period when British manufacture was in the ascendancy.

As well as taking issue with Adam Smith, List had a different view of the future of industrialism from his much more famous fellow countryman, Karl Marx. It is always dangerous to reduce a great philosopher's views to simple propositions, but it is fair to say that Marx envisaged industrialism destroying not only traditional cultures and economies but nation-states as well. Instead of national rivalry, there would be rivalry between social classes and, in the end, all countries would be more or less the same: 'The country that is more developed industrially only shows to the less developed the image of its own future.'³ Marx had no time for List, whom he regarded as a minor 'bourgeois' figure, although List's seminal work, *The National System of Political Economy*, published in 1841, was well regarded in the nineteenth century.

However, all the attempts in the first half of the nineteenth century to understand the economic and social mechanisms which gave rise to industrial advance and what the future might hold can be regarded as failures. Technological innovation was in reality so far-reaching that it could not have been built into any model of the future – the rapid development of the oil industry is as good an example as any – and there were developments so bizarre that anybody who predicted them would have been thought mad and, no doubt, incarcerated. The most notable of these was the astonishing result of the opening up of Japan by the United States and the European powers. All the latter wanted were safe havens for their whaling ships and an extension of the established China trade. What they got was a new industrial nation so powerful it was able to defeat Russia in 1904–5 and, some four decades later, to challenge the military supremacy of the United States itself with the attack on Pearl Harbor in 1941.

There is no agreed account of why Japan should have been so successful in adopting and adapting the industrial system to its own culture. Essentially, industrialism was something its rulers were forced to accept after the visit of Commodore Matthew Perry and his fleet of 'Black Ships' in 1853–4, as their attempts to stave off economic subjection and retain their isolation with treaties failed to convince a younger generation of proud Japanese that this was a workable strategy. The illegal and dangerous explorations in the West of the Choshu and, later, Satsuma samurai brought home to them just how far behind Japan was industrially and that in any conflict it would be defenceless, a point made abundantly clear by the British bombardment of the Satsuma port of Kagoshima in 1863. In some ways, the Japanese response to the arrival of industrialism was similar to that of the United States almost a century earlier: the realization that the alternative to developing indigenous industry was to remain a lowly supplier of raw material to be turned into high-value goods by British or European machines.

The Japanese economic miracle, as it was once known, is the more remarkable, however, since it involved technological plagiarism on a truly heroic scale and the adoption of critical aspects of a completely alien culture, whereas the American colonialists were mostly British and European emigrés. And Japan had nothing like the natural resources of the post-1850 United States. In fact, it seems incontrovertible that the key to Japanese industrialization was cultural, which is to say that it was brought about by the sheer will of the reformers of the Meiji Restoration.

The idea that the key to industrialization was not inventiveness or technological genius but was rooted in values and culture goes back to Arnold Toynbee's *Lectures on the Industrial Revolution* of 1884. It was an approach developed in the early twentieth century by Max Weber, who wrote *The Protestant Ethic and the Spirit of Capitalism*, in which he argued that there was a 'fit' between the requirements of what he called 'sober bourgeois capitalism' and the work ethic of non-conformist sects. And it is fashionable again now as contemporary historians and economists try to puzzle out why it is that so many countries, which they imagined in the 1960s were on the verge of economic 'take-off', have remained poverty-stricken. For example, Lawrence E. Harrison argues in *The Central Liberal Truth: How Politics Can Change a Culture and Save It From Itself* that certain belief systems are incompatible with economic advance. In an article in the *Washington Post*, he stated:

> Some religions and cultures do better than others at promoting personal responsibility, education, entrepreneurship and trust – all

values that shape political and economic development. When it comes to democracy, prosperity and rule of law, Protestant societies – above all, the Nordic countries of Denmark, Finland, Iceland, Norway and Sweden – have generally done better than Catholic nations, particularly those of Latin America. Confucian societies such as Japan, Singapore, South Korea, Taiwan and now China have produced transforming economic growth. Islamic countries, even those with oil, have not.[4]

Harrison, who teaches at Tufts University in the United States, gives a startling example from his own experience working for the US Agency for International Development in South America and the Carbibbean.

In the late 1970s, I worked in Haiti, which shares the island of Hispaniola with the Dominican Republic. In 1804, when Haiti became independent, it was vastly richer and more powerful than the Spanish colony to the east. But today Haiti is by far the poorest country in the hemisphere – in 2003, its per capita income was $1,740, compared with $6,820 for the Dominican Republic, according to UN estimates. Adult literacy was 51 per cent in Haiti vs. 88 per cent in the Dominican Republic. And while Dominicans have experienced substantial democratic continuity in the past forty years, authoritarianism has been the norm for Haiti.

The Dominican Republic's evolution has been typical of Latin America, while Haiti's has been typical of Africa. Why the difference? The dominant religion in Haiti is voodoo, which nurtures mistrust and irrationality. Its roots are in the Dahomey region of West Africa – what is today Benin. The levels of income, child malnutrition, child mortality, life expectancy and literacy are virtually identical today in Haiti and Benin.[5]

An argument diametrically opposed to that of Harrison and those who believe culture is significant is that of Jared Diamond, a Professor of Geography and Environmental Health Sciences at UCLA. In his book *Guns, Germs and*

Steel: The Fate of Human Societies, published in 1997, Diamond argues that the Eurasian dominance of the world is a result of the environmental advantages enjoyed by the ancestors of modern Europeans and has nothing to do with ability or intelligence or culture. It is a thesis which he developed while pursuing one of his fascinations, the bird life of the islands of New Guinea. His premise is that apparently 'primitive' peoples are just as sophisticated as any other and that their apparent 'backwardness' is a consequence of the limited environmental opportunities their ancestors possessed, and particularly the range of plants and animals they had which might have been cultivated or domesticated. Unable to develop a sophisticated form of agriculture, they could not support cities in which the forerunners of modern industry were developed.

The logic of Diamond's argument is that if the ancestors of his friends in New Guinea had been born in Mesopotamia, they would have been the forerunners of modern industrialism, and if the ancestors of James Watt or Thomas Edison had been born in New Guinea, they would still be living as hunter-gatherers. Given the severe limitations presented by an environment like that of New Guinea, this proposition does not seem far-fetched. On the other hand, it tells us absolutely nothing about how Western industrialism developed. The arguments of Adam Smith, Karl Marx, Max Weber and, more recently, Lawrence Harrison are not concerned with innate intelligence but with political and social culture, which is quite different.

Grand theories about the rise of industrialism and the Eurocentric dominance of the world are appealing, but really tell us very little about how technology actually developed. Was it inevitable, for example, that someone in Europe would devise a steam locomotive? Was it inevitable, given the geographical advantages of the Europeans, that they, with their American rivals, would invent the light bulb? Was it inevitable that someone would realize that you could fuel an engine with oil drilled from the ground? To all such questions the answer must be that we cannot know what might have happened; we can only know what did happen. However, there is a tendency to regard what did happen as inevitable, and, having accepted its inevitability, to devise a thesis which explains why it was bound to happen. This is a kind of historical tautology which enjoys wide popularity.

The tales of industrial endeavour outlined in this book should serve as an antidote to the view that the transformation of agricultural societies into modern industrial nations was driven by some impersonal force. Indeed, to attribute this astonishing process, as Jared Diamond appears to do, to the simple fact that Europeans were in the right place at the right time seems a little harsh, if not downright misguided. If it was anything, the long industrial revolution was surely, for good or for ill, the result of a colossal amount of human endeavour, much of it quite breathtaking in its brilliance.

NOTES

Introduction
1 'To the Hon. Mrs. Richard Watson', 11 July 1851 in Graham Storey, Kathleen Tillotson and Nina Burgis (eds), *The Letters of Charles Dickens*, vol. 6, Clarendon Press, 1988, pp. 427–9.

Chapter One: Spies
1 *Universal Register*, Tuesday, 12 April 1785, Issue 91, p. 2, col. B.
2 Josiah Wedgwood the Elder, *An Address to the Workmen in the Pottery, on the subject of entering into the service of foreign manufacturers*, Newcastle, 1783.
3 Daniel Defoe, *A Plan of the English Commerce. Being a compleat prospect of the trade of this nation, as well the home trade as the foreign, etc.*, Charles Rivington, 1728.

Chapter Two: Mad About Iron
1 Quoted in François, duc de La Rochefoucauld, *Innocent Espionage: the La Rochefoucauld brothers' Tour of England in 1785*, edited and translated by Norman Scarfe, Boydell Press, 1995.
2 Quoted in J. R. Harris, *Industrial Espionage and Technology Transfer: Britain and France in the eighteenth century*, Ashgate, 1998.
3 Letter in Boulton & Watt Collection, Birmingham Public Library; quoted in W. H. Chaloner, 'Hazards of Trade with France in time of War', *Business History*, 6, 1963/64.
4 In C. Bruyn Andrews (ed.), *Torrington Diaries*, London, 1934; quoted in Richard Barker, 'John Wilkinson and the Paris Water Pipes', *Wilkinson Studies*, vol. II, Merton Priory Press, 1992, pp. 57–76.
5 Quoted in A. P. Woolrich, *Mechanical Arts & Merchandise: industrial espionage and travellers' accounts as a source for technical historians*, De Archaeologische Pers, Eindhoven, *c.*1986.

6   Erasmus Darwin to Watt, 29 March 1775, in Birmingham Archives.
7   Quoted in Norbert C. Soldon, *John Wilkinson (1728–1808), English Ironmaster and Inventor*, Edwin Mellen Press, 1998.
8   Quoted in ibid.

Chapter Three: The Toolbag Travellers

1   Quoted in David Jeremy, *Artisans, Entrepreneurs and Machines: essays on the early Anglo-American textile industries, 1770–1840s*, Ashgate, 1998, p. 40.
2   The 1776 edition of Adam Smith, *Wealth of Nations*, can be found online at <http://www.adamsmith.org/smith/won-intro.htm>
3   Quoted in Darwin H. Stapleton, *The Transfer of Early Industrial Technologies to America*, American Philosophical Society, 1987.
4   Quoted in Richard Shelton Kirby, *William Weston and his Contribution to Early American Engineering*, The Newcomen Society, 2004.
5   Karl Marx, *Capital: A Critique of Political Economy*, 3 vols, edited by Friedrich Engels, translated by Ernest Untermann, Charles H. Kerr and Co. Cooperative, Chicago, 1909, 1910; also online at <http://oll.libertyfund.org/Home3/Set.php?recordID=0445>

Chapter Four: The Cornishman's Puffer

1   Quoted in Anthony Burton, *Richard Trevithick: Giant of Steam*, Aurum Press, 2000.
2   H. W. Dickinson and Arthur Titley, *Richard Trevithick. The Engineer and the Man*, Cambridge University Press, 1934.

Chapter Five: They Kept Their Heads

1   Quoted in Richard Cobb (General ed.), *The French Revolution: Voices from a Momentous Epoch 1789–1795*, Simon & Schuster, 1988.
2   Letter quoted in Bessie Gardner Du Pont, *Life of Eluthère Irénée Du Pont from Contemporary Correspondence*, University of Delaware Press, 1923–6.

Chapter Six: Some Yankees in the Works

1   *The Times*, Friday, 18 October 1805, p. 3.
2   Quoted in R. A. H. Smith, 'Robert Fulton: a letter to Lord Nelson', *British Library Journal*, 25 February 1999.
3   H. W. Dickinson, *Robert Fulton, Engineer and Artist. His Life and Works*, John Lane, 1913.
4   Ibid.
5   Quoted in ibid.
6   Quoted in *The Times*, Wednesday, 2 September 1807, p. 3.
7   Thomas W. Knox, *The Life of Robert Fulton and a History of Steam Navigation*,

G. P. Putnam's & Sons, New York, 1886.

8   Basil Hall, RN, *Voyages and Travels of Captain Basil Hall*, T. Nelson & Sons, 1895.

9   Quoted in Jeanette Mirsky and Allan Nevins, *The World of Eli Whitney*, Collier Books, 1962.

10 Hall, *Voyages and Travels of Captain Basil Hall*.

11 Samuel Griswold Goodrich, *Recollections of a Lifetime: or, men and things I have seen in a series of letters to a friend*, 2 vols, New York and Auburn, 1857.

12 Quoted in Greville and Dorothy Bathe, *Jacob Perkins – His Inventions, His Time and His Contemporaries*, Historical Society of Pennsylvania, 1943.

Chapter Seven: The Railway Men

1   Quoted in Robert E. Carlson, *The Liverpool and Manchester Railway Project 1821–1831*, David & Charles, 1969.

2   Quoted in L. T. C. Rolt, *George and Robert Stephenson: the railway revolution*, Longmans, 1960.

3   Quoted in Carlson, *Liverpool and Manchester Railway Project*.

4   Quoted in ibid.

5   Anthony Burton, *The Rainhill Story: the great locomotive trial*, BBC Books, 1980.

Chapter Eight: Cowcatchers and Timber Tracks

1   Charles Dickens, *American Notes: American Notes for General Circulation*, Chapman and Hall, 1842; also online at <http://www.online-literature.com/dickens/americannotes/>

2   Quoted in Robert E. Carlson, 'British Railroads and Engineers and the Beginnings of the American Railroad Development', *Business History Review*, 34 (1960).

3   Quotes from Horatio Allen's diaries at <http://www.dudleymall.co.uk/loclhist/agenoria.htm>

4   Ibid.

5   Ibid.

6   John H. White, *The Civil Engineering of Canals and Railways before 1850*, edited by Mike Chrimes, Ashgate, 1997.

7   Quotes from Horatio Allen's diaries at <http://www.dudleymall.co.uk/loclhist/agenoria.htm>

8   Originally published in John H. B. Latrobe, *The Baltimore and Ohio Railroad: Personal Recollections*, 1868; reprinted in Albert B. Hart (ed.), *American History Told by Contemporaries*, vol. 3, 1927; also online at <http://www.eyewitnesstohistory.com/tomthumb.htm>

9   Quoted in Darwin H. Stapleton, *The Transfer of Early Industrial Technologies to America*, American Philosophical Society, 1987.

10 Ibid.

Chapter Nine: Les Rosbifs Go To Work

1 Quoted in K. H. Vignoles, *Charles Blacker Vignoles: Romantic Engineer*, Cambridge University Press, 1982.
2 Ibid.
3 Michel Chevalier, *Society, Manners and Politics in the United States being a series of letters on North America*, translated from 3rd Paris edition by Thomas G. Bradford Weeks, Jordan & Co., Boston, 1839.
4 Ibid.
5 Edwin Chadwick, *Papers Read Before the Statistical Society of Manchester on the Demoralisation and Injuries Occasioned by the Want of Proper Regulations of Labourers Engaged in the Construction and Working of Railways*, Simms and Dinham, 1846.
6 *The Times*, 9 September 1843, p. 3, abridged from 'The Paris and Rouen Railway' in *Journal des Débats*.
7 Ibid.
8 Frederick S. Williams, *Our Iron Roads: their history, construction and social influences*, Ingram Cooke, 1852.
9 Ibid.
10 Ibid.
11 Ibid.
12 Ibid.

Chapter Ten: A Prophet Without Honour

1 Quoted in W. O. Henderson, *Friedrich List: the making of an economist*, Hammer, 1977.
2 Ibid.
3 Ibid.
4 Ibid.

Chapter Eleven: A Blast of Hot Air

1 Quote from <http://www.buffalohistoryworks.com/ptracks/chapter5/chapter5.htm>

Chapter Twelve: Morse Decoded

1 Quoted in Alfred Vail, *The American Electro-Magnetic Telegraph: with the reports of Congress and a description of all telegraphs known, employing electricity or galvanism*, Philadelphia, 1845.
2 Quoted in ibid.
3 Quoted in Kenneth Silverman, *Lightning Man: the accursed life of Samuel F. B. Morse*, Alfred A. Knopf, New York, 2003.

Chapter Thirteen: The Palace of Wonders

1 Michel Chevalier quoted in Dionysius Lardner, *The Great Exhibition and London in 1851*, Green and Longmans, 1852.
2 Quoted in ibid.
3 Quoted in ibid.
4 Quoted in ibid.
5 Quoted in Jeffrey A. Auerbach, *The Great Exhibition of 1851: a nation on display*, Yale University Press, 1999.
6 Quoted in Robert F. Dalzell, *American Participation in the Great Exhibition of 1851*, Amherst College Press, 1960.
7 Quoted in ibid.
8 Quoted in ibid.
9 *The Times*, 4 September 1851, p. 5.
10 Quoted in Charles T. Rodgers, *American Superiority at the World's Fair*, Philadelphia, 1852.
11 Quoted in ibid.
12 Quoted in Dalzell, *American Participation in the Great Exhibition of 1851*.

Chapter Fourteen: 'A Very Handsome Tail'

1 Quoted in John Manjiro, *Drifting Towards the South East: the story of five Japanese castaways*, translated by Junya Nagakuni and Junji Kitadai, Spinner Publications, New Bedford, 2003.
2 Extract from Herman Melville, *Moby Dick,* 1st edn, *The Whale*, 3 vols, Richard Bentley, 1851.
3 *The Times*, Friday, 26 March 1852, p. 5.
4 Ibid.
5 Ibid.
6 Reprinted in *The Times*, 26 March 1852, p. 8.
7 Ibid.
8 *Narrative of the Expedition to the China Seas and Japan 1852–1854*, compiled from original notes and journals of Commodore Perry and his officers, at his request, and under his supervision by Francis L. Hawks, facsimile of original 1856 publication by Dover Publications, Mineola, New York, 2000.
9 Ibid.
10 Ibid.
11 Quoted in ibid.
12 Ibid.

Chapter Fifteen: The Petroleum Pioneers
1 Abraham Gesner, *A Practical Treatise on Coal, Petroleum, and Other Distilled Oils*, New York, 1861; 2nd edn, revised by G.W. Gesner, 1865.

Chapter Sixteen: The Steel Revolution
1 Sir Henry Bessemer, FRS, *An Autobiography*, Offices of 'Engineering', London, 1905; available online at < http://www.history.rochester.edu/ehp-book/shb/start.htm>
2 Ibid.
3 Quoted in William Manchester, *The Arms of Krupp 1587–1968*, Michael Joseph, 1969.

Chapter Seventeen: Of Scots and Samurai
1 Quoted in Olive Checkland, *Britain's Encounter with Mejii Japan, 1868–1912*, Macmillan, 1989.
2 Quoted in Alexander McKay, *Scottish Samurai: Thomas Blake Glover, 1839–1911*, Canongate, 1997.
3 Richard Henry Brunton, *Schoolmaster to an Empire 1868–1876*, Greenwood Press, 1991.
4 Ibid.
5 Quoted in Francis H. Trevithick, 'The History and Development of the Railway System in Japan', *Asiatic Society of Japan Transactions*, vol. 22, 1874.
6 Ibid.
7 Brunton, *Schoolmaster to an Empire 1868–1876*.
8 Ibid.

Chapter Eighteen: Horsepower
1 Quoted in Jennifer Davies, *Tales of the Old Horsemen*, David & Charles, 1997.
2 William Plowden, *The Motor Car and Politics 1896–1970*, The Bodley Head, 1971.
3 Quoted in John Boyd Dunlop, *The History of the Pneumatic Tyre*, A. Thom & Co., Dublin, 1924.
4 Quoted in James M. Laux, *In First Gear: the French automobile industry to 1914*, Liverpool University Press, 1976.
5 Robert Louis Jefferson, *Awheel to Moscow and Back. The Record of a Cycle Ride*, Sampson Low & Co., 1895.
6 Quoted in Eugen Diesel, Gustav Goldbeck and Friedrich Schildberger, *From Engines to Autos: five pioneers in engine development and their contribution to the automotive industry*, Henry Regnery Company, Chicago, 1960.
7 Quoted in ibid.
8 Quoted in ibid.

Chapter Nineteen: **The Wizard of Menlo Park**

1   Arthur Conan Doyle, *The Great Boer War*, Smith, Elder & Co., 1902, Ch. 1.
2   H. G. Wells, *Mr Britling Sees it Through*, Cassell, 1916.
3   Quoted in T. C. Barker and M. Robbins, *A History of London Transport: Passenger Travel and the Development of the Metropolis*, vol. 2, Allen & Unwin, 1974.
4   Quoted in Paul Israel, *Edison: a life of invention*, John Wiley, 1998.
5   Quoted in ibid.
6   George Bernard Shaw, *The Irrational Knot, Being the Second Novel of his Nonage* (1880), Brentano's, New York, 1905.
7   Quoted in Robert Friedel, Paul Israel, with Bernard S. Finn, *Edison's Electric Light*, Rutgers University Press, 1988.
8   Quoted in R. A. S. Hennessy, *The Electric Revolution*, Oriel Press, 1972.

Chapter Twenty: **The Terror of the Torpedo**

1   Quoted in Walter Wood, *North Sea Fishers and Fighters*, Kegan Paul & Co., 1911.
2   *The Times*, Monday, 24 October 1904, p. 7.
3   Quoted in Edwyn Gray, *The Devil's Device: the story of Robert Whitehead, inventor of the torpedo*, Seeley, 1975.
4   *The Times*, obituary of Mr Robert Whitehead, 15 November 1905, p. 3.
5   *The Times*, editorial, 12 June 1905, p. 7.

Chapter Twenty-One: **The Synthetic World**

1   Quoted in W. H. Brock, *Justus von Liebig: the chemical gatekeeper*, Cambridge University Press, 1997.
2   Quoted in ibid.
3   Quoted in ibid.
4   Quoted in ibid.
5   Quoted in ibid.
6   Quoted in ibid.
7   Quoted in *The Life and Work of Professor William Henry Perkin*, The Chemical Society (Great Britain), London, 1932.
8   Quoted in ibid.
9   Quoted in ibid.
10 F. M. Perkin, 'The Artificial Colour Industry and its Position in this Country', *Journal of the Society of Dyers and Colourists*, 10 November 1914.
11 W. J. Reader, *Imperial Chemical Industries: A History*, Oxford University Press, 1970.

Postscript

1   Adam Smith, *Wealth of Nations*; the 1776 edition can be found online at <http://www.adamsmith.org/smith/won-intro.htm>

2   Ibid.

3   Karl Marx, *Capital: A Critique of Political Economy*, 3 vols, edited by Friedrich Engels, translated by Ernest Untermann, Charles H. Kerr and Co. Cooperative, Chicago,1909, 1910; also online at <http://oll.libertyfund.org/Home3/Set.php?recordID=0445>

4   Lawrence E. Harrison, 'Hearts, Minds and Schools', *Washington Post*, 17 December 2006.

5   Ibid.

BIBLIOGRAPHY

———◆◆◆———

I have listed below all the major works consulted, as well as one or two articles in journals on key topics and individuals.

Assad, Matt, Mike Frassinelli, David Venditta, *Forging America: the story of Bethlehem Steel*, Andrews McMeel, 2004

Barker, Richard, 'John Wilkinson and the Paris Water Pipes', *Wilkinson Studies*, vol. ll, Merton Priory Press, 1992

Barkhouse, Joyce, *Abraham Gesner*, Fitzhenry & Whiteside, 1980

Bathe, Greville and Dorothy, *Jacob Perkins – His Inventions, His Time and His Contemporaries*, Historical Society of Pennsylvania, 1943

— *Oliver Evans: a chronicle of early American engineering*, Historical Society of Pennsylvania, 1935

Beamish, Richard, *Memoir of the Life of Sir Marc Isambard Brunel*, Longman, 1862

Beaton, Kendall, 'Dr Gesner's Kerosene: The Start of American Oil Refining', *Business History Review*, 29, 1 March 1955

Bessemer, Sir Henry, *Sir Henry Bessemer FRS, An Autobiography*, Offices of 'Engineering', 1905; also at <http://www.history.rochester.edu/ehp-book/shb/>

Brock, W. H., *Justus von Liebig: the chemical gatekeeper*, Cambridge University Press, 1997

Brooke, David (ed.), *The Diary of William MacKenzie, the First International Railway Contractor*, Ashgate, 1997

Brown, Sidney DeVere, 'Nagasaki in the Meji Restoration: Choshu Loyalists and British Arms Merchants', *Crossroads*, No. 1, 1993 (Nagasaki)

Brunton, Richard Henry, *Schoolmaster to an Empire 1868–1876*, Greenwood Press, 1991

Burton, Anthony, *Richard Trevithick: giant of steam*, Aurum Press, 2000

— *The Railway Empire*, John Murray, 1994

— *The Rainhill Story*, BBC Books, 1980

Butt, John, *James 'Paraffin' Young: founder of the mineral oil industry*, Scotland's Cultural Heritage, Edinburgh, 1983

Carlson, Robert E., *The Liverpool and Manchester Railway Project 1821–1831*, David & Charles, 1969

— 'British Railroads and Engineers and the Beginnings of the American Railroad Development', *Business History Review*, 34, 1960

Chaloner, W. H., 'Builders of Industry: John Wilkinson, Ironmaster', *History Today*, May 1951

Checkland, Olive, *Britain's Encounter with Meiji Japan, 1868–1912*, Macmillan, 1989

The Chemical Society, *The Life and Work of Professor William Henry Perkin*, 1932

Clark, Ronald W., *Edison: the man who made the future*, Macdonald and Jane's, 1977

Clements, Paul, *Marc Isambard Brunel*, Longmans, 1970

Coad, Jonathan, *The Portsmouth Block Mills: Bentham, Brunel and the start of the Royal Navy's industrial revolution*, English Heritage, 2005

Dalzell, Robert F., *American Participation in the Great Exhibition of 1851*, Amherst College Press, 1960

Davies, Hunter, *A Biographical Study of the Father of Railways George Stephenson*, Weidenfeld and Nicolson, 1975

Davies, Ron, *John Wilkinson*, Dulston, 1987

Diesel, Eugen, Gustav Goldbeck and Friedrich Schildberger, *From Engines to Autos: five pioneers in engine development and their contribution to the automotive industry*, Henry Regnery Company, Chicago, 1960

Dickinson, H. W., *A Short History of the Steam Engine*, University Press, 1938

— *James Watt and the Steam Engine*, Clarendon Press, 1927

— *Robert Fulton, Engineer and Artist. His Life and Works*, John Lane, 1913

Dunlop, John Boyd, *The History of the Pneumatic Tyre*, A. Thom & Co., 1924

Du Pont, Bessie Gardner, *Life of Eluthère Irénée Du Pont from Contemporary Correspondence*, University of Delaware Press, 1923–6

Faujas de Saint-Fond, Barthélemi, *A Journey through England and Scotland to the Hebrides in 1784*, edited and translated by Sir Archibald Geike, Hugh Hopkins, Glasgow, 1907

Ferguson, Niall, *The House of Rothschild: money's prophets 1798–1848*, Penguin, 2000

Fitton, Richard and Alfred Wadsworth, *The Strutts and the Arkwrights 1758–1830: a study of the early factory system*, Manchester University Press, 1964

Fitton, Richard, *The Arkwrights: spinners of fortune*, Manchester University Press, 1989

Fox, Robert, 'Diversity and Diffusion: the transfer of technologies in the Industrial Age', *Journal of the Newcomen Society*, 70, 1988–99

Friedel, Robert, Paul Israel with Bernard S. Finn, *Edison's Electric Light*, Rutgers University Press, 1988

Gardner, Walter M. (ed.), *The British Coal-tar Industry*, Williams and Norgate, 1915

Garfield, Simon, *Mauve: how one man invented a colour that changed the world*, Faber and Faber, 2000

Giddens, Paul H., *The Birth of the Oil Industry*, Macmillan Company, New York, 1938

Gray, Edwyn, *The Devil's Device: the story of Robert Whitehead, inventor of the torpedo*, Seeley, 1975

Green, Constance, *Eli Whitney and the Birth of American Technology*, Little Brown, 1956

Haber, Ludwig, *The Chemical Industry during the Nineteenth Century*, Clarendon Press, 1958

Hall, Basil, RN, *Voyages and Travels of Basil Hall*, Nelson & Sons, 1895

Harris, J. R., *Industrial Espionage and Technology Transfer: Britain and France in the eighteenth century*, Ashgate, 1998

— 'John Holker: a Lancashire Jacobite in French Industry', The First Chaloner Memorial Lecture, Newcomen Society, 2004

Helps, Sir Arthur, *Life and Labours of Mr Brassey 1805–1870*, Bell and Daldy, 1872

Henderson, W. O., *The Industrial Revolution on the Continent: Germany, France, Russia 1800–1914*, Frank Cass, 1961

— *Friedrich List: the making of an economist*, Hammer, 1977; Cass, 1983

— *The Rise of German Industrial Power 1834–1914*, Temple Smith, 1975

— *The Zollverein*, Cambridge University Press, 1939; republished by Cass, 1984

Hough, Richard Alexander, *The Fleet That Had to Die*, Hamish Hamilton, 1958

Israel, Paul, *Edison: a life of invention*, John Wiley, 1998

Jefferson, Robert L., *Through a Continent on Wheels*, Simpkin, Marshall & Co London, 1899

Jeremy, David, *Transatlantic Industrial Revolution: the diffusion of textile technologies between Britain and America 1790–1830s*, Basil Blackwell, 1981

— *Artisans, Entrepreneurs and Machines: essays on the early Anglo-American textile industries 1770s–1840s*, Ashgate, 1998

Kieve, Jeffrey L., *The Electric Telegraph: a social and economic history*, David & Charles, 1973

La Rochefoucauld, François, duc de, *Innocent Espionage: the La Rochefoucauld brothers' Tour of England in 1785*, edited and translated by Norman Scarfe, Boydell Press, 1995

Landes, David S., *The Unbound Prometheus: technological change and industrial development in Western Europe from 1750 to the present*, 2nd edn, Cambridge University Press, 2003

Lakwete, Angela, *Inventing the Cotton Gin: machine and myth in antebellum America*, Johns Hopkins University Press, 2003

Lardner, Dionysius (ed.), *The Great Exhibition and London in 1851* (includes essay by Michel Chevalier), Green and Longmans, 1852

Laux, James M., *In First Gear: the French automobile industry to 1914*, Liverpool University Press, 1976

List, Friedrich, *The National System of Political Economy* (translated from the German by S. Sampson), Lloyd Longmans, Green, 1905

McKay, Alexander, *Scottish Samurai: Thomas Blake Glover, 1839–1911*, Canongate, 1993

Manjiro, John, *Drifting Towards the South-East: the story of five Japanese castaways* (translation by Junya Nagakuni and Junji Kitadai), Spinner Publications, New Bedford, 2003

Mirsky, Jeannette and Allan Nevins, *The World of Eli Whitney*, Macmillan, New York, 1952

Musson, Albert Edward and Eric Robinson, *Science and Technology in the Industrial Revolution*, Methuen, 1972

O'Brien, Patrick, *Economic Growth in Britain and France 1780–1914: two paths to the twentieth century*, Allen and Unwin, 1978

Perkin, F. M., 'The Artificial Colour Industry and its Position in this Country', *Journal of the Society of Dyers and Colourists*, 10, November 1914

Pleshakov, Konstantin, *The Tsar's Last Armada: the epic journey to the Battle of Tsushima*, Perseus Press, 2002

Remond, André, *John Holker, manufacturier et grand fonctionnaire en France au XVIIIème siècle 1719–1786*, M. Rivière, Paris, 1946

Rodgers, Charles T., *American Superiority at the World's Fair*, Philadelphia, 1852

Rolt, L. T. C., *George and Robert Stephenson: the railway revolution*, Longmans, 1960

Faujas de Saint-Fond, Barthélemi, *A Journey through England and Scotland to the Hebrides in 1784*, edited and translated by Sir Archibald Geike, Hugh Hopkins, Glasgow, 1907

Schwartz, Sharron P., *A 'Professor' in Peru: Trevithick and the transatlantic migration of the industrial revolution*, Institute of Cornish Studies, 2002

Silverman, Kenneth, *Lightning Man: the accursed life of Samuel F. B. Morse*, Alfred A. Knopf, New York, 2003

Soldon, Norbert C., *John Wilkinson (1728–1808), English Ironmaster and Inventor*, Edwin Mellen, 1998

Stapleton, Darwin H., *The Transfer of Early Industrial Technologies to America*, American Philosophical Society, 1987

Szostak, Rick, *The Role of Transportation in the Industrial Revolution: a comparison of England and France*, McGill-Queen's University Press, 1991

Thomas, Samuel, 'Reminiscences of the Early Anthracite-Iron Industry', *Transactions of the American Institute of Mining Engineers*, 29, 1899

Thompson, F. M. L., 'Nineteenth-Century Horse Sense', *The Economic History Review*, New Series, Vol. 29, No. 1 (February 1976)

— *Victorian England: the horse-drawn society*, Bedford College, University of London, 1970

Thompson, L. G., *Sidney Gilchrist Thomas: an invention and its consequences*, Faber and Faber, 1940

Tolf, Robert W., *The Russian Rockefellers: the saga of the Nobel family and the Russian oil industry*, Hoover Institution Press, Stanford University, 1976

Tompkins, Eric, *The History of the Pneumatic Tyre*, Dunlop Archive Project, Eastland, 1981

Travis, Anthony S., *The Rainbow Makers: the origins of the synthetic dyestuffs industry in Western Europe*, Associated University Presses, 1993

Tunzelmann, G. N. von, *Steam Power and British Industrialization to 1860*, Oxford Clarendon Press, 1978

Vail, Alfred, *The American Electro-Magnetic Telegraph: with the reports of Congress and a description of all telegraphs known, employing electricity or galvanism*, Lea & Blanchard, Philadelphia, 1845

Wachhorst, Wyn, *Thomas Alva Edison, an American Myth*, MIT Press, 1981

Walker, Charles, *Thomas Brassey: railway builder*, Muller, 1969

Weible, Robert (ed.), *The World of the Industrial Revolution: comparative and international aspects of industrialization*, Museum of American Textile History, 1986

Whitten, David O. (ed.), *Eli Whitney's Cotton Gin 1793–1993 Symposium Selected Papers*, University of California, 1993

Williams, Frederick S., *Our Iron Roads: their history, construction and social influences*, Ingram, Cooke and Co., 1852

Williams, Peter N., *From Wales to Pennsylvania: the David Thomas story*, Glyndwr Publishing, 2002

Williamson, H. F. and A. R. Daum, *The American Petroleum Industry: the age of illumination 1859–1899*, North-western University Press, 1959

INDEX

Aberdeen 290, 291
Académie Royale des
    Sciences 271
Adams, John Quincy 183
Admiralty (British) 5, 75, 77,
    90, 97, 99, 202, 356
AEG 341
Africa, scramble for 348
Aix-en-Provence 377
Alabama 104–5
Albany Evening Journal 226
Albert, Charles 16, 372
Albert, Prince Consort 215,
    220–21, 271, 373, 378–9
Albert County, New
    Brunswick 256
Albertite 256
Alcock, Sir Rutherford 290
Alexander, William 206
Alexander I, Tsar 77
alizarin dyes 377, 378
alkalis 257
Allen, Horatio 5, 141–5, 147,
    149–50, 153
Allen, Richard and William
    272
Alsace-Lorraine 281, 282
alternating current 341
ambergris 239, 241
American Civil War (1861–5)
    329, 350
American Revolution
    (1776–83) 29, 177, 183, 386
'American System' 182
American Tobacco Company
    326

American War (1812–15) 141
American War of
    Independence (1773–6)
    37, 38, 105, 124, 179, 254,
    327, 336
Andrews of Manchester 376
Angier, J.D. 260, 262
aniline 372, 373, 375, 377,
    378
animal chemistry 371
anthracite *see also* coal
anti-Semitism 175
arc lamps 336, 337
Ardwick, Manchester 258
Argand, François Pierre Ami
    253
Argentina: railways 170
Arkwright, Richard 11, 12,
    13, 19–20, 38, 39, 40, 57
Armstrong 356–7
Armstrong, John W. 113
Ashley, J.L. 330
asphalt 256, 257
Asphalt Mining and Kerosene
    Gas Company 256
aspirin 362, 380
Atlantic and Pacific Telegraph
    Company 332
Attwick, William 191
Atwood, Luther 258, 259, 261
Australia and the Great
    Exhibition 222
    railways 170
Austria, annexation of (1938)
    357
Austria Lloyd, Trieste 353

Austro-Hungary, first railway
    line in 186

Bacon, Joshua Butters 115,
    116
Baird, Charles 32, 103–4
Baku oilfields, Azerbaijan
    264–8
Baldwin, Ruth 95
Baltimore-Ohio line 147, 209
Bank of England 5, 114
banknote engraving 113–14
bar iron *see* pig iron
Barbados: 'tar springs' 255
Barbary Pirates 86
Barbier, Aristide 307
Barcelona 169
Barker, George 335
Barlow, Joel 95, 99
BASF (Badische Anilin-und-
    Soda Fabrik) 380
Batchelor, Charles 330–31,
    339, 341
Bathgate, near Edinburgh
    258, 259, 268
batteries 202
Battersea sawmill, London 76,
    77
Belgian railways 186
Belgrave Institute, London
    204
Bell, Alexander Graham 332
Bell Telephone Company 333
Benin 391
Bentham, Brigadier-General
    Samuel 73–4, 75, 112

Benz, Bertha (née Ringer) 317

Benz, Hanns Georg 316–17

Benz, Josephine 317

Benz, Karl 316, 317–20, 323

Benz & Cie 318
 Velo 20, 321
 Viktoria 320
 Vis-à-Vis 320

benzene 253

Bergmann, Sigmund 331

Berliner, Emile 333

Berne River 276

Bersham foundry, North Wales 26, 28

Berthollet, Claude Louis 367

Bessember, Anthony 271

Bessemer, Sir Henry 270–75, 276, 277, 278, 279, 282, 283, 333, 380

Bessemer, Miss (Henry's sister): *Studies of Flowers from Nature by Miss Bessemer* 271

Bessemer converters 277, 278, 279, 282

Beveridge, William 315

bicycles 302–310, 323

Bidermann, Jacques Antoine 89

Billingsgate Fish Market, London 337

Biot, Jean-Baptiste 367

Bird (Hurricane) Island, South Pacific 234–5

Birkbeck College, London 282

Birkenhead, Cheshire 160, 161

Birkinshaw, John 122, 127

Birley and Kirk spinning mill, Manchester 153–4

Birmingham 18, 33, 56

Birmingham Canal 153

Birmingham–London line 134–5, 156, 370

Bismarck, Prince Otto von 281

Bissell, George H. 260, 261

bitumen 255

black band ironstone 192, 193

Blackett, Christopher 119

Blenkinsop, John 120, 127

Board of Health report (1850s) 301

boats: first iron boat 33–4

Boer War (1899–1902) 324

Bolivar, Simon 63, 157

Bolton-Leigh goods line 133

Booth, Henry 133

boots, army 76

Boulton, Matthew 18, 21, 29, 31, 32, 33, 55–6, 57, 61, 150, 252, 333, 363

Boulton & Watt 22, 27, 57, 58, 97, 99, 150, 252, 253
 engines 46, 56, 65, 98, 100, 101, 103, 131

Bovril 380

Bradley, Staffordshire 36

Braithwaite, John 134, 217

Bramah, Joseph 73

Bramah of Birmingham 217, 224–5

Bramall Lane football ground, Sheffield 337

Brandywine River 85, 86, 87

Brassey, Maria (née Harrison) 161

Brassey, Thomas 6, 159–70, 273

Brazil: railways 170

Breguet, Louis 336

Brewer, Francis B. 260–61, 262

Brewer and Watson lumber company 260, 261

bridges
 cast-iron 160
 first Russian iron bridges 32
 Japan 294, 296
 Laguna Veneta, Italy 171
 tunnelling technique 79
 world's first iron bridge 18, 33, 294
 wrought-iron 191

Bridgewater, Francis Egerton, Duke of 42

Bridgewater Canal 42, 150

Bridgewater Canal Company 134

Bristol Channel 41, 94

Bristol Copper and Brass Works 53

Britain
 American engineers visit to gain expertise 139–43, 149–50
 canal-building 41–3
 as a consumer of dyestuffs 362
 craftsmen and 'indentured' servants emigrate 37
 first railway mania 134–5, 156, 159
 loses ground to United States and Germany 7, 284
 outlaws slave trade 110
 over-confidence 382
 population 2, 218
 railways 117–34, 296–7
 rapid rise of industrial towns 2
 reliance on coal 2
 second bout of railway mania 167, 217
 tidal rivers 41
 urbanisation 2

Britannia Nail Works 113

British Association for the Advancement of Science 369

British Library, London 300

Broadstairs, Kent 3

Brosely ironwork, Shropshire 23, 26, 27

broughams 310, 322

Bruderhaus factory, Germany 315

Brunel, Isambard Kingdom 6, 76–7, 79, 206, 217

Brunel, Marc Isambard 6, 69–80, 112, 116, 124, 157–8, 315, 352

Brunton, Richard Henry 7, 292–5, 297–8
Buddicom, William 164
Buffalo and Niagara Falls Railway 194
buses
horse-drawn 310, 322
motor 322
Bushnell, David 96
Byng, Hon. John 30

Calais-Calcutta line 171–2
Calder & Barrett 337
calico riots 12
Calicut, India 12–13
California 241, 246, 247
Calley, John 51
Camborne, Cornwall 5, 58, 62
camera obscura 208
camphene 253–4, 255
Canada: railways 170
Canal du Midi 42
canals 41–7, 94–5, 118, 119–20, 123, 126, 139, 141, 150, 160, 189, 190, 327
cannon 22–4, 26–9, 32, 34, 64, 115, 178
steam 114–15
steel 277, 279, 281
Cannstatt, Germany 316, 321
Canterbury & Whitstable Railway 129
card-shuffling machine 79
Carnegie, Andrew 283
Caro, Heinrich 380–81
Carron ironworks, Scotland 24, 32, 55, 103, 384
Cartwright, Edmund 95
cast iron 33, 58, 118, 122, 217
Castlehead, Cumberland 35
Catasauqua, Pennsylvania 194
Catherine the Great 31, 32, 73
Catholicism 175
Chadwick, Edwin 162
Chaloner, George 282

Chamberlain, Joseph 340
charcoal
iron smelted with charcoal 10, 24, 25, 193, 195, 214
timber supplies 25
Charenton forges, near Paris 163–4
Charlemagne 174–5
Charles Stewart, Prince ('Bonnie Prince Charlie') 14, 15
Charleston Mercury 224
Charlton, Hertfordshire 271
Chat Moss, near Manchester 132
Chatham dockyard 153
Chatsworth, Derbyshire 216
Chevalier, Michel 155, 213–15, 219, 221, 388
Chicago World's Fair (1893) 322
China
isolationism 241
steel-making 275
Choshu clan 285, 286, 287, 290, 390
Choshu Five 1–2, 7, 288–92, 345
Christianity 233
Chubb 225
Church, Arthur 375
Churchill, Sir Winston 315
cinchona tree 374
Clément, Nicolas 368
Clemm, Carl and August 380
coal 2, 5, 20, 24–5, 36, 41, 42, 54–5, 118, 125–6, 153, 189, 190–96, 240, 247, 255, 257, 258, 259, 348
anthracite 129, 141, 191, 192, 193, 195
bituminous 191, 193, 196
sea 152
coal tar 255, 362, 363, 372, 374, 375, 377, 378
Coalbrookdale, Shropshire 18, 24, 26, 27, 30, 32, 33, 52, 195, 294

Cochrane, Thomas, tenth Earl of Dundonald 255–6
Cockerill, John 320
Code Napoleon 177
Coffin, Isaac 209
coke
coal turned into 24
smelting 10, 24–7, 188, 191, 195, 196, 384
Cole, Henry 115–16, 217, 229
collodion 338
Colombia 130, 131, 132
Colquhoun, Patrick 45
Colt, Samuel 209, 228
Colt revolver 229, 249
Columbus, Christopher 34
Commercial Docks, London 157
Compagnie de l'Alliance 336
Compagnie des Eaux de Paris 30
Congleton, Cheshire 154
Congreve, William 114, 178–9
Continental System 179, 185
Cook, Captain James 25
Cooke, Dr William 204
Cooke, William Fothergil 204–6, 208
Cooke-Wheatstone patent 204, 205–6
Cooper, Peter 147–8, 149
copper mines 51, 53, 56
Cort, Henry 191, 195, 214
Costa Rica 63
cotton gin 8, 92–3, 108–112
cotton industry 11–13, 15, 16, 17, 95, 104, 108–111, 146, 153, 220, 241, 353, 376
'counterfactual horse' 300, 301
'coup oil' 258
Courtenay, William, Earl of Devon 94
Coventry 322
cowcatchers 139

Cowes Regatta 229
Crane, George 192, 193, 195–6
Crawshay, Richard 59, 60
'creek oil' 260
Crimean War (1854–5) 265, 273, 274
Cromford Mill, Derbyshire 11–12, 13, 18, 39
Crompton, Samuel 38
Crosby, Albert 260
Crossley Brothers 313
Crystal Palace, Hyde Park, London 212, 213–31, 232, 279
Cycloped 133

Daguerre, Louis 208–9
daguerreotype 208, 249
Daimler, Emma (née Kurz) 315
Daimler, Gottlieb 7, 313–17, 317, 320–23
Daimler Motor Company 322
Dalmas, Charles 82, 87
Darby, Abraham 24, 26, 33, 195
Darby family 294
Darmstadt 364, 367
Darwin, Charles, *The Descent of Man* 281
Darwin, Erasmus 32
Daubrée, André 307
Daubrée, Edouard 307
Daubrée, Elizabeth Pugh (née Parker) 307
Davis, Ira 237
Davy, Edward 203–4, 208
Davy, Sir Humphry 253, 363
Davy's Diamond Cement 203–4
Day and Newell 224, 225
De Boer, Captain 266
de la HouliÈre, Marchant 27, 28
De Luppis, Giovanni 354
Defoe, Daniel: *A Plan of the*

English Commerce 19
Delaware & Hudson Canal Company 141, 143
Derbyshire, textile industry in 11, 177
Derwent River 11
Devonshire, Duke of 216
Diamond, Jared 393
Guns, Germs and Steel: The Fate of Human Societies 391–2
'Dick, Captain' 61, 62
Dickens, Charles 3–4, 77, 136–9, 145, 167, 220, 301
Dickinson, Henry Winram 64–5, 96–7
diorama 208
direct current 341
Dogger Bank fishing grounds 342–5
Dolly Pit, Black Callerton 121
Dominican Republic 391
Dover line 162
Doyle, Sir Arthur Conan 324
Drake, Edwin L. 262–3
draught horses 299, 303
Droz, Jean-Pierre 18
drugs, synthetic 362, 380
du Cros, Harvey 306, 308
du Pont de Nemours, Irénée 81–9
du Pont de Nemours, Pierre Samuel 80–82, 83, 85, 87–8
du Pont de Nemours, Victor 82, 86, 89
Du Pont family 6, 86, 89
Duke, James Buchanan ('Buck') 326
Dulong, Pierre Louis 367
Dumas, Alexandre 69
Dunlop, Jean 307
Dunlop, John Boyd 305–7
Dunlop, Johnnie 305–6
Dunlop Rubber Company 307

Dupont (Du Pont) chemical company 6, 80, 87, 189
Dutton viaduct, Grand Junction railway 161
Dyer, Joseph Chessborough 113
dyes, synthetic 361–2, 374–81

East India Company 12
Eclectic Review, The 172
eclipse of the sun (1878) 335
economic slump (1860s) 170
Edgehill tunnel, Liverpool 132
Edison, Mary (née Sitwell) 331
Edison, Nancy 327, 329
Edison, Sam 327, 328, 329, 331, 332
Edison, Thomas Alva 327–36, 380, 392
Edison Phonograph Company 334
Ediswan light bulb 340
Edlin and Sinclair 306
Edo (Yedo) (modern Tokyo), Japan 233, 247, 291
Egypt: cotton industry 12
Elbe River 188
Elbing, Prussia 187
Elbing Wednesday Club 187
electric cars 321
electric current 201–6
electric light 7, 335–40
Electric Lighting Act (1882) 340
electric motors 7
electric telegraph 196, 197–212, 213, 220, 230–31, 249, 291, 328–9
electrical generator 203
Electrician, The 336–7
electricity
  ability to generate a current artificially 197
  alternating current 341
  American attitude to electricity 196, 200

direct current 341
properties of 197
Eleutherian Mills 85, 88
Ellicott's Mills, Maryland 148
Ellis, Lister 129
Engelhorn, Friedrich 380
English Channel 152, 158, 159, 170, 212, 343, 344, 352
Ericsson, John 134, 217
Erie Canal 46–7, 149
Esperance, L' (pigeon-fanciers club) 280
Essen foundry, Ruhr 275, 276, 277
Etruria, Staffordshire 18, 154
Euston Station, London 217
Evans, Oliver 92, 102–3, 112, 114
Eveleth, J.G. 260, 261

Fairhaven, Massachusetts 238, 239
Fairman, Gideon 114
Faraday, Michael 203, 363, 370
Experimental Researches 329
Faujas de Saint-Fond, Barthélemy 17–18
Felkerzam, Dimitri von 350
Ferranti, Sebastian Ziani de 326
fertilizers, artificial 372
Fillmore, Millard 242, 245–8
First World War 7, 322, 339, 360, 361
Fiume shipyard (now Rijeka in Croatia) 353–7
Flachat, Eugene 155
flax 12
Ford, Henry 322
Forth Street Works, Newcastle-upon-Tyne 127
Foster, Rastrick and Company 133, 143, 153
Fox, Charles 217, 218
Fox, Henderson & Co. 217

Fox-Pitt, St George Lane 339
France
Britain's greatest rival 10
coalfields 20
as a consumer of dyestuffs 362
emigration of skilled artisans to United States 5, 6
guillotine 67–9
industrialization 34, 283
iron industry 22
'Iron Mad' Wilkinson's Loire factory 5
railways 6, 151, 154–6, 158–9, 162–71, 186
seeks to emulate Britain's industrial successes 3
theoretical science 6
underachievement at beginning of industralism 6, 150–51
Franco-Prussian War (1870–71) 250, 279–81, 313
Frankfurt
Judensau mural 175
Judenstrasse ghetto 175–8, 180
Franklin, Benjamin 17, 44, 45, 386
Franklin Institute 140
Franz Josef, Emperor of Austria 354
free trade 185, 187, 188, 379, 382, 388–9
French Revolution (1789–99) 3, 6, 29, 31, 66, 67–71, 80, 82, 173, 175, 177
Friedrich Wilhelm IV, King of Prussia 221
fulminates 365
Fulton, Robert ('Robert Francis') 5, 90–101, 103, 104, 112, 113, 178, 249, 264–5, 350, 354
Fürth, near Nuremberg 270
fuschine dye 380

Gale, Professor Leonard 201, 207, 209
Galvani, Luigi 202, 325, 326
Garbett, Samuel 32
Garrett, George William Littler 350
Garrett, Richard 224
gas engine, Lenoir 311, 312, 313
Gas Light and Coke Company 253
gas lighting 154, 219, 252–3, 337, 339
Gascoigne, Charles 32
Gasmotoren-Fabrik Deutz AG 313
Gasmotorenfabrik Mannheim 318
Gauss, Carl Friedrich 203, 210
Gay-Lussac, Joseph Louis 6, 150, 257, 363, 367, 368
George Miller & Company 258
Gerard, James 63
Germany
collapse of economy after defeat in 1918 381
as a consumer of dyestuffs 362
and electricity 340–41
emigration of skilled artisans to United States 5
fragmentation of administration 186
and the Great Exhibition 222
industrial take-off after unification 187, 279, 283
meteoric rise of chemical industry 360
railways 186, 188
reviving chemical industry 381
seeks to emulate Britain's industrial successes 3
synthetic dyes 361

unification 279, 281, 313, 360

Gerstner, F. von 171

Gesner, Dr Abraham 254–7, 268, 269
   A Practical Treatise on Coal, Petroleum and Other Distilled Oils 268

Gesner, Harriet (née Webster) 254

Gesner, Henry 254

Gilbert (Giddy), Davies 57, 58, 59, 60, 62

Gilchrist, Percy C. 282

Giles, Francis 132

Girard, Philippe Henri de 220

Glasgow University 55, 290

Glover, Jim 291

Glover, Thomas Blake 7, 286–92, 295, 296, 298

Godalming, Surrey 337–9

Goeman (fisherman friend of John Manjiro) 235, 237–8

gold 237

'gold' paint powder 269, 270–73

Goodrich, Samuel G. 115

Goodyear, Charles 227, 230

Gould, Jay 331

Gouraud, François 209

Government Stamp Office 271

governors 57

Graham, Lieutenant Governor John 105

Graham, Thomas 257, 370

Grand Allies 122

Grand Junction Canal 43

Grand Junction line 158, 160, 161

Grand Union canal 377

Gray, Thomas 120

Great Exhibition (London, 1851) 3, 4, 94, 212, 213–31, 232, 241, 257, 277, 279, 312, 323, 375

Great Northern line (France) 170

Great Siberian Railway 346

Great Western Railway 206

Greeks 49–50

Greene, Catherine ('Caty') 105, 106, 107

Greene, General Nathanael 105, 106

Greenford Green works, Middlesex 377, 378

greenhouses 216, 217

Grosvenor Art Gallery, London 340

guano 374

Guillotin, Dr Joseph-Ignace 68

guillotine 6, 67–71

gunpowder manufacture 6, 83–9, 202

guns
   Colt revolver 229, 249
   machine-gun 5, 115, 339
   repeating pistol 228
   rifles 273–4

Guppy, William 113

Hackworth, Timothy 4, 121, 134, 142–3, 171

Hague, Joseph 38, 39

Haiti 391

Hall, Captain Basil 104–5
   Travels in North America 110–111

Hall, John 65

Hall, Thomas 373

Hamburg-Amerika line 348

Hampton Court Palace, East Molesey, Surrey 50

Hancock, Thomas 227

hansoms 322

Hargreaves, James 13, 19

Harrison, Joseph 161

Harrison, Lawrence E. 390–91, 392
   The Central Liberal Truth: How Politics Can Change a Culture and Save It From Itself 390

Hartford, Connecticut 228

Hawaii 236, 237
   see also Sandwich Islands

Hawks, Francis L. 243, 244, 250

Hazard, Erskine 193

Heath, Frederick 116

'heavy chemical' industries 362–3

Hedley, William 120–21

Heilbronn, Württemberg 173, 182

Henderson, John 217

Henry, Charles 369, 370

Henry, Joseph 201, 211

Henry, William 369

Hetton colliery, Durham 133

Hill, Sir Rowland 115–16

Hillman 304, 325

Hillman, William 303

Historien, L' (journal) 81, 83

Hitler, Adolf 357

Hobbs, A.C. 224, 225, 228

hobbyhorse 302–3

Hofmann, August Wilhelm von 6–7, 372–9

Hohenasperg fortress, Württemberg 182

Hokendauqua, Pennsylvania 196

Holborn Viaduct, London 337, 340

Holker, John 4, 11, 14–17, 24

Holme, Ryle 291

Holmes, Professor F. H. 336

Holy Roman Empire 173–8, 180, 185, 211, 388

Homfray, Samuel 58–9, 60

'Honeymoon Sociable' 303–4

Honolulu, Hawaii 236, 237, 240

Hornblower, Jonathan 53, 56, 57, 58

Hornblower, Josiah 53–4

horse buses 310, 322

horse feed 119, 300–301

horses as transport 299–302

hot-air balloons 280, 281

hot-blast furnace 192–6
House of Commons Select
    Committee on Highways
    124
Hoyos, Count George 355
Hubbard, O. P. 260
Hudson River 5, 46, 47, 93,
    98, 100, 240
Huguenots 154, 271
Hull fishermen, Russian
    attack on (1904) 342–5,
    348–9, 350
Humber 304, 325
Humboldt, Alexander von
    368
Huntsman, Benjamin 25, 275
Huskisson, William, MP 144
Hutton, Dr 157
hydrocarbons 363

Illustrated London News 245
Imperial Chemical Industries
    (ICI) 380
Imperial Tobacco Company
    326
incandescent lamps 337–8,
    340
India
    cotton industry 12
    and the Great Exhibition
        222
    khaki first adopted in 361
    railways 170, 172
    and synthetic dyes 377
    indigo 258, 375, 376, 377
Industrial Revolution, first
    2–3, 4
inoculation 107
Inoue Kaoru 288, 290, 292,
    295
Irish Cyclist magazine 306
iron industry 22–36, 194,
    196, 214, 269
    founders 11
    iron ore mining 2, 196
    see also cast iron; pig iron;
        scrap iron; wrought iron
ironclads 353–4

ironstone 191–2
    black band 192, 193
Isle Indret, Loire 28, 29
Isle of Wight 229
Italy
    and the Great Exhibition
        222
    industrialization 8, 284
    and railways 170
    and unification 353
Ito Hirobumi 288, 290, 292

Jablochkoff, Paul 336
Jablochkoff Candles 336
Jablochkoff lamps 336
Jackson, Andrew 183, 184
Jackson, Dr Charles 200–201
Jacobins 70, 81
James, William 4, 117–18,
    122–3, 126–7, 128, 129,
    131, 132, 133, 188
James, William Henry 122
James Muspratt and Sons 257
James River Canal Company
    149
Japan
    Bafuku 234, 285–8, 291,
        345
    bridges 294, 296
    Choshu Five 1–2, 7
    earthquakes 294
    education 7, 298
    and the Great Exhibition
        221–2
    industrialization 2, 3, 7,
        249–50, 284, 298, 345,
        382, 387, 390
    isolationism 1, 232, 241
    Jesuit missionaries 232
    lighthouses 7, 292–5, 298
    Pearl Harbor attack (1941)
        389
    Perry's mission 242–51
    potentially a very wealthy
        nation 241
    power of 389
    railways 293, 294, 295–7
    roads 293

ship-building 298
    shipwrecked fishermen
        232–8
    Shogunate 1, 7, 232, 242,
        286, 290
    steamships 293
    steel-making 275
    treaty ports opened 285
    use of foreign expertise 7
    xenophobia 232
Japan Commercial News 289
Jardine Matheson 286, 288,
    289, 290
Jars, Gabriel 24, 384
Jefferson, Robert Louis
    309–310, 387
    Awheel to Moscow and Back
        309–310
Jefferson, Thomas 17, 85
Jellicoe, Adam 191
Jellinek, Emil 323
Jenner, Edward 107
Jervis, John B. 141–2, 143
Jessop, William 46
Jews: in Frankfurt ghetto
    175–8, 180
Jiel-Laval, Jacques 308
Johnson, B.P. 226
Johnson, Samuel 385
Journal des Débats 163–5
Judd, Gerrit Parmele 236
Jumbo generator (Edison) 339

Kagoshima, Japan 289–90,
    295, 345, 390
Kaiser-Ferdinands Nordband
    186
Karlsruhe Railway 317
Kastner, K.W. G. 365, 366,
    367, 368
Kay, John 20
Keir, Samuel 259, 260, 262
Keith, Thomas 377
kerosene 255, 256, 259, 264,
    266, 267
khaki dye 361–2
Killingworth, Tyne & Wear
    121

Killingworth colliery, Tyne & Wear 121, 122, 126, 133
Kingdom, Sophia (Mrs Marc Isambard Brunel) 6, 70–73, 75, 77, 80
Kinzuke, Endo 288
Kneass, Samuel 140
Knox, Thomas W. 100–101
Kobe, Japan 297
Korea 292, 345
Kracow, Poland 186
Kruesi, John 331, 334
Krupp, Alfred 275–81, 282
Krupp, Friedrich 275, 276
Krupp, Hermann 276
Kuchler, Conrad Heinrich 18
Kufstein, Tyrol 188
Kugler, Mr (postmaster of Speyer) 319–20
Kuper, Vice-Admiral 289
Kure naval yard, Japan 347

La Rouchefoucauld, François 23
La Rouchefoucauld brothers 23
La Seyne ship-building yard, near Toulon 352
Lafayette, Marquis de 182, 207
Lafitte, Charles 158
Laguna Venta, Italy 171
Lake Erie coastal railway 328
Lake Ladoga, Russia 267
Lake Onega, Russia 267
Lancashire: textile industry 12, 15, 16, 177
Lancet, The (journal) 372
Langen, Eugene 312, 313, 315, 316
Lardner, Dionysius 220
Latrobe, Henry 40, 46, 47, 140
Latrobe, John 147, 148
'laughing gas' (nitrous oxide) 228
Lavoisier, Antoine 6, 67, 71, 80, 81, 83, 84

Laws, Dr 329, 330
Lawson, Harry J. 304
Le Creusot foundry, near Montcenis 29, 34, 352
Le Havre 158, 159, 165
Le Turc, Monsieur (a traveller) 17–18
Lebon, Philippe 219, 252–3
Leeds, west Yorkshire 220, 314
Leeds and Liverpool Canal 160
Lefferts, General 330
Leggett, William Arthur 342
Lehigh Coal and Navigation Company 193
Lehigh Crane Iron Company 193
Lehigh Valley, Pennsylvania 190, 194
Leipzig-Dresden line 184, 186
Lenoir, Etienne 310–311
Lenoir engine 311, 312, 313
Levassor, Emile 320, 321
Levinstein, Herbert 362
Levinstein, Ivan 362
Lew Chew islands 248, 249
Leyden jar 201, 202
Liddell, Sir Thomas 122
Liebig, Henriette (née Moldenauer) 369
Liebig, Johann 364, 365
Liebig, Justus von 6, 257, 363–73, 376, 378–80
Chemistry in its Applications to Agriculture and Physiology 371–2
On the decomposing products of uric acid 370
Liebig, Louis 364
Liebig family 364
lighthouses 7, 292–5, 298, 336
Lima Gazette 62
Lime Street tunnel, Liverpool 160
linen 12, 219–20
List, Friedrich 173–4, 175, 180–89, 316, 388, 389

The National System of Political Economy 389
List, Johannes 174
Little Schuylkill River Navigation, Railroad and Canal Company 182–3
Liverpool 2, 142, 153, 190, 370
Liverpool and Manchester Railway Company 132, 133
Liverpool-Birmingham line 370
Liverpool-Manchester line 117–18, 128–30, 132–5, 136, 142, 144, 147, 153, 155–61, 164, 167, 205, 214
Liverpool-Manchester Railway Bill 128, 130, 131, 152
Livingston, Chancellor Robert R. 96–7, 98, 100
Livingstone, David 257
'lock controversy' 224–5
Locke, Joseph 132, 158–64, 166, 168–9
Locke, William 132, 158
Locomotive Acts 302
locomotives
  Blenkinsop 120, 127
  Braithwaite and Ericsson 134
  Daimer and 314
  demonstrated in Japan 249, 250, 251
  Hackworth 134
  Hedley 121
  manufacturers 126
  Rastrick 133, 143
  Steel 60, 119
  Stephenson 60, 64, 121–3, 127–8, 133, 143, 186
  to 'consume their own smoke' 131
  Trevithick's Cornish 'puffer' 48, 58–60, 119, 121, 131

London
    first electric underground
        326–7
    gas lighting 154
    Moncure Robinson on 150
    population 218
    railway speculation 186
    and sea coal 125
    and tidal rivers 41
    World's Fair (1862) 312, 315
London and North-Western
    Railway 296
London and North-Western
    Railway Company 65
London and South-West
    Railway Company 169
London and South-Western
    Railway 158, 292
London-Birmingham
    Railway 215, 217, 370
London-Paris railway 151,
    152, 156, 158, 159, 165–6,
    170
London-Southampton line
    161–2
Longridge, Michael 129
Longsdon, Alfred 278
Longsdon, Robert 278
Losh, William 122, 127
Losh, Wilson & Bell 122
Louis, Dr Antoine 68
Louis XVI, King 67, 68–9
Louis-Philippe, King of
    France 152–3, 185, 208,
    352
Louisiana Purchase 96, 101,
    105, 110, 386–7
Lowell textile works, New
    England 137
Ludwig I, Grand Duke 364,
    365
Ludwigshafen, Germany 380
Luther, Martin 175

Macadam, John Loudon
    123–5
McCormick, Cyrus 225–6,
    228

machine-gun 5, 115, 339
Macintosh, Charles 227, 307,
    370
Macintosh, George 192
Mackenzie, H. 310
MacKenzie, Ross 286
Mackenzie, William 6,
    159–67, 168, 170
madder 375, 376, 377
Maidstone Gazette 229
Makarov, Stepan 346–7,
    349
Manby, Aaron 351–2
Manby, Charles 351–2
Manchester 1, 14, 15, 17, 42,
    95, 153–4, 178, 381
Manchester Examiner
    newspaper 258
Manchester Guardian
    newspaper 113
Manchuria 345, 346, 358
Manjiro, John and Shoryo,
    Kawada: A brief account of
    drifting towards the south-
    east: The story of Five
    Japanese. A very Handsome
    Tail (Hyoson Kirykau) 234
Manjiro (Mung), John 232–9,
    245, 250, 285
Mannheim gas works 380
marble-cutting machine 94
Marconi, Guglielmo 325,
    326, 357, 358
marine mine 264–5
Mars Works, Philadelphia 103
Marshall, Charles 201
Marshall, John 220
Martin, Pierre and Emile 278
Marx, Karl 111, 182, 389, 392
    Das Kapital 47
Masaru, Inoue 288
Matheson, Hugh 289
Maudslay, Henry 73, 74, 75,
    78, 80, 112, 315
Mawson, John 338
Maxim, Sir Hiram 339
Maybach, Wilhelm 315, 316,
    320

Mayhew, Henry 301
meat extract 380
Melville, Herman 231
    Moby Dick 238, 239
Menai Bridge 153
Menlo Park, New Jersey 332,
    380
Menzel, Wolfgang 181
Mercedes-Benz 323
Merrill, Josepha 258
Metcalf, Robert 128
methylene blue 381
Mexican War (1846) 228,
    241, 242
Michaux, Pierre 302–3
Michelin, André 308
Michelin, Edouard 308
Michelin, Jules 307, 308
micro-photography 281
Middleton Colliery, Yorkshire
    120, 122
Middleton Colliery Railway
    120, 122, 133
mild steel 273
Milk of Magnesia 369
Miller, E. L. 146
Miller, George 258, 259
Miller, Phineas 106–9,
    111–12
Minié, Commandant 274
Mississippi River 5, 101, 104,
    105, 240
Mitsubishi shipping company
    291
Montelegre, José Maria and
    Mariano 63
Mony, Stephane 155
'mordants' 375
Mori, Arinori 291
Morning Chronicle newspaper
    223
Morris, Robert 44
Morrison, George 287
Morse, Lucretia Pickering
    (née Walker) 207
Morse, Samuel Finley Breese
    196, 197–201, 205–211,
    228, 230

Morse, Sarah Elizabeth (née Griswold) 211
Morse family 226
Morse system 199, 208, 210, 211–12, 249, 328, 329, 331, 332, 357
Moscow-St Petersburg line 171
Moss, Peter 14
motor buses 322
motor cars
electric 321
four-wheeler 320
motor tricycle 316, 318–20
opposition to a petrol-powered vehicle 299
Mount Fuji, Japan 296
Mulberry Grove plantation, Georgeia 105–6, 107, 109
Murdoch, William 57, 58, 150, 252, 253
murexide 374, 375, 377
Muspratt, James 257

N. A. Otto & Company 312
Nagasaki, Japan 1, 286, 287, 296
nail-making 106, 113
naphtha 227, 258
Napoleon Bonaparte 5, 34, 59, 71, 76, 85, 87–8, 95, 96, 99, 101, 173, 174, 177, 178, 179, 185, 202–3, 219–20, 255, 275, 364, 367, 387, 388
Napoleon III, Emperor of France (previously Prince Napoleon) 274, 280, 313
Napoleonic Wars 119, 122, 178–9, 180, 274, 364
National, Le newspaper 155
National Efficiency movement 324, 325–6
'navvies' 6, 162–5, 169, 273
Nazis 357
Neath Abbey ironworks 192
Neckar Zeitung newspaper 182
needle telegraph 203–4, 210

Neilson, James 192, 193, 195
Nelson, Admiral Horatio, Lord 74, 75, 91, 92, 99, 358
New Bedford, Massachusetts 236, 237, 238, 239, 240
New Guinea 392
New Lanark, Scotland 95
New Monthly Magazine 115
New York City
Edison's electricity station 340
Stock Exchange 329
water supply 45–6
New York Courier and Enquirer 242
New York Herald newspaper 222
New York Observer 197
New York Sun 335
New York Tribune 223
New York University 197, 201, 207
Newcastle, Duke of 17
Newcastle Courant newspaper 52–3
Newcomen, Thomas 50–51, 53
Newgate prison, London 4, 14
Nicholas, Grand Duke (later Tsar Nicholas I) 120, 203
Nicholas II, Tsar of Russia 345, 348, 349
Nightingale, Florence 273
nitrous oxide ('laughing gas') 229
Nobel, Alfred 265, 266
Nobel, Immanuel 264–5
Nobel, Ludwig 265–8
Nobel, Robert 264–7
Nobel family 284
Nobel Prizes 265
Nollet, Abbé 201
North Sea 41
Nuremberg-Fürth line 186

Oates, James 258
Observer 229

ocean liners 171, 326, 357
Oested, Hans 202
Ogden's tobacco firm 326
Ohio River 104, 147
oil industry 252–69, 283, 284
oil shale 257, 258, 259, 268
Oppenheim, Wolf Jacob 176
organic chemistry 363
Osaka 296
Otto, Anna (née Gossi) 312
Otto, Nikolaus August 311–12, 315, 322
Otto, Philipp Wilhelm 311
Otto-Langen 320, 321
Otto-Langen engine 313
Otto engine 313, 315, 316, 318, 320–21
Overton, George 126
Owen, Robert 95
Oxo cubes 380

Pacific Ocean 238
paddle-steamers 101, 104
Paddockhurst, Worth, Berkshire 355
Page, Richard 62–3
Panhard and Levassor company 323
Papin, Denis 50, 310
paraffin 258, 261, 302
Paraffin Light and Mineral Oil Company 259
'parallel motion' mechanism 57
Parent, Charles François 86–7
Paris
Gare du Nord 336
gas lighting demonstration 252
Grand Magasins du Louvre 336
population 218
siege of (1870–71) 280–81
World's Fair (1889) 320
Paris Electrical Exhibition (1881) 339
Paris Exhibition (1849) 214, 215

Paris Exhibition (1867) 313
Paris St Lazare-St Germain-en-Laye line 155, 156, 208
Paris-Rouen line 158–9, 163–5
Paris-Versailles lines 156
Parkes, Sir Harry 292–3
Parsees 264, 267
Paxton, Joseph 216–18
Peabody, George 223
Pearl Harbor attack (1941) 389
Pease, Edward 126
Pease, Joseph 126
Peel, Sir Robert 372
Pell, William 199–200
Penkridge viaduct 161
Pennsylvania Germans 182, 183
Pennsylvania Railroad 283
Pennsylvania Rock Oil Company of Connecticut 261
Pennsylvania Society for the Promotion of Internal Improvement 140
Penny Black 5, 116
penny-farthings 303
Penydarren, Wales 59, 60, 118, 119, 144
Péreire, Emile 155, 156
Péreire, Constantin and Augustin-Charles 29, 30, 98
Perin, Jean-Louis 314
Perin and Panhard 320–21
Perkin, Frederick 378, 379
Perkin, Thomas 375, 377
Perkin, W. H. 361–2
Perkin, William 362, 373–8, 381
Perkin & Sons 378, 379
Perkins, Bacon and Petch (later Perkins and Bacon) 115–16
Perkins, Jacob 5, 92, 112–16
Perry, Commodore Matthew Calbraith 242–51, 285, 389

Peru silver mines 60–62
Peto, Morton 170, 273
petrol engines 7
    Otto engine 313, 315, 316, 318, 320–21
    Otto-Langen engine 313
    Otto's patent application 311–12
two-cylinder 316
petroleum
    industry 323
    Japan's ample supplies 295
    petroleum oils as medicine 259–60
    Young's discovery 258
Peugeot 304, 321
phenols 363
Philadelphia
    Centennial Exhibition (1876) 336
    US first city 86
'Philadelphia Plan' 45
Philadelphia Waterworks 46
Phillips, Benjamin H. 38–9
phonograph 334, 341
phosphoric ores 278, 279, 281, 282
Pickersgill haulage firm 128
pig iron (bar iron) production 24, 25, 26, 191, 193, 194, 195, 277, 278, 282
pigeon post 280–81
pitch 255, 256, 257, 267
'Pitch Lake', Trinidad 255, 256
pitch pine 253
Pitt, William, the Younger 90
plant chemistry 371, 372
Platen, August Graf von 367, 368
Playfair, Lyon 257, 372
Pneumatic Tyre and Booth's Cycle Agency 307
polygraph 72
Pope, Franklin L. 329, 330
population 2, 218–19
Port Arthur (Lushun), China 346, 347, 349, 358
'port-rule' apparatus 201

Portsmouth, Treaty of (1905) 359
Post Office 116, 332, 334
postage stamps 5, 116
pottery 18–19
power loom 95
Powers, Hiram: *The Greek Slave* 223
Preece, William 334
Priestley, Joseph 35
Prince-Smith, John 187
Protestantism 175, 271
Prout, William 374
Prussia 184, 185, 187, 188
Prussian army 279
puddling 191
Pullar, Robert 376
Pullar of Perth 376, 377
pulley-block machines 72, 74, 75, 79, 315
Punch magazine 230

quinine 374, 375

Raglan, Lord 273
railways
    in America 5, 136–49, 171, 172, 185, 186, 189, 190, 193, 237
    atmospheric 155
    Belgian 186
    British 117–34, 296–7
    built by British worldwide 6, 7, 126
    and canals 120, 123
    cog-wheel system 120, 122, 127
    cowcatchers 139
    and electric telegraph 212
    finances 3
    first British railway boom 134–5, 156, 159
    French 6, 151, 154–6, 158–9, 162–71, 186
    German 186, 188
    horse-drawn 101, 118, 119, 140, 141, 143, 146, 147, 181, 183

and increased demand for horses 134
Indian 170, 172
Japanese 293, 294, 295–6
Paxton invests in 216
promoters 4, 126, 128–9, 131, 137, 145, 153
Russian 120, 171
second British railway boom 167, 217
steam 58–60, 64
Rainhill trials 132–4, 143, 157
Ransomes & May of Ipswich 224
Rastrick, James 130, 133, 143
Reader, W. J. 379–80
Red Flag Act (1865) 302
Redtenbacher, Ferdinand 317
Regent's Park, London 114–15, 116, 304
Renault 304
Rennie, George 131, 157
Rennie, John 126, 131, 157
repeating pistol 228
Reuleaux, Professor Franz 313
Reutlingen, Germany 173, 174, 180
Revolutions of 1848 220, 353
revolver pistol 209
Rhine River 173, 187, 188
Rhineland 184
Rhode Island system 40
Rhone River 20
Richard Ormerod & Son 351
Richards, Sir Frederick 350–51, 355
Richardson, Charles Lennox 287
rifles 273–4
right whales 239, 252, 253
road-building 123–5, 160, 293
Robert Stephenson & Company 127, 132, 143
Roberts, Dale and Company 381

Roberts, Solomon White 193
Roberts and Company 314–15
Robespierre, Maximilien 67, 69, 81
Robinson, Moncure 149–51, 183, 214, 371
Robison, John 32
'rock oil' 259–60
rockets, military 114, 178–9
Roebuck, John 32, 55, 56, 384
Roget, Dr Peter Mark 205
rolling 191
Rolls, Charles 325
Roman Purple see also murexide
Ronalds, Francis 202, 204
Descriptions of an Electric Telegraph and other electrical apparatus 202
Roosevelt, Theodore 359
Rothschild, Amschel Mayer 176, 178
Rothschild, Gutle 176
Rothschild, Isaac de 156
Rothschild, Jakob (James) 177
Rothschild, James de 155, 156, 178, 179, 186
Rothschild, Kalman 176
Rothschild, Kalman (Carl) 176, 178
Rothschild, Mayer Amschel 176, 177, 178
Rothschild, Nathan Mayer 176, 178, 179–80, 185–6
Rothschild, Salomon 176, 178, 186
Rothschild family 176–80, 186
Rouen, Normandy (Holker's factory) 4, 15, 17
Rouen–Le Havre line 165–7
Rover 304, 325
Royal Arsenal, Woolwich 355
Royal College of Chemistry 372–7

Royal Commission on the Great Exhibition 215, 217
Royal Dockyards 73, 74
Royal Mint 33, 271
Royal Navy 22, 23, 24, 74, 75, 287, 315, 355, 357
Royal Society 50, 202, 205, 370
Royal Society for the Encouragement of Arts, Manufactures amd Commerce 215
Royce, Frank 332
Royce, Henry 325
Rozhdestvenski, Admiral Zinovi Petrovich 344, 347–50, 357, 358, 359
Rualt, Nicholas 67
rubber 227–8, 230, 258
Russia
first iron bridges 32
first steamships 32, 103–4
foreign expertise 7, 31, 231, 284
oil industry 264–8, 284
railways 120, 171
seeks to emulate Britain's industrial successes 3
Russian Baltic Fleet 345, 347
Russian Revolution (1917) 359
Russo–Japanese War (1904–5) 2, 7, 341, 342–50, 357, 358–9, 389
Russo–Turkish War (1877–8) 346

Sadler, Samuel 109–110
St Augustine, Florida 157
St Helens–Widnes Railway 153
St Paul's cathedral, London 218, 253
St Petersburg 32
Sampachi ('Sam Patch'; Japanese castaway) 245
samurai 285–92, 345, 346, 383, 390

Sandars, Joseph 128, 129, 130
Sandwich Islands 236, 240, 242
  see also Hawaii
Sankey canal 160
Sarazin, Edouard 320, 321
Satow, Ernest 290
Satsuma clan 285, 286, 287, 289, 295, 345, 390
Savery, Thomas 50, 51, 52, 53
  The Miner's Friend 50
Schilling, Baron Pavel Lwowitch 202–3, 204, 209, 210
Schnapper, Wolf Salomon 176
Scholes, Geoffrey 16
Schuckert, Sigmund 331
Schuyler, Colonel John 53
Scientific American 334
Scots Magazine 201
Scott, William 326
scrap iron 191
sea coal 152
Seacole, Mary 273
Seine River 29, 53, 96, 98, 156, 158, 164, 165, 166, 352
Selden, George B. 321–2
semaphore system 202, 203
Seneca oil 260
Seneca Oil Company of Connecticut 262
Seven Weeks' War (1866) 279
Seven Years War (1756–63) 23
Severn River 18, 24, 26, 33, 41, 294
Shaw, George Bernard: *The Irrational Knot* 333–4
Sheffield
  and Bessemer steel 277
  cutlery industry 25, 214
  home of crucible steel 276
Shinbashi, Japan 297
shipworms 78
Shoin, Yoshida 285–6, 287
Siemens, Werner and William 279

Siemens, William 338
Siemens alternator 337
Siemens–Martin process 279, 283
silk dyeing 377
silk production 12, 105, 107, 154, 241, 298, 353
Silliman, Benjamin 261
silver mines 60–63
Simpson, Maule & Nicholson 378
Sino-Japanese War (1894–5) 346
Sivers, Natalia 349
skilled workmen
  bribery of 10, 13–14
  emigration of 5, 6, 11
  enticed abroad 11, 14, 15, 16, 18–19, 139–40, 177, 220
Slater, Samuel 39–40
slavery 5, 8, 24, 84, 105, 106, 108, 110, 111, 198
smallpox 107
Smeaton, John 46, 54
Smith, Adam 44, 182, 183, 187, 384–5, 387, 388, 392
  An Inquiry into the Nature and Causes of the Wealth of Nations 43, 183, 383–4, 385–6
Smith, C. A. 308–9
Smith, Francis O. J. 207, 208, 209
Smith, Henry (skipper of the *Crane*) 342
Smith, Peacock and Tanner 314
Smith, William 'Uncle Billy' 263
'snake heads' 194
Société Générale Éléctrique, La 336, 337
Society for the Encouragement of Arts, Manufactures and Commerce 94
Society of Arcueil 367

Society of Arts and Manufactures 271
Society of Dyers and Colourists 378
soda 363
Soho Works, Birmingham 18, 29, 55
Solling, Friedrich Heinrich 276
Sommerling, Samuel Thomas von 202
Sorbonne University, Paris 150, 200
Sotteville, Rouen 164
Sound of Music, The (film) 357
South Carolina Railroad 145–7
South-Western railway 166
Southampton 158, 165, 222
Soyer, Alexis 273
Spain
  industrialization 8, 284
  railways 168–9, 170
Speedwell works, New Jersey 207
Spencer, George John, 2ne Earl 73, 74
sperm whales 239, 253
spies
  in disguise 10, 139
  Holker's spying on the textile industry 4, 11, 15–17
  imprisoned 16
  and the secrets of Britain's industrial success 10
  and textile developments 11
spinning bullets 273–4
spinning jennies 11, 13, 15, 16, 37–8, 39
spinning mills 11, 108, 153–4, 177, 188, 189, 331, 381
spinning mules 16, 38, 40
Spitalfields, London 12, 154
Springwell colliery, Durham 133
Stabilimento Tecnico Fiumano 353, 355

Stafford-Wolverhampton line 161
stagecoaches 134
stallion-walkers 300
Stapleton, Darwin H. 140
Starley, James 303, 304
State Railway Bureau, Japan 297
Steam (poem) 115
steam cannon 114–15
steam engines 7, 20, 48–65, 220
  'atmospheric' 52, 57, 61, 102
  and coal 2
  'Columbian' 103
  dangers 49, 50
  Evans 92, 102–3
  first commercial 60
  high-pressure 58, 92, 101, 102, 103, 114, 297
  Hornblower 53–4, 57
  moving 48, 58
  Newcomen 51–7, 102, 131, 312
  rotary 57, 58
  Savery 50–53, 56
  'self-acting' 52
  textile industry 11, 188
  Trevithick 58, 59, 61, 64–5, 101, 119, 120, 123, 144
  Watt 4, 18, 55, 56, 57, 311
steamboats 96–103, 113, 249
steamships 158, 171, 240, 242, 247
  first all-iron 352
  Japan 293, 294
  screw-propeller 134
  transatlantic 190
steel
  crucible 275, 276, 277
  industry 33, 196, 214, 269, 270–83
  mild 273
Steel (Steele), John 60, 119
Steinway, William 322
Stephenson, Fanny (née Henderson) 121

Stephenson, George 4, 60, 64, 114, 121–3, 126–33, 142, 144, 157, 158, 160–61
Stephenson, James 128
Stephenson, Robert 4, 60, 64, 114, 119, 121, 127, 130, 131, 132, 133, 134, 156, 158, 186, 215, 216, 217
Stevenson, Robert 126
Stevenson, Robert Louis 126
Stevensons (Scottish firm) 292
Stiles, Reverend Ezra 107, 111
Stockton & Stokes 148
Stockton-Darlington line 64, 125–8, 130, 135, 141, 142–3
Stockton-Darlington Railway Act (1821) 126, 127
Stourbridge, Worcestershire 143, 153
Stourton, Staffordshire 160
Strabilimento Strudhoff 353
Straits of Shimonoseki, Japan 290
strap-rails 194
Strathmore, Earl of 122
Strickland, William 140, 149–50
'strong steam' 49, 58
Strutt, Jedediah 11, 13, 39, 40
submarines 5, 95–8, 178, 350
Suez Canal 348
sugar
  beet 219, 307
  cane 219
sugar cane press 270–71
sulphuric acid 363
'sun and planet' cog system 57
Surrey Iron Railway 118, 123, 181
Sussex, Duke of 114, 115
Swan, Joseph 338, 340
Swan lamps 338–9, 339
Sweden: iron foundries 33
Swift, William 351, 352

synthetic dyes 361–81

'tar springs' (Barbados) 255
tasimeter 335
taxi cabs 310
Taylor, Philip 352, 353
technology, built-in obsolescence of 7
Telegrapher, The 330
telemachon 335, 336
telephone 332, 333–4
Telford, Thomas 125, 153, 160
Tennant, Clow & Co. 258
Terashima Munenori 294
Terront, Charles 308
Thames Embankment, London 337
Thames River 41, 50, 53, 79, 94, 125, 352
Thames Tunnel 78–80, 153, 157–8
Thames Tunnel Company 352
Thénard, Louis Jacques 367
Theophilus (a German monk) 272
thermolampe 252
Thiers, Adolphe 152–6, 185
Thomas, David 190–96
Thomas, Samuel 190, 193, 194, 195, 196
Thomas, Sidney Gilchrist 281–2, 283
Thomas-Gilchrist converters 282, 283
Thomas Iron Company 196
Thompson, F. M. L. 299–300
  Nineteenth-Century Horse Sense 299
  Victorian England: the Horse-Drawn Society 299
Thomson, Robert William 304, 307
Thomson, Thomas 370
Times, The (London) 17, 73, 114, 163, 167, 212, 220, 223–4, 225, 241, 281, 289, 298, 343, 344–5, 355

tin mines 51, 56
Titley, A. 64–5
Titusville, Pennsylvania 260, 261, 262, 263
Togo, Admiral Heihachiro 345–6, 347, 357, 358, 359
Tokyo 286, 291
  British legation attacked (1861) 287
Toraemon (fisherman friend of John Manjiro) 235, 237–8
Tornquist, Alfred 267
torpedoes 5, 90–92, 95–100, 178, 342, 346, 350, 354–8
Tourville bridge, Normandy 164
Toussard, Colonel Louis de 84
Townley, Colonel 14
Townsend, James M. 261, 262
Toynbee, Arnold: Lectures on the Industrial Revolution 3, 20–21, 390
Trafalgar, Battle of (1805) 74, 75, 92, 99, 350, 358, 387
trams 310
Trans-Siberian railway 359
'transfer of technology' 89
Trevithick, Francis 64, 65, 296, 297
Trevithick, Richard 48–9, 53, 58, 61–6, 76, 78–9, 92, 100, 102, 114, 118, 123, 131, 133, 297
Trevithick, Richard, Jr. 297
Trinidad: Pitch Lake 255
Trudaine, Daniel Charles 15, 16
Tsushima, Battle of (1905) 7, 358, 359
turnpike roads 134
turnpike trusts 118, 125
turpentine 254
Tyne River 24, 41

tyres, pneumatic 304–8
Tyrian Purple 375

U-boat (Unterseeboot) 350
underwater cables 209, 212
Unger, William 330
Union of Merchants 180
United States
  'accidental wealth' 223
  canals 5, 43–7, 139, 189, 190, 327
  and coal 5, 36, 193, 196
  and electricity 196, 340
  engineers visit Britain to gain expertise 139–43, 149–50
  first Newcomen-type engine 53
  and funding of London's transport 326–7
  gas industry 340
  and the Great Exhibition 222–3, 229–30
  independence 3, 5, 17, 36
  industrialization 36, 92, 283
  influx of skilled artisans 5, 6
  iron industry 194, 196
  manufacturing industries 80
  and new technologies 3
  population 218–19
  railroads 5, 136–49, 171, 172, 185, 186, 189, 190, 193, 212, 237
  rapid transformation of 183–4
  riverboats 5
  roads 139
  slavery 5, 8
  textile industry 37, 39
United States Chemical Manufacturing Company 258
United States Electric Lighting Company 339
Universal Register 17
University College London 1, 289, 291
University of Erlangen 366–7

University of Giessen 368, 369, 372, 373
uric acid 374
US Agency for International Development 391
Uville, Francisco 61

Vail, Alfred 207, 209–210, 211
Vail, George 207
Vail family 226
Vanderbilt, Cornelius 332
vegetable oils 253, 254, 268
Vickers 356–7
Victoria, Queen 215, 220, 221, 379
Victoria Regia giant water lily 216
Vignoles, Camilla (née Hutton) 156, 157
Vignoles, Captain Charles 156, 157
Vignoles, Charles Blacker 131, 152–8, 185
Vincennes firing range, France 274
Vitgeft, Admiral Wilgelm 347
Vladivostock 346, 347
Volta, Alessandro 202, 325, 326
Voltaire 174
von Trapp, Georg Ritter 357
von Trapp, Maria Augusta (née Jutschera) 357
von Trapp family singers 357
vulcanization 227, 230

Wallace & Sons 335, 336, 339
War Department (UK) 273, 274
War of 1812 114
Warsaw 220
Washington, George 44, 72, 105, 182
Washington Post 390
watchmakers 10, 11
water frames 11, 12, 13, 15, 16, 20, 38, 40, 57, 61
Waterloo, Battle of (1815) 179, 273, 387

Watson, Sir William 201
Watt, James 4, 18, 29, 31, 32, 33, 49, 55–8, 150, 252, 297, 312, 333, 384, 392
see also Boulton & Watt
Watt, James, Jr. 252
Weber, Max 392
The Protestant Ethic and the Spirit of Capitalism 390
Weber, Wilhelm 203, 210
Webster, Dr Isaac 254
Wedgwood, Josiah 18, 21, 38, 363
An Address to the Workmen in the Pottery on the subject of Entering into Service of Foreign Manufacturers 18–19
Wedgwood factory, Etruria 18, 154
Wellington, Arthur Wellesley, Duke of 5, 76, 77, 78, 114, 115, 120, 157, 178, 179
Wells, H. G. 324, 326, 340
Mr Britling Sees it Through 324–5
West, Benjamin 94
West Indies 37
West Moor colliery, Tyne & Wear 121, 122
West Point Foundry Works, New York City 143, 146
West Point military academy, New York 140
Western Union 329, 330, 332, 333
Westinghouse, George 341
Weston, William 40, 45–7
Wey River 337, 338, 339
W. G. Armstrong, Mitchell & Company 268
whale oil 237, 238, 239, 252, 253, 254

whalebone 239
whaling industry 233, 235–40, 247, 250, 251, 253, 389
Wheatstone, Professor Charles 204, 205, 206, 208
White, John H. 145
White, Josiah 193
Whitehead, Agathe 357
Whitehead, Ellen (née Swift) 351
Whitehead, Frances Maria (née Johnson) 351
Whitehead, John 355, 357
Whitehead, Robert 350–57
Whitfield, Captain William H. 235–9, 250
Whitney, Eli 92–3, 106–113, 228
Whitney, William 321–2
Whitneyville, Connecticut 228
Whitworth, William 315
Wilhelm II, Kaiser 348
Wilkinson, Isaac 26
Wilkinson, John 'Iron Mad' 5, 21, 22–36, 56, 195, 294, 333, 352
Wilkinson, William 22, 28, 29, 33, 36
William, Prince, of Hesse-Kassel 176, 177
William I, King of Wurttemberg 180–81
Williams, Frederick Smeeton: Our Iron Roads: Their History, Construction and Social Influences 136, 167–8, 169, 170, 171–2
Williams, Captain John 29–30
Williamson, Alexander 289
Willington, Tyne & Wear 121

Winzer (Windsor), Frederick 252, 253
wireless telegraphy 212, 326, 357–8
Wood, Nicholas 127
wool industry 10, 12, 15, 95
Worcester, Marquess of 50
Worsley, near Manchester 42
Wortley, Stuart 122
wrought iron 122, 191, 214, 217, 277, 282, 354
Wurts, Maurice and William 141
Württemberg 173–4, 180, 181, 182, 184, 185, 188
Wylam Colliery, Northumberland 60, 119, 121, 133, 134

Yazoo Land Purchase 109
Yellow Sea, Battle of the (1904) 347
Yerkes, Charles Tyson 326, 327
Ynyscedwyn ironworks, South Wales 192, 193
Yoko, Yamao 288
Yokohama, Japan 286, 292–3, 294, 295
Yokohama-Tokyo line 296
Yokosuka naval yard, Japan 347
Young, James 'Paraffin' 254, 257–9, 261, 268, 269, 370, 372

Zimmermann, Wilhelm 369
Zollverein (customs union) 180, 185–8, 222
Zons, Michael 311, 312